SOCIAL WORK Matters

THE POWER OF LINKING POLICY AND PRACTICE

Elizabeth F. Hoffler and Elizabeth J. Clark, Editors

NASW PRESS

**National Association
of Social Workers**
Washington, DC

Jeane W. Anastas, PhD, LMSW
President

Elizabeth J. Clark, PhD, ACSW, MPH
Executive Director

Cheryl Y. Bradley, *Publisher*
Sarah Lowman, *Senior Editor*
John Cassels, *Staff Editor and Project Manager*
Amanda Morgan, *Copyeditor*
Lori J. Holtzinger, *Indexer*

Cover by Eye to Eye Design Studio
Interior design by Electronic Quill
Printed and bound by Sheridan Books, Inc.

First impression: March 2012

Library of Congress Cataloging-in-Publication Data

Social work matters: the power of linking policy and practice / edited by Elizabeth F. Hoffler
and Elizabeth J. Clark.
    p. cm.
  Includes bibliographical references and index.
  ISBN 978-0-87101-441-2
  1. Social service. I. Hoffler, Elizabeth F. II. Clark, Elizabeth J., 1944–
  HV40.S6616 2012
  361.3—dc23

                                       2012002947

Printed in the United States of America

CONTENTS

COMMUNITIES

CORRECTIONS AND THE COURTS

DIRECT PRACTICE

HIV/AIDS

PARITY

RESEARCH

About the Editors

Elizabeth F. Hoffler, MSW, ACSW, works in the executive office of NASW in Washington, DC, where she advises the executive director on key planning, strategic, and policy issues and assists in managing, analyzing, and implementing special projects and important issues within the office of the executive director. She is the chief speechwriter for the executive director and represents the national office at external events and meetings. She is also the executive office congressional liaison, coordinating congressional meetings and events for the executive director.

In addition, Hoffler works in NASW's Government Relations Department as lobbyist for the Social Work Reinvestment Initiative. This workforce initiative seeks to secure federal and state investments in professional social work to enhance societal well-being. Hoffler oversees the full initiative, which includes 56 NASW chapter reinvestment plans across the country as well as state and federal legislation that affects professional social workers, including the Dorothy I. Height and Whitney M. Young, Jr. Social Work Reinvestment Act.

Hoffler is a member of the Academy of Certified Social Workers; she has an MSW from the University of Illinois at Chicago's Jane Addams College of Social Work and a BSW from the University of Kentucky. Her interest areas are macro social work, nonprofit administration, social work workforce issues, public policy, and political social work.

Elizabeth J. Clark, PhD, ACSW, MPH, is executive director of NASW in Washington, DC. During her career, Dr. Clark has served in numerous administrative positions in social work, health care, and academia. Previously, she was executive director of the New York State chapter of NASW; chief operating officer for The March: Coming Together to Conquer Cancer, a national public awareness and grassroots organizing campaign; and director of diagnostic and therapeutic services at Albany Medical Center, Albany, NY, and associate professor of medicine, Division of Medical Oncology, Albany Medical College. Dr. Clark's other professional experience includes terms as deputy departmental chair and associate professor of health professions, Montclair State University, Monclair, NJ, where she also served as assistant to the dean of the School of Professional Studies and vice president of the faculty senate.

She also developed and administered the Cancer Care Program of St. Luke's Hospital in Bethlehem, PA.

Dr. Clark is a member of the Academy of Certified Social Workers and the National Academies of Practice. She holds a bachelor's and a master's degree in social work and an MPH from the University of Pittsburgh as well as a master's degree and a doctorate in medical sociology from the University of North Carolina at Chapel Hill. Dr. Clark is the recipient of an Honorary Doctor of Humane Letters from Wartburg College in Waverly, IA.

About the Contributors

Jeane W. Anastas, PhD, LMSW, is president of the board of directors of NASW. She has been a long-standing and active member of NASW and has also served as convener for the Action Network for Social Work Education and Research and a member of the NASW Workforce Research Advisory Workgroup. Previously, she served on the boards of directors of the Institute for Advancement of Social Work Research and the Society for Social Work and Research. Dr. Anastas has served as chair of the National Committee on Lesbian, Gay, Bisexual, and Transgender Issues; chair of the National Committee on Women's Issues; and a member of the National Committee on Nominations and Leadership Identification. She is active in her local NASW chapter, has served as president of the Massachusetts chapter of NASW, and was named that chapter's Social Worker of the Year in 1995.

Dr. Anastas is a professor at the New York University Silver School of Social Work and is highly regarded in the field of social work doctoral education and research. She was named a Council on Social Work Education (CSWE) Visiting Scholar for 2006–07 and received CSWE's Greatest Recent Contribution to Social Work Education Award in 2007. In 2007, Dr. Anastas was elected to the National Academies of Practice in Health Care.

Dr. Anastas has published extensively in the areas of women's issues, GLBT rights, mental health, and social work education, including the recently published *Teaching in Social Work: Theory and Practice for Educators* and the forthcoming *Doctoral Education in Social Work.* She received her BLS in social work from Boston University, her MSW from Boston College, and her PhD from Brandeis University.

Gary Bailey MSW, ACSW, received his BA from the Eliot Pearson School of Child Study, Tufts University, and his MSW from Boston University's School of Social Work. Currently, he is a professor of practice at the Simmons College School of Social Work and the Simmons School of Nursing and Health Sciences. Bailey is an award-winning professor who has played top leadership roles in the social work field. He is president of the International Federation of Social Workers, representing over 700,000 thousand social workers from over 80 countries. He was president of NASW from 2003 to 2005 and was named Social Worker of the Year by both the Massachusetts chapter of

NASW and the national organization in 1998. He was made a Social Work Pioneer by NASW in 2005.

Bailey is a past president of the board of directors of the AIDS Action Committee of Massachusetts. In June 2010, he was selected as one of 25 people who have made a difference in Massachusetts in the fight against HIV/AIDS and whose contributions to the fight against AIDS over the last two-and-a-half decades have been invaluable.

Audrey L. Begun, PhD, MSW, received her social work and research training at the University of Michigan, taking a doctorate in social work and the social sciences (developmental psychology). From 1997 to 2008, she served on the social work faculty of the Helen Bader School of Social Welfare at the University of Wisconsin–Milwaukee and as both a center scientist and administrator with the school's Center for Addiction and Behavioral Health Research. In 2009, she joined the faculty of the Ohio State University College of Social Work, where she continues to conduct research concerning substance abuse and other behavioral health concerns and to educate social workers at the BSSW, MSW, and PhD levels.

She was the primary editor of the National Institute on Alcohol Abuse and Alcoholism curriculum for social work education on alcohol abuse and dependence, which is still available to social work educators online. Her recent publications include articles and book chapters concerning social work intervention to address substance abuse–related needs among women during incarceration and community reentry, sibling relationships, and a life-course context for alcohol change attempts. She is currently working with a colleague to produce a book for social workers about conducting substance abuse research.

Tricia B. Bent-Goodley, PhD, MSW, LICSW, is professor of social work at Howard University. Dr. Bent-Goodley's research and writing have focused on developing community and faith-based interventions in the areas of domestic violence, dating violence, HIV prevention, and healthy relationship education. She is a member of the NASW Committee on Women's Issues. Dr. Bent-Goodley received her PhD in social policy, planning and analysis from Columbia University and her master's degree in social work from the University of Pennsylvania.

S. Megan Berthold, PhD, LICSW, CTS, is an assistant professor in casework at the University of Connecticut's School of Social Work. She holds a PhD in social welfare and for the past 24 years has specialized in the cross-cultural assessment and treatment of refugees and asylum seekers from many countries who are survivors of political persecution, torture, war traumas, human trafficking, female genital cutting, and other traumas. Before coming to the University of Connecticut in 2011, Dr. Berthold worked with the Program for Torture Victims in Los Angeles for 13 years as a psychotherapist and later as the director of research and evaluation. She has worked in refugee camps in Nepal and the Philippines and on the Thai–Cambodian border. Currently, she is conducting research funded by the National Institute of Mental Health with colleagues at the RAND Corporation examining the prevalence of torture and its mental and physical health consequences among Khmer refugees in southern California. She has also conducted federally funded clinical outcomes research with torture survivors, and she co-chairs the National Consortium of Torture Treatment Programs' data project. She has testified on numerous occasions since 1998 as an expert witness in U.S. immigration court.

Katharine Briar-Lawson, PhD, MSW, is dean and professor in the School of Social Welfare at the University at Albany, State University of New York. Among her books (coauthored) are *Family-Centered Policies and Practices: International Implications* and (coedited) *Innovative Practices with Vulnerable Children and Families; Evaluation Research in Child Welfare; Charting the Impacts of University–Child Welfare Collaboration; Social Work Research; Social Work Practice Research;* and *Globalization, Social Justice and the Helping Professions.* She co-chairs the Gerontological Task Force for the National Association for Deans and Directors and has served as a past president of the association. In addition, she is a co–principal investigator of the National Child Welfare Workforce Institute.

Karen Bullock, PhD, MSW, is an associate professor in the Department of Social Work at North Carolina State University. She holds a clinical appointment at the Institute of Living at Hartford Hospital, Hartford, CT, and serves on a number of community and professional boards. Dr. Bullock earned a BSW degree from North Carolina State University, an MSW from Columbia University, and a PhD from Boston University. She is a John A. Hartford Faculty Scholar and a member of the Social Work Hospice and Palliative Care Network board of directors and the NASW Mental Health Section Committee. She has published and presented nationally and internationally on health care disparities and end-of-life care issues with older adults.

Joseph E. Chicas, MSW, is a macro-level social worker, working with various agencies to improve organizational performance, develop programs, improve service delivery, and increase funding capacity. He recently worked for Congresswoman Karen Bass (D-CA), enhancing the federal casework program to meet the urgent needs of service members and their families. Currently, Chicas serves as a project specialist for the University of Southern California Center for Innovation and Research on Veterans and Military Families. He works with a senior research team to implement the Reintegration Partnership Project, an 18-month research and training effort to help National Guard soldiers transition from combat to civilian and family life. Chicas earned his bachelor's degree from University of California, Los Angeles, and his MSW from University of Southern California.

King Davis, PhD, is director of the Institute for Urban Policy Research and Analysis at the University of Texas at Austin (UTA). He served as the executive director of UTA's Hogg Foundation for Mental Health Services, Research, Policy and Education from 2003 to 2009. Since 2000, he has held the Robert Lee Sutherland Chair in Mental Health and Social Policy in the School of Social Work at UTA. He was a professor of public mental health policy and planning at the Virginia Commonwealth University from 1984 to 2000. As the Galt Scholar, he held full professorships at each of Virginia's three medical schools from 1985 to 1988. He was awarded a PhD from the Florence G. Heller School for Social Policy and Management at Brandeis University in 1971.

Dr. Davis is a former commissioner (1990–1994) of the Virginia Department of Mental Health, Mental Retardation, and Substance Abuse Services. At UTA, he teaches courses in mental health policy, planning, and theory. He is conducting a study of the policies that led to the development of the Central Lunatic Asylum for Colored Insane, the first mental institution for Africans in the United States. He is coauthor of *The Color of Social Policy,* and his most recent articles were published in *American Psychologist,* the *Journal of Social Policy,* and the *International Journal of Social Policy.*

Peter J. Delany, PhD, LCSW-C, Rear Admiral Lower Half in the U.S. Public Health Service Commissioned Corps, is currently director of the Center for Behavioral for Behavioral Health Statistics and Quality at the Substance Abuse and Mental Services Administration, Rockville, MD, and is the strategic lead for the data, outcomes, and quality initiative. He is also an adjunct professor of social work at the Catholic University of America.

Gina Fedock, MSW, is a doctoral student in social work at Michigan State University. Her clinical and research interests focus on interventions for the health and mental health needs of marginalized women, particularly those who are incarcerated.

Marilyn Flynn, PhD, MSW, was first appointed dean of the University of Southern California School (USC) of Social Work in 1997 and was reappointed in 2011. Under her leadership, the school significantly expanded its Hamovitch Center for Science in the Human Services and recruited a nationally recognized faculty to conduct clinical and intervention studies in health, mental health, aging, and child maltreatment. She established new graduate academic centers in San Diego and at the Skirball Cultural Center in West Los Angeles and then, in 2010, launched a full Web-based MSW degree program through the USC School of Social Work's new Virtual Academic Center. The school now graduates nearly 40 percent of all social workers in California and, with the Virtual Academic Center, has become the first truly national program in the profession. In addition, under Dr. Flynn's leadership, the school has received three congressionally directed appropriations to establish the Center for Innovation and Research on Veterans and Military families, focusing on the mental health needs of service members and their families.

Melissa Frey, MA, LCSW, is a community- and hospital-based social worker with interests in mental health, geriatrics, trauma, minority health disparities, and couples therapy. As a social worker, Frey has worked in various settings, including inpatient and outpatient behavioral health, community mental health, and public health centers. She currently works at Rush University Medical Center in Chicago as program coordinator of the BRIGHTEN Heart program in the Department of Preventive Medicine. Frey was selected to participate in the national Practice Change Fellowship Program, a grant-based leadership development program. As a fellow, she works as the developer, coordinator, and researcher on the UNIDOS (United in Identifying and Developing Our Strengths) program, which provides trauma treatment for Spanish-speaking older adults. Frey received her undergraduate degree from the University of Wisconsin–Madison, during which time she spent a year studying at the Universidad de Sevilla in Spain. Her master's degree is from the University of Chicago School of Social Administration, where she was awarded the Jane Mullenbach Moore Scholarship. She completed a postgraduate fellowship in evidence-based psychotherapy at Rush University Medical Center.

Irwin Garfinkel, PhD, is the Mitchell I. Ginsberg Professor of Contemporary Urban Problems at the Columbia University School of Social Work, co-founding director of the Columbia Population Research Center, and the co–principal investigator of the Fragile Families Study. He has authored over 200 scientific articles and 16 books and edited volumes on poverty, income transfer policy, program evaluation, single-parent families, and child support. His most recent book (with Lee Rainwater and Timothy Smeeding) is *Wealth and Welfare States: Is America a Laggard or Leader?*

Sarah Gehlert, PhD, is the E. Desmond Lee Professor of Racial and Ethnic Diversity at the George Warren Brown School of Social Work and professor in the Department of Surgery at Washington University in St. Louis. Until 2009, she was the Helen Ross Professor at the School of Social Service Administration at the University of Chicago. At Washington University, she is the co-leader of the Prevention and Control Program of the Siteman Cancer Center, co-director of the Transdisciplinary Center on Energetics and Cancer, and training program director for the Program for the Elimination of Cancer Disparities. Dr. Gehlert serves on the executive committee of Washington University's Institute for Clinical and Translational Science and co-chairs the Center for Community-Engaged Research. She is a member of the Board of Scientific Counselors of the National Human Genome Research Institute. She chaired the National Institutes of Health's (NIH) Summer Institute on Community-Based

Participatory Research in 2007 and 2009 and serves as a chartered member of NIH's Community-Level Health Promotion Study Section. She is a member of the Oncology Social Work Peer Review Committee at the American Cancer Society, a past president of the Society for Social Work and Research, and a fellow in the American Academy of Social Work and Social Welfare.

Leon H. Ginsberg, PhD, teaches social work at Appalachian State University, where he has served as interim chair of the Department of Social Work. He was formerly distinguished professor and dean at the College of Social Work, University of South Carolina; dean of the School of Social Work, West Virginia University; and West Virginia's Commissioner of Human Services. He was also formerly a board member and national secretary of NASW. He is the editor of the journal *Administration in Social Work.*

Robyn Golden, MA, LCSW, serves as the director of older adult programs at Rush University Medical Center in Chicago, where she also holds academic appointments in the Departments of Preventive Medicine and Health Systems Management. She is responsible for the expansion of services and oversees the health and aging, mental health, and transitional care programs. Golden has worked in the field of aging for more than 25 years. She has been actively involved in service provision, program development, education, research, and public policy aimed at developing innovative initiatives and systems integration to improve the health and well-being of older adults and their families. In 2003–04, Golden was the John Heinz Senate Fellow, based in the office of Senator Hillary Rodham Clinton (D-NY) in Washington, DC. Prior to this, she worked at the Council for Jewish Elderly for 18 years, serving for much of that time as their director of clinical service. She is past chair of the American Society on Aging and is a fellow of the Gerontological Society of America. She co-chairs the National Coalition on Care Coordination, housed at the New York Academy of Medicine. Golden has a master's degree from the School of Social Service Administration at the University of Chicago and a bachelor's degree from Miami University. She and her coauthor Melissa Frey acknowledge Gayle Shier, with gratitude, for assistance in editing their chapter.

Seana Golder, PhD, MSW, received her BA from the University of Maryland, her MSW from Louisiana State University, and her PhD in social welfare from the University of Washington. Dr. Golder's clinical practice experience has included work with adult women and men in the criminal justice system, substance abuse treatment, and addressing high-risk behaviors among adolescent and young adult women. She joined the faculty of the University of Louisville's Kent School of Social Work in 2003, where she is currently an associate professor, teaching primarily in the area of practice. Her research focuses on women's engagement in high-risk behaviors (substance abuse, law-breaking, risky sexual behavior), with a particular emphasis on understanding the intersection of victimization, substance abuse, and psychological distress, especially among women in the criminal justice system.

Stephen H. Gorin, PhD, received his doctorate in social welfare policy from the Heller School, Brandeis University. He is professor in the Social Work Department at Plymouth State University in Plymouth, NH, and executive director of the New Hampshire chapter of NASW. He is currently serving his second term as editor-in-chief of the journal *Health & Social Work.* He served as a delegate to the 1995 and 2005 White House Conferences on Aging and the 1998 White House Conference on Social Security. He was elected to membership in the National Academy of Social Insurance and been appointed to the standing editorial board of *Oxford Bibliographies Online: Social Work.* He is also serving a second term as a member of the New Hampshire State Committee on Aging.

Laura W. Groshong, MSW, received her master's in social work in 1974 from the School of Social Service Administration at the University of Chicago. She also has advanced training in adult psychotherapy from the Seattle Psychoanalytic Institute, receiving her certificate in 1979. Groshong has been in private practice with individuals, couples, and families for 35 years. Since 1996, she has also worked as a registered lobbyist in Washington state for eight mental health groups, passing several bills promoting access to mental health treatment. Since 2006, she has served as the director of government relations for the Clinical Social Work Association, a national organization that advocates on behalf of clinical social workers.

Groshong was inducted into the National Social Work Academy of Practice in November 2004 for her clinical, legislative, and organizational work. She has also written several articles on legislative activity and coauthored social work licensure laws in 10 states. Groshong is the author of *Clinical Social Work Regulation and Practice: An Overview,* which compared clinical social work licensure laws and scopes of practice across all states and jurisdictions in the United States. She spoke to the Council on Social Work Education as an invited presenter at their national conference in Portland, Oregon, in October 2010.

Lisa P. Gwyther, MSW, LCSW, is a social worker with 40 years of experience in aging and Alzheimer's services. She is an associate professor in the Department of Psychiatry and Behavioral Sciences at Duke University Medical Center, director of the Duke Aging Center Family Support Program, and education director of the Bryan Alzheimer's Disease Research Center at Duke University Medical Center. In 1999, Duke's Family Support Program was named the Agency of the Year by NASW's North Carolina chapter. Gwyther was the 2008 president of the Gerontological Society of America. She received her graduate training in social work at Case Western Reserve University. She has published over 130 articles, book chapters, and books on

Alzheimer's care and family caregiving research. She served on the U.S. federal advisory panel on Alzheimer's disease for nine years and, during that time, provided expert testimony for several congressional hearings on Alzheimer's disease. In June 1998, Gwyther was recognized in the 20th anniversary issue of *Contemporary Long-Term Care* as one of 20 people who made a difference in U.S. long-term care in those two decades. She has received two major North Carolina awards for leadership in aging services. In 1993, as the first recipient of the John Heinz Congressional Fellowship in Aging and Health, she spent six months on the health staff of U.S. Senate Majority Leader George J. Mitchell.Jodi Hall, EdD, MSW, is a clinical assistant professor and director of field education in the Department of Social Work at North Carolina State University. She earned an EdD from North Carolina State University and an MSW from the University of North Carolina at Chapel Hill. Her direct practice experience includes abuse investigations and treatment and public health social work. Dr. Hall was also the staff development manager for a large county human services agency and administered a partnership program between large county government agencies. Her primary research focus is education and access for ethnic minorities and disadvantaged groups. She has written and presented on issues of health and social justice in relation to improving access to services and opportunities.

Anthony M. Hassan, EdD, LCSW, is director of the Center for Innovation and Research on Veterans and Military Families at the University of Southern California. Dr. Hassan is a retired Air Force officer who brings 25 years of experience in military social work and leadership development to this project. He was chief executive officer of the MacDill Air Force Base community mental health center, which was ranked first out of 10 community mental health centers in its region for productivity and "best clinic." Dr. Hassan served during Operation Iraqi Freedom in 2004 on the first-ever Air Force combat stress control and prevention team embedded with an Army unit. His unique combination of experiences contributes greatly to his success as a leader, educator, researcher, and clinician, which has been recognized with over $17 million in grant funding in 2009–10.

Anne Hoffman, LCSW-C, serves as a supervisor for Montgomery County, MD, Child Welfare Services and is in her 17th year with the department. Her tenure has included four years as a sexual abuse investigator; 10 years as the sexual abuse investigation unit supervisor; and her current position as supervisor of several in-home services programs, in accordance with Maryland's family-centered practice policy initiatives. Hoffman also serves as the agency liaison with the Department of Juvenile Services, Emergency Services, Homeless Services, and the Maryland State's Attorney's Office to facilitate interagency collaboration and seamless service delivery.

Hoffman is a member of the State Council on Child Abuse and Neglect and the Children's Justice Act Committee. She has appeared as an expert witness in various jurisdictions around the state of Maryland and has collaborated with the U.S. Attorney's Office at the federal level. She is one of the founding faculty members of the Finding Words/Child First initiative in Maryland, an intense, five-day training course directed at social workers, law enforcement personnel, prosecutors, victim/witness coordinators, and other professionals involved in child abuse investigations. She is also an adjunct professor at Hood College. Hoffman conducts trainings on a variety of child welfare issues throughout the state and is currently involved in crafting a training for Maryland's Juvenile Court judges to be presented in May at the annual CANDO Conference.

Ebony Jackson is the digital media and online community manager at the NASW national office, where she manages a social networking presence of over 50,000 engaged social workers and students connecting via social media channels. An avid blogger and early social media proponent, she has over 10 years of Web development and content management experience, with a focus on usability and functional design. She received her BA in communications from Howard University.

Jessica L. Katz graduated from Penn State University in 2009 with a BA in psychology and minors in gerontology and human development and family studies. While at Penn State, Katz completed a research assistantship with Steven Zarit, an internationally recognized clinical investigator in dementia caregiver assessment and services. Katz is currently in her final year in the MSW program at the University of North Carolina at Chapel Hill. She is working toward a certificate in aging and is a fellow in the Hartford Partnership Practicum for Aging Education program, with a field placement at the Duke Family Support Program. She is scheduled to receive her MSW in May 2012 and anticipates state licensure in clinical social work and a career working with older adults with memory impairment and their family caregivers.

James J. Kelly, PhD, MSSW, is the president of Menlo College, Atherton, CA, and the immediate past president of NASW. For 27 years prior to joining Menlo, he worked as a professor of social work, provost, associate vice president, dean, and director in the California State University system. His areas of expertise include social work, continuing, international, and business education; gerontology; program development; and higher education administration. Dr. Kelly earned his PhD from the Heller School for Social Policy and Management at Brandeis University, his MSSW from the University of Tennessee, and his BS from Edinboro University in Pennsylvania. He is a fellow of the Gerontological Society of America.

Susan Kosche Vallem, EdD, LISW, is a professor in the Social Work Department at Wartburg College, Waverly, IA, and currently serves as field education director. She has been active in legislative advocacy at the state and federal levels, advocating particularly for families and children, social work education, the Social Work Reinvestment

Act, and health care policy. She currently serves as convener of the ANSWER Coalition, member of the Baccalaureate Program Directors Nominations and Advocacy and Outreach Committees, and chair of the Waverly Health Center board of trustees. Along with teaching undergraduate social work, Dr. Kosche Vallem serves as a disaster mental health worker for the American Red Cross and the state of Iowa.

Sheryl Pimlott Kubiak, PhD, is associate professor and director of doctoral education at the School of Social Work, Michigan State University. Her research interests include the intersections between criminal justice, mental health, and substance abuse, with a primary focus on women in jails and prison who have experienced traumatic events, particularly interpersonal violence.

Vicki Lens, PhD, JD, MSW, is currently associate professor at the Columbia University School of Social Work. Her primary research interest is in exploring the intersection of law, social work, and social policy, with a focus on welfare reform and administrative justice in public welfare bureaucracies. She is also interested in advocacy and the policy-making process and has published several articles drawing on linguistics and other disciplines to teach social work practitioners how to frame issues in the public arena.

Charles E. Lewis Jr., PhD, MSW, is the deputy chief of staff and communications director for Congressman Edolphus Towns (D-NY). He is also an adjunct professor at the University of Maryland Baltimore School of Social Work. Dr. Lewis completed his BA in psychology at the College of New Rochelle, his MSW in clinical counseling at Clark Atlanta University, and his PhD in social policy analysis at Columbia University. He is the former president and a current member of the board of the Mental Health Association of the District of New York.

Kathy Lopes, MSW, is a licensed independent clinical social worker with many years of experience dedicated to the health and care of youths and families. She received her MSW from Simmons College School of Social Work and her BA from the University of Massachusetts, Amherst. She is a clinical supervisor and manager at the Massachusetts Society for the Prevention of Cruelty to Children. Her social work experience includes case management, clinical, and managerial roles, with training in cognitive–behavioral, trauma-focused cognitive–behavioral, and child-centered play therapies. Her involvement in a nationally publicized case, *United States v. Banita Jacks,* inspired her work in advocacy and policy reform within the field. She is also a part-time instructor at Simmons College, teaching graduate courses on social policy and political action. She received the Justice for Victims of Crime award from the U.S. Department of Justice in 2010 and the Simmons College Recent Graduate Award in 2008. She is an active member of the Simmons College School of Social Work Alumni Board.

Mayra Lopez-Humphreys, PhD, MSW, is an assistant professor and field coordinator of the undergraduate social work department at Nyack College. She has taught undergraduate and graduate courses in diversity, social welfare policy and field practice, and her research interests include critical multiculturalism and restorative practices. She has coauthored a number of peer-reviewed scholarly articles, including "The Social Construction of Client Participation: The Evolution and Transformation of the Role of Service Recipients in Child Welfare and Mental Disabilities." Dr. Lopez-Humphreys has over 10 years of practice/organizational leadership experience in both youth development and community organizing and has designed a number of asset-based programs that focus on fostering and integrating both communities' and participants' social, spiritual, and cultural capital. In 2002, she received the Children's Aid Society Excellence Award for her leadership in program innovations and partnerships with immigrant families. In the Harlem community in New York City, she is currently involved in the development of and research on a local food cooperative that offers affordable, healthy, locally grown meals and facilitating the social benefits of preparing and sharing group meals.

Mark Lusk, EdD, LMSW, ACSW, is professor of social work at the University of Texas at El Paso. He has spent much of his career working in Latin America on social development. Dr. Lusk is currently carrying out a program of research on trauma among Mexican refugees. He volunteers with civil rights and immigration advocacy organizations on the border.

Romel Mackelprang, DSW, MSW, LICSW, has been a social work educator for 30 years. He is the director of the Eastern Washington University Center for Disability Studies and Universal Access. For decades, he has been active in disability rights advocacy; he currently chairs the Washington State Independent Living Council, and he is the principal investigator in a study of the long-term impact of donated wheelchairs in several sub-Saharan African countries.

Ruth G. McRoy, PhD, MSW, became, in September 2009, the first holder of the Donahue and DiFelice Endowed Professorship at Boston College Graduate School of Social Work. Before joining the Boston College faculty, Dr. McRoy was a member of the University of Texas at Austin (UTA) School of Social Work faculty for 25 years and held the Ruby Lee Piester Centennial Professorship. She received her BA and MSW degrees from the University of Kansas and her PhD from UTA. As part of the federally funded AdoptUSKids project, Dr. McRoy and her research team at UTA recently completed two nationwide studies on barriers to adoption and factors associated with successful special-needs adoptions. Currently, she is leading a team conducting a five-year evaluation of AdoptUSKids. Dr. McRoy has served as president and board member of the North American Council on Adoptable Children and is a senior research fellow and member of the Evan B. Donaldson Adoption Institute Board. She has published numerous articles and book chapters, and nine books, including *Transracial and Interracial Adoptees: The Adolescent Years* (with Louis A. Zurcher Jr.), *Special Needs Adoptions: Practice Issues,* and *Openness in Adoption: Family Connections* (with Harold D. Grotevant).

Terry Mizrahi, PhD, MSW, is professor at the Silberman School of Social Work, Hunter College, City University of New York, where she chairs the Community Organization, Planning and Development (COP & D) practice method and teaches both COP & D and social and health policy. She is also director of the Education Center for Community Organizing. Dr. Mizrahi was co-editor-in-chief of the 20th edition of the *Encyclopedia of Social Work.* She is the author of five books and monographs and 70 articles, book chapters, reviews, and manuals. Among her publications are *Women, Organizing and Diversity: Struggling with the Issues* (coauthor); *Getting Rid of Patients: Contradiction in the Socialization of Physicians; Community Organization and Social Administration* (coeditor and author); and *Strategic Partnerships: Building Successful Coalitions and Collaborations* (coauthor).

Her areas of research, training, and consultation include professional socialization, coalition building, community organizing practice, and health policy. Dr. Mizrahi is continuing a longitudinal study of 26 physicians that began in 1980, and she and colleagues are also examining the role of professional background in interdisciplinary community health collaborations; she is also engaged in a cross-country study with Israel of the role of gender and organizing—the perspectives of male and female community organizers.

Dr. Mizrahi served as the national president of NASW from 2001 to 2003. She is a founder of the Association for Community Organization and Social Administration's (ACOSA) *Journal of Community Practice.* Among her many awards are the Hunter Presidential Award for Excellence in Applied Research (2008) and Hunter's Community Leadership Award (1992). She also won the Lifetime Career Achievement Award from ACOSA in 2004. She completed a Fulbright fellowship in Israel in 2006 and continues to train and consult there with various academic and professional leaders.

Linda S. Moore, PhD, ACSW, LMSW-AP, is professor of social work at Texas Christian University (TCU). Her MSW is from Virginia Commonwealth University, and her PhD is from Texas Woman's University. She has published on the impact of social work education on student values and attitudes, gatekeeping, community practice, using the Myers–Briggs Type Inventory in social work education, social workers' contributions to the emergence of the NAACP, and the legacy of Whitney M. Young Jr. Dr. Moore has been president of the Association of Baccalaureate Social Work Program Directors (BPD), NASW's Texas chapter, and the Texas Association of Social Work Deans and Directors and chair of the Nominating Committee of the Council on Social Work Education, the Nominations Committee of BPD, and NASW's National Committee on Nominations and Leadership Identification. She is a certified accreditation site team chair and was editor-in-chief of the *Journal of Baccalaureate Social Work*. Dr. Moore received the TCU College of Health and Human Sciences Distinguished Research Award and the TCU Deans' Teaching Award twice and was nominated for the Chancellor's Award for Distinguished Teaching on three occasions. She is a member of Phi Kappa Phi honor society, Alpha Delta Mu and Phi Alpha (social work honor societies), Alpha Kappa Delta (the international sociology honor society), and Golden Key International Honor Society.

Frederic G. Reamer, PhD, is a professor in the graduate program of the School of Social Work, Rhode Island College, where he has been on the faculty since 1983. His research and teaching have addressed a wide range of human service issues, including mental health, health care, criminal justice, and professional ethics. Reamer received his PhD from the University of Chicago in 1978 and has served as a social worker in correctional and mental health settings. He has served as director of the National Juvenile Justice Assessment Center of the U.S. Department of Justice, Office of Juvenile Justice and Delinquency Prevention; senior policy advisor to the governor of Rhode Island; and commissioner of the Rhode Island Housing and Mortgage Finance Corporation. Since 1992, he has served on the State of Rhode Island Parole Board. He was also editor-in-chief of the *Journal of Social Work Education* and associate editor of the 20th edition of the *Encyclopedia of Social Work*. Reamer is the author of many books and articles. He chaired the national task force that wrote the current NASW *Code of Ethics*.

Deirdra Robinson, MSW, graduated from the University of Kentucky, completing her BSW in 1993 and her MSW in 1994. She grew up in a rural town in eastern Kentucky, and her passion for promoting social justice led her to work in community development. In 1999, she accepted an appointment with the University of Kentucky College of Social Work as clinical faculty member and administrative coordinator of the southeast Kentucky MSW program. In 2010, she accepted an instructor position at Morehead State University in the Department of Sociology, Social Work and Criminology. Her research and community development work focuses on health disparities and rural health issues. She is currently the president-elect of the NASW Kentucky chapter. Robinson is a member of the National Health Service Corps, the Kentucky Fairness Alliance, and NASW. She has presented research at local, state, and national conferences and mentors student trainees. She is also working on her PhD dissertation.

Sunny Harris Rome, JD, MSW, is an associate professor in the Department of Social Work, George Mason University. She earned her MSW from the University of Michigan and her JD from Georgetown University Law Center. Prior to joining the George

Mason faculty, she worked as a litigating attorney in the General Counsel's Office of the U.S. Department of Education and as a senior lobbyist for NASW's national office. She teaches courses on social policy, legislative advocacy, social work and the law, and community practice. Her research interests include child welfare policy, immigration, and political action. She is a faculty fellow with the Cochrane Collaboration College for Policy, under whose auspices she is completing a project on the mental health status of immigrant children and youths. She is the author of the textbook *Social Work and Law: Judicial Policy and Forensic Practice,* which is currently in press.

Trina R. Williams Shanks, PhD, MSW, is currently associate professor at the University of Michigan School of Social Work. She completed her PhD in social work at Washington University in St. Louis and is a faculty associate with its Center for Social Development. She earned a master's degree in comparative social research from the University of Oxford as a Rhodes Scholar. Her research interests include asset-building policy and practice across the life course, the impact of poverty and wealth on child well-being, and community and economic development in urban areas. She has several active research projects, including serving as co-investigator for the SEED Impact Assessment study, which has established a quasi-experimental research design to test the impact of offering 529 college education plans to Head Start families; an NICHD-funded study to conduct secondary data analysis examining how the financial situation of households influences child outcomes from early childhood into adulthood; and an evaluation, which she is overseeing, for Detroit's Summer Youth Employment Program. As of May 2010, Dr. Shanks was appointed by Governor Jennifer M. Granholm to serve on Michigan's Commission on Community Action and Economic Opportunity.

Joseph J. Shields, PhD, is an associate professor at the National Catholic School of Social Service, Catholic University of America, Washington, DC. He also has a joint appointment with the Center for Behavioral Health, Statistics and Quality, the Substance Abuse and Mental Health Services Administration, Rockville, MD, where he serves as a senior research scientist.

Tracy Soska, LSW, is assistant professor, chair of the Community Organization and Social Administration Program, and director of continuing education at the University of Pittsburgh's School of Social Work. He also co-directs the university's Community Outreach Partnership Center and, in 2000, received the university chancellor's Faculty Public Service award. In addition to serving as immediate past chair of the Association for Community Organization and Social Administration, he serves as an editor of the *Journal of Community Practice.* Prior to joining the Pittsburgh faculty in 1993, Soska was a nonprofit executive for over 15 years, leading such initiatives as the Westinghouse Valley Human Services Center and the Mon Valley Providers Council during the era of Pittsburgh's industrial decline, the Urban League of Pittsburgh's Youth Employment System and Ex-Offender Programs, and the Pittsburgh Neighborhood Alliance and its citywide crime prevention program.

Evelyn P. Tomaszewski, MSW, is a senior policy associate in NASW's Human Rights and International Affairs Division. She is responsible for implementation of the NASW HIV/AIDS Spectrum Project, which addresses a range of health and behavioral health issues, with a focus on HIV/AIDS and co-occurring chronic illnesses. She promotes the NASW Global HIV/AIDS Initiative through collaboration with domestic and international groups and agencies, having implemented capacity and training needs assessments addressing the social work workforce, volunteers, and health and mental health care providers in sub-Saharan Africa. She staffs the NASW National Committee on Lesbian, Gay, Bisexual, and Transgender Issues and previously staffed the International Committee. She has expertise in policy analysis and implementation addressing gender equity, violence prevention and early intervention, the connection of trauma and risk for HIV/AIDS, and public health approaches to community health. Tomaszewski has over two decades of social work experience as a counselor, community organizer, educator/trainer, and administrator. She holds a BSW and an MSW from West Virginia University and a graduate certificate in procurement and contracts management and a certificate in leadership development from the University of Virginia.

Adrienne Walnoha, MSW, is the chief executive officer of Community Human Services (CHS), Pittsburgh, a private community benefit organization that operates the Lawn Street Community Center and social service programming for youths and families, primary and behavioral health care, and supported community housing. Under Walnoha's leadership, CHS has expanded its housing assistance programs to include atypical shelter, housing first, eviction prevention, and rapid rehousing programs, which previously had not been available in Allegheny County, PA. CHS also acts as the housing crisis provider for Allegheny County Department of Human Services. Walnoha serves as an advisor on the Allegheny County Homeless Advisory Board and the Emergency Food and Shelter Program Board. She is also a therapist and licensed social worker and part of the adjunct faculty at the University of Pittsburgh School of Social Work.

Katherine Walsh, PhD, MSW, is a professor of social work in the MSW program at Westfield State University and maintains a private practice in Northampton, MA. She is a past board member and past president of the Association of Oncology Social Workers, author of the text book *Grief and Loss: Theories and Skills for the Helping Professions* (2nd ed.), coauthor of the C-Penn award–winning *Cancer Survival Toolbox,* and author of more than 30 book chapters and peer-reviewed journal articles.

She has led social work exchanges to Cambodia, China, and Hungary and has won numerous professional awards, such as the Trish Greene Award from the American Cancer Society.

Carmen D. Weisner, LCSW, ACSW, graduated from the Louisiana State University School of Social Work in 1974. She retired from public service in 2004. Before her retirement, she was appointed by Governor Mike Foster to be the assistant secretary for the Louisiana Department of Social Service's Office of Community Services, and, under her leadership, the agency became the third public statewide system to achieve accreditation by the Council on Accreditation (COA). On her retirement from public service, Weisner was hired by the Louisiana chapter of NASW as its executive director; it was during her first year in that position that Louisiana was hit by Hurricanes Katrina and Rita. She was a keynote speaker at the 2005 COA Public Agency Roundtable and the 2006 Child Welfare League of America Conference. In 2010, she was named the NASW executive director of the year.

Tracy Robinson Whitaker, DSW, ACSW, is director of NASW's Center for Workforce Studies and Social Work Practice. She directed the 2004 national benchmark study of licensed social workers and was the lead author of five reports that emanated from that study. She also led the first compensation and benefits study of the social work profession in 2009 and has conducted multiple studies of the NASW membership. Dr. Whitaker is the lead author of *Workforce Trends Affecting the Profession 2009* and *The Results Are In: What Social Workers Say About Social Work,* both published by the NASW Press.

Dr. Whitaker's career has included work with individuals, organizations, and community systems. She has served as the executive director of a transitional center for homeless women; as a court monitor overseeing the deinstitutionalization of St. Elizabeths Hospital, Washington, DC; and as the deputy director of a federally funded national resource center addressing the behavioral health needs of women across the life cycle. Dr. Whitaker received a BA in political science and an MSW and a DSW from Howard University. She also holds certification from NASW's Academy of Certified Social Workers.

Reeta Wolfsohn, CMSW, is founder of the Center for Financial Social Work (http://www.financialsocialwork.com) and a nationally known motivational speaker. She is a certified social worker, author, and expert on money from a psychosocial perspective. Wolfsohn's work began in 1997 with a focus on "femonomics—the gender of money," based on the feminization-of-poverty approach. Over time, it grew less gender specific, and in 2003 she renamed her approach "financial social work" and founded the Center for Financial Social Work, which has since certified hundreds of men and women across the United States and around the world in financial social work. Wolfsohn gives keynote speeches and trainings at national and state conferences and has taught at numerous universities and colleges.

Joan Levy Zlotnik, PhD, ACSW, is the director of the NASW Social Work Policy Institute and previously served as the executive director of the Institute for Social Work Research. She is nationally recognized for her leadership work on building university–agency collaborations, addressing policy and practice issues related to the enhancement of the child welfare and aging workforces, and developing strategies for building and sustaining social work research infrastructure and capacity. For more than two decades, she has worked in national social work organizations, successfully garnering federal and foundation funds to enhance the delivery of social work services.

INTRODUCTION

Elizabeth F. Hoffler and Elizabeth J. Clark

> *The good we secure for ourselves is precarious and uncertain until it is secured for all of us and incorporated into our common life.*
>
> —Jane Addams

This book is titled *Social Work Matters* for a variety of reasons. Social work matters because the profession is absolutely necessary for a healthy society. The primary mission of the social work profession is to enhance human well-being and help meet the basic needs of all people, with particular attention to those who are vulnerable, oppressed, and living in poverty. As we continue to deal with the consequences of a devastating economic recession, the looming fear of instability, and a government that is no longer able to meet the needs or fulfill the promises made to millions of people at risk of falling through the cracks, the social work profession continues to pick up the pieces of a broken system and determine how to make that system whole again.

To this end, social justice is the fuel that drives social workers and is what sets social work apart from other professions. *Social justice* is defined as "an ideal condition in which all members of a society have the same basic rights, protections, opportunities, obligations, and social benefits. . . . Social justice entails advocacy to confront discrimination, oppression, and institutional inequities" (Barker, 2003, pp. 404–405).

Social workers work with individuals, families, communities, and systems and can be found in almost every corner of our lives, including schools, prisons, hospitals, mental health clinics, addiction recovery centers, skilled nursing facilities, hospices, private practice, and state and federal government, to name but a few. They form the front line and make up the threads of society's social safety net. Social workers are first responders to natural disasters, are officers in the military, and are members of the U.S. Congress. They own their own businesses and work in and run foundations, nonprofits, and corporate organizations and companies throughout the country.

The profession of social work has existed for over a century, since its founding in settlement houses like Jane Addams' Hull House in Chicago. Social workers—like Frances Perkins, Harry Hopkins, Dorothy I. Height, and Whitney M. Young

Jr.—have been key architects on groundbreaking social initiatives like civil rights legislation, Social Security, unemployment insurance, and Medicaid and Medicare and provide the majority of mental health services throughout the country. Social workers assist people when they face emotional, difficult, and seemingly insurmountable obstacles. These social work *matters* are the issues that our nation struggles with and are challenges that we must overcome. They include poverty, inequality, insecurity, fear, violence, trauma, loss, and pain. Our world would be radically different without the contributions of social workers.

The idea for this book emerged, in part, from recognition of the breadth and depth of social work services just described. We created the book with two goals in mind. First, we wanted to portray what social workers accomplish in different fields on a daily basis. The work of social workers can seem overwhelming in the variety of positions they hold, the tasks that they accomplish, and the intensity and gravity of the work that they do. The profession is often misunderstood and undervalued. This does a disservice to the profession as well as to clients and society as a whole.

Second, this publication seeks to link the traditional, direct practice side of social work with the critical policy and advocacy components of the profession. The book explores the transition from micro-level service, working directly to improve the lives of individuals, to the macro-level work of altering our social systems and institutions through broad social action and advocacy.

Social workers have advocated for social justice and promoted equality since the founding of the profession. In the *Encyclopedia of Social Work,* Schneider, Lester, and Ochieng (2008) stated that "the term *advocacy* was first evidenced in the [1917] *Proceedings of the National Conference of Charities and Corrections*" (p. 61). Furthermore, "social work advocates fought for basic human rights and social justice for oppressed, vulnerable, and displaced populations" (Schneider et al., 2008, p. 61). The *Social Work Dictionary* defines *advocacy* as "the act of directly representing or defending others. . . . championing the rights of individuals and communities through direct intervention and *empowerment*" (p. 11).

Advocacy is the cornerstone on which social work is built. It is so important that it is framed in three sections of the NASW (2008) *Code of Ethics.* Advocacy for individuals, communities, and systems is not just a suggested activity for social workers—it is a requisite. Social workers are ethically obligated to "engage in social and political action that seeks to ensure that all people have equal access to the resources . . . they require to meet their basic human needs and to develop fully" (NASW, 2008, p. 27). The *Code of Ethics* further notes that "social workers should be aware of the impact of the political arena on practice and should advocate for changes in policy and legislation to improve social conditions" (NASW, 2008, p. 27). Without advocacy, there would be no social work profession (Clark, 2009). Social workers acquire resources for clients, organize communities for causes, and coordinate grassroots advocacy campaigns.

In this book, we explore the direct connection of practice to policy and the ethical obligation of social workers to understand and foster the relationship between the two. Each of the contributors provides a personal narrative that was, or could have been, influenced by the application of a particular policy or piece of legislation. They provide analyses of broad implications and describe the importance of advocacy at organizational, local, state, or federal levels to the achievement of maximum client opportunity and benefit. In short, they illustrate the intricacies of the linkage of practice and policy.

Although the majority of social workers practice directly with clients, determining how to achieve successful outcomes on an individual basis, their understanding of the challenges facing their clients puts them in an excellent position to advocate for broader social change. Social workers with practice experience make excellent advocates because they understand clearly the challenges facing their clients, including clients' presenting problems, holistic environmental factors, and client strengths that can be drawn on so as to help them.

At this time of incredible demand for social work services, combined with ever-diminishing resources, the professional role of advocate is more critical than ever before. The chapters of this book illustrate what social workers do each day to improve the lives of others and the macro-level action that can be taken to help systems better serve those for whom they were created. We hope this book increases public understanding of the value of social work services, and we hope that it inspires all helping professionals to recognize the potential they have to create positive change.

Social worker Dorothy I. Height (1990) once said, "We hold in our hands the power to shape, not only our own, but the nation's future" (p. 75). Height's social work colleague and fellow civil rights advocate Whitney M. Young Jr. said during his tenure as NASW president,

> There is a lot to tell the public. The important thing now is that we can begin saying something as persistently as we can. The media and the government, regardless of their reasons, cannot continue to disregard the findings of current research and the knowledge of thousands of social workers who know as much or more as the so called experts on the social problems draining the spirit and resources of this nation. (Young, 1971, p. 7)

We wholeheartedly believe that social work is not just "value added," but is necessary to ensure that our country continues to provide opportunity, ensure equity, and help millions of individuals as they seek to fulfill their potential, whether that means battling addiction, escaping poverty, caring for loved ones, accessing education, or overcoming a variety of life's obstacles. As you read these narratives, you will understand that social workers are the professionals to help them do just that.

REFERENCES

Barker, R. L. (2003). *The social work dictionary* (5th ed.). Washington, DC: NASW Press.

Clark, E. J. (2009). *A broader vision for the social work profession.* Retrieved from http://www.social workers.org/nasw/VisionSpeech0809.pdf

Height, D. I. (1990). 1990–2035: 45 years from today. *Ebony, 46,* 75.

National Association of Social Workers. (2008). *Code of ethics of the National Association of Social Workers.* Washington, DC: NASW Press.

Schneider, R. L., Lester, L., & Ochieng, J. (2008). Advocacy. In T. Mizrahi & L. E. Davis (Eds.), *Encyclopedia of social work* (20th ed., Vol. 1, pp. 59–65). Washington, DC, and New York: NASW Press & Oxford University Press.

Young, W. M. (1971, March). From the president. *NASW News, 16,* 7.

Note: The narratives in this book are based on real-life cases of clients served by professional social workers. Names and identifying details have been changed to ensure the confidentiality and safety of these clients.

ADMINISTRATION

CHAPTER 1

THE BUSINESS
OF SOCIAL WORK

Elizabeth J. Clark

SOCIAL WORK MATTERS

During my social work career, I often have been surprised by the number of people who believe that social work should avoid the term "business" and that business principles do not apply to our profession. Somehow, the concept of nonprofit has been mistakenly defined as non*business*. This is a misperception that can limit the impact of what social workers do and on the services they provide.

If you examine the two concepts of for-profit business and nonprofit business, you will find that the differences are few. The main issue is the purpose for which an organization or corporation has been established. The designation of for profit or nonprofit is awarded by tax code, and to open a business, everyone needs a tax identification number (also called an EIN, or employer identification number). The determination of whether your organization is tax exempt is made on the basis of its purpose and its mission.

To be tax exempt, you must have a mission in the line of charitable or educational activities. The mission cannot be to make a profit for yourself, your company, or your stockholders. In fact, the dollars you make must mainly be used for your nonprofit activities. This does not, however, mean that you cannot make a profit or have a positive bottom line.

There are many similarities between for- and nonprofit businesses. Unless a business is owned by one person (sole proprietorship), it must be incorporated in a state. To incorporate, you need to have a board of directors and officers. You are required to keep specific data and records. You must pay employment taxes for any employees and, depending on size, must offer mandated benefits such as family medical leave and follow all required policies such as paying overtime for nonexempt employees. Regardless of tax status, you must adhere to antidiscrimination and other employee protections. You must also comply with occupational, health, and labor regulations (Edwards & Yankey, 2006). Both for- and nonprofit businesses may be challenged legally by individuals, groups, or the government, and it is important to have directors' and officers' liability insurance to protect nonprofits as well.

Regardless of purpose (for profit or nonprofit), an organization needs to conduct audits, file annual tax returns, and pay state and federal income tax. The form of filing differs, but the function is the same. For a nonprofit organization, management must file what is referred to as IRS Form 990. Because of the nonprofit status, this form must be made available to the public and is listed on a Web site called GuideStar (http://www2.guidestar.org). If a nonprofit has revenue from activities not considered central to its mission (for example, selling member address lists), it must pay UBIT (unrelated business income tax).

Just as for-profit businesses have varied forms (for example, privately held, publicly traded), nonprofits have numerous designations under U.S. Tax Code (U.S.C. 26, Sec. 501). We generally refer to these as "C" designations. There are 28 different designations, but it is the 501(c)(3) that is especially germane here.

The 501(c)(3) is a charitable designation. This designation means that an organization can give a tax-deductible receipt when funds (donations) are received. Most social service programs are 501(c)(3) organizations. This includes food pantries, shelters, and other community support programs as well as large national organizations like the American Cancer Society, the United Service Organizations, and the United Way.

The structure and funding of social work agencies and programs also vary. Some are government, community, or grant funded. Others depend on individual and organizational contributions. A few have endowments that earn enough annual interest to pay operational costs. Others are operated on a fee-for-service basis.

Assumptions about a program or organization can be faulty. Just as we have private and public colleges and universities, there are for-profit and nonprofit hospitals and nursing homes. About half of all hospices are now for profit. Most assisted living facilities are for profit. There are public and private adoption agencies, prisons, rehabilitation centers, and mental health clinics. Their stated goals may be similar, but their financial structures differ. It is the structure that dictates who is served, the way programs operate, the level and credentials of staffing, personnel policies, and the way outcomes are evaluated.

The one commonality is the bottom line. Whereas a large profit margin may not be the overarching goal, even the smallest nonprofit agency must have enough income to operate. They are all businesses. Business principles are seldom taught in social work programs. In fact, many social workers claim they chose social work because they did not want to be involved in business. We talk about social justice goals, about client and community advocacy, about helping others to have a better quality of life. These goals cannot be realized without adequate funding, and that takes us back to business.

So what do social workers need to know about business? Understanding the structure of and the funding stream for an agency or program is an important first step, because that dictates the mission and the program goals.

Next, every social worker should have a basic understanding of budgeting and should be able to read a "balance sheet" (for-profit term) or "statement of activities" (nonprofit term). It is necessary to know what percentage of a budget is spent on program activities versus what is spent on fundraising to keep doors open and a program operational. Understanding the difference between restricted funds that can only be used for a specified purpose and unrestricted funds that can be used as needed is critical for audit and fundraising purposes. All of these things are basic and should be a routine part of social work training.

Perhaps even more important is the ability to make a business case for the existence of your program or agency. Although anecdotes and case examples are helpful (particularly in public fundraising), they are not sufficient for most business decisions. What is important is data. Can you show the value of your work in dollar-and-cent terms?

NARRATIVE

The Social Work Department at a large nonprofit medical center had been well staffed and well regarded for many years. The social workers were highly skilled and enjoyed a good reputation as problem solvers and team players. As the medical center experienced cutbacks in funding, management began to discuss cutting "nonessential" staff. Unlike many other professional health care workers whose services are billable, social work services in hospitals are not reimbursable. Instead, they are considered part of bundled services. That means they are not revenue generating.

When asked to defend retaining all 12 social work staff, the director's thoughts turned first to the wonderful successes that her staff had achieved that year. She asked each person to write one case example showing the benefits of his or her work. The anecdotes were touching—great human interest stories. The director went to the next management meeting thinking she had prepared a good argument. She was rather shocked when the president of the hospital said that her case examples were wonderful descriptions of "value-added" services but that the medical center could not afford that luxury any longer. Could she show him any convincing data about why they should keep the entire department?

The director brought her social work staff together again and said that they had to rethink their argument. Because social workers could not be revenue generating, they had to reframe their collective value in terms of cost savings. The department was required to keep annual statistics. How could they be used?

There had been several difficult placement cases that year. One was a young patient who had been paralyzed and was on a ventilator. Rehabilitation beds for this type of patient are difficult to find. Yet, working as a team, social workers had found a placement in record time, saving the hospital a great deal of money.

Another patient without insurance who needed ongoing care had no family in this country. The patient wanted to go home to his own country and his family wanted him to come home, but the family had no money for ambulance transportation. The social worker suggested that the hospital pay the expense. At first, this suggestion was met with resistance, but the social worker had been able to show that it would take less than two weeks of unreimbursed inpatient stay to equal the cost of sending the patient home. The hospital paid, and the cost savings was significant.

The social workers looked at other activities such as helping patients acquire needed medications and other services so they could prevent unnecessary, and expensive, readmissions. They had documented the large number of patients they had assisted in this fashion. This was a timely example, because health care reform is mandating accountable care and will soon stop paying for patients who are readmitted within 30 days.

The Social Work Department also served a patient navigation function. It made certain patients got to their outpatient clinic appointments for assessment and follow-up. Missed appointments equal lost revenue for hospitals. Again, the department had kept good statistics on numbers of patients contacted and the ratio of kept-to-missed appointments. It was an impressive number.

Although the department's final report could not be stated in precise numbers, it was a good estimate. It was calculated that the Social Work Department had saved the medical center over $2 million in the past year. The department could now argue that social workers provided essential, not simply value-added services.

POLICY MATTERS

Every social work program and agency keeps statistics, yet they are not always used effectively to highlight the importance of services provided. In a tight budget situation, this can be a major disadvantage.

At the second Congress of Social Work in 2010, social work leaders determined 10 imperatives for the future of the profession (Clark et al., 2010). One of these imperatives addressed the business of social work and recommended that we "infuse models of sustainable business and management practice in social work education and practice" (Clark et al., 2010, p. 5). This is especially true if we want our organizations to reflect social work values so that we can maintain and grow social work services. Many services traditionally offered by social workers are now being provided by other professionals, paraprofessionals, or volunteers. We must be able to explain why these services would be more effective clinically or more cost-effective if provided by a professional social worker. Managing nonprofit and human service organizations is not easy. Managerial positions require a combination of skills, many of which social workers already possess. Edwards and Austin (2006) noted that there are four sectors of skills needed by managers: (1) boundary-spanning, (2) human relations, (3) coordinating, and (4) directing skills. Other authors have added to this list. Menafee (2000) included innovation, evaluation, facilitation, team building, and advocacy. These, again, are skills that many social workers possess. What is not always present are the business and financial skills, such as budgeting, forecasting, financial operations and fundraising (Perlmutter & Crook, 2004). Some schools of social work do offer macro practice and courses in administration. Another possibility is dual-degree programs (for example, MSW/MBA, MSW/MPA) that help social workers acquire needed business expertise. For social workers already in practice, there are executive training programs available to help offset any gaps in financial planning and management knowledge and skills. Another excellent resource is the American Society of Association Executives, which offers a certified association executive certificate (see http://www.asaecenter.org). The business of social work is too important to be left to those without a social work focus.

DISCUSSION QUESTIONS

1. Most of us came to the profession of social work to work with individuals and communities to bring about positive change and improve the quality of people's lives. If we are working in nonprofit organizations, why isn't being value-added enough? How can we maintain our value system if we have to worry about the bottom line?

2. The social work literature consistently speaks about evidence-based practice. How can we most effectively link evidence-based practice and nonprofit social service agencies?

REFERENCES

Clark, E. J., Hoffler, E., Jackson, E., Loomis, R., Myers, R. S., Rothblum, M., et al. (Eds.). (2010). *2010 Social Work Congress—Final report.* Retrieved from http://www.socialworkers.org/2010congress/documents/FinalCongress-StudentReport.pdf

Edwards, R. L., & Austin, D. M. (2006). Managing effectively in an environment of competing values. In R. L. Edwards & J. A. Yankey, J. A. (Eds.), *Effectively managing nonprofit organizations* (pp. 3–25). Washington, DC: NASW Press.

Edwards, R. L., & Yankey, J. A. (Eds.). (2006). *Effectively managing nonprofit organizations.* Washington, DC: NASW Press.

Menefee, D. (2000). What human services managers do and why they do it. In P. J. Rino (Ed.), *The handbook of human service management* (2nd ed., pp. 102–116). London: Sage Publications.

Perlmutter, F. D., & Crook, W. P. (Eds.). (2004). *Changing hats while managing change: From social work practice to administration* (2nd ed.). Washington, DC: NASW Press.

CHAPTER 2

SOCIAL MEDIA FOR SOCIAL WORKERS:

AN IMPERATIVE FOR THE PROFESSION

Elizabeth F. Hoffler and Ebony Jackson

> *We don't have choice on whether we do social media, the question is how well we do it.*
>
> —Eric Qualman

Social media is the number one activity on the Web (Qualman, 2010). The U.S. Census Bureau has observed that over 50 percent of the world's population is under 30 years old, and 96 percent of those in this younger half have joined a social network (Grunwald Associates, 2007). The United Nations stated that it took radio 38 years to reach 50 million users and television 13 years to reach the same number, whereas it took the Internet four years to accomplish that feat (Qualman, 2010). According to social media Web site Socialnomics (see http://www.socialnomics.net/), Facebook is the number one Web site in the world, with almost 1 billion users; it took less than one year for 200 million users to join the site. Facebook outpaces Google for weekly traffic, and if it were a country, it would be the world's third largest and would be twice as large as the United States. Furthermore, there are over 200 million blogs on the Web, and 34 percent of bloggers post opinions about products and brands (Qualman, 2011).

In response to the rapid emergence and development of these "Web 2.0" tools, most nonprofit organizations, large and small, are seeking to define, or refine, their organizational presence on the Internet, particularly through social media outlets. Having an online presence was once just an option, and added value to an organization's efforts to market and inform potential members and other stakeholders about programs and initiatives. However, participation in a variety of Web sites is now a requirement for relevancy as competition in every field, and for every dollar, becomes increasingly fierce. For instance, 78.6 percent of consumers have joined a company's online community to get more information about that company, and 66 percent of those users are more loyal to the brand as a result (Universal McCann, 2011). Businesses and organizations must go further than the standard Web site to have a significant impact online today, particularly if they expect to be embraced by younger generations. However, the concept that only younger generations engage online is quickly becoming outdated—the fastest growing segment on Facebook is 55- to 65-year-old women (Smith, 2009). The expectations of Web-savvy users of all ages are formed by their online experiences as a whole, and they assume that companies and organizations will be up to par in terms of Web offerings and digital communications.

SOCIAL WORK (AND NONPROFIT ORGANIZATION) MATTERS

To be seen and understood, nonprofit organizations (many of which are run and staffed by social workers) must have profiles, feeds, group pages, fundraising efforts, and professional presences on numerous Web sites. These new channels do not replace traditional methods, like print media and e-mail, but serve to give nonprofits reach and visibility within the social media world.

Social media expectations are high, regardless of whether you are running a Fortune 500 corporation or a small nonprofit organization. Although nonprofit organizations may have limited finances and smaller staffs than their corporate counterparts, they are still responsible for presenting professional, timely, and constantly updated social media presences. This includes communicating everything from the overall management and direction of the organization to governance, marketing, communication, advocacy, and membership efforts. Along with staffing and time resource challenges come new legal and privacy concerns and new considerations involving digital publications, e-commerce, and mobile app technologies.

The following narrative provides a glimpse into the online opportunities and challenges faced by many nonprofit organizations and employees as they navigate the ever-evolving world of social media.

NARRATIVE

A national nonprofit organization with 50 staff members and a tight budget was behind the curve in terms of their social media efforts and online presence. For the past decade or so, the organization functioned under the assumption that their official Web site would be enough to educate the public about their services and convince individuals and organizations to donate to support their work. Furthermore, they believed that their solid reputation and quality services would be enough to sustain them. The organization's executive director and staff members were extremely busy with their day-to-day responsibilities, and, thus far, college interns were tasked with creating and updating the organization's Facebook page, which was its only attempt at web 2.0 engagement.

As other organizations launched Twitter feeds, YouTube accounts, RSS feeds, and Linke-dIn pages, it became increasingly obvious that the organization could no longer expect individuals to simply find its Web site for information. Its paltry Facebook page basically went untouched when the interns finished their placements. The expectations of consumers and the public had shifted, and the organization now had to deliver information to them.

First, the organization decided to reevaluate its Facebook page and determine how it could best leverage its "brand" on this major social networking Web site. It focused on engagement and increasing the amount of content it posted, including activities and events it was involved with, fundraising and Facebook causes promotional efforts, photos, and relevant news stories. Another tactic the organization used was "liking" other Facebook pages that were similar to it in focus and posting information to those pages to attract attention to its own page and build relationships with page owners. By using the link-shortening service Bit.ly and Facebook's "Insights" analytics reports, the organization was able to see the metrics on how much reach its Facebook presence was creating. It quickly gained more "fans" and found that the exposure created by its Facebook presence interested reporters, students, potential funders, policymakers, and consumers, among others. The organization was thrilled that its efforts appeared to be paying off.

It did not take long, however, for staff to realize that Facebook posed an opportunity for people to post unfiltered opinions, good or bad. Every now and then, someone disagreed with a stance of the organization or posted misinformation about its work on the Facebook wall. This feedback was often instantaneous and sometimes encouraged others to contribute to the conversation. Occasionally, people would disagree with each other's comments and engage in arguments. Initially, this seemed like terrible publicity, and the executive director immediately directed staff to delete these comments. However, that quickly backfired, encouraging the naysayers to post more commentary about the organization on their own Facebook pages and blogs.

Staff determined that they had to set organizational policy to deal with these negative comments. They petitioned the executive director to allow any comments as long as they were not offensive or inappropriate. They concluded that it was best to have access to the concerns and opinions of individuals and would provide factual rebuttals when necessary. They also recognized when they made a mistake, admitted it, and worked to rectify their missteps. A Disclaimer and Code of Conduct was created for the page so that page fans would have some guidelines and understand the organization's stance on comments in general and on disagreements among page members. If a post was removed, the individual was notified and provided with an explanation.

After it felt more comfortable with Facebook, the organization branched out into Twitter with an official presence. It found that Twitter provided a simple and quick method to update followers. The organization provided information on breaking advocacy updates and national conference developments and even engaged with its followers who tweeted about the organization. It was difficult to communicate the complex issues the organization dealt with in 140 characters, but it provided succinct and abbreviated information and linked to Web sites where more information was available. The organization also launched its own organizational blog where it could elaborate on its tweets.

The organization launched a LinkedIn page, which served as a professional networking tool and was geared toward colleagues, job seekers, and other professionals. All of these avenues created additional opportunities for interaction and feedback, which served to improve the organization as it adapted and evolved in response.

Many staff members also maintained professional social media profiles in an effort to disseminate information about the work of the organization as broadly as possible. Different staff provided more detailed information on their areas of expertise, such as research, advocacy, fundraising, and publications. The organization set policy mandating that staff be respectful at all times, cite external references, refrain from posting any confidential or legal information, and provide information only within their realms of expertise. Staff found that their pages provided additional promotion for the organization as well as exposure for their own careers.

Unfortunately, one staff member in the Government Relations Department posted information about a controversial advocacy issue that was outside the scope of the organization. Because of the staff person's affiliation with the organization, the executive director received numerous e-mails and phone calls from individuals who did not agree with the staff person's opinion and were offended that the organization was taking a stand on an issue that was outside of its mission. A funder even called to express dismay and explore the possibility of pulling funding if the situation was not remediated. The executive director determined that staff with professional profiles, claiming to represent the organization, had to refrain from posting their personal opinions and information about controversial issues with no relevancy to their work. Social media presences were also clearly posted on the official organizational Web site and in all staff e-mail signatures. Further, staff members were free to maintain personal profiles without organizational affiliation.

One staff member decided that she would not affiliate with the organization but had maintained her own personal profile for several years. Vivian enjoyed using her profile to keep up with old friends and colleagues. She was also a licensed clinical social worker and ran a private practice on nights and weekends. It did not take long for Vivian's clients to begin trying to "friend" her on Facebook. Vivian did not post anything inappropriate on her page, but she still felt that this situation posed an ethical dilemma for her. She was concerned about crossing boundaries, but when she did not respond to client requests, they would ask at their next session why she had not accepted them as friends on the Web site. Vivian was concerned that they might not understand why she could not accept their seemingly innocuous request, but she determined that she had to outline her own social media policy and present it to all clients on their first session. This helped her to meet her ethical responsibilities and decrease any ambiguity or confusion with her clients regarding her role as a clinician.

Vivian also refrained from "friending" her coworkers and professional contacts. She wanted to keep her professional and personal lives separate and was clear regarding her personal boundaries when discussions about social networking sites arose at work. She set her privacy settings to reflect this decision and felt relatively insulated as she responded to friends' comments or posted pictures. However, Vivian did not take into account that her interactions with friends on their public profile pages or pictures that they posted could be found easily by others.

At a bachelorette party, she was not concerned about the constant flash of cameras and cell phones as she celebrated with close friends. However, the following Monday, a coworker made a flippant comment and laughed regarding Vivian's "wild weekend." Vivian asked what he meant, and he informed her that he was a friend of a friend and had viewed the pictures on Facebook. She was mortified and realized that she had to be more careful with her online presence. She realized that the lines between professional and personal lives had become blurred, and she had to be more cognizant of the image that she wanted to project to others at all times. She also realized that not only would coworkers and clients find her online, but potential future employers could easily form an opinion about her based solely on her online persona.

POLICY MATTERS

Social media provides outstanding, and often free (in terms of belonging to an online community, although $4.26 billion will be spent on social media marketing globally in 2011 [Esposito, 2011]), opportunities to engage with stakeholders, disseminate information, and promote the products or services of nonprofit organizations or individuals. It is a natural extension of the work that social workers do on a daily basis; reaching out to communities, guiding people to information and resources, and promoting good in as many ways as possible. However, these outlets also pose some risks and can reduce the ability of individuals or organizational staff to control the conversation. In addition to those depicted in the narrative, there are a range of ethical concerns to address for professional social workers and nonprofit organizations when engaging with the public through social media. Issues for individual practitioners include privacy, confidentiality, duty to warn, boundary concerns, and personal safety. Challenges for organizations include constantly developing current and relevant content and developing policies and protocols to guide outreach efforts.

Regardless of the potential risks, social media is no longer just an option. Individuals and organizations must behave in an ethical and transparent manner, using these tools to fulfill their mission and goals.

DISCUSSION QUESTIONS

1. Why is it important for organizations and agencies to set social media policies to guide their efforts?

2. What are some examples of excellent social media efforts by nonprofit organizations? What did the organizations get out of these efforts?

3. What are some pros and cons to engaging consumers in social media outreach? Policymakers? The public? The media? Potential members and donors?

REFERENCES

Esposito, J. (2011). *23 social media facts to share with executives.* Retrieved from http://jeffesposito.com/2011/02/14/social-media-facts-share-executives/

Grunwald Associates. (2007). *Kids social networking study.* Retrieved from http://www.grunwald.com/reports/sn/index.php

Qualman, E. (2010). *Social media revolution.* Retrieved from http://www.socialnomics.net/2010/05/05/social-media-revolution-2-refresh/

Qualman, E. (2011). *10 WOW social media statistics.* Retrieved from

Smith, J. (2009). *Fastest growing demographic on Facebook: Women over 55.* Retrieved from http://www.insidefacebook.com/2009/02/02/fastest-growing-demographic-on-facebook-women-over-55/

Universal McCann. (2010). *Wave 5: The socialisation of brands* [Slide]. Retrieved from http://www.slideshare.net/Olivier.mermet/universal-mccann-wave-5-the-socialisation-of-brands

CHAPTER 3
FUNDRAISING AS SOCIAL WORK PRACTICE

Marilyn Flynn

We make a living by what we get, we make a life by what we give.

—Sir Winston Churchill

In 2008, individuals and corporations made charitable gifts exceeding $307 billion, or 2.2 percent of U.S. gross domestic product—the highest level of giving in the world (Bond, 2009). The majority of these donations were made by individuals, particularly through estate bequests; foundations provided approximately $47 billion. Human services ranked first among all beneficiary groups, receiving about 27 percent of funding. These gifts acted as an engine for policy and program innovation in the nonprofit sector, mitigated some of the worst immediate effects of the recession, and filled in some of the gaps left by deficient social policy.

The nature of philanthropy has changed in some dramatic ways over the past century. Beginning from the general idea of helping people with their expressed needs for relief from pain or poverty, foundations and donors have grown more concerned with underlying causes, testable interventions, and policy solutions. Government has also followed this trend, moving well beyond public assistance, Social Security, and charity hospitals as responses to social need. The newest generation of private philanthropists has taken on the mission of reducing some of the world's most intransigent problems, such as HIV/AIDs in Africa and failing urban schools in the United States. New collaborations between foundations and government have made long-term, complex social projects more viable than ever before. Charitable resources are being used in ways that reflect the influence of social science, professional social work, and savvy investment strategies, increasing the likelihood of positive social benefit. Social policy experimentation is now possible on a scale and in forms never previously imagined. Fundraising by social workers has never been more important, nor has it been more potentially consequential.

POLICY MATTERS

Parallel with these developments, fundraising has emerged as a recognized profession with technical, legal, and ethical dimensions and demands. Social workers have, throughout this period, emphasized the need for expertise and scientific understanding of society in charitable work. They have helped both government and private charities maintain a focus on *why* programs or policies are necessary. Today, fundraisers are expected to understand existing policy contexts and arrays of services, identify emergent or unaddressed social problems, offer scientific rationales for interventions, and ensure that interventions will be sustainable. The making of this case is one of the most important responsibilities of modern fundraisers and requires a level of expertise that many social workers possess. Fundraising has become a vital aspect of social work practice, and an exciting means of driving social change. It is one of the most formidable tools for actualizing a vision and affecting social policy.

FUNDRAISING DEFINED

The concept of fundraising includes allocations or gifts from private individuals for private purposes; grants from private organizations, such as foundations; grants from governmental authorities; and almost every other kind of exchange between people in which there is no expectation of formal return. The goal of fundraising is to generate interest in, and perhaps ongoing commitment by others, to a civic or social purpose.

The goal of fundraising is, of course, to increase resources. It is easy to forget that there are other kinds of resources—for example, volunteer time, activities and events that build credibility and social acceptability for a cause, free media exposure, and personal help with connections to new supporting networks in the community. These nonmonetary "gifts" produce expanded relationships, legitimacy, and broadened social engagement for a program or project. They represent an implicit but critical aspect of fundraising success.

FUNDRAISING, SOCIAL POLICY, AND SOCIAL CHANGE

Social policies serve both as guidelines for action and as statements of social aspirations—to end poverty, for example. Together with leadership and vision, there is perhaps nothing more potent for achievement of policy objectives than adequate resources. Successful fundraising, at its best, helps to ensure that policies are implemented in the most timely, effective, and compelling ways.

For more than a century, social workers have understood the importance of resource development and have been central in the creation of some of today's most enduring community philanthropies. The United Way of America stands as one widely recognized example in which social work leadership, at both the local and national level, has played an essential role for almost a century. Social workers serve as program officers in many of the nation's most important charitable foundations, work as advancement staff in universities and other nonprofit organizations, and are lead fundraisers in organizations that they administer. Social work executives often are the single most compelling spokespersons for the problems and populations with which their agencies are associated. When they speak, donors often listen.

Although fewer in number, social workers also act as lobbyists with local, state, and national legislative bodies, helping to generate funds through direct appropriation and other political mechanisms. This goes well beyond advocacy and combines knowledge of policy gaps, ability to communicate needs to a variety of audiences in spoken and written form, understanding of political and appropriations processes, ability to listen, and capacity for relationship building at the highest levels.

NARRATIVE

As an example, I would point to fundraising initiatives that I began with the U.S. House of Representatives in 2008. By that time, it had become clear that there were no effective policies in place to ensure adequate treatment for soldiers returning from the wars in Afghanistan and Iraq. The problem was not so much poor policy as the absence of organized public and private attention. Further, it was unclear how national policy leadership could be established, because responsibility was divided into so many disparate parts—the Pentagon, the individual regular armed forces, the Reserves and Guard, the benefits and health divisions of the Department of Veterans Affairs, state governments, and other veterans organizations. In general, public institutions such as schools, mental health clinics, and legal services for the poor were negligibly oriented to military experience. Equally serious, it was unclear how a national professional workforce could be rapidly prepared to address the special needs of veterans with posttraumatic stress or other combat-related reactions, the problems of their families and children, and the general issues of community reentry.

Over a period of six months, I prepared a white paper that highlighted policy issues, especially those related to social work and behavioral health workforce development. I met with staffers from the appropriations committees in both the House of Representatives and the Senate, representatives from the state of California, where my university was located, Pentagon officials—including the chairman of the Joint Chiefs of Staff—research leaders in the National Institute of Mental Health, the newly created Defense Centers of Excellence, and the Army. I talked with strategic workforce planners in the Department of Defense and policy analysts in key Washington think tanks. I hired a social worker newly retired from the Air Force Academy to work with me in this effort and to give a credible military face to this issue.

As a result, Congress subsequently allocated nearly $15,000,000 within the space of about 18 months to support innovative training approaches in graduate social work education and model data-based interventions for children with deployed parents. Subsequently, *two major foundations contributed an additional $4,000,000 to strengthen these programs. At present, these are the largest community-based, civilian projects in the United States and give social work a continuing role of advocacy on behalf of the nation's returning service members.*

DISCUSSION

This example is meaningful because it is emblematic of the powerful impact social workers can—and do—have in the shaping of policy solutions; creation of new resources desperately needed by vulnerable populations; and, ultimately, implementation of these solutions. In this case, fundraising brought together both public and private resources; combined new clinical interventions for returning soldiers with community-level public, university, and military partnerships; advanced innovative teaching technology; and undergirded all with a solid scientific research core.

Fundraising in this case was particularly effective, because it brought a social work perspective on family and community to the nation's dialogue on military issues. The need for service providers to understand military culture as part of culturally competent professional practice was stressed. The involvement of civilian community institutions as partners in the social reintegration of soldiers and their families to civilian life was highlighted, and the particular psychological vulnerability of Reserve and National Guard members was emphasized. All of these individual elements had, of course, been part of the national dialogue, but the disciplinary framework of social work brought these themes together in a compelling way that attracted both public and private support.

SOCIAL WORK MATTERS

Fundraising in the hands of a social worker is quite distinct from the same activity conducted by a professional fundraiser. At its best, resource development is never an end in itself but, rather, is driven by a compelling idea concerning human need. The best fundraisers do succeed in obtaining money, volunteers, and enhanced reputation for the organizations they serve. However, perpetuation of the organization itself is the least valuable aspect of their work. The enhancement of human life and strengthening of human potential, expressed in program ideas and policies, is the true objective. Social workers often excel at fundraising, because they are so closely in touch with human stories at the grassroots level and can translate these experiences in a convincing way to larger audiences. And social workers are often among the first to recognize unmet need, as was the case in the narrative.

Fundraising is also connected to an honest appreciation and use of data. The presentation of an idea, together with a request for financial support, requires deep ethical commitment, a hallmark of the social work profession. When resources are limited, social workers have increasingly recognized that appeals for help must be tied to defensible purposes, not simply ideology. Calls for funding must be supported by adequate evidence, with the promise of consequential outcomes, and where possible, grounded in science. This is consistent with the historic grounding of social work from its inception in research and systematic understanding of social behavior.

Relationship building lies at the core of fundraising. A gift represents a donor's response not only to the inherent worth of a cause but to a fundraiser's ability to make an appealing connection to the donor's values or priorities. Because social workers are highly skilled at relationship building, they bring an indispensable skill to grant making and grant development.

Conclusion

Fundraising is an integral aspect of policy development and clinical intervention, the underlying pump-priming element that makes social transformation and innovation possible. As a process, it draws on long-established social work values and skills. As a highly evolved professional activity, it reflects the influence of social work leadership in both public and private sectors.

Over the coming decade, the continued advancement of human welfare and social justice will depend to a far greater degree than ever before on a mix of resources from government, philanthropic organizations, and private donors. Jostling for fiscal support among competing needs will only intensify. With their ability to understand complex environments, their relationship-building proficiency, and their keen eye for human need, social workers will continue to occupy key roles in the fundraising arena—roles that will perhaps be more important than ever before.

Discussion Questions

1. How does the approach of a social worker to fundraising differ from that of any professional fundraiser in general?

2. Why is fundraising such a powerful tool for connecting social policy and clinical work individuals?

Reference

Bond, S. (2009). *U.S. charitable giving estimated to be $307.65 billion in 2008*. Retrieved from http://www.givingusa.org/press_releases/gusa/GivingReaches300billion.pdf

CHAPTER 4
WORKPLACE BULLYING

Tracy Robinson Whitaker

The world of work is full of interesting dynamics. Not only is it a place where people earn a living, but it is also often the place where people define themselves as adults. It is a place where people invest their time toward a common goal and the place where they craft and hone their professional skills and reputations. Work provides income, structure, and an environment where people interact with a relatively constant group of individuals for extended periods of time.

Across all settings, employers have expectations of workers, and, likewise, workers have expectations of employers. Whether in blue collar or white collar environments, employers generally expect that workers will be honest about the skills they possess, that they will provide a fair day's work for a day's pay, and they will not engage in behaviors that are illegal or dangerous. On the other side, workers expect fairness in compensation, hiring and promotions, scheduling, and workload. In addition to these expectations, workers also expect to feel safe at work. However, despite numerous worker safety regulations, the workplace can be an increasingly hostile and, in some instances, dangerous place.

Coupled with the daily stressors associated with earning a living, countless employees also experience a range of hostile behaviors from incivility to violence. The perpetrators of these noxious behaviors are not strangers but, rather, bosses, colleagues, and subordinates of employees. These hostile interactions can occur in all work environments, including those of helping professionals; however, they are not all equally harmful. For instance, incivility (such as rude and obnoxious behavior, withholding information, or checking e-mail or texting during a meeting) can be annoying and irritating, but it is usually harmless. In fact, most employees encounter some form of incivility in their jobs. However, numerous employees experience more serious hostile workplace interactions that involve nonphysical, psychological violence that have been generally described as "workplace bullying" (Namie, 2003). The Workforce Bullying Institute defines *workplace bullying* as "status-blind interpersonal hostility that is deliberate, repeated, and sufficiently severe as to harm the target's health or economic status" (Namie, 2003, p. 1). Workplace bullying can manifest as physical assaults and threats, sexual harassment, and verbally and emotionally abusive interactions.

Bullying is an equal opportunity offense. Bullying is not limited to high-powered corporate environments—it can occur anywhere. In fact, the National Institute for Occupational Safety and Health (NIOSH) (2004) found that one-quarter of the 516 U.S. companies surveyed acknowledged that some degree of bullying had occurred in their organization. Despite common views about nonprofits being "warm and fuzzy" work environments, workers in these settings, including social workers, can also be subjected to bullying behaviors (Whitaker, in press).

Targets of workplace bullying can experience health problems such as depression, insomnia, ulcers, posttraumatic stress disorders, anxiety and migraines, and suicidal thoughts (Bond, Tuckey, & Dollard, 2010; McKay & Fratzl, 2011). For some employees, workplace bullying is a severely debilitating experience. And unlike random criminal violence, workplace bullying is particularly harmful because of the continuous and economic relationship with the target. Targets of workplace bullying may fear they will lose their jobs in ways that make finding another job very difficult, and many often do (McKay & Fratzl, 2011; Namie, 2003). They may also be ostracized or isolated in the workplace by colleagues (Whitaker, 2011). In addition, workplace bullying is not prohibited under federal employment discrimination laws, leaving targets with few avenues of redress.

Part of the dilemma facing targets of workplace bullying is the minimization of what they are experiencing (Namie, 2003). However, when people are derided or humiliated by their employers, an abuse of power occurs that closely resembles the phenomenon of domestic violence (Namie, 2003). Like domestic violence, workplace bullying is a repetitive behavior. Targets and victims are subjected to repeated attacks that occur over time. Some of the same problems that plague victims of domestic violence likewise are experienced by targets of workplace bullying. Domestic violence was once considered a *personal* problem, whereas workplace bullying is often considered a *personnel* problem. Victims of partner violence are often blamed for instigating the violence; targets of workplace bullying are often scrutinized by friends and colleagues for their roles in antagonizing their bullies. Domestic violence victims are often blamed for staying in abusive relationships; similarly, bullying targets are often advised to find another job and blamed when they do not leave their current place of employment. In addition, both groups experience societal indifference and silent bystanders (Workplace Bullying Institute, n.d.).

NARRATIVE

The following example illustrates some of the dynamics of workplace bullying.

Kelly Drexler was an ambitious, confident social worker. She'd been on a fast career track, and she was thrilled when she accepted a management position at a nonprofit organization reporting to a manager who had worked at the organization for over 20 years. However, she soon found herself in an untenable situation. Despite having a stellar work history before this position, she was unable to meet her boss's increasingly unreasonable demands in her new job.

Within months of starting her new job, she experienced a series of incidents that initially seemed inconsequential but left her feeling disrespected and confused. She was excluded from important meetings in her department, her work was criticized publicly, other staff members were given credit for her work, she was given impossible deadlines, and her boss spoke to her in a rude and disrespectful tone. When she was at work, Kelly often felt humiliated and isolated.

At first, Kelly thought that she was being overly sensitive; however, these incidents quickly grew into a pattern of hostile and abrasive interactions. Hoping to turn the situation around, Kelly threw herself into the work, working longer hours and weekends, but the situation became worse.

Kelly was dismayed to learn that she had been labeled a troublemaker and that her boss was gossiping about her to other coworkers. Her colleagues, afraid that the wrath of their boss would turn on them if they associated with Kelly, began to isolate her. They also seemed to benefit from the disproportionate amount of attention directed at Kelly, as it allowed them more freedom and less oversight in their positions. Kelly was confused about why she had been singled out for such hurtful behavior.

She contemplated leaving the job, but the economy was bad, and good jobs were hard to come by. She also contributed significantly to her family's income. Kelly had never encountered anything like this in her professional life, and she tried to counter the hostility in traditional ways. On several occasions, she talked to her boss about these behaviors, assuming that there had been a misunderstanding, but these discussions were futile. She kept meticulous records and met with the human resources (HR) department. Because she was not in a "protected status group" of employees, the HR department had no recourse to offer her except "try to deal with it."

Kelly sought the advice of an attorney but was told that there was no legal recourse available to her. She also talked to friends and family members, who sympathized but conveyed the sentiment "that's why they call it work." Lacking legal, organizational, and informal supports, Kelly began to blame herself. She became discouraged and depressed. She struggled with insomnia and had constant headaches. Her confidence plummeted. She lost interest in hobbies and began to be reclusive on the weekends. After a year on the job, Kelly's husband insisted that she quit to protect her health. Afraid that she would encounter more bullying in her next position, Kelly's efforts to find a new job were inconsistent.

POLICY MATTERS

Public policy can be a powerful tool for prevention and intervention. Legislation not only provides motivation to change behavior, it also provides consequences for unacceptable behavior (Bent-Goodley, 2011; Namie, 2003). For instance, negative workplace behavior, including sexual harassment and racial discrimination, were rampant until state and federal laws provided sanctions for such actions. Just as the Occupational Safety and Health Administration ensures safe and healthful working physical conditions for working men and women by setting and enforcing standards, attention needs to be paid to the safety of the psychological environment of the workplace (NIOSH, 2006).

To this end, 21 states have introduced the "Healthy Workplace Bill" (Workplace Bullying Institute, n.d.). This bill fills the gap in current state and federal legislation by defining an abusive work environment and giving employers the power to terminate or sanction offenders. In addition, adoption of this legislation would hold employers accountable for health-harming cruelty at work and provide an avenue for legal redress for such behaviors.

SOCIAL WORK MATTERS

Not only are social workers called on to help professionals who encounter workplace bullying, they can also be targets of such bullying themselves (Whitaker, in press). As such, the social work community can play an important role in addressing this insidious issue as advocates, employee assistance program (EAP) specialists, employees, and supervisors. As advocates, social workers can support legislation that addresses the harm that workplace bullying can cause. Occupational social workers and EAP specialists can help individuals and organizations identify bullying behaviors and develop policies and programs that promote healthy work environments. As supervisors and employees, social workers can uphold their ethical obligations by refraining from engaging in bullying behaviors and by assisting colleagues who are targets of bullying (NASW, 2008). Social workers also can do what they have always done in the face of injustice—identify perpetrators, acknowledge the harm, affirm the targets, and strive to make a difference.

DISCUSSION QUESTIONS

1. In addition to limiting harm to individual employees, what other arguments can be made in support of bully-free workplaces?

2. Would passage of healthy workplace legislation result in frivolous or unfounded litigation? Why or why not?

REFERENCES

Bent-Goodley, T. B. (2011). *The ultimate betrayal: A renewed look at intimate partner violence.* Washington, DC: NASW Press.

Bond, S. A., Tuckey, M. R., & Dollard, M. F. (2010). Psychosocial safety climate, workplace bullying, and symptoms of posttraumatic stress. *Organization Development Journal, 28*(1). Retrieved from http://findarticles.com/p/articles/mi_qa5427/is_201004/ai_n53078459/

McKay, R., & Fratzl, J. (2011). A cause of failure in addressing workplace bullying: Trauma and the employee. *International Journal of Business and Social Science, 2*(7), 13–27.

Namie, G. (2003, November/December). Workplace bullying: Escalated incivility. *Ivey Business Journal,* 1–6.

National Association of Social Workers. (2008). *Code of ethics of the National Association of Social Workers.* Washington, DC: Author.

National Institute of Occupational Safety and Health. (2004, July 28). *Most workplace bullying is worker to worker, early findings from NIOSH study suggest.* Retrieved from http://www.cdc.gov/niosh/updates/upd-07-28-04.html

National Institute of Occupational Safety and Health. (2006). *Workplace violence prevention strategies and research needs.* Retrieved from http://www.cdc.gov/niosh/docs/2006-144/pdfs/2006-144.pdf

Whitaker, T. (2011). The high costs of workplace bullying. *NASW Specialty Practice Sections Inter-Sections in Practice, 1*(1), 20–21.

Whitaker, T. (in press). Social workers and workplace bullying: Perceptions, responses and implications. *WORK: A Journal of Prevention, Assessment and Rehabilitation.*

Workplace Bullying Institute. (n.d.). *The Healthy Workplace Bill—Quick facts about the legislation.* Retrieved from http://www.healthyworkplacebill.org/bill.php

ADVOCACY

CHAPTER 5

LINKAGES BETWEEN CLINICAL AND POLICY PRACTICE IN SOCIAL WORK

King Davis

SOCIAL WORK MATTERS

Social work organizations are often asked to provide input on governmental policies and prospective programs that focus on human services. For example, a senior member of an incoming governor's transition team asked several faculty members in my school of social work to meet to discuss social welfare policy issues that could be addressed by the new administration. This invitation was based on the extensive knowledge and experience that social work educators and practitioners have in social welfare. Social work education provides a variety of skills to analyze, interpret, and recommend changes in policy. In this case, the emphasis on social justice within social work education and practice provided the basis for protecting human rights.

NARRATIVE

L. Douglas Wilder, the first African American governor in Virginia since Reconstruction, was due to take office in January 1990. His successful run for the governor's office followed four years as lieutenant governor and 20 years as an influential state senator and advocate for social and economic justice. Wilder's administration was soliciting input from social work faculty to identify unresolved human service questions that could be translated into a viable social policy platform that would obtain bipartisan support in the legislature.

In mental health, there were a number of related questions: How well was Virginia doing compared to other southern states in its treatment of people with severe mental disabilities? Why were so many children with mild to moderate developmental delays in residential placements outside of the state? What would be the impact on service quality if there was a 15 to 20 percent reduction in funding for mental health and substance abuse care? Would merger of the health and mental health departments achieve improvements in services and cost savings? Could Virginia develop a community Medicaid program that would access federal funding for local community mental health care? How could the state improve its ability to recruit, educate, and retain a competent mental health workforce?

Following conversations with Wilder's lead transition staff about these issues, I was offered an opportunity to become commissioner of the Virginia Department of Mental Health, Mental Retardation, and Substance Abuse Services. Other social workers were asked to manage the Departments of Social Services, Medicaid, Juvenile Justice, and Aging. I had started my social work career in the Virginia Department of Mental Health as director of community mental health services in the early 1970s, and had had numerous opportunities to observe how intense differences between the governor and the legislature on policy and financial issues limited decisions that could change the locus of care from large institutions to communities. Within a few weeks, I accepted the position, after meeting with Governor Wilder and learning more about his vision and goals for the state during his four-year term in office.

What was most attractive about the commissioner's position was the opportunity to combine my interests and social work background in mental health policy, advocacy, research, teaching, management, disparities, finance, and quality clinical practice. The governor assured me that I would have an opportunity to contribute to future state policies on mental disabilities that would have an impact on quality of care. The commissioner's position seemed to offer the ideal opportunity to find ways to implement a broader vision of integrated approaches to service delivery, policy, and social work practice. However, I did not anticipate that major health and safety problems within the 17 state hospital facilities would cause death and injury and lead to a federal investigation under a relatively unknown federal civil rights policy.

In 1990, Virginia's philosophical orientation and its fiscal resources remained focused on maintenance and expansion of these 17 traditional institutions, as opposed to further investments in community-based care through its 40 community mental health programs. In the 18th and 19th centuries, Virginia had developed the first mental institutions for both blacks and whites in the United States (Dain, 1968), but it was among the last states to adopt a community mental health orientation (Kennedy, 1963), use federal funding, or racially integrate services.

Virginia's reluctance to pursue federal community mental health funding was partly a reflection of the long-standing belief that federal funding was tantamount to federal intervention and control. Remnants of a states' rights stance and unresolved questions about the constitutional interpretation of federalism influenced Virginia's unwillingness to pursue the multiple service and funding opportunities offered by federal community mental health legislation (Davis, 2008). Maintenance of its 17 large mental institutions also helped stabilize the economies of the rural legislative districts where they were located, which reinforced local resistance to efforts to reduce the size of the staff within the institutions, lower their censuses, or consider permanent closure.

However, a severe recession that reduced state tax revenue provided the new governor an opportunity to promote a more robust community-based system of services that would use federal Medicaid funding to offset shortfalls in the state's budget. At the same time, the state was being forced by federal policy to decide how to use its limited funding to fix staff shortages and the aging infrastructure within the state mental hospitals.

Near the end of the second year of the Wilder administration, the Virginia attorney general received a certified letter from the U.S. Department of Justice (DOJ) that had been sent to Governor Wilder about harmful and dangerous conditions in one of the state's large hospital facilities. The letter was written by Deval Patrick (1992), then a member of the DOJ's Civil Rights Division and later governor of Massachusetts. It was assumed that the contents of the letter would soon reach the local and regional press, and the governor's office wanted to develop a transparent set of strategies before the issues and conditions outlined in detail in the letter became public.

In the letter, Patrick and the DOJ charged that one, and perhaps more, of our state mental health and developmental facilities were in violation of the constitutional rights of 800 residents. Although the language in the initial charge was global, it alleged that my new department was not providing acceptable clinical services to vulnerable populations. More specifically, the DOJ indicated that conditions in the hospitals "pose a danger to residents" and had resulted in deaths at more than one facility (Patrick, 1992, p. 1). The director of Eastern State Hospital developed a report that identified each of the charges and the responses by the hospital. The specific charges were (Favret, 1994)

- *failure to provide adequate psychiatric and psychological treatment;*
- *failure to provide adequate medical care for residents;*
- *failure to ensure that living conditions were safe;*
- *absence of measures to prevent individuals from harming themselves or others;*
- *absence of an adequate number of trained staff to meet the needs of residents;*
- *failure to provide treatment and training when necessary; and*
- *failure to ensure that each resident is evaluated to determine whether continued placement in the facility is appropriate.*

The DOJ letter indicated that the state could admit that it was in violation of patients' constitutional rights, sign a consent order to improve the conditions, or contest the charges in federal court. Regrettably, Virginia selected to contest the charges, although few states had successfully challenged the DOJ on such constitutional violations (National Council on Disability, 2005).

As part of its investigation, the DOJ sends a group of national experts in all aspects of mental health practice to examine a hospital's intake and diagnostic procedures, medical care and treatment, use of pharmaceuticals, discharge preparation, environmental conditions, and patient safety. The specific Virginia facility that was cited in Patrick's letter was considered the premier mental hospital in the state; the quality of care, protection of its 800 residents, and overall quality of life was considered by my staff to be the best. The obvious implication was that if this facility was replete with constitutional violations, similar conditions would likely be found at other institutions. The immediate issue was to determine quickly how the institution contributed to unsafe conditions that could result in death or injury to the 800 persons in our care. The second issue was to identify the requisite ethical, legal, clinical, administrative, policy, workforce, and fiscal strategies and implement them to save lives.

POLICY MATTERS

The DOJ is responsible for enforcement of the Civil Rights of Institutionalized Persons Act (P.L. 96-247). Congress passed this relatively unknown law to ensure that the civil rights of people who lived in jails, prisons, hospitals, mental institutions, and nursing homes were protected. Concerns about the loss of these rights stemmed from prior lawsuits and national reports (Joint Commission on Mental Illness and Health, 1961; *Wyatt v. Stickney*, 1971).

The DOJ has the authority under this act to bring charges against a state or private facility where there is clear evidence that constitutional rights have been abrogated. However, it cannot file charges for violations of the constitutional rights of a single individual. When such cases occur, whether in a psychiatric, medical, or correctional facility, it would be the responsibility of the individual or his or her relative or other advocate to seek legal redress (Barczyk & Davis, 2010). The DOJ looks for broad patterns of rights violations that appear to be pervasive throughout a facility, in which it concludes that there are large groups or classes of individuals whose rights are being denied and whose lives or safety are at risk.

In its letter to the governor, the DOJ charged that all 800 patients in the identified facility constituted a clinical class of individuals who were not receiving an acceptable standard of psychiatric or medical care and that this could result or had resulted in an absence of an accurate diagnosis, implementation of a quality treatment plan, periodic reevaluation to determine effectiveness, or development of a discharge plan that would restore their functioning and would lead to a timely discharge to the least restrictive environment (Patrick, 1992).

Essentially, the DOJ charged in 1990 that Virginia's mental institutions evidenced an array of constitutional concerns similar to those that had sparked a landmark case in Alabama (*Wyatt v. Stickney*, 1971) and would again in Georgia (*Olmstead v. L. C.*, 1999) and that were later addressed in the Americans with Disabilities Act of 1990 (P.L. 101-336). In both of these lawsuits, the courts ruled that an absence of clinical care that results in misdiagnosis, prolonged stays in a restricted environment (such as a state hospital), and a limited opportunity to recover are egregious violations of a person's constitutionally guaranteed rights. Both decisions required that individuals be treated to restore their ability to function in their community.

By 1996, the Commonwealth of Virginia had agreed to sign a consent agreement that would bring about major changes in the quality of care within the identified mental hospital (Patrick, 2011). Virginia simultaneously agreed to make similar improvements in one of its largest facilities for people with developmental delays. Although the consent decree resolved this issue for two of Virginia's facilities, federal suits were brought against other mental health facilities in the state.

The problem that has been described includes overlapping administrative, clinical, policy, advocacy, ethical, and financial components. Philosophically, the focus by the DOJ on the failure to maintain clinical care standards in the institutions is consistent with my working definition of social justice:

> Social justice is a basic value and desired goal in democratic societies and includes equitable and fair access to societal institutions, laws, resources, opportunities, rights, goods, services for all groups and individuals without arbitrary limitations or barriers based on observed or interpretations of the value of differences in age, color, culture, physical or mental disability, education, employment status, gender, income, language, marital status, national origin, race, religion, residence, sexual identity, or sexual orientation. (Davis, 2004, p. 1)

This definition rests on the assumption that individuals have the right to access quality of care regardless of their characteristics. Quality in this instance equates to accurate diagnosis and treatments that are designed to assist the individual to recover and return to the least restrictive environment possible.

In the Virginia case, mentally disabled citizens were being placed at great risk of harm and death because of the failure of the state to provide quality care or safekeeping. The federal policy appears to have been the only mechanism that was available to both identify the extent of the problem and force the state to resolve it. Once an unconstitutional incident is claimed, the DOJ is obligated to investigate and alert the state authority of the conditions that have been reported. The state must then grapple with a lengthy investigatory process that is designed to determine whether there is evidence to support the charges of unconstitutional conditions.

DISCUSSION QUESTIONS

The following questions are based on the problem situation as it occurred and efforts to understand the extent of the problem and find ways to resolve it.

1. Will changes in policy aimed at protecting constitutional rights resolve the problem of injury, deaths, safety, and poor quality of care?

2. Is there an optimum relationship between mental disabilities, human rights, social justice, and the role of government?

3. Does the DOJ intervention strategy have the risk of reinforcing short-term solutions rather than long-term solutions to issues of quality care?

4. What are the social work issues that this set of policy problems highlights?

REFERENCES

Americans with Disabilities Act of 1990, P.L. 101-336, 104 Stat. 327 (1990).

Barczyk, A. N., & Davis, K. (2010). Analysis of the Civil Rights of Institutionalized Persons Act (CRIPA) of 1980. *Journal of Policy Practice, 8,* 188–203.

Civil Rights of Institutionalized Persons Act, P.L. 96-247, 94 Stat. 349 (1997).

Dain, N. (1968). *History of Eastern State Hospital.* Williamsburg, VA: Colonial Williamsburg Foundation.

Davis, K. (2004). Social work's commitment to social justice. In K. Davis & T. Bent-Goodley (Eds.), *The color of social policy* (pp. 229–244). Alexandria, VA: Council on Social Work Education.

Davis, K. (2008). New federalism, new freedom, and states' rights: The uncertain and fragmented direction of public mental health policy in the United States. In I. C. Colby (Ed.), *Comprehensive handbook of social work and social welfare: Social policy and policy practice* (pp. 145–176). Hoboken, NJ: John Wiley & Sons.

Favret, J. M. (1994). *Eastern State Hospital report to the U.S. Justice Department.* Williamsburg, VA: Eastern State Hospital.

Joint Commission on Mental Illness and Health. (1961). *Action for mental health.* New York: Science Editions.

Kennedy, J. F. (1963). *Special message to the congress on mental illness and mental retardation.* Retrieved from http://www.presidency.ucsb.edu/ws/?pid=9546#axzz1jDDIFXla

National Council on Disability. (2005). *The Civil Rights of Institutionalized Persons Act: Has it fulfilled its promise?* Washington, DC: National Council on Disability.

Olmstead v. L.C. (98-536) 527 U.S. 581 (1999) 138 F. 3rd 893.

Patrick, D. (1992, May 10). [Unpublished letter to Governor L. Douglas Wilder]. Washington, DC: U.S. Department of Justice, Civil Rights Division.

Patrick, D. (2011). *Virginia agrees to improve conditions at two institutions for the mentally disabled* [Department of Justice press release]. Retrieved from http://www.justice.gov/opa/pr/1996/July96/347cr.htm

Wyatt v. Stickney, 325 F. Supp 781 (M.D. Ala. 1971).

CHAPTER 6

REINVESTING IN THE PROFESSION TO SECURE THE FUTURE

Elizabeth F. Hoffler

SOCIAL WORK MATTERS

The profession of social work was founded in the United States in the 1800s, and social workers have historically cared for the most vulnerable and oppressed clients, families, and communities in the country. For over 100 years, social work has built a reputation as *the* helping profession, and social workers have striven to reduce poverty, prevent homelessness, organize communities, and help people get back on their feet. Beginning with the settlement houses, and playing major roles in movements such as those for civil and women's rights and the war on poverty, social workers have consistently been an integral part of society's safety net. Social workers have been essential to a healthy society and have long been the professionals who guide people to critical resources, counsel them on important life decisions, and help them reach their full potential.

However, in 2007, the profession was at a crossroads, and the social safety net was fraying. Although the services provided by social workers had become increasingly necessary, there was evidence that the current and projected supply of professional social workers would not keep pace with demand. The U.S. Bureau of Labor Statistics (2011) stated that employment of social workers was expected to increase faster than average (18 percent to 26 percent) for all occupations through 2014. At the time, approximately 600,000 professional social workers were serving 10,000,000 clients per day (Whitaker, Weismiller, & Clark, 2007), and that number was quickly growing. Social workers not only provided the traditional social work services already mentioned and the majority of mental health services in the country (Substance Abuse and Mental Health Services Administration, 2008), they also branched out into many new fields of practice. They were providing care for the nation's military and veterans after a decade of war. They were responding to national and international disasters such as hurricanes and tornadoes. Social workers worked in all branches of government, serving in Congress and state legislatures and managing major cities and agencies. In an era of health care reform, social workers fulfilled new roles in care coordination and found innovative and creative ways to reduce hospital readmissions and ensure accountability. Social workers were navigating a world of emerging societal challenges and seemingly intractable problems.

The economic recession that began in 2008 created an even more untenable situation. In 2011, the time of this writing (a full three years after the recession began and was addressed by numerous pieces of federal law and state-led efforts to assuage its repercussions), the unemployment rate stood at 9.1 percent, with even higher rates for communities of color, young workers, and those with little education (Weller, 2011). In 2010, the poverty rate rose to 15.1 percent, the highest since 1993 (Weller, 2011). Furthermore, one in eight mortgages were delinquent or in foreclosure (Weller, 2011). Those clients who struggled prior to the recession were hit hardest; as Weller (2011) stated, "the crisis had taken a massive toll on the most vulnerable." However, people from all walks of life struggled to provide for their families and stay afloat. Since the Great Depression, there had perhaps never been a time when social work was needed more, as unprecedented economic insecurity contributed to the incidence of mental illness; violence; suicide; substance abuse; crime; and diminished capacity for health, family, and community functioning (Dorothy I. Height and Whitney M. Young, Jr. Social Work Reinvestment Act, 2008).

SOCIAL WORK WORKFORCE CHALLENGES

At the same time that the need for social work services was so great, recruitment and retention of social workers became a serious concern due to a host of workforce challenges, including competing policy priorities, fiscal constraints, significant educational debt, comparatively insufficient salaries, safety concerns, limited research capacity, increased administrative burdens, and unsupportive work environments.

Social work salaries are among the lowest for professionals in general and for those with master's education in particular. According to the NASW Center for Workforce Studies, 60 percent of full-time social workers earn between $35,000 and $59,999 per year (Whitaker et al., 2007). Social workers who earn lower salaries are more likely to work in challenging agency environments, serve more vulnerable clients, and leave the profession (Dorothy I. Height and Whitney M. Young, Jr. Social Work Reinvestment Act, 2008).

In 2010, approximately 72 percent of students graduating from MSW programs had incurred debt to earn their degree, and the average debt was approximately $35,500 (Watkins, 2010). When low salaries are added to this equation, a social work degree becomes an impossible pursuit for many. The U.S. Public Interest Research Group (2006) stated that "37 percent of public four year graduates have too much debt to manage as a starting social worker." The profession is personally fulfilling to many; however, due to high loan debt and low income, many social workers struggle financially.

Further, safety is a concern for many social workers as clients are often dealing with emotional or traumatic situations. The NASW Center for Workforce Studies (Whitaker et al., 2007) found that 44 percent of survey respondents faced personal safety issues on the job. The Occupational Safety and Health Administration (2004) stated that 48 percent of assaults occur in the health care and social services industry.

These challenges contributed to potential social work students choosing other degree options and to experienced social workers leaving the field. At a time of significant social and economic strain, a strategic, comprehensive plan to reinvest in the profession was necessary.

NARRATIVE

Adrianne Walters was a graduate student working toward her MSW. Adrianne's parents divorced when she was an infant and Adrianne was raised by her mother, a teacher's aide. Adrianne's father held odd jobs and was never financially secure. They both encouraged Adrianne, the first in her family to attend college and graduate school, to pursue a career that would lead to a high salary, such as business or law. Adrianne understood their concerns but had also witnessed the important impact that professional social workers had had on their lives, in her school when she was dealing with the emotional repercussions of the divorce, when her mother sought government assistance, and when her father entered an alcohol recovery program. She believed strongly in the power of social work to influence people's lives for the better.

Adrianne was going to graduate with roughly $30,000 in educational debt, and although she had already researched state and federal loan forgiveness programs, she knew that she was still going to have a significant amount of debt to pay off. Once Adrianne graduated, she took her first job in an organization dedicated to eradicating homelessness, where she served as policy coordinator, advocating for state and local policy initiatives to benefit her clients. Her starting salary, in a large U.S. city, was $35,000, and she purchased low-cost health insurance through her organization.

After several years of working for her organization, Adrianne realized how ironic it was that she was working extremely hard to prevent homelessness and economic inequality for others, but after paying her rent and bills, she had little money left over each month. Adrianne realized that she had to seek a position with a higher salary if she was ever going to pay off her educational debt and eventually lead a middle-class lifestyle. She knew that she could no longer effectively serve her clients while she was so concerned for her own future. She had to make the tough decision if that future would be as a professional social worker.

POLICY MATTERS

In response to social work workforce challenges, the Action Network for Social Work Education and Research (ANSWER Coalition) created the Social Work Reinvestment

Initiative, which sought to secure federal and state investments in professional social work to enhance societal well-being. It consisted of three major components: (1) state-level reinvestment plans (led by NASW chapters); (2) relevant federal legislation; and (3) the cornerstone of the initiative, the Dorothy I. Height and Whitney M. Young, Jr. Social Work Reinvestment Act.

State plans addressed issues such as title protection, licensure, reimbursement, public education, and the establishment of social work education programs, among many other issues. NASW chapters held reinvestment symposiums across the country; surveyed members regarding their most pressing workforce concerns; advocated for state and local changes that would affect social workers and the clients they served; and worked with employers of social workers, schools of social work, and state government to ensure that necessary changes were implemented. Chapters secured millions in state-level loan forgiveness dollars, obtained grants that invested in their workforces, fought off possible closures of schools of social work in uncertain economic times, and successfully passed state legislation urging their congressional delegations to pass the Dorothy I. and Whitney M. Young, Jr. Social Work Reinvestment Act at the federal level.

Meanwhile, the ANSWER Coalition worked in support of several pieces of federal legislation aimed at strengthening the workforce. These included the National Center for Social Work Research Act (reintroduced as the National Office for Social Work Research Act), which would establish a National Institutes of Health center focused exclusively on the important societal research being done by professional social workers. The ANSWER Coalition also focused on the Strengthen Social Work Training Act (reintroduced as the Strengthen Social Work Workforce Act), which would amend the Public Health Service Act to include support for social work training. Additional federal legislation included the Teri Zenner Social Worker Safety Act, named after a social worker slain in the line of duty, which would invest in safety measures and equipment intended to provide an environment in which social workers could best serve their clients. Finally, loan forgiveness legislation, including the College Cost Reduction and Access Act (P.L. 110-84) and the 2008 reauthorization of the Higher Education Act of 1965 (P.L. 89-329), addressed one of the most problematic issues for social workers, allowing them to focus on their careers instead of the educational debt they had accumulated.

In an effort to comprehensively address all of the issues previously mentioned, the ANSWER Coalition worked with Congressman Edolphus Towns (D-NY) and Senator Barbara Mikulski (D-MD) to introduce the Dorothy I. Height and Whitney M. Young, Jr. Social Work Reinvestment Act in the 110th Congress. The legislation consists of two major components.

In an effort to address the long-term concerns facing the profession, the legislation would establish a Social Work Reinvestment Commission, which would analyze the current state of the profession and develop long-term recommendations and strategies to maximize the ability of the nation's social workers to serve their clients with competence and care. Demonstration projects would also address the immediate needs of the profession and would be established in the areas of workplace improvements (providing funding in areas such as social work supervision, incomparable salaries, and high caseloads), education and training (to fund the education of social workers at the BSW, MSW, and doctoral levels), research (to support postdoctoral social workers in their research pursuits), and community-based programs of excellence (providing funding to replicate successful social work agencies and organizations so as to provide clients and communities across the country with leading-edge services). Together, these components would create the foundation from which the social work profession could continue to serve as a voice for not only the most vulnerable in our country, but for individuals from all walks of life in need of social work services. Social workers are indispensible in a nation that prides itself on the American dream, for without social work, it is arguable that there would be no sustainable force for social justice.

The Social Work Reinvestment Initiative has mobilized the social work community as never before. Over 100,000 social workers have communicated with their members of Congress in support of the Dorothy I. Height and Whitney M. Young, Jr. Reinvestment Act. The legislation continues to gain support and has been reintroduced in the 111th and 112th Congresses. Every social worker in Congress has signed on as a cosponsor of the legislation, along with other notable cosponsors, including then-Senators Barack Obama and Hillary Clinton. The legislation also enjoyed bipartisan support in the 110th Congress.

In addition to pushing for passage of the legislation in full, the ANSWER Coalition galvanized support for a number of strategies, including

- urging President Obama to establish the Social Work Reinvestment Commission through executive order;
- urging Secretary of Health and Human Services Kathleen Sebelius to establish the Social Work Reinvestment Commission independently;
- submitting appropriations report language to be considered in the Labor, Health and Human Services, Education, and Related Agencies appropriations bill;
- working with Congressman Towns as he sought to have the Social Work Reinvestment Commission considered on the House of Representatives suspension calendar; and
- supporting Congressman Towns as he sought to have the Social Work Reinvestment Commission included in broader legislation, such as the 2010 Affordable Care Act and the 2010 Economic Stimulus package.

Numerous milestones have been reached as a part of social work reinvestment efforts, including the following:

- The House of Representatives Committee on Education and Labor held the first ever congressional hearing on the profession, "Caring for the Vulnerable: The State of Social Work in America," in 2008.
- Support for the Social Work Reinvestment Act came from a variety of social work and allied organizations, including the Association of Baccalaureate Social Work Program Directors, the Association of Oncology Social Work, the Clinical Social Work Association, the Council on Social Work Education, the Group for the Advancement of Doctoral Education in Social Work, the Latino Social Work Organization, the National Association for the Advancement of Colored People, the National Association of Black Social Workers, NASW, the National Council of Negro Women, the National Urban League, the Social Welfare Action Alliance, the Society for Social Work and Research, the Society for Social Work Leadership in Health Care, and the Young Women's Christian Association.
- The NASW Foundation launched the Social Work Policy Institute (see http:// www.socialworkpolicy.org/).
- NASW submitted congressional testimony in support of the Dorothy I. Height and Whitney M. Young, Jr. Social Work Reinvestment Act on several occasions.
- Congressman Towns included the legislation as his one "bill to watch" in the biannual report of Congressional Black Caucus of the 111th Congress (2009), *Opportunities for All—Pathways Out of Poverty.*
- The bipartisan Congressional Social Work Caucus was established and held a briefing on the Social Work Reinvestment Initiative in 2010.

For a full listing of efforts in support of the Social Work Reinvestment Initiative, please visit http: www.socialworkreinvestment.org.

The Social Work Reinvestment Initiative has been a strategic, systematic effort on behalf of hundreds of thousands of professional social workers across the country. Regardless of the final outcome of the cornerstone federal legislation, the effort has garnered widespread support from social work and other allied organizations, and it has cultivated enhanced public understanding of the profession from the public and media outlets, fostering collective professional pride. It has allowed a profession that has always cared for others to advocate and stand up for its own needs, which in turn will allow us all to reinvest in the future of our country.

DISCUSSION QUESTIONS

1. What would our nation look like if social work no longer existed? Do you think this is a possibility?

2. This chapter mentions that social workers serve people across the life span and in all social classes, but why do many people believe that social work services are only

for people with limited resources? Could you provide examples of how people with middle-class incomes might benefit from the services of a social worker?

3. In addition to the efforts mentioned in this chapter, what can be done to attract more students to select social work as a career? What makes a social work degree unique?

REFERENCES

College Cost Reduction and Access Act, P.L. 110-84, 121 Stat. 784 (2007).

Congressional Black Caucus of the 111th Congress. (2009, January–June). *Opportunities for all—Pathways out of poverty.* Retrieved from http://thecongressionalblackcaucus.lee.house.gov/reports/Bi_Annual_Report_June_2009.pdf

Dorothy I. Height and Whitney M. Young, Jr. Social Work Reinvestment Act. (2008). Retrieved from http://www.socialworkreinvestment.org/SWRA/

Higher Education Act of 1965, P.L. 89-329, 79 Stat. 1219 (1965).

Occupational Safety and Health Administration. (2004). *Guidelines for preventing workplace violence for health care & social service workers.* Retrieved from http://www.osha.gov/Publications/OSHA3148/osha3148.html

Substance Abuse and Mental Health Services Administration. (2008). *Mental health, United States, 2008.* Retrieved from http://store.samhsa.gov/shin/content/SMA10-4590/SMA10-4590.pdf

U.S. Bureau of Labor Statistics. (2011). Social workers. In *Occupational outlook handbook, 2010–11 edition.* Retrieved from http://www.bls.gov/oco/ocos060.htm#outlook

U. S. Public Interest Research Group. (2006). *Student debt.* Retrieved from http://www.uspirg.org/higher-education/student-debt

Watkins, J. M. (2010, August 13). [*Letter to Office of the Assistant Secretary for Planning and Evaluation, Office of Planning and Policy Support, U.S. Department of Health and Human Services*]. Retrieved from http://www.cswe.org/File.aspx?id=43515

Weller, C. E. (2011). *Economic snapshot for September 2011.* Retrieved from http://www.americanprogress.org/issues/2011/09/econsnap0911.html

Whitaker, T., Weismiller, T., & Clark, E. J. (2007). *Assuring the sufficiency of a frontline workforce: A national study of licensed social workers.* Retrieved from http://workforce.socialworkers.org/studies/nasw_06_execsummary.pdf

CHAPTER 7

FROM THE TOUGH STREETS OF EAST NEW YORK TO CAPITOL HILL

Charles E. Lewis Jr.

NARRATIVE

When I returned to school to complete my education in 1992 at the age of 42, I had no idea that I would become a social worker. I had been in therapy for three years and found my experience very helpful, and I wanted to acquire the same skills and knowledge so I could use them in working with the men at the church where I was employed. I was working full-time at the Saint Paul Community Baptist Church in the East New York section of Brooklyn as the communications director and coordinator of a vibrant ministry to African American boys and men. It was an exciting and rewarding experience, but a challenging and often discouraging one as well.

Saint Paul Community Baptist Church, located at 859 Hendrix Street in the heart of the East New York community, was surrounded by a number of housing developments that were overwhelmed by crime and drugs. There were 110 murders in the 75th precinct in 1993, and some officers began referring to the neighborhood as the "killing fields."

With hundreds of men coming to a church that welcomed them with open arms, there was a sense of hope that something could be done to turn things around. However, while the fellowship was healing for these men, it soon became clear that the church was not equipped to address many of the issues they were bringing with them. Many had problems with substance abuse and had had various encounters with the criminal justice system. Some arrived straight from jail or prison as the word spread about the church's outreach to African American men.

This was the beginning of my long-time quest to address the disproportionate impact of incarceration on African American men and their families. Articles in the Boston Globe, Washington Post, *and* New York Times, *among others, had begun referring to black boys and men as an endangered species (Ball, 1989; Lee, 1990; Raspberry, 1990). I decided that this prognosis did not have to be the final word. I returned to school to better equip myself to become part of the solution.*

In September 1992 I entered the College of New Rochelle to complete my undergraduate education, which I had interrupted almost 20 years before after four years at City College in New York—two years of mechanical engineering and another two of journalism. For a while, I was a ship without a rudder. Having lost both of my parents at an early age—my mother died when I was five years old and my father when I was 16—I had been drifting from one job to the next with no real plan for the future. With two failed marriages behind me, I sought meaning in the only place I knew I could regain my compass: the church.

Several years after joining the church, I left my job as a communications specialist for the borough president of Brooklyn to put my skills to work for the Saint Paul Community Church and its dynamic pastor, Rev. Johnny Ray Youngblood. Little did I know at the time that I was heading toward a career in social work. I was attracted to the church because of its willingness to welcome men into the church regardless of their history. With a congregation of about 5,000 people, it had an unusually large contingent of boys and men for a local church. About 40 percent of the congregants at Sunday morning services were men and boys.

Unlike many of the men who were finding their way to Saint Paul Community, I was not a stranger to the church. My father had been the pastor of the New Canaan Baptist Church in Brooklyn for 11 years, until his untimely death in 1966. Working in the church, playing piano and organ and directing choirs, was an integral part of my early life. However, that all changed after my father died. I lost my faith in the church until I found Saint Paul Community. It was different than any church I had attended before. This church was involved in the community, and that was inspiring to me.

The church and its pastor were key members of a consortium of churches known as the East Brooklyn Congregations under the umbrella of the Industrial Areas Foundation, an organization founded by radical organizer Saul Alinsky. The Industrial Areas Foundation had organized churches in a number of cities to address social problems in the communities they served. Building affordable housing was a primary focus of the coalitions, and Saint Paul Community Baptist Church led the effort in Brooklyn with its Nehemiah Project, which erected more than 5,000 single-family owner-occupied houses in the blighted blocks of East New York.

Rev. Youngblood had gained fame for his leadership in negotiations with the New York City government that secured land and subsidies for the housing effort. But he also began to receive attention for his work with African American men. An article in the New York Times *put the spotlight on the ministry to men, which led to former* Times *reporter Samuel Freedman (1993) writing a book about the church.*

SOCIAL WORK MATTERS

When I began my studies at the College of New Rochelle, I was firmly entrenched in the Saint Paul Community experience. I thought that I would be at the church for years to come. I saw my undergraduate studies leading to seminary and master's-level studies in pastoral counseling, which I could use in my work with the men's ministry. As I neared completion of my degree and began contemplating the future, the dean at the College of New Rochelle suggested I consider social work as a next step.

After several courses of religious studies, the idea of seminary had begun to lose its luster. I wanted to gain theoretical knowledge and skills that would be useful in addressing the needs of African American boys and men. But I had my reservations about a career in social work. I saw the profession as casework more than anything else. My therapist had an MSW, but I thought he was an exception to the rule. However, after talking to several social workers, including Morris Jeff, a past president of the National Association of Black Social Workers, I began to appreciate the value of social work.

Jeff not only convinced me to pursue studies in social work, he convinced me to enroll at Clark Atlanta School of Social Work, his alma mater. I began my studies in clinical counseling there in 1995, still with the idea that I would return to Saint Paul Community and resume my work with the men's ministry. My studies in clinical counseling not only opened up my mind to a whole new means of helping people, it helped me to better understand myself. I put everything I had into becoming the best possible therapist.

POLICY MATTERS

However, a new interest in policy had taken hold during a course in social welfare policy. I had never considered social work as a profession that addressed social ills at the policy level. I devoted my semester to following the evolving negotiations on the enactment and implementation of the Personal Responsibility and Work Opportunity Reconciliation Act of 1996 (P.L. 104-193), known colloquially as welfare reform. I was dismayed when I realized that the people who would be most affected by the new legislation had little voice in its design and implementation. It was also evident that churches were completely absent from the conversation.

Because of my work with black men, I also became very interested in the emerging focus on fatherhood issues spurred by David Blankenhorn's (1995) book *Fatherless America*. I was invited to speak at conferences and carried the persistent message that something had to be done about the burgeoning numbers of male African Americans being scarred by their involvement with the criminal justice system. The troubling plight of black men gained national attention in the wake of the Million Man March in October 1995. I was extremely disappointed that a clear set of policy initiatives was not generated from this monumental effort.

I began looking for scholars of color addressing policy issues affecting African American boys and men. When I found few, I decided that I would shift my focus from clinical counseling to policy and was accepted into the doctoral program at Columbia University School of Social Work. There I had the opportunity to work with Ronald

B. Mincy, a professor with deep roots in black male issues and the nascent fatherhood movement. I collaborated with him on a chapter in a book published by the Urban Institute Press, *Black Males: Left Behind* (Mincy, Lewis, & Han, 2006), and other research affecting black men.

My work with Irv Garfinkel at Columbia University afforded me the opportunity to research the impact of incarceration on fathers in the Fragile Families Study (Bendheim-Thoman Center, n.d.). Using these data, I found that fathers who had been incarcerated earned significantly less and had a harder time finding employment than fathers who had never been incarcerated (Lewis, Garfinkel, & Gao, 2007). In addition to economic penalties, incarceration was also associated with relational penalties. Conventional wisdom obviously suggests that incarceration negatively affects people, but now I was among those who were providing evidence. The next step was finding a means to influence policies that would address these problems.

The sobering reality about policy and politics is that they are slow-moving trains. I got my first chance to be involved in policy discussions after joining the faculty of Howard University School of Social Work, when I was invited to be on the planning committee for the State of the African American Male Initiative sponsored by Chicago-based Congressman Danny K. Davis. The initiative addressed several areas of concern regarding African American men, including our disproportionate involvement in the criminal justice system.

This effort led directly to the introduction and passage of the Second Chance Act of 2008 (P.L. 110-199). This legislation, signed into law by President George W. Bush on April 9, 2008, is designed to provide support to people leaving prison that would allow their successful reintegration into society and reduce recidivism.

In January 2011, I took another step toward realizing my goal of influencing policy when I was appointed deputy chief of staff for Brooklyn Congressman Edolphus "Ed" Towns (D-NY), a 15-term veteran in the U. S. House of Representatives who is also a professional social worker. With his leadership, the Congressional Social Work Caucus was established; it included all members of the House who were professional social workers—Susan Davis (D-CA), Luis Gutiérrez (D-IL), Barbara Lee (D-CA), Allyson Schwartz (D-PA), Niki Tsongas (D-MA), and Edolphus Towns. The Caucus added 58 members during the first year of its existence, including the two U. S. senators who were professional social workers, Barbara Mikulski of Maryland and Debbie Stabenow of Michigan.

In 2011, I co-edited *Ministry to Prisoners and Families: The Way Forward* with former Philadelphia mayor W. Wilson Goode and Harold Dean Trulear, an associate professor at Howard University School of Divinity (Goode, Lewis, & Trulear, 2011). In the book, I offer policy prescriptions that would reduce the probability of young people becoming entangled in the criminal justice system. Trulear and I also published a journal article encouraging African American churches to ramp up their advocacy efforts (Lewis & Trulear, 2008).

Working with African American men in one of the most devastated communities in Brooklyn has resulted in an opportunity to influence policy on Capitol Hill. This happened because of my decision to embrace social work. I am a proud social worker with plans to use this opportunity to promote policies that will reduce the likelihood of children and youths having their lives destroyed by a criminal justice system with little mercy.

DISCUSSION QUESTIONS

1. Is social work a viable option for students seeking a career in social welfare policy?

2. How has social work addressed issues of relevance to the unique plight of African American boys and men?

3. How has forensic social work contributed to efforts to reduce the impact of incarceration on individuals and families?

4. Are there examples of working relationships between the social work profession and faith-based organizations?

REFERENCES

Ball, J. (1989, June 4). Endangered: Black men, AIDS, drugs, crime lower life expectancy. *Boston Globe*.

Bendheim-Thoman Center for Research on Child Well-being. (n.d.). *The fragile families and child well-being study*. Retrieved from http://crcw.princeton.edu/ff.asp

Blankenhorn, D. G. (1995). *Fatherless America: Confronting our most urgent social problem*. New York: Basic Books.

Freedman, S. G. (1993). *Upon this rock: The miracles of a black church*. New York: HarperCollins.

Goode, W. W., Lewis, C. E., Jr., & Trulear, H. D. (Eds.). (2011). *Ministry to prisoners and families: The way forward*. Valley Forge, PA: Judson Press.

Lee, F. E. (1990, June 26). Black men: Are they imperiled? *New York Times*. Retrieved from http://www.nytimes.com/1990/06/26/nyregion/black-men-are-they-imperiled.html

Lewis, C. E., Jr., Garfinkel, I., & Gao, Q. (2007). Incarceration and unwed fathers in fragile families. *Journal of Sociology and Social Welfare, 34*(3), 77–94.

Lewis, C. E., Jr., & Trulear, H. D. (2008). Rethinking the role of African American churches as social service providers. *Black Theology: An International Journal, 6*, 354–376.

Mincy, R. B., Lewis, C. E., Jr., & Han, W.-J. (2006). Left behind: Less-educated young black men in the economic boom of the 1990s. In R. B. Mincy (Ed.), *Black males: Left behind* (pp. 1–10). Washington, DC: Urban Institute Press.

Personal Responsibility and Work Opportunity Reconciliation Act of 1996, P.L. 104-193, 110 Stat. 2105 (1996).

Raspberry, W. (1990, January 17). Black help for black males. *Washington Post*.

Second Chance Act of 2008, P.L. 110-199, 122 Stat. 657 (2008).

CHILDREN AND FAMILIES

CHAPTER 8

From a Staffing Crisis to the Building of a National Workforce Agenda for Social Work

Katharine Briar-Lawson

Narrative

A number of years ago, I had the honor of being recruited away from an academic post in social work to be a state-level assistant secretary for Children, Youth and Families. Crack and cocaine had hit U.S. communities, and tragedies, including high-profile child abuse and neglect deaths, were occurring. Child welfare agencies were being attacked by the media and the public for not being able to protect children. Social workers were blamed, even though very few trained social workers were implicated.

Early on in my new state role, I participated in a conference involving representatives from national child welfare associations. Presenters were to focus on competencies in child welfare. Yet as each of us spoke, the agenda turned from competencies to recognition that there was a nationwide staffing crisis. Some counties and states reportedly had vacancy rates for Child Protective Services caseworkers of up to one-third. It was clear that a workforce agenda was needed and that this, indeed, was a social work agenda.

Shortly after this conference, I was appointed to chair a new NASW Commission on Families. This national body provided a strategic base from which to address the workforce crisis in child welfare (Zlotnik, Pecora, & Briar, 1989). Staffed and essentially advanced on all fronts by Joan Levy Zlotnik at NASW, this commission helped to spearhead a series of workforce conferences addressing the staffing crisis in child welfare.

This commission and NASW began to make the case that trained social workers are needed in child welfare. Once the backbone of services and the workforce for public sector families, social workers had dropped from being about 58 percent of the public-sector services workforce to less than 30 percent. Yet child welfare work was then, and continues to be, one of the most challenging and complex jobs in the country. Even more, the effects of crack and cocaine addiction were taking their toll, with many parents unable to protect their children as they were living with drug-addicted partners and were also, often, victims of domestic violence. The complexity of co-occurring risk factors in many child welfare families—including poverty, domestic violence, mental health, and addiction challenges— underscored the need for well-trained social workers. Nonetheless, many, if not most, state and county hiring criteria involved a college degree unrelated to human services. In fact, there were counties in the United States that required only a high school diploma.

NASW's commission, co-led the campaign to address workforce issues. The activities included meetings in the latter part of the 1980s with the U.S. Children's Bureau to advance the model introduced by Illinois with Title IV-E funds deployed for social work education in schools of social work. Title IV-E was introduced as an amendment to the Social Security Act stipulating that funds could be used for education, training, and the administration of training-related activities in public child welfare. These entitlements, along with Title IV-B 426 funds deployed by the U.S. Children's Bureau, constituted a basis and funding source for the professionalization of child welfare.

The U.S. Children's Bureau funds made it possible to hold forums on the workforce crisis and to help forge more strategic partnerships between agencies and universities. Moving this workforce agenda forward involved the brokering of formal agreements between schools of social work and state and county child welfare agencies.

Such reprofessionalization initiatives required that a consensus emerge among national organizations regarding the need to bring social workers back into public child welfare. Supporters included the National Association of Public Child Welfare Administrators, the American Public Welfare Association, the Child Welfare League of America, the Children's Defense Fund, the American Humane Association, and the Council on Social Work Education. Their leadership, along with that of the U.S. Children's Bureau, helped to advance the NASW-led reprofessionalization agenda. This work was bolstered by a Booz-Allen & Hamilton, Inc. (1987) study showing the benefits of trained social workers in public child welfare.

POLICY MATTERS

The *Federal Register* in the early 1990s cited Title IV-E as a resource for reprofessionalization. Schools of social work and state and county child welfare agencies were joining forces around the staffing crisis. Partnership agreements and Title IV-E funds enabled staff members to get degrees in social work and students to be educated and hired in public child welfare (Briar, Hansen, & Harris, 1992). New field units were developed in public child welfare offices. Joint grant proposals were generated. Some schools of social work assumed the training for all child welfare workers as well as evaluation research. Some prominent consortiums were the California Social Work Education Center, the Texas IV-E Roundtable, and the New York State Social Work Education Consortium. Now, more than two decades later, about $300 million in

Title IV-E training funds are drawn down each year, with about 80 schools of social work participating in these partnerships (NASW, 2004). Such mature and substantive partnerships involve innovations in education and training as well as evaluation. In addition, in a few cases, Medicaid funds help to underwrite some of the workforce developments in child welfare education, training, and service pilots.

In the past decade, when Title IV-E funding was threatened by some members of Congress, two special issues of journals (reprinted as books: Briar-Lawson & Zlotnik, 2002a, 2002b) were published delineating the discernible benefits of the IV-E and IV-B 426-funded partnerships. Simultaneously, the Annie E. Casey Foundation (2003) published its report on the workforce crisis. A U.S. General Accounting Office (2003) report to Congress addressed retention and turnover concerns in public child welfare. The Child Welfare League (Alwon & Reitz, 2000) and the American Public Human Services Association (2005) also focused on workforce issues. Retention barriers and problems have been increasingly attributed to high human and financial costs (Dorch, McCarthy, & Denofrio, 2008; Mor Barak, Nissly, & Levin 2001) and have been shown to have detrimental effects on child safety (National Council on Crime and Delinquency, 2006). In addition, permanency issues are of major concern, as time limits in child welfare and service gaps due to caseworker attrition may impede reunification, resulting in children being adrift in foster care or placed for adoption (Flower, McDonald, & Sumski, 2005; Marsh, Ryan, Choi, & Testa, 2006).

Paralleling these developments were increasing investments by the U.S. Children's Bureau in recruitment and retention innovations. More recently, explicit workforce grants have been funded, including a National Child Welfare Workforce Institute (see http://www.ncwwi.org). This data-driven and knowledge-generating institute is dedicated to leadership development for middle managers and supervisors and the promotion of innovative traineeships grants in child welfare at 12 universities and colleges.

SOCIAL WORK MATTERS

Workforce development remains at the forefront of social work, with the NASW Center for Workforce Studies focusing in part on public child welfare. The National Association of Deans and Directors of Schools of Social Work focuses efforts on reprofessionalization through a Child Welfare Task Force. Most recently, the U.S. Department of Health and Human Services Commissioner on Children, Youth and Families, Bryan Samuels, challenged deans and directors of schools of social work with the fact that too many youths with trauma go untreated and then age out of the system, unprepared to overcome many of life's trials. He appealed for workforce developments, education, and training in social work addressing trauma treatment and argued for social work treatment units in child welfare. His goals reinforce the reprofessionalization agenda, and he argued that public child welfare needs to use the clinical, and not just the case management, skills of social workers.

Despite the fact that workforce policy, training, and clinical practice issues have moved to the forefront among some public child welfare leaders, dilemmas remain. First, the field lacks a systematic, multistate study of the differential benefits of social work skills in child welfare practice. Although studies have shown impact (Flower et al., 2005; Fox, Burnham, Barbee, & Yankeelov, 2000; Hess, Folaron, & Jefferson, 1992; Leung, Willis, Cheung, & Walijarvi, 2011), more-state-of-the-art contributions are required in support of a systematic reprofessionalization agenda. Second, although state and county administrators increasingly attribute problematic practice and service outcomes to workforce issues, there is no national campaign within public child welfare to hire social workers into every new frontline and supervisory job in public child welfare. Third, few states require a social work degree for public child welfare employment. If there were such mandates, a supply-and demand-challenge would confront schools of social work. Currently, schools do not produce a sufficient number of graduates to fill these vacancies. And the field faces other workforce challenges, such as that in aging services. For example, although John A. Hartford Foundation's $74 million investment in workforce development in aging has had a far reach, gerontology, like child welfare, remains profoundly underserved by trained social workers (John A. Hartford Foundation, 2010).

Despite sustained efforts in workforce preparation and focus, such as those in child welfare and aging, the numbers of students graduating with social work degrees have not kept pace with the demand and need. To address shortages and to foster more recruitment, NASW has worked with Congressman Edolphus "Ed" Towns (D-NY) and Senator Barbara Mikulski (D-MD) to introduce to Congress the Dorothy I. Height and Whitney M. Young, Jr. Social Work Reinvestment Act (2008) (see also NASW, 2008). This is one key policy initiative that might move the workforce agenda to a more prominent profile in Congress. It could also build on the priority given to workforce development by such federal agencies as the U.S. Children's Bureau and foundations such as the John A. Hartford Foundation. This act requires a national effort among all in the profession to foster its passage.

Often, public policy is initiated if not generated by county, state, and federal agencies, not elected officials. Thus, the leadership role of the U.S. Children's Bureau in advancing workforce development might inspire other federal agencies, such as the Administration on Aging and the U.S. Department of Veterans Affairs, to follow suit. If more federal agencies joined with the U.S. Children's Bureau, such efforts in turn might help to reinforce the NASW campaign to pass the Dorothy I. Height and Whitney M. Young, Jr. Social Work Reinvestment Act (2008).

DISCUSSION QUESTIONS

1. Why should workforce development in the profession be a nationally significant public policy concern?

2. What are some of the consequences of having untrained workers doing social work jobs?

3. What might be some of the consequences of caseworker turnover and retention problems in child welfare?

4. How might the profession recruit and attract more workers into public child welfare jobs?

5. In what ways might the Dorothy I. Height and Whitney M. Young, Jr. Social Work Reinvestment Act be beneficial to workforce development in your state or county?

REFERENCES

Alwon, F., & Reitz, A. (2000). *The workforce crisis in child welfare*. Washington, DC: Child Welfare League of America.

American Public Human Services Association. (2005). *Report from the 2004 Child Welfare Workforce Survey: State agency findings*. Washington, DC: Author.

Annie E. Casey Foundation. (2003). *The unsolved challenge of system reform: The condition of the frontline human services workforce*. Baltimore: Author.

Booz-Allen & Hamilton, Inc. (1987). *The Maryland Social Work Services Job Analysis and Personnel Qualifications Study*. Baltimore: Maryland Department of Human Resources.

Briar, K., Hansen, V., & Harris. N. (Eds.). (1992). *New partnerships*. Miami: Institute on Children and Families at Risk, Florida International University.

Briar-Lawson, K., & Zlotnik, J. L. (Eds.). (2002a). *Charting the impacts of university–child welfare collaboration*. Binghamton, NY: Haworth Press.

Briar-Lawson, K., & Zlotnik, J. L. (Eds.). (2002b). *Evaluation research in child welfare*. Binghamton, NY: Haworth Press.

Dorch, E., McCarthy, M., & Denofrio, D. (2008). Calculating child welfare separation, replacement, training costs. *Social Work in Public Health, 23*(6), 39–54.

Dorothy I. Height and Whitney M. Young, Jr. Social Work Reinvestment Act. (2008). Retrieved from http://www.socialworkreinvestment.org/SWRA/

Flower, C., McDonald, J., & Sumski, M. (2005). *Review of turnover in Milwaukee County: Private agency child welfare ongoing case management staff*. Retrieved from http://louisville.edu/kent/projects/iv-e/turnoverstudy.pdf

Fox, S. R., Burnham, D., Barbee, A. P., & Yankeelov, P. A. (2000). School to work—Social work that is: Maximizing agency/university partnerships in preparing child welfare workers. *Journal of the National Staff Development and Training Association, 1*(1), 13–20.

Hess, P. M., Folaron, G., & Jefferson, A. B. (1992). Effectiveness of family reunification services: An innovative evaluation model. *Social Work, 37,* 304–311.

John A. Hartford Foundation. (2010). *2010 annual report*. Retrieved from www.jhartfound.org/pdf%20files/JAHF_2010_AR.pdf

Leung, P., Willis, N. D., Cheung, A., & Walijarvi, C. (2011, October). *The impact of Title IV-E training on case outcomes*. Paper presented at the 57th Annual Program Meeting of the Council on Social Work Education, Atlanta.

Marsh, J., Ryan, J., Choi, S., & Testa, M. (2006). Integrated services for families with multiple problems: Obstacles to family reunification. *Children and Youth Services Review, 28,* 1074–1087.

Mor Barak, M., Nissly, J., & Levin, A. (2001). Antecedents to retention and turnover among child welfare, social work, and other human service employees: What can we learn from past research? A review and metanalysis. *Social Service Review, 75,* 625–661.

National Association of Social Workers. (2004). *Fact sheet: Title IV-E child welfare training program.* Retrieved from http://www.socialworkers.org/advocacy/updates/2003/081204a.asp

National Association of Social Workers. (2008, February 14). *Statement of National Association of Social Workers (NASW) executive director Dr. Elizabeth Clark in support of H.R. 5447, the Dorothy I. Height and Whitney M. Young, Jr. Social Work Reinvestment Act.* Retrieved from http://www. socialworkers.org/pressroom/2008/0214act.asp

National Council on Crime and Delinquency. (2006). *The relationship between staff turnover, child welfare system functioning and recurrent child abuse.* Houston: Cornerstones for Kids.

U.S. General Accounting Office. (2003). *Child welfare: HHS could play a greater role in helping child welfare agencies to recruit and retain staff.* Washington, DC: Author.

Zlotnik, J. L., Pecora, P., & Briar, K. (1989). *Addressing the program and personnel crisis in child welfare.* Silver Spring, MD: National Association of Social Workers.

CHAPTER 9

AN ADVOCACY PLAN ON BEHALF OF FOSTER FAMILIES

Susan Kosche Vallem

SOCIAL WORK MATTERS

When social workers put together a plan, positive changes can and do happen. Advocacy on behalf of clients and constituents often requires a plan of action to best make policy changes. Social work practice should lead to policy changes, and who better to advocate for needed changes than social work practitioners.

The NASW *Code of Ethics* states, "Social workers should advocate for living conditions conducive to the fulfillment of basic human needs and should promote social, economic, political, and cultural values and institutions that are compatible with the realization of social justice" (NASW, 2008, p. 26). Social workers are called on to be advocates as well as clinicians, to ameliorate social problems as well as individual problems. We cannot do one without the other.

Hoefer (2001) identified the following effective advocacy: be knowledgeable about and proactive in the policy process; learn timely and policy-related information; build a relationship with decision makers; and build coalitions with other interest groups and policy actors.

NARRATIVE

Extensive research has been carried out related to meeting the needs of children in the welfare system generally and in the foster system specifically. A dilemma facing foster families in Iowa is a state law that requires that foster children stay with licensed foster parents for respite care, services for children when foster parents must be absent. The current restrictive state law means that many relatives and family friends do not qualify.

> *The service area manager or designee may authorize respite for a family foster care for up to 24 days per calendar year per placement. Respite care shall be provided by a licensed foster family. (Iowa Code, §156.8(7))*

The need for respite care often means foster children having to stay with another foster family, and sometimes have to change schools if a licensed provider does not live near the family. Finding foster homes that are not already at licensed capacity is also a dilemma.

To address the need for more foster respite care, a four-county foster care association and the Wartburg College Social Work Department received a $5,000 grant from Adopt Us Kids to develop and implement a pilot respite foster care project to identify and train respite foster care providers. The project worked in conjunction with the Department of Human Services (DHS). Currently, the program operates successfully in four counties, and the next step is to expand the program statewide.

Expanding the program will require permanent funding through the DHS and an amendment to state law to permit certified respite providers to assist with respite foster care. An action plan to expand the program was developed by an undergraduate social work student from the practice class and social work faculty who had experience working with foster families. The action plan will be presented to the 2012 Iowa Legislature.

POLICY MATTERS

This five-step action plan can serve as a model for advocacy with federal, state, and local governments and agencies.

Step One

The first step is to change the state law that governs respite foster care. The plan uses data from the pilot project. Foster parents who participated in the program were asked to complete a survey to measure their level of satisfaction. A social work premise is to build on client or community strengths, and families identified the pilot respite program as a strength. The data will also be useful in demonstrating to legislators the success of the program. The inclusion of constituents is valuable when approaching legislators to advocate policy change. Materials displaying the success of the pilot program can be a primary tool for educating legislators and advocating for change.

Step Two

The second step is to deal with the potential costs of establishing the program statewide. Legislators evaluate proposed legislation partially on the basis of what it will cost. Consider potential ways of meeting the costs of expanding the program. Currently, Iowa foster parents use an average of six days of their allotted 24 days of respite a year (Walker, 2011). Changing policy to allow certified respite providers to supply respite care would enable families to use more respite care, thus increasing the cost of the program.

Other costs of expanding the program would include the necessary staff and related expenses to allow the program to be functional. For example, DHS may need to hire more caseworkers to interview potential respite care providers, carry out background checks, and train and certify those who are selected. During the pilot program, the interviews and background checks were carried out by the social work practice class at no expense; many students also applied for and were trained as respite care providers following the same protocol. If the program is expanded, the administrative and financial responsibility for the program will fall on DHS. Any advocacy program must look at what the legislation will cost and consider additional sources of funding to suggest.

Step Three

Once the necessary materials explaining the program and its costs and benefits are generated, the next step would be contacting DHS administrators to enlist their support. Because DHS would administer and fund an expanded respite care program, its support would be critical. A good advocacy plan is well organized and involves all the stakeholders. For advocacy to be successful, a coalition of interested parties is usually the most effective way to carry it out.

Other stakeholders from the private sector who work in the area of child welfare and foster care would be encouraged to join this interest group. Many of these foster care organizations support a bill to extend Iowa foster care licensure to two years. These agencies also support adding the respite care project to the pending bill, or at least bringing the subject to legislators' attention. The goal is to gain as much diverse support for an issue as possible. Using a coalition of stakeholders adds strength to proposed legislation. Including a variety of stakeholders also minimizes potential opposition. Determining who might be opposed to proposed legislation is essential in any advocacy plan.

Step Four

Once support for the change in the law is gained from DHS, private child welfare agencies, and foster care groups, the next step is to contact legislators. Three different categories of legislators will be contacted: those holding positions on key committees and councils focused on children's issues, those representing areas served by the Certified Respite Program and other stakeholders, and those most likely to support the proposal.

When working with legislators, initial contact should be made by e-mail or phone. If possible, set a time to meet in person with the legislator to discuss the proposal. The best approach is by a small group of stakeholders who bring printed materials about the proposal, but individuals can be effective as well. If personal meetings with key legislators cannot be arranged, phone interviews can be used to educate legislators and ask for their opinions and their support. When the legislature is not in session, members of the respite care coalition can visit with legislators in their respective districts.

Step Five

As soon as state law is changed to make certified respite providers eligible to provide respite care for foster children, the program has the opportunity to expand throughout the state. Administrators of each of the five DHS service areas will then be contacted and encouraged to adapt their services and launch the program to meet the needs of foster families living in their respective areas.

In summary, changing state laws and policies takes organization, data collection, inclusion of stakeholders, and legislative advocacy. Gathering support from stakeholders and constituents goes a long way toward bringing about legislative and policy change. Practicing social workers are ideal advocates because they know the needs, know how to solve problems and build on strengths, and can bring diverse populations together to reach a common goal.

DISCUSSION QUESTIONS

1. What foster care policies need to be changed or revised in your agency or state or nationally?

2. How can social workers become effective advocates using the advocacy plan outlined in this chapter?

REFERENCES

Hoefer, R. (2001). Highly effective human services interest groups: Seven key practices. *Journal of Community Practice, 9*(2), 1–13.

National Association of Social Workers. (2008). *Code of ethics of the National Association of Social Workers.* Washington, DC: NASW Press.

Walker, C. (2011). *Foster respite care advocacy plan.* Waverly, IA: Wartburg College.

CHAPTER 10

CHILD WELFARE:
DOES SOCIAL WORK MATTER?

Joan Levy Zlotnik

SOCIAL WORK MATTERS

In my first job as a new MSW graduate, I worked at a state institution for people with intellectual disabilities. Although each of the units had a "social worker," it turned out that I was the only one with an actual social work degree. I was shocked. How could these people without social work degrees be doing their job? I was fresh out of graduate school and had completed three different field placements, all in specialized units where a group of social work students did fieldwork under the tutelage of a field instructor employed by the university. I had not encountered any of the many settings in which people without a social work degree perform social work and are called social workers. I was concerned: if a degree was not required for a social worker position, how would the public or policymakers distinguish between those who hired workers especially educated to perform the job and those who just hired anyone?

The state institution was dealing with a class action lawsuit and under the scrutiny of the media, becoming an early leader in deinstitutionalization. It had nurses without BAs and physicians who did not instill confidence in their skills, and I thought that service delivery would be improved if the best qualified social workers, nurses, physicians, psychologists, and other relevant professionals would be employed in such settings. But hiring professionals, especially experienced professionals, raises staffing costs.

Six years later, I was running a small specialized foster care program in Virginia. This was at a time when increasing numbers of specialty foster care programs were being developed, in the shadows of deinstitutionalization, for people with physical, intellectual, and behavioral limitations. Because therapeutic interventions and creation of a treatment milieu were aspects of these placement programs, the Association of Licensed Child Placing Agencies, of which I was a member, advocated for broadening the staffing requirements for the state's licensed child placement agencies beyond the MSW or a related degree requirement. I recall one of my colleagues saying, "what would NASW say?"

Another six years later, in 1987, I was hired by the national office of NASW to work on the implementation of the NASW presidential initiative to promote professional social work practice in public child welfare agencies. There I was confronted each day with the challenges of documenting the importance of a social work degree for quality child welfare practice. Years of declassification had occurred in public child welfare services, and the common belief in social work education programs was that public child welfare agencies were not attractive work sites for new BSW and MSW graduates.

Soon after coming to NASW, I found myself on a panel on workforce issues at a conference of the National Association of Public Child Welfare Administrators, an affiliate of the American Public Welfare Association (now the American Public Human Services Association). The panelists included representatives from NASW and the Child Welfare League of America, a dean of a school of social work, a state director of child welfare, and a university-based child welfare trainer. We all discussed the challenges of recruitment and retention that public child welfare agencies were facing and highlighted the need to ensure that child welfare staff members have the competencies to perform their jobs. Rather than blaming each other for the problem, we committed on that panel to work together, and over the past 20-plus years, representatives from those entities have worked together to address staffing issues. Partnerships have been forged at the state and national levels to address workforce issues and to work toward child welfare service delivery improvement.

NARRATIVE

The challenges faced by child welfare administrators, and the ways that partnerships between social work education and professional associations can be useful, are highlighted in the following example.

Jane Smith has recently been appointed child welfare director of a midwestern state where the child welfare services are directly administered by the state and there is limited involvement by private agencies that contract with the state, except for specialized services. Ms. Smith has 20 years of experience as a child advocate and is a lawyer. She has never worked in a public child welfare agency, nor has she managed a large and complex agency. She was appointed to this job after her predecessor was fired by the governor following a horrific case in which a child died due to maltreatment and three siblings were found malnourished and locked in a room. That case had been known to the child welfare agency due to previous maltreatment reports. However, visitation records were sparse, and no services had been provided to the family after the previous instances of abuse were substantiated.

After the story of the child's death gained a great deal of media attention, the governor appointed an independent panel, chaired by the dean of one of the two schools of social work in the state, to investigate how this could have happened. The panel's report highlighted several problems, including caseloads that were four times higher than those recommended by the Child Welfare League of America; supervisors who had little training because they were being promoted from frontline jobs relatively soon after being hired, due to high turnover; and limited training for frontline workers (such as three days of preservice training and an annual requirement of eight hours of training on completing agency forms or a specialized topic like dealing with natural disasters).

The report also raised concerns because the agency selected staff through the generic civil service list, hiring anyone with a bachelor's degree and an interest in child welfare work. The panel recommended lowering caseloads, raising qualifications for both frontline workers and supervisors, implementing a structured risk assessment and safety decision-making protocol, increasing documentation and analysis of case data, restructuring and expanding both preservice and in-service training, and creating evidence-based home visiting and parent training programs.

Ms. Smith is faced with a daunting task. The agency morale is low due to the firing of the previous director and the current public scrutiny. The current workforce is not only demoralized but also skeptical that Ms. Smith has the experience and expertise to make things better for the workers, or for the children and families that the agency serves.

What should Ms. Smith do? What information will be helpful to her? What policies might she advocate? What supports does she need, and who will be her partners in achieving the necessary reforms?

POLICY MATTERS

This story is unfortunately common in the United States. A plan of action to improve service delivery and address workforce issues requires many partnerships and the development of strategic alliances. Addressing service delivery improvements needs to take place concurrently with addressing the competencies and qualifications of frontline staff and supervisors and the organizational culture and climate (APHSA, 2011; Zlotnik, 2009; Zlotnik, Strand, & Anderson, 2009). A policy workgroup convened by the Children's Defense Fund and Children's Rights and supported by the Annie E. Casey Foundation's Human Services Workforce Initiative identified 14 interlocking components that need to be considered when working to improve the child welfare workforce (Children's Defense Fund, 2007):

1. strong and consistent leadership,
2. supportive organizational environment,
3. manageable caseloads and workloads,
4. meaningful supervision and mentoring,
5. quality education and professional preparation,
6. competency-based training and professional development,
7. timely and accurate data and information,
8. practice-enhancing research and evaluation,

9. effective quality assurance and accountability,
10. useful technological resources,
11. safe and suitable working conditions,
12. equitable employment incentives,
13. authentic cultural competence, and
14. significant family and community connectedness.

To accomplish these goals, child welfare administrators need to work with their advisory boards and create strong partnerships with BSW and MSW programs in their states that can prepare students for child welfare careers, undertake research and information gathering projects, analyze data, present evidence before the legislature to support quality child welfare practice, and help to engage in long-range planning. Although traineeships supported by federal or state funding can provide financial incentives for students to pursue child welfare careers (Zlotnik, 2003), funding alone is not sufficient. There needs to be relevant training in providing culturally competent child welfare services.

An enhanced child welfare curriculum is especially important, as a degree by itself does not necessarily prepare social work graduates for the challenges of child welfare work. Thoughtful use of data is also extremely important to promote service delivery improvements. For example, the child welfare research center at the University of California, Berkeley, provides key data reports and analysis to California counties for county child welfare directors and their staff to understand case outcomes and target service delivery enhancements and for supervisors to work with frontline workers to improve case outcomes (Institute for the Advancement of Social Work Research, 2008).

Professional associations like NASW also have an important role to play. In many years of working in national social work organizations, I have learned that it is not enough to advocate for hiring professional social workers in leadership, middle management, supervisory, and frontline positions in child welfare. Although those are great goals, there needs to be more. NASW needs to work with schools of social work, child advocates, the executive branch of government, and Congress to seek child welfare improvements and to provide evidence of the value of professional social workers.

NASW also needs to develop information and resources that can influence policymakers at the state and national level. For example, the NASW Center for Workforce Studies has produced a number of valuable reports, including *"If You're Right for the Job, It's the Best Job in the World"* (Whitaker, Reich, Reid, Williams, & Woodside, 2004) and *Assuring the Sufficiency of a Frontline Workforce: A National Study of Licensed Social Workers: Special Report: Social Work Services for Children & Families* (National Association of Social Workers Center for Workforce Studies, 2006). Information on the links between staff turnover and social work degrees, and the sense of self-efficacy of professional social workers in child welfare, is critical information to provide to policymakers (Ellett, Ellett, & Rugutt, 2003; Zlotnik, DePanfilis, Daining, & Lane, 2005). A social work degree can ensure that staff have the necessary competencies for child welfare practice (Rittner & Wodarski, 1999) and can help provide a pipeline to career advancement in child welfare, as more agencies may require the MSW for supervisors than they do for frontline staff (Social Work Policy Institute 2011).

Beginning in 1994, Illinois had the same child welfare director for nine years, an exceptionally long tenure for this position. One of the critical decisions made early, as the agency dealt with numerous class action lawsuits and clamors for reform, was to increase engagement with the social work education programs in the state. This included partnering with the Child and Family Research Center for the necessary data and research, and partnering with social work deans and faculty on providing supervisors with MSW degrees as the agency sought to meet Council on Accreditation standards (McDonald, 2005; McDonald & McCarthy, 1999; Testa, 2010; Zlotnik, 2010).

If Ms. Smith is truly an experienced and effective advocate, she will know that working with NASW, other child welfare advocates, and the universities will be essential to her success. Even if she is not a social worker, she can come to understand that social work education programs and the social work profession can be important resources for her success. If the concerned parties work together, they can help influence the legislature and the executive branch to secure the necessary funding, implement legislation to decrease caseloads and increase staffing standards, and put in place an improved training system. Hiring trained social workers may not be all that is needed to improve child welfare practice, but it is one of the important steps that an agency can take in addressing the complex needs for system improvements.

Discussion Questions

1. What role can NASW take in promoting professional social work practice in child welfare?

2. What can be done to advocate for social work staffing requirements in child welfare agencies?

References

American Public Human Services Association. (2011). *Positioning public child welfare guidance: Workforce.* Retrieved from http://www.ppcwg.org/workforce-overview.html

Children's Defense Fund. (2007). *14 components to support an effective child welfare workforce.* Retrieved from http://www.childrensdefense.org/child-research-data-publications/data/effective-child-welfare-workforce-diagram.pdf

Ellett, A., Ellett, C., & Rugutt, J. K. (2003). *A study of personal and organizational factors contributing to employee retention and turnover in child welfare in Georgia: A report prepared for the Georgia Department of Human Resources/Division of Family & Children Services: Executive summary.* Retrieved from http://louisville.edu/kent/projects/iv-e/ExecSummary.pdf

Institute for the Advancement of Social Work Research. (2008). *Strengthening university–agency/ research partnerships to enhance child welfare outcomes: A toolkit for building research partnerships.* Washington, DC: Author. Retrieved from http://www.socialworkpolicy.org/wp-content/ uploads/2007/06/9-IASWR-CW-Research-Partners.pdf

McDonald, J. (2005). *Lessons learned from the Illinois child welfare system turnaround.* Retrieved from http://www.jessmcdonald.a25hourdaysites.com/f/Lessons_Learned_from_Illinois_-_7-22-05. pdf

McDonald, J., & McCarthy, B. (1999). Effective partnership models between the state agencies, the university and community service providers. In *Changing paradigms of child welfare practice: Responding to opportunities and challenges* (pp. 43–72). Washington, DC: Children's Bureau.

National Association of Social Workers Center for Workforce Studies. (2006, March). *Assuring the sufficiency of a frontline workforce: A national study of licensed social workers: Special report: Social work services for children & families.* Retrieved from http://workforce.socialworkers.org/studies/ children/children_families.pdf

Rittner, B., & Wodarski, J. (1999). Differential uses for BSW and MSW educated social workers in child welfare services. *Children and Youth Services Review, 21,* 217–238.

Social Work Policy Institute. (2011). *Supervision: The safety net for front-line child welfare practice.* Retrieved from http://www.socialworkpolicy.org/news-events/supervision-the-safety-net-for-front-line-child-welfare-practice.html

Testa, M. (2010). Introduction. In M. Testa & J. Poertner (Eds.), *Fostering accountability* (pp. 3–34). New York: Oxford University Press.

Whitaker, T., Reich, S., Reid, L. B., Williams, M., & Woodside, C. (2004). *"If you're right for the job, it's the best job in the world."* Retrieved from http://www.socialworkers.org/practice/children/ NASWChildWelfareRpt062004.pdf

Zlotnik, J. L. (2003). The use of Title IV-E training funds for social work education: An historical perspective. *Journal of Human Behavior and the Social Environment, 7*(1/2), 5–20.

Zlotnik, J. L. (2009, September). *Social work and child welfare: A national debate.* Retrieved from ssw.umich.edu/events/fauri/FauriLecture_ChildWelfare.pdf

Zlotnik, J. L. (2010). Fostering and sustaining university-agency partnerships. In M. Testa & J. Poertner (Eds.), *Fostering accountability: Using evidence to guide and improve child welfare policy* (pp. 328–356). New York: Oxford University Press.

Zlotnik, J. L., DePanfilis, D., Daining, C., & Lane, M. M. (2005). *Factors influencing retention of child welfare staff: A systematic review of research.* Washington, DC: Institute for the Advancement of Social Work Research.

Zlotnik, J. L., Strand, V., & Anderson, G. (2009). Introduction: Achieving positive outcomes for children and families: Recruiting and retaining a competent child welfare workforce. *Child Welfare, 88*(5), 7–22.

CHAPTER 11

Care Coordination for the Well-Being of Children

Kathy Lopes

Social Work Matters

Social workers are often considered the gatekeepers of client care and services. Regardless of the diversity or specialization of the profession, case management and care coordination have remained an integral role for social workers.

In recent years, care coordination has become a more refined and specific function within the social work field. "Care coordination is a client-centered, assessment-based, interdisciplinary approach to integrating health care and psychosocial support services in which a care coordinator develops and implements a comprehensive care plan that addresses the client's needs, strengths, and goals" (NASW, 2009, p. 1).

The significance of care coordination has often been highlighted when discussing work with older adults or those living with advanced illness or multiple chronic conditions. It is only within the last decade that we have seen policy shift to incorporate and fund care coordination not only for these clients but for all, regardless of age or disability (NASW, 2009).

As we better understand the correlation of physical and mental health, the multiple benefits of coordinating health and psychosocial services for children and families become clear. Providing care coordination as an option to all clients increases provider communication and decreases duplication of services, ultimately resulting in better quality of service. In addition, research has shown that failure to share information reduces those safety net redundancies that are necessary to catch an individual in crisis before it becomes too late (Council of the District of Columbia on Human Services, 2010, p. 2).

Narrative

The following example illustrates the significance of care coordination and how failure to share information can be detrimental to the provision of preventative care.

Brittany was a 15-year-old student in her freshman year of high school. She attended school every day, working hard to maintain good grades, and appeared to have a typical high school social life.

It wasn't until Brittany had been absent from school for several weeks without an excuse that members of the student support team became concerned. Following the school's unsuccessful attempts to contact her mother by phone and letter, the team decided that the school social worker would make a visit to the home to try to get more information on Brittany's absence.

When the social worker and a colleague arrived at Brittany's home, they were met by Brittany's mother, who appeared agitated, although they explained that the visit was out of concern that Brittany had missed so many days of school. She denied their request to enter the home and speak to Brittany, and it was from the front steps that they noticed three young children looking on from the living room. When they asked her about the children and why they weren't in school, Brittany's mother explained that they were her daughters and she had withdrawn all four of her children from school, including Brittany, and would take on the responsibility of home-schooling.

Throughout the conversation, the social worker expressed apprehension regarding the woman's irrational responses to questions, her defensive posture, and the unkempt appearance of the other children in the living room. The mother deflected all of the social workers' concerns and made it clear that their presence was unwelcome. They left without seeing Brittany.

Immediately upon leaving Brittany's home, the social worker made a report to the city's child welfare agency, citing indications of abuse and educational neglect of several children in the household. The hotline worker said that a staff member would go to the home and investigate.

The social worker also contacted the elementary school where the younger children had been enrolled to verify the information she received from Brittany's mother. School staff informed her that they received a verbal withdrawal notice for the three children from a family friend and that they had no follow-up process for student withdrawal.

Several days later, the child welfare agency closed the investigation after not receiving an answer at the identified address and obtaining unconfirmed reports that the family had moved to a different city.

The social worker continued to make calls to the director of the child welfare agency, the court system, and the police department, only to be transferred from one agency to the next. After numerous attempts by the social worker to identify the appropriate agency to check up on the children, the police department sent an officer to the home. Following the officer's visit, he called the social worker to confirm that he had gone to the home and seen all of the children and sensed no immediate concerns. (In later reports, the officer denied seeing Brittany—Alexander, 2009.)

At this point, the social worker felt that she had exhausted all options, as it appeared that each system had followed its agency protocol. The end of the school year arrived and Brittany never returned.

Nine months later, during a routine eviction procedure, fire marshals entered the home that the social worker had previously visited and found the dead bodies of four children, identified as Brittany and her three sisters. Their bodies were so heavily decomposed that it was impossible to determine the exact time and cause of their deaths, but it was apparent that they had been dead for several months. Brittany's mother was later convicted of the murder of her four daughters and is now serving a sentence of 120 years in prison.

DISCUSSION

Following the shocking discovery, the city's investigation produced overwhelming information detailing the family's long history of contacts with "no less than 20 agencies and community providers"(Council of the District of Columbia on Human Services, 2010, p. 2). The social worker's documented efforts to check on Brittany's welfare were publicized, exposing how a lack of communication and information-sharing had contributed to the devastating outcome.

Although tragic, this story is not the first of its kind, as agencies across the country have struggled to maintain a system for sharing valuable information to prevent similar tragedies rather than react after they occur. This narrative highlights the discrepancies and numerous breakdowns that led many to speculate as to whether this could have been prevented if such a system had existed. The public's reaction was the beginning of what became the focus of litigation and shifts in policy for several of the agencies involved (Cauvin, 2010).

POLICY MATTERS

The details of the incident provoked outrage within the community and prompted policymakers to respond with a sense of urgency. They recognized that the existing system allowed agencies to work in isolation and offer treatment to children and families without knowing the full context of their experiences and needs. Critical information was frequently lost between providers, compromising quality of care to an already vulnerable population. City representatives and council members proposed a reassessment of the current system to incorporate the sharing of valuable information when children and families receive several services and interact with multiple providers (Child Welfare League of America, 2009).

Proposals for change ultimately resulted in new legislation: the Data-Sharing and Information Coordination Amendment Act of 2010 (the Coordination Amendment Act), designed to address the failure of communication across agency and provider lines, while also ensuring effective and timely delivery of social services to individuals and families in crisis. The act details a number of policy changes with regard to sharing health and human services information between agencies and service providers, with three specific goals: (1) amending privacy and confidentiality laws to allow for use and disclosure of information, (2) creating a combined data system to house protected information, and (3) creating a case coordination program to improve administration and management of services.

The Coordination Amendment Act is an important step in addressing gaps and creating a more supportive structure for a preventive model. The legislation removes legal barriers that have previously restricted the sharing of information, but further assessment will find that additional barriers to managing the system will unfold and need to be addressed for this act to be most effective. This is where the social worker's role is critical in the long-term success of this policy, particularly in the efforts to expand the implementation of a true system of care coordination.

Care coordination highlights the importance of an interdisciplinary approach and requires a facilitator to work with a variety of specialists to share information and integrate a plan to meet the child and family's needs (Fink-Samnick, 2011). The effectiveness of the model relies heavily on the ability of the coordinator (often a social worker) to build a team that incorporates not only the family's needs, but also historical information and understanding of their strengths. Social workers, particularly those with case management and clinical experience, are trained with the necessary skills to guide this process and bring the best of their practices to improve the delivery of care.

The hopes of those who supported implementation of the Coordination Amendment Act are that it will mend a failed system and foster collaboration across agencies. It will require the efforts of all agencies and providers to shift old practices, but it opens the door for social workers to be instrumental in the process. With a supported system in place to increase provider communication and advocacy for clients, the risk of another tragedy similar to the one that befell Brittany and her sisters is significantly diminished.

DISCUSSION QUESTIONS

1. Had the Coordination Amendment Act been in place prior to the tragedy, in what specific ways could the social worker in the narrative have used the system?

2. What supports need to be considered to address potential barriers to a successful implementation of this act, and how can social workers play a part in the sustainability of this policy?

3. What other systems were responsible, and where could policy reform in those agencies have helped?

REFERENCES

Alexander, K. (2009, July 23). At murder trial, D.C. police sergeant recants story of seeing Jacks girl healthy. *Washington Post*. Retrieved from http://www.washingtonpost.com/wp-dyn/content/article/2009/07/22/AR2009072203315.html

Cauvin, H. E. (2010, May 27). D.C. child welfare agency showing improvement but problems persist, report says. *Washington Post.* Retrieved from http://www.washingtonpost.com/wp-dyn/content/article/2010/05/26/AR2010052603592.html?nav=emailpage

Child Welfare League of America. (2009). Moving forward after tragedy. *Children's Voice.* Retrieved from http://www.cwla.org/voice/0907national.htm

Council of the District of Columbia on Human Services. (2010, April 28). *Committee report for Bill 18-0356.* Retrieved from http://dcclims1.dccouncil.us/images/00001/20110218112329.pdf

Data-Sharing and Information Coordination Amendment Act of 2010, 57 D.C. Register 7171 (August 13, 2010).

Fink-Samnick, E. (2011). Understanding care coordination: Emerging opportunities for social workers. *New Social Worker.* Retrieved from http://www.socialworker.com/home/Feature_Articles/Professional_Development_%26_Advancement/Understanding_Care_Coordination%3A_Emerging_Opportunities_for_Social_Workers/

National Association of Social Workers (NASW). (2009). *Social work and care coordination.* Retrieved from http://www.socialworkers.org/advocacy/briefing/CareCoordinationBriefing Paper.pdf

Adoption Practices and Policies Affecting Children and Families in Child Welfare:

In Whose Best Interests?

Ruth G. McRoy

Policy Matters

State and national adoption and foster care policies have evolved significantly over the past several decades and have increasingly affected social work decision making about children and families in the child welfare system. For example, in 1980, in an attempt to reduce the number of children in foster care, the Adoption Assistance and Child Welfare Act of 1980 (P.L. 96-272) was passed. This law required courts and administrative bodies to make reasonable efforts to prevent child removal; to hold six-month case reviews of children in foster care to determine their best interests, with most emphasis placed on returning children to their homes; and if return to the home is not possible, to make efforts to find permanent homes through adoption. The law defined "child with special needs" as a child who has a special condition such that he or she cannot be returned to the parent's home and cannot be placed without providing assistance (Child Welfare Information Gateway, Administration for Children and Families [CWIG, ACF], 2011a).

The disproportionately high representation of children of color in the child welfare system who are awaiting adoption has resulted in additional federal legislation. Although African Americans only represented about 15 percent of the U.S. population in 2010, African American children represented 29 percent or 30,812 of children needing adoption (U.S. Department of Health and Human Services, Administration for Children and Families [HHS, ACF], 2011). This disproportionate representation of African American children in child welfare has existed for many years. To increase the likelihood of these children being adopted, two laws were passed: the

Multiethnic Placement Act of 1994 (part of the Improving America's Schools Act of 1994 [P.L. 103-382]) and the Interethnic Provisions Act of 1996 (part of the Small Business Job Protection Act of 1996 [P.L. 104-188]). The Multiethnic Placement Act called for the "diligent recruitment of foster and adoptive families that reflect the ethnic and racial diversity of children in the state for whom foster and adoptive homes are needed" (McRoy, Mica, Freundlich, & Kroll, 2007, p. 51) and prohibited federally funded foster care and adoption agencies from delaying or denying placements or discriminating in placement decision making based solely on the race, color, or national origin of the parents or child (Hollinger, 1998). The Interethnic Provisions Act removed the word "solely" from the Multiethnic Placement Act provisions and prohibited any consideration of race, color, or national origin (McRoy et al., 2007).

To accelerate adoption permanency, another law was passed in 1997: the Adoption and Safe Families Act (P.L. 105-89), which required states to initiate court proceedings to terminate parental rights if a child had been in care for at least 15 of the last 22 months, unless there was an exception (for example, the child had been in foster care with a relative for the past 15 months) (U.S. Government Accountability Office, 2002). The law also gave states incentive payments if they increased the number of completed adoptions from foster care. The implementation of this law has raised a number of issues, as parental rights are often terminated before an adoptive family has been found and the children become essentially "legal orphans" (Ellis, Malm, & Bishop, 2009). This is an ethical issue that many social work professionals must address. In 2010, about 64,000 of the children in foster care had the parental rights of all living parents terminated (HHS, ACF, 2011). These are children for whom adoption or another planned permanent living arrangement must be sought.

In 2010, there were approximately 107,000 children in the U.S. foster care system awaiting adoption; almost 18,000 of these children have been waiting five years or longer (HHS, ACF, 2011). Despite legislation to increase, the adoption of older children still continues to be a challenge. Of the children awaiting adoption, 37 percent were 10 years or older, and unfortunately, as children age, their likelihood of adoption seems to decrease. In 2010, about 64,000 children were legally freed from their birth parents and had been awaiting adoption for an average of two years (HHS, ACF, 2011).

Partly due to the ongoing challenges of finding both foster and adoptive families for children, many states have begun to not only encourage but also facilitate placement of children in the foster care system with the children's relatives. In 2008, the Fostering Connections to Success and Increasing Adoptions Act (P.L. 110-351) was passed, which included strategies to help children in care reconnect with family members. It allowed for kinship guardianship assistance payments under Title IV-E (under the Social Security Act) for children who had been in kinship foster care, and the relative could take legal guardianship of the child. This law also required Title IV-E-funded agencies to make reasonable efforts to ensure that siblings removed from their home were placed together in the same foster care, adoption, or guardianship placement (CWIG, ACF, 2011b).

State laws differ on many issues such as who can adopt, marital status preferences, termination of parental rights, access to records, and consent to adoption. For example, some states allow single-parent adoptions, but not adoption by same-sex or unmarried couples. In those instances, the second parent may have to pursue a second parent adoption. A *second parent* is defined as a partner (unmarried to the legal parent) who lives in the home and adopts the child without negatively affecting the rights of the other adoptive parent (CWIG, ACF, 2011b). However, other states allow both same-sex marriages and adoptions by same-sex couples. All of these legal considerations can deter some families from seeking to adopt from foster care and limit options for many children needing a permanent placement through adoption.

It is clear that practitioners must be well versed in the state and national adoption laws that govern the provision of services to families seeking to adopt from foster care and children in care needing adoption. The following case illustrates how policies affect adoption practice by child welfare professionals today.

NARRATIVE

Johnny, a 16-year-old African American, has been in foster care since the age of 10. At that time, Johnny and his three half brothers—ages 8, 6, and 4—were removed from their birth mother after numerous reports to the county child welfare agency that the children were being left alone at home while the mother was out drinking. Johnny's father was in prison serving a term for assault with a deadly weapon, and Johnny had not seen him since the age of five.

When he was first removed from his home, Johnny was placed on an emergency basis with an African American foster family that was caring for three other foster children. At that time, the agency did not have a family available that would take Johnny along with his three brothers. The siblings were placed separately in two other homes. Being separated from one another was a big loss for all the children, as they had been very close. In fact, Johnny had been largely responsible for taking care of his younger siblings, as neither of his parents was around much of the time. However, the agency worker was unable to find a foster home that would take all four brothers. The agency tried to arrange visits with Johnny's mother and siblings periodically, but transportation and other logistical issues created barriers, and the visits rarely occurred. Efforts to get Johnny's mother into a treatment program were also unsuccessful.

Over the next four years, Johnny experienced 12 foster home placements, attended six schools, and was assigned seven different caseworkers. On a couple of occasions he became very angry toward one of his foster families and acted out, making threats and throwing furniture and the telephone down the stairs. The foster mother became frightened and told the placing agency that Johnny had to go immediately. In several of his other foster placements, he and the children in the home fought, and he was removed again. Johnny's angry behavior continued to escalate; eventually he was placed in a therapeutic group home.

By the time Johnny was 14, his mother and father's parental rights had terminated, and his three younger brothers had been adopted by their foster parents. The foster parents refused to consider adopting Johnny because they were aware of his angry outbursts and did not feel comfortable with him in their home. Johnny remained in group care for the next two years, and his angry outbursts subsided somewhat.

When Johnny turned 16, he was assigned a new caseworker who began exploring with him the option of adoption. He was aware that his siblings had been adopted, and he had talked with them by phone a couple of times. When Johnny's caseworker asked if he wanted her to try to find him an adoptive family, Johnny initially agreed. For the next few months, she worked with him to create a life book, and she took pictures of him to be posted on the Heart Gallery (an exhibit featuring the pictures and stories of foster care youths in need of adoption) and on the state Web site which lists children needing a placement. Since Johnny was African American, she knew that all placement decisions would have to comply with the Multiethnic Placement Act and the Interethnic Provisions Act. Therefore, she was open to considering families of all ethnic backgrounds who inquired about Johnny. One day, she came to the group home to visit Johnny to let him know that she had talked with three prospective adoptive families, two white and one African American, who had seen his picture on the state adoption Web site and expressed an interest in learning more about him. His worker was shocked to hear Johnny say that he had changed his mind and did not want to be adopted anymore. He said he was fine in his current group home placement and did not want to move again.

In the state where Johnny lived, the law stipulated that adoptions require the child's consent if the child is 12 years or older. Despite his worker's urging him to reconsider, Johnny insisted that he had talked with other children in the group home about adoption and about moving again. He was firm in his decision that adoption was not for him. He told his worker not to continue seeking an adoptive family and to give him the papers to sign that verified that his permanency goal would be independent living. Basically, this meant he would age out of foster care without a permanent family.

SOCIAL WORK MATTERS

The foregoing case highlights policy and practice issues that may arise in handling adoptions from the public child welfare system. For example, Johnny decided not to be adopted. What are the implications for the social worker involved in the case? State laws vary about the age of consent to adoption. In 25 states and the District of Columbia, the age of consent is 14, while 18 states set it at 12, and six states require consent beginning at age 10 (Louisiana is currently the only state that does not address the issue of child's consent in their statute) (CWIG, ACF, 2010). Social workers must be aware of how state law governs the approach they can take in making adoption plans for a child.

Johnny lived in a state that required that children of his age consent to adoption, and when he indicated he did not want to be adopted, another plan was considered. However, it is also important to consider the reasons Johnny made this decision. As mentioned earlier, Johnny had experienced many early life stressors, including lack of consistent caregivers, feelings of rejection, an alcoholic mother, an absent father, unstable housing, and a general feeling of being worthless and unlovable. All of these factors may have influenced his decision not to be adopted.

Moreover, recent neurological research on the brain development of children and adolescents suggests that youths who have experienced early trauma as a result of abuse, or who have experienced family separations, multiple moves, and "relationship disruptions in foster care may find it difficult to trust that adults will be there for them. Their brains are 'wired' to expect a non-supportive environment or sudden, arbitrary moves" (Jim Casey Youth Opportunities Initiative, 2011, p. 25).

However, although policy in almost all states stipulates that at certain ages, children must give consent to adoption, have we considered to what extent a child's decision is influenced by his or her stage of brain development? Research suggests that not only does an adolescent brain function differently from an adult brain, but there are gender differences in brain development as well. According to recent research findings, girls' brain development reaches its midpoint just prior to age 11 and is complete between ages 21 and 22. Boys' brain development, however, does not arrive at its midpoint until just before age 15 and is not complete until almost the age of 30 (Lenroot et al. 2007). Therefore, it is critical that social policies allowing children to make adult decisions be reconsidered, given the expanded knowledge and evidence about the variety of factors influencing a child's brain development and decision-making ability.

Not only are policies related to child welfare important to consider in cases like Johnny's, but in many instances, other systems affect family and child outcomes. It is estimated that at least 8 percent of children in the nation's child welfare system have an incarcerated parent. A recent report by the U.S. Government Accountability Office (2011) noted that often child welfare systems and judicial systems may serve the same populations, yet very little is done to facilitate linkages between the agencies. When a parent is incarcerated, child welfare workers need to be able to communicate with corrections agencies to improve opportunities for family connections by exploring options for communication, visitation, and involvement in decision making, as well as the use of technology to facilitate virtual visits between children and incarcerated parents. Perhaps if the child welfare staff and state corrections officials had attempted to collaborate, Johnny might have had more opportunities for ongoing contact with his father and perhaps members of his father's extended family. Through these connections, perhaps a kinship placement might have been a possibility for Johnny.

We must move toward evidence-informed and developmentally appropriate adoption decision making that takes into consideration the specific situation of the child and the impact of trauma, loss, and grief on the decision-making process. Social workers must continually be updated on the state and federal laws that guide their actions. Even more important, they need to be more involved in legislative advocacy to promote the passage of more evidence-informed policies and practices that can lead to better outcomes for positive youth development.

DISCUSSION QUESTIONS

1. What could the social workers in this case have done earlier and differently to expedite permanent placements for Johnny and his siblings?

2. How could knowledge of state and federal adoption policies have affected the workers' decision making and efforts in this case?

3. What policy changes are needed to expedite permanent placements for older children in the foster care system? What can social workers do to advocate for policy changes that are in line with trauma-informed child welfare practice?

REFERENCES

Adoption and Safe Families Act of 1997, P.L. No. 105-89, 111 Stat. 2115 (1997).

Adoption Assistance and Child Welfare Act of 1980, P.L. 96-272, 94 Stat. 500 (1980).

Child Welfare Information Gateway, Administration for Children and Families. (2010). *Consent to adoption.* Retrieved from http://www.childwelfare.gov/systemwide/laws_policies/statutes/consent.cfm

Child Welfare Information Gateway, Administration for Children and Families. (2011a). *Adoption Assistance and Child Welfare Act of 1980, P.L. 96-272.* Retrieved from http://www.childwelfare.gov/systemwide/laws_policies/federal/index.cfm?event=federalLegislation.viewLegis&id=22

Child Welfare Information Gateway, Administration for Children and Families. (2011b). *Major federal legislation concerned with child protection, child welfare, and adoption.* Retrieved from www.childwelfare.gov/pubs/otherpubs/majorfedlegis.cfm

Ellis, R., Malm, K., & Bishop, E. (2009). *The timing of termination of parental rights: A balancing act for children's best interests.* Washington, DC: Child Trends.

Fostering Connections to Success and Promoting Adoptions Act, P.L. 110-351, C.F.R. (2008).

Hollinger, J. H. (1998). A guide to the Multiethnic Placement Act of 1994 as amended by the Interethnic Adoption Provisions of 1996. Retrieved from http://www.acf.dhhs.gov/programs/cb/pubs/mepa94/mepachp1.htm.

Improving America's Schools Act of 1994, P.L. 103-382, 108 Stat. 3518 (1994).

Jim Casey Youth Opportunities Initiative. (2011). *The adolescent brain: New research and its implications for young people transitioning from foster care.* Retrieved from http://www.jimcaseyyouth.org/adolescent-brain-study-full-report

Lenroot, R. K., Gogtay, N., Greenstein, D. K., Wells, E. M., Wallace, G. L., Clasen, L. S., et al. (2007). Sexual dimorphism of brain developmental trajectories during childhood and adolescence. *NeuroImage, 36,* 1065–1073.

McRoy, R., Mica, M., Freundlich, M., & Kroll, J. (2007). Making MEPA-IEP work: Tools for professionals. *Child Welfare, 86*(2), 49–66.

Small Business Job Protection Act of 1996, P.L. 104-188, 110 Stat. 1755 (1996).

Social Security Act, Title IV, Part E-Federal Payments for Foster Care and Adoption Assistance, §470, 42 U.S.C. 670. (1980).

U.S. Department of Health and Human Services, Administration for Children and Families. (2011). *The AFCARS report: Preliminary estimates for FY 2010 as of June 2011 (18).* Retrieved from http://www.acf.hhs.gov/programs/cb/stats_research/afcars/tar/report18.htm

U.S. Government Accountability Office. (2002). *Foster care: Recent legislation helps states focus on finding permanent homes for children, but long-standing barriers remain.* Retrieved from http://www.gao.gov/products/GAO-02-585

U.S. Government Accountability Office. (2011). *Child welfare: More information and collaboration could promote ties between foster care children and their incarcerated parents.* Retrieved from http://www.gao.gov/products/GAO-11-863.

COMMUNITIES

CHAPTER 13

How I Became a Community Organizer as a Casework Social Work Student:

The Interrelationship between Case and Cause Advocacy

Terry Mizrahi

I shifted the focus of my budding social work career from individual casework to community organizing while I was still a student, and that made all the difference in my career. It all began when I was in college and volunteered to run a girls' group at a local settlement house that I later learned exemplified the social group work method. It was there that I discovered the value of community-based services in the lives of poor and working class populations. The settlement house never compartmentalized its services; rather, it focused on programs that would link the "case to the class." Direct services, such as help with housing or government benefits, always informed the types of programs and strategies developed; the staff members who I learned were called "social workers" evaluated and improved services on the basis of how a program affected the lives of the neighborhood residents. The settlement house and its social group work supervisors provided me with excellent foundational group work skills that I found invaluable later on in community practice. It provided necessary, critical, and even transformative strategies for affecting the lives of people.

When I decided right then to attend a graduate social work school, I was assigned to the casework method by requirement. The MSW program I attended did not allow just-out-of-college students to apply in the community organizing (CO) method. Retrospectively, it was this beginning direct service social work experience, albeit imposed, that taught me early about the connections between policy and practice, and moving from the "case to the cause" or as Schwartz (1969) named it "from the personal to the political." I was assigned for my field work to a family agency in a low-income, mixed ethnic neighborhood in New York City. It was there that I learned how different policies adversely affected the daily lives of my two assigned clients and those of their families and neighbors. My intensive, emotion-filled work with them is what, ironically, propelled me toward the systems-change orientation of CO.

NARRATIVE

Ms. T was a young Puerto Rican mother with five children under the age of eight whose common law husband was in jail for drug dealing; Mr. H was an 18-year-old African American man caring for a schizophrenic mother and trying to keep his 12-year-old brother in school and out of trouble. Both of them lived in run-down tenement buildings. The narrative about my two clients I received from the "case record" and my supervisor was that they were viewed by the agency as, respectively, "dependent" and "resistant." In the case of Ms. T, not getting her children to a clinic for preschool immunizations was presented as a psychological issue ("perhaps an unresolved Oedipal Complex," my field instructor speculated), and in the case Mr. H, dropping out of a job-readiness program for adolescents who did not complete high school was viewed as his avoiding responsibilities. Ms. T and Mr. H were perceived by the systems they encountered—schools, welfare, private landlords, health care, public housing, and even the family agency—through a lens of class and racial/ethnic deficits (Gunewardena, 2009). As I learned more about and immersed myself in their lives through home and office visits, they taught me about their strengths and resilience indirectly, even before those concepts came into the social work vernacular (Greene, Lee, & Hoffpauir, 2005; McMillen, Morris, & Sherraden, 2004).

Although they let me into their lives, it took months to gain their confidence, as I experienced how the core principles of "self-awareness" and "conscious use of self" were revealed in my student practice (Burghardt, 2010a, 2010b); I asked myself how a young, white middle-class woman with good intentions could positively affect the lives of people from different cultures, classes, and races/ethnicities. Was there a positive role for the outsider? the professional? the privileged? I want to be of help, but I realized that Ms. T and Mr. H needed to see me as an ally who neither imposed my will on them nor withheld timely advice and advocacy.

My incipient social work skills began to have an impact on Ms. T and Mr. H's situations, the first and foremost of which emphasized building a relationship based on trust and authenticity. My most effective roles over time included the ability to stand by Ms. T and Mr. H and just be present, to "bear witness" to their struggles, and reveal to them their hidden strengths amidst their struggles; to provide them with information-gathering and navigation skills; to gather and present resources and opportunities to them; and to be an advocate who presented an alternative perspective on their circumstances to those officials and policymakers who shaped the quality of their lives and determined their future prospects.

Discussion

And there were multiple oppressors—intentional or not—whose collective impact I began to understand profoundly over time (Mullaly, 2007): In no particular order, these were the landlord not providing heat and hot water; the creditor extracting additional payments for inferior merchandise; the welfare clerk demanding inordinate amounts of proof of need to receive special clothing and furniture allowances; the public housing official denying single mothers (as Ms. T was classified) a place in the development across the street from her fifth-floor walkup apartment; the school registrar demanding proof of immunizations without understanding the lack of availability of accessible and culturally competent health facilities; the vocational employment program not providing flexible hours for Mr. H to complete a training program because of his caretaking responsibilities; the overcrowded and understaffed psychiatric facilities temporarily housing Mr. H's mother after she drank a bottle of Clorox, which might have been an act of desperation or an accident attributable to her confused mental state; and, finally, the streets teeming with drug dealers waiting to prey on stressed young adults operating under enormous pressures. Ms. T and Mr. H encountered a slew of obstacles as they tried to survive and raise their families against incredible odds.

Social Work Matters

There were certain strategies I learned to use individually to affect the lives of Ms. T and Mr. H immediately and in the short term, and other strategies that required my joining with other social workers and their allies to influence system change targets in the long term. As a first example, Ms. T kept her children entertained at home with the help of the television and stereo; she was understandably afraid of the streets (they lived in a high drug and crime area) and therefore would not use the local settlement house's programs for toddlers and school-age children. I contacted the settlement house staff about providing an escort service home for the children after dark or at least to certain key locations. I also learned that the after-school program was underused. The agency was willing to make that program change, which helped them increase their enrollment, and Ms. T had some respite from her older children for a few hours a day, four days a week.

As a second example, tenants' rights and protection organizations was contacted about the deplorable conditions in which both clients lived. These housing organizations, with data gathered by caseworkers like me, began to put pressure on the local government code enforcement agency to tighten its tenant habitability regulations. The local neighborhood association was also alerted to pay more attention to code enforcement. An ad hoc coalition was formed with local elected officials, and together we developed an outreach strategy. It included a sticker campaign—a self-adhesive sticker was to be placed in every tenement apartment in the area that simply stated, "No heat and hot water? No secure locks on doors and windows?" and provided the numbers of the New York City housing enforcement agency and the tenants' rights organization. We knew these stickers were having a collective impact when they began being torn off mailboxes. We engaged a youth group in a settlement house along with other organizations to continue each week to put new stickers on the buildings and also distribute other housing information. Equally important, to counter landlord resistance, we located a landlord ally who demonstrated to the community and in public testimony that a landlord could still earn a profit and keep his or her buildings up to standard.

One a third front, I and many others at the time were reporting to the consumer protection agency on the practices of store owners, like the owner of an appliance store who convinced Ms. T to purchase a new television that was way beyond her means. At the same time, not coincidentally, the expose *The Poor Pay More* (Caplovitz, 1967), created with the help of social workers at the local settlement house, was published (Hall, 1971). With the help of local elected officials, this led to the passage of city council legislation and regulations strengthening consumer protection laws and establishing a new unit in city government to enforce the newly instituted statutes.

In a fourth arena, during the same period, social workers from the parent organization in which I was placed were beginning to collect stories of seemingly unwarranted denials of benefits for public assistance and were also uncovering large numbers of people in the community who were eligible for certain benefits but had not received them, including people like Ms. T and Mr. H's disabled mother. I was witnessing, then, the beginning of the "welfare rights movement," right in my backyard (Piven & Cloward, 1972; Pope, 1989), and the push for the right to a "fair hearing" by legal and social work advocates. Without data from individual and family social workers, the neglect of thousands of poor residents would probably have gone unnoticed or been ignored. Moreover, not only were social workers taking the lead in organizing welfare recipients, they were also empowering many recipients to themselves become leaders and spokespeople on their own individual and collective behalf.

FROM CASE TO CAUSE

Social workers are often privy to the actual transactions between their clients and oppressive systems. They can be the bridges and catalysts for change. Even as a casework intern, I saw the need to focus on systems and policies that, if revised or strengthened, would improve the lives and conditions of the thousands of Ms. Ts and Mr. Hs struggling in untenable situations. I was also available to provide alternative explanations when questions were raised about the behavior or attitudes of Ms. T or Mr. H by those intruding in their lives; often, those in control put an unfair onus of responsibility on clients. People in Ms. T's and Mr. H's situation are often pejoratively labeled as "weak" (at best) and "corrupt" (at worst), and along with those labels came stigma and shame and, perhaps, in some circumstances, self-fulfilling destructive behavior ("why bother?").

The conclusion I ultimately came to, through contentious dialogues with my field instructor, was that neither of us would know if the psychological diagnoses assigned to my clients (through the *Diagnostic and Statistical Manual of Mental Disorders* or equivalent) were accurate *until* the external obstacles in the clients' lives were ameliorated or minimized. The tendency was to see these clients through a lens of pathology rather than one of coping; the clients used mechanisms that were rational from their perspectives—given their struggle and survival needs (Brown, Westbrook, & Challagalla, 2005)—if not always effective. This perspective of assuming goodwill and common cause does not mean that we overromanticize poor or oppressed populations but, rather, that we examine the frameworks for coping and adaptation that could make a difference in people's lives today. The question for our profession is this: How can social workers become agents for empowerment and change—individually and collectively (Hardcastle, Powers, & Wenocur, 2010; Haynes & Mickelson, 2009)? To be sure, clinical social workers can have an impact on the lives of individuals in "chronic crisis" (the oxymoron I came to use to characterize their often chaotic lives) (case advocacy); but, also, these social workers on the ground have such a profound understanding of their clients that it can—when collected, compiled, and categorized—provide a foundation for making systemic and policy change (class advocacy).

POLICY MATTERS

I was working with these families when President Lyndon Johnson announced his "Great Society" program as the solution to his declared "War on Poverty" in 1964 (Boyer, 2001; ushistory.org, 2012). He proposed transformative social programs that would allow the Ms. Ts and Mr. Hs of the country to take advantage of the opportunities, supports, and protections that were then being created and implemented. Though not perfect, among the programs that would have had (and maybe did have) enormous positive impact on goal of "equality of opportunity" were the Head Start program; Section 8 (of the Housing Act of 1937 [P.L. 75-412]) housing; the Elementary and Secondary Education Act of 1965 (P.L. 89-10); Community Health Centers; and the all-important Legal Service Program, which allowed poor people for the first time to sue in civil courts for their rights and benefits. Poor people flocked to take advantage of these services to redress grievances and obtain their entitlements. Others gained opportunities for employment and volunteer leadership in community action programs and were able to move up the ladder from lower to middle class. And perhaps most important were the myriad class-action lawsuits aimed at system reform of the public and private entities that were neglecting or abusing people without power, resources, or voice (Legal Services Corporation Act of 1974 [P.L. 93-355]; see also http://www.classactionlitigation.com/faq.html). Some of these cases originated in the community in which I interned and later practiced as a community organizer; others gained national attention, which encouraged Congress to create Food Stamps and, during the years of President Nixon, federalized many of the public relief programs into Supplemental Security Income.

Specifically, neither Ms. T nor Mr. H and their families had access to affordable health care, and they were unaware of the few health and mental health resources that had been newly created then. All I could do at that time was provide them with information, escort them to the clinic, and at the same time encourage the one community health program to reach out more aggressively into the neighborhood. Plans for a new community hospital had been on the drawing board for almost a decade thanks to the advocacy of social workers and other community leaders, but they were slow in coming to fruition until I was assigned as a community organizer in my first job to begin a community campaign to complete the facility, which would include a community health center (Chowkwanyun, 2011; Mizrahi, 1993). Because the right to good health was viewed as one factor in bringing people out of poverty, neighborhood health centers were created with government support by teams of physicians, social workers, and consumer advocates that allowed poor people access to preventive and primary care after generations of neglect of their health (Merten & Nothman, 1975).

And the very first one sponsored by a community-based organization, at the time when I was in the area, got its foundation indirectly because of the tragic instance of a woman from the neighborhood who died during the 1965 New York City transit strike as a result of not being able to be transported to the public hospital a few miles away (Dumois, 1971). Because of community organizers' close contact with the hospital social workers in the same area, they were able to pool ideas, experiences, and resources and develop proposals for new models of family-based health care with community input. The community eventually got its new hospital with the assistance of social work community organizers and others working with the health authorities. This was the result of organized and sustained community participation both "at the table" and "at the door," with rallies and public demonstrations (Mizrahi, 1993, 1999).

Social workers are often viewed as being both the social conscience of society (from the right wing) and social control agents (from the left wing). In the extreme, on the one hand (the right), we have been viewed as sympathizers and even "dupes" of the poor and underprivileged and, at times, have been criticized for creating dependency (for example, Ronald Reagan's observation, "Some of you may remember that in my early days, I was sort of a bleeding-heart liberal. Then I became a man and put away childish ways" ["Every Party Needs a Pooper," 2007]); on the other hand (the left), we have been portrayed as pawns of the capitalist power structure, preventing fundamental structural change toward a more just and equal society (Specht & Courtney, 1995; Wagner, 1990). It seems that this is a contradiction with which we have to live; in reality, we are probably both. We are a tough and vibrant profession that has a complex role in society, especially in economically and socially conservative times. Are we up for the challenge? If we pool the millions of social work transactions with clients like the ones represented by Ms. T and Mr. H, we are all already engaged in transformative change. We just have to claim and demonstrate it.

DISCUSSION QUESTIONS

1. Hardcastle et al. (2010) identified a spectrum of advocacy: self-advocacy, individual, group, community, political/policy, and system. Identify and apply one or more of these types of advocacy to your practice.

2. What additional strategies and skills could you have used in working with Mr. H and Ms. T and their families.

3. Can you identify a situation where you did or could apply the "case to cause" framework to your practice?

4. How can you tell the story (to the public and policymakers) of the ways you have made a difference in the lives of individuals, families, groups, communities, and organizations in compelling ways?

REFERENCES

Boyer, P. S. (2001). *Great Society.* Retrieved from http://www.encyclopedia.com/topic/Great_Society.aspx

Brown, S. P., Westbrook, R. A., & Challagalla, G. (2005). Good cope, bad cope: Adaptive and maladaptive coping strategies. *Journal of Applied Psychology, 90,* 792–798.

Burghardt, S. (2010a). Framing the issues within the community: The social construction of practice as micro meets macro. In *Macro practice in social work for the 21st century* (pp. 97–131). Thousand Oaks, CA: Sage Publications.

Burghardt, S. (2010b). Macro practitioners undertake community assessments: Tactical self-awareness. In *Macro practice in social work for the 21st century* (pp. 36–70). Thousand Oaks, CA: Sage Publications.

Caplovitz, D. (1967). *The poor pay more: Consumer practices of low-income families.* New York: Free Press.

Chowkwanyun, M. (2011). The new left *and* public health: The Health Policy Advisory Center, community organizing, and the big business of health, 1967–1975. *American Journal of Public Health, 101,* 238–249.

Dumois, A. (1971). Organizing a community around health. *Social Policy, 1*(5).

Elementary and Secondary Education Act of 1965, P.L. 89-10, 79 Stat. 27 (1965).

Every party needs a pooper: People love to talk trash about Republicans, Democrats. (2007, February 11). Retrieved from http://www.sfgate.com/cgi-bin/article.cgi?f=/c/a/2007/02/11/INGQ6O1BA11.DTL

Greene, G. J., Lee, M. Y., & Hoffpauir, S. (2005). The languages of empowerment and strengths in clinical social work: A constructivist perspective. *Families in Society, 86,* 267–277. Retrieved from http://www.familiesinsociety.org/Show.asp?override=true&docid=2465

Gunewardena, N. (2009, Winter). Pathologizing poverty: Structural forces versus personal deficits theories in the feminization of poverty. *Journal of Educational Controversy.* Retrieved from http://www.wce.wwu.edu/Resources/CEP/eJournal/v004n001/a005.shtml

Hall, H. (1971). *Unfinished business: In neighborhood and nation.* New York: MacMillan.

Hardcastle, D., Powers, P. R., & Wenocur, S. (2010). *Community practice: Theory and skills for social workers* (3rd ed.). New York: Oxford University Press.

Haynes, K. S., & Mickelson, J. S. (2009). *Affecting change: Social work in the political arena* (7th ed.). Boston: Allyn & Bacon.

Housing Act of 1937, P.L. 75-412, 50 Stat. 888 (1937).

Legal Services Corporation Act of 1974, P.L. 93-355, 88 Stat. 378 (1974).

McMillen, J. C., Morris, L., & Sherraden, M. (2004). Ending social work's grudge match: Problems versus strengths. *Families in Society, 85,* 317–324. Retrieved from http://www.familiesinsociety.org/Show.asp?override=true&docid=1492

Merten, W., & Nothman, S. (1975). The neighborhood health center experience: Implications for project grants. *American Journal of Public Health, 65,* 248–252. Retrieved from http://www.ncbi.nlm.nih.gov/pmc/articles/PMC1778030/pdf/amjph00790-0026.pdf

Mizrahi, T. (1993, Summer). Coming full cycle: Lessons from health care organizing. *Health PAC Bulletin, 23*(2), 12–15.

Mizrahi, T. (1999). Strategies for effective collaborations in the human services. *Social Policy, 29*(4), 5–20.

Mullaly, R. P. (2007). *Structural social work: Ideology, theory and practice* (3rd ed.). New York: Oxford University Press.

Piven, F. F., & Cloward, R. A. (1972). *Regulating the poor: The functions of public welfare.* New York: Random House.

Pope, J. (1989). *Biting the hand that feeds them: Organizing women on welfare at the grass roots level.* New York: Praeger.

Schwartz, W. (1969). Private troubles and public issues: One job or two? In *Social welfare forum, proceedings of the national conference on social work* (pp. 22–43). New York: Columbia University Press.

Specht, H., & Courtney, M. E. (1995). *Unfaithful angels: How social work has abandoned the poor.* New York: Free Press.

ushistory.org. (2012). *Lyndon Johnson's "Great Society."* Retrieved from http://www.ushistory.org/us/56e.asp

Wagner, D. (1990). *The quest for a radical profession: Social service careers and political ideology.* Lanham, MD: University Press of America.

CHAPTER 14

DISASTER POLICY AND THE HUMAN RESPONSE

Carmen D. Weisner

Each person defines a disaster from his or her own perspective. Many people view a disaster differently depending on the type of impact it has—the number of individuals injured, killed, or suffering loss or displacement; the extent of community destruction; and whether the disaster is man-made or natural. Disasters can be defined as having an identifiable beginning and end, adversely affecting a relatively large group of people, being public and experienced by members of more than one family, being out of the realm of ordinary experience, and being psychologically traumatic enough to induce stress in almost anyone (Rosenfeld, Caye, Ayalon, & Lahad, 2005; Saylor, 1993).

In recent years, it appears that we have been continually bombarded by the scope and frequency of these events and their effect on the individuals whose images are reflected in local, national, and international reporting in 24-hour media coverage. The story of a disaster's impact can help us focus on the immediate needs of individuals, families, and communities. We are often transfixed by these events and can experience secondary trauma through continued exposure. From a social worker's perspective, the long-term effects of these significant events overlay on recovery. This is the area in which systems need to take a serious look at current local, state, and federal disaster-response protocols.

POLICY MATTERS

The Robert T. Stafford Disaster Relief and Emergency Assistance Act (P.L. 100-707) (the Stafford Act) is the statutory authority for most federal disaster response activities, especially as they pertain to the Federal Emergency Management Agency (FEMA) and its programs. It became law on November 23, 1988, and amended the Disaster Relief Act of 1974 (P.L. 93-288). It was designed to establish an orderly and systematic means for federal natural disaster assistance to be provided to state and local governments carrying out their responsibility to aid citizens following the declaration of a federal disaster. The intention of the legislation was to encourage states and localities to develop comprehensive disaster preparedness plans, prepare for better intergovernmental coordination in the response to a disaster, encourage the use of insurance coverage, and provide federal assistance to address losses due to a disaster (FEMA, 2007).

Following the deficiencies in the federal government's response to Hurricane Katrina, the Post-Katrina Emergency Management Reform Act of 2006 (P.L. 109-295) was passed into law. It amended sections of the Stafford Act and overhauled the federal government's preparedness protocols (FEMA, 2008).

Public policy that drives and directs the response to disasters needs to be evaluated and refined to ensure that the individuals served by social workers following disasters have their immediate and long-term needs met. If health care and service delivery systems need to be rebuilt, they need to work in tandem, recognizing the mental health needs and the physical health needs of those directly affected by the event (Calderon-Abbo, 2008). Communities should prepare disaster plans that are comprehensive, realistic, and focused on *when* not *if* disaster strikes. A disaster plan should separately address the first three days of a disaster, the first month, and the two years following. Life-altering events do not end overnight; they may continue to affect individuals and communities for several decades.

To fully understand the impact of a disaster, one must use an integrated model that examines its effects on the family, the larger community, and the mental health needs of the survivors (Rosenfeld et al., 2005). Such a model acknowledges that to understand, plan for, and develop an effective and comprehensive response that will address the multilevel needs of individuals, families, and the community, we must seek the input of people at various levels of the service continuum. This includes those individuals who should and must be served in a response.

NARRATIVE

The following narrative reflects how one community responded to the immediate needs of its state following landfall of Hurricane Katrina in August 2005.

The residents of coastal Louisiana and Mississippi were transfixed by the television weather reports. Many had survived earlier storms and envisioned that this time once again they would evacuate for several days, return home, and clear debris, and life would return to normal. For those who lived in the greater New Orleans area, the drill was part of their routine. They boarded up their homes, fueled up their cars, and took in outdoor furniture. They knew that many of their neighbors would decide to stay and ride out the storm in their homes or in public shelters.

Those of us living further inland prepared for family and friends evacuating to "ride out the storm" with us, anticipating that we might lose electrical power and have some minor damage but that in two or three days all would return to normal. We knew the drill. As the busy day before the storm progressed, the skies over our city took on a foreboding color. We knew that this would be a much larger storm than we had seen in the past few decades. Maybe this time, the city of New Orleans would take the catastrophic direct hit that forecasters had warned about. Before we went to bed that evening, we watched on television as many of those who had stayed in New Orleans took shelter in the Super Dome. Some decided to remain in their homes and ride it out. For many in the low-lying areas of the metropolitan area, the decision to remain was influenced by their lack of resources to evacuate or their need to try and save the few possessions that they owned. The storm had taken an ever-so-slight turn to the east. New Orleans did not seem likely to experience the full force of the storm.

Landfall came. By late afternoon, the storm was making its way through northern Mississippi and Alabama. We relied on telephone calls from friends and family members who lived out of state or further north to relay to us how serious the damage had been along the Gulf coast and in New Orleans.

The day after the storm, media reports said water was rising in New Orleans. The levees had been compromised, and major sections of the city were taking on water. People who had stayed would need to be evacuated. Many were rescued over the following days by helicopters, small boats, and buses that could make their way to the outlying suburbs that still had accessible roadways. Many of those being evacuated required medical attention.

Eighty-five miles north of New Orleans, on the campus of Louisiana State University, the state and city set up the largest acute-care field hospital in U.S. history. Local members of the medical community, including a contingency of social workers and students from the Louisiana State University School of Social Work, embarked on an odyssey that would affect the lives of both evacuees and service providers. A mass appeal for medical help was made to the local community and to national groups. We had lots of donations coming in, but we had no way of knowing what further donations would arrive, so we acted as though we were starting from scratch, building an emergency facility under extreme conditions.

Social workers helped in several ways. Initially, they helped establish a method of tracking patients from their entrance into the facility to their discharge location. We located space to allow for confidential conversations with patients who did not want their stories overheard by the patient in the next cot. Telecommunications in the area were compromised, and we relied on cell phones to help patients make contact with family members. For some of the less seriously injured patients, we located family members in the area who could pick them up. For those who needed to be treated further, we located facilities for them, reaching out to neighboring states that still had capacity.

During the one week this facility remained open (August 31 to September 7, 2005), we saw 25,000 patients and treated 6,000 (Cagley, 2005). Many were screened for serious medical and mental health conditions. All of the patients had experienced the trauma of the disaster and were in various stages of grief. Our efforts were charted, creating a record for those who would provide care once patients left that facility. Many of the patients had lost friends, family, community, and all of their worldly possessions. In the months and years that followed, recovery for these individuals was plagued by a variety of obstacles.

For those of us who worked in the facility, it was an experience we will never forget. By the end of that week, we began to see members of the health care community from other states arriving to give us some relief. The first 72 hours of an organized response to a disaster, no matter how large, remains the responsibility of the individuals in the local community.

SOCIAL WORK MATTERS

Social workers are not immune from disasters, and in fact, they play an important role in recovery. When disaster occurs in their communities, they are often called on to serve in a first-responder role. As the days and weeks go by after the initial event, the role of the social worker changes to one of therapist, agency administrator, policy advisor, and advocate. In evaluating the impact of the way human services are being delivered and sustained, one must look to the responsibility of government entities to respond and support citizens during these difficult times. The coordination of supports and services is vital.

States and local jurisdictions rely on the timely and effective administration of federal funds that are set aside as directed by the Stafford Act. These dollars assist in infrastructure repair and provide loans to homeowners and small businesses affected by the disaster. Post-disaster evaluations have noted that disaster survivors have struggled with the long application process, the need to interface with insurance companies, and the need for local matching funds. Individuals, businesses, and local government entities do not have line items built into their budgets for post-disaster expenses. By their very nature, disasters are unplanned and unpredictable events that are out of the realm of ordinary experience. The void in resources at all of these levels must be recognized in the effective administration of time and responses. The larger federal infrastructure has implemented some of the changes recommended following Hurricanes Katrina and Rita of 2005. However, each disaster is different. Flexibility in some of the protocols is needed to make them responsive and effective (Moss & Shelham, 2007).

This country has been challenged by large disasters in the past decade. The federal government has responded with significant allocation of resources to help the affected areas. However, in the current financial climate, concerns about limiting assistance to communities and individuals affected by disasters would need to be tied to corresponding reductions in other government programs. For many of the individuals who are struggling to recover from disaster, a reduction in the supports that are critical to their overall well-being would be viewed as a revictimization.

Social workers have a vital role to play in response to and recovery from a disaster. From the initial contact, social workers approach the work with individuals and families in a family systems context. They value the whole environment and recognize that each member of the family plays a valuable role in helping the individual and family regain balance. Initially, the role of the social worker is to help individuals explore their informal and formal resources. People need to recognize that it is normal to be overwhelmed by a disaster, and they need to begin the process of identifying their supports as they move toward long-term adjustment to a changed environment. Social workers have the unique skills and values to support clients beginning in the immediate aftermath of a disaster, when practical support is often needed, and continuing through long-term support for grief and loss and posttraumatic stress. It is critical that social workers seek specialized training in disaster response. Such training is offered by the American Red Cross, crisis intervention agencies, local government organizations, and NASW chapters.

It is not unusual for social workers themselves to be affected by a disaster (Pascale, 2011). It is vital that social workers deal with their own personal experiences before they actively engage in this work. In a major disaster area, the potential for shared trauma is a reality. Professionals must practice self-care, and supervisors need to remain vigilant in identifying the impact of shared trauma on their staff and take appropriate action to protect their staff, patients, and clients.

Service delivery should be culturally competent and recognize the dignity of the individual (NASW, 2008, section 1.05). Social workers also need to recognize their role in working with the media during disasters to keep the needs of the community visible while preserving the confidentiality rights of individuals.

When they serve in administrative positions, social workers have an ethical responsibility to advocate within and outside their agencies for adequate resources to meet clients' needs. When they establish or administer guidelines, administrative social workers have a duty to advocate for resources to be distributed in an open and fair manner. When not all clients' needs can be met, a resource allocation protocol should be developed that is nondiscriminatory and based on appropriate and consistently applied principles (NASW, 2008, section 3.07).

DISCUSSION QUESTIONS

1. How can individual social workers prepare for a disaster that may affect their community?

2. What is the social worker's role in refining disaster response policy at the local, state, and national level to ensure that services are humane and recognize an individual's dignity and rights to confidentiality?

3. Is there a role for social workers in advocating for changes to the Stafford Act and the management of services after a disaster?

REFERENCES

Cagley, T. (2005, October). The largest acute-care field hospital in U.S. history. *Journal* (Baton Rouge, LA), p. 17.

Calderon-Abbo, J. (2008). The long road home: Rebuilding public inpatient psychiatric services in post-Katrina New Orleans. *Psychiatric Services, 59,* 304–309. doi: 10.1176/appi.ps.59.3.304

Disaster Relief Act of 1974, P.L. 93-288, 88 Stat. 143 (1974).

Federal Emergency Management Agency. (2007). *Robert T. Stafford Disaster Relief and Emergency Assistance Act, as amended, and related authorities as of June 2007.* Retrieved from http://www.fema.gov/library/viewRecord.do?id=3564

Federal Emergency Management Agency. (2008, September). *On call: Disaster reserve workforce news.* Retrieved from http://www.fema.gov/pdf/dae/200809.pdf

Moss, M. L., & Shelham, C. (2007). *The Stafford Act: Priorities for reform.* Retrieved from http://www.nyu.edu/ccpr/pubs/Report_StaffordActReform_MitchellMoss_10.03.07.pdf

National Association of Social Workers. (2008). *Code of ethics of the National Association of Social Workers.* Retrieved from http://www.socialworkers.org/pubs/code/default.asp

Pascale, A. (2011, March 23). 9/11 a decade later: Study finds shared trauma still a factor. *NY1 News.* Retrieved from http://manhattan.ny1.com/content/top_stories/136113/9-11-a-decade-later--study-finds-shared-trauma-still-a-factor

Post-Katrina Emergency Management Reform Act of 2006, P.L. 109-295, 120 Stat. 1394 (2006).

Robert T. Stafford Disaster Relief and Emergency Assistance Act, P.L. 100-107, 42 U.S.C. § 5121 *et seq.* (1988).

Rosenfeld, L. B., Caye, J. S., Ayalon, O., & Lahad, M. (2005). Introduction to disasters. In *When their world falls apart: Helping families and children manage the effects of disasters* (pp. 3–27). Washington, DC: NASW Press.

Saylor, C. F. (1993). Children and disasters: Clinical and research issues. In C. Saylor (Ed.), *Children and disasters* (pp. 1–9). New York: Plenum Press.

CHAPTER 15

POLICY AND PRACTICE IN RURAL SOCIAL WORK

Deirdra Robinson

Rural social work is often associated with particular social problems, such as poverty, fatalism, and geographic isolation. It is true that rural areas generally have lower incomes, higher poverty rates, and lower education levels. However, with more than a quarter of the U.S. population living in rural areas, the challenges of these areas affect a significant percentage of the nation and create unique practice and knowledge frameworks for the social work profession. NASW (2009) offers a strong policy statement on rural social work, recognizing social workers as being capable of helping rural people use their strengths to create positive changes in their lives and in their communities.

Perhaps the most well-known rural area of the nation is the region known as Appalachia. Its 205,000 square miles make up the spine of the Appalachian Mountains from southern New York to northern Mississippi.

> It includes all of West Virginia and parts of 12 other states: Alabama, Georgia, Kentucky, Maryland, Mississippi, New York, North Carolina, Ohio, Pennsylvania, South Carolina, Tennessee, and Virginia. Forty-two percent of the region's population is rural, compared with 20 percent of the national population. (Appalachian Region Commission, 2011, para. 1)

Although this region is well known for being the place where President Lyndon Johnson launched the War on Poverty in 1964, the people of Appalachia are often described as resilient and proud. Jones (1994) described Appalachian people as independent, self-reliant, proud, neighborly, hospitable, humble, modest, patriotic, and having a good sense of humor.

Social work in rural communities, especially in Appalachia, often requires building on the strengths of the people to address daunting challenges in their communities. Belanger (2005) suggested rural communities need to focus on the development of financial, physical, and human capital. She suggested building on the vast amount of social capital that exists within rural communities to promote positive changes for the community whatever the challenge.

In rural Appalachian communities, the growing prevalence of chronic disease is more than just a problem for individuals; the whole community is affected. Rural social work is the quintessential example of systems theory. The social worker may be in a micro practice setting, working on issues such as brokering services or navigating the health care system, while simultaneously identifying gaps in services, making strong networking connections with providers, and advocating for policy change to improve the system of health care.

DIABETES: A RURAL CHALLENGE

The Centers for Disease Control and Prevention (CDC) (2011) estimated that close to 8.3 percent of Americans, approximately 26 million people, are affected by diabetes. More than 1.9 million people in the United States age 20 years or older were diagnosed for the first time with diabetes in 2010. Even more staggering is that an estimated 5.7 million people are unaware that they have the disease (Health Day, 2008). Experts and officials, from federal to local levels, have identified the prevalence of diabetes as a major health epidemic. It is the largest and fastest-growing chronic disease in the nation (CDC, 2011).

The medical and economic cost of treating diabetes is estimated to be $218 billion annually, when factoring in costs of undiagnosed and untreated diabetes (Dall et al., 2009). A rising concern is the estimation that the number of people with diabetes in the United States and worldwide will double by the year 2025, creating a greater burden on our already strained health care system (*Facts about Diabetes and Insulin*, 2010).

For Americans in rural Appalachia, the scope and impact of diabetes is even more pronounced. New research by the CDC has shown higher rates of diabetes and obesity (a leading contributor to type 2 diabetes) in Appalachian counties, with 10 percent of residents in southern Appalachia diagnosed with diabetes and 30 percent considered obese (Health Day, 2008). Geography, environment, economy, and culture are major factors that lead to higher diabetes rates in Appalachian communities. A higher poverty rate results in a lack of education, a poor diet, a more sedentary lifestyle, and limited access to health care. The following case was identified through a focus group conducted by social work students working with the community-based project described in this chapter and is all too common in the rural areas of our nation.

NARRATIVE

Jim is a coal truck driver in eastern Kentucky. He is married and has two children, ages four and six. He owns a house and considers himself middle class. His truck company paid him a high salary. He was one of the best drivers in the state, with quick deliveries and no wrecks, for the last 11 years. His company didn't offer health insurance because there are only five trucks and it's too expensive for the owner.

Jim recently had an accident while driving the coal truck; he passed out and crashed into a cliff. He went to the local emergency room and was told he probably fell asleep rather than passed out, since he was on the last of three deliveries for the day. A week later, he crashed another truck and was fired. The emergency room doctor ordered blood tests and found Jim's glucose level to be 620. He had passed out as a result of diabetes. Now, Jim is looking for another job as a coal truck driver, but with his driving record, he is often turned down before he can explain that his diabetes caused the crashes.

POLICY MATTERS

With health care reform and health care cost-saving analyses, many social policies are being created in an attempt to minimize the burden placed on the health care system by patients with diabetes. According to the National Conference of State Legislatures (2011), 46 states and the District of Columbia have a law that requires health insurance policies to cover diabetes treatment. Most states require some level of coverage both for direct treatment and for diabetic equipment and supplies that are used by the patient at home. However, four states have no such requirement: Alabama, Idaho, North Dakota, and Ohio, all of which have significant rural areas.

Nationally, improvements have been made in clinical standards of care and management of diabetes. However, clinical guidelines and best practice models are only as effective as the patient's ability to access and use them. Rural areas continue to face special challenges in this regard. Federal and state legislatures nationwide are exploring policy options to deal with the issues related to this health epidemic, but the extent to which social policies are successful in enhancing communities is largely dependent on the evidence and information gathered about the issue.

COMMUNITY INVOLVEMENT

No one knows the complexity of an issue better than those who work on the front lines with patients daily. After years of working with few resources, a high population of uninsured or underinsured people, and escalating health care costs, a group of health professionals and community representatives from three counties in a rural Appalachian state began meeting to share information, network, and build the capacity needed to assess the continuum of diabetes care. With a small amount of funding from the state health department, the group became more formalized, developing a vision and mission statement and setting goals for the project's work for the next calendar year.

The community-informed decision-making model of community social work practice was the basis for the group's work. Calico wrote (1999), "Community Initiated

Decision-Making (CIDM) is a process successfully applied in obtaining qualitative information and gaining community ownership of the process. It is a two-way learning process with an effective community health care council, or coalition" (p. 3). A project coordinator was hired who was a social worker from one of the counties and had extensive health research and community organizing experience. Additionally, community encouragers (two of whom were social workers) were hired to facilitate and organize the work in each of the counties. These community encouragers were either retired professionals who had worked their entire careers in the county or individuals who were from the county and had a passion for improving it. Two of the three community encouragers worked from the county health departments.

One of the first priorities of the group was to improve communication between the counties. Most research has found that people in Appalachia base their ideas about health care largely "upon discussion among community members about their experiences with disease and health care" (Behringer & Friedell, 2006, p. 113). Many of these professionals are so busy with patients and services that they don't get a chance to learn about new programs or community events. An electronic mailing list was created and became the catalyst for sharing ideas and brainstorming about next steps. It also was the forum for discussion of social policies affecting the health care system in the area. This line of communication created multiple opportunities for advocacy and resource sharing.

The individual members of the group were already connected to the state's diabetes network and were active in multiple coalitions and groups working on the issue of diabetes. What made this group different was its focus on strengthening the system of care (such as the practices and processes) by working together on the local level to address their own issues.

For example, the group wanted to gather information from patients who were part of a formal diabetes management health system available in the region in order to gain an empirical understanding of the practice and policy issues related to diabetes. They created a survey for diabetes patients who had been diagnosed for at least two years. Working with the graduate social work program in the region, the group distributed the survey to more than 300 people at diabetes-related events and support groups throughout the three counties. Social work students analyzed the data and presented their findings. The group had evidence to share with the providers and legislators in their own counties about gaps in services, issues of access to health care, gaps in professional services (such as the lack of certified diabetic educators), and other issues highly germane to creating healthier communities. By sharing the findings with key stakeholders, the group played a role in legislative accomplishments in the state addressing the lack of insurance coverage for diabetes self-management classes and the creation of a statewide diabetes plan.

The group continues to work to address diabetes-related health disparities in the three rural counties. Beginning in September of 2010, with support from pharmaceutical companies and local providers, the group is launching a screening project for individuals over the age of 65. Screening will start with that age group because it has the highest incidence of type 2 diabetes (26.9 percent have diabetes and 50 percent have pre-diabetes) (CDC, 2011), and once a patient has been identified through the screening process, the costs of care will be covered by Medicare. The group has reviewed national data showing that although Medicare will pay for screening and any needed subsequent care, only 11 percent of those who are eligible are screened (American Diabetes Association, 2010). The challenge is to screen the other 89 percent, and this accomplished group, led by social workers with the help of social work students, is certainly up to the challenge.

SOCIAL WORK MATTERS

One of the core values of the social work profession is that we work to maximize the potential of our clients and our communities. Unfortunately, clients and communities in rural areas can sometimes feel isolated and powerless when trying to cope with a complex and overwhelming problem, especially if social policies do not adequately address the issue. There are certainly additional challenges and barriers to working in rural areas. However, those challenges are often overcome by the tenacious work of rural social workers. Whether it is behind-the-scenes preparatory work or grassroots legislative advocacy, rural social workers are equipped to handle the unique challenges that accompany the beautiful geography.

DISCUSSION QUESTIONS

1. Although rural areas often pose unique challenges for social work practice, discuss the assets found in these communities and how a social worker might build on those to improve policies.

2. When working from the person-in-environment perspective, how do the cultural values of rural cultures affect social work practice?

3. What are some ethical considerations when working in rural areas?

REFERENCES

American Diabetes Association. (2010, March 29). *Screening for diabetes highly cost effective, study finds.* Retrieved from http://www.diabetes.org/for-media/2010/screening-for-diabetes-highly-cost-effective.html

Appalachian Region Commission. (2011). *The Appalachian region.* Retrieved from http://www.arc.gov/appalachian_region/TheAppalachianRegion.asp

Behringer, B., & Friedell, G. H. (2006). Appalachia: Where place matters in health. *Prevention of Chronic Disease, 3*(4), A113.

Belanger, K. (2005). In search of a theory to guide rural practice: The case for social capital. In L. H. Ginsberg (Ed.), *Social work in rural communities* (4th ed., pp. 4–7). Alexandria, VA: Council on Social Work Education.

Calico, F. (1999). Changing our minds about health care. *Foresight, 6,* 3.

Centers for Disease Control and Prevention. (2011). *National diabetes surveillance system.* Retrieved from http://www.cdc.gov/diabetes/statistics/index.htm

Dall, T., Zhang, Y., Chen Y., Quick, W., Yang, W., & Fogli, J. (2009). The economic burden of diabetes. *Health Affairs, 29*(2), 1–7.

Facts about diabetes and insulin. (2010). Retrieved from http://nobelprize.org/educational_games/medicine/insulin/diabetes-insulin.html

Health Day. (2008). *Appalachia, southeast hit hardest by obesity and diabetes.* Retrieved from http://www.drugs.com/news/appalachia-southeast-hit-hardest-obesity-diabetes-21030.html

Jones, L. (1994). *Appalachian values.* Ashland, KY: Jesse Stuart Foundation.

National Association of Social Workers. (2009). Rural social work. In *Social work speaks: National Association of Social Workers policy statements, 2009–2012* (8th ed., pp. 297–302). Washington, DC: NASW Press.

National Conference of State Legislatures. (2011). *Providing diabetes health coverage: State laws & programs.* Retrieved from http://www.ncsl.org/default.aspx?tabid=14504

CORRECTIONS AND THE COURTS

CHAPTER 16

WOMEN, DRUGS, CRIME, AND POLICY:

THE UNANTICIPATED CONSEQUENCES OF WOMEN'S SUBSTANCE USE

Seana Golder

NARRATIVE

Monica and her two older siblings grew up with her paternal grandparents in a low-income urban neighborhood. Her mother had died when she was two, and her father could not take care of her or her siblings on his own. Monica had her first child at 14, and by the time she was 19, she had three children under the age of five. School had always been a challenge for Monica, and taking care of small children did not make it any easier. Missed days of school turned into missed weeks at a time, until Monica stopped attending school altogether when she was 17. The father of Monica's children, Marcus, was four years older than her and had worked himself up in the ranks of an illegal drug distribution network operating in their neighborhood. Drugs, particularly marijuana and crack, were prevalent in Monica's neighborhood and readily available due to Marcus's drug dealing. Monica began smoking marijuana with Marcus when they started dating, when she was about 13 years old. Initially, her substance abuse was mostly limited to marijuana and alcohol. Over the course of their relationship, Marcus would occasionally smack Monica in the face or push her down, demanding to know where she was at all times, and would call her nasty names in front of the children. The physical violence and psychological abuse became more frequent as time went on. After the birth of her third child, Monica broke up with Marcus.

In order to relieve the stress and boredom of caring for three young children on her own, and to show Marcus that she could "have a life" without him, she began leaving her children at home with her grandparents and going out to party on the weekends at neighborhood social clubs and house parties. During this time, Monica began experimenting with a variety of different drugs in addition to her now daily marijuana smoking. At first, her drug use was confined to the weekends and parties; then Monica tried crack and found that she really liked it. Crack was relatively cheap, even free if she was getting high with the right guys, and it gave her energy and made everything seem more fun. Eventually the weekends extended into Monday and then Tuesday. Soon she was leaving her children with her grandparents for days at a time and getting high on crack several times each day.

Having enough money to feed her growing crack addiction was a challenge. Monica "dated" a number of guys in order to get drugs or money to buy drugs. When Monica couldn't get enough money for her drugs, one of the guys she bought from, Alex, would let her "hold" for him. Holding meant that Monica would put the crack (or other drugs) that were for sale in her pocket or purse while she and Alex walked up and down on the corner where Alex sold his drugs. Buyers paid Alex while Monica handed off the drugs. For her work, Monica could earn enough crack to keep her high for the day.

Monica did not consider herself a drug dealer; rather, she worked to keep getting high. She held for Alex once or twice a month for about six months. Then, one afternoon as she was leaving her grandparents' apartment, Monica was arrested and later charged with conspiracy to distribute a controlled substance. Ultimately, she was sentenced to 63 months in federal prison with no parole and five years' supervised release. She was 24 years old.

Monica's grandparents were appointed as legal guardians for her children while she was incarcerated. During her incarceration she remained drug-free, participated in a 12-week substance abuse course, and earned her GED. Upon release, Monica returned to her home town, an urban area in a moderate-sized midwestern city. Due to her prior behavior, her grandparents would not permit her to move back into their apartment. Monica took up residence in the city's homeless mission. The mission offered a year-long, peer-led residential recovery program for homeless men and women, providing an invaluable safety net for individuals who would otherwise fall through the gaps with other nonprofit and fee-for-service substance abuse treatment providers.

Monica is grateful to have found a safe place to stay at the mission. She is excited to be free and near her children and family again, but she is also concerned about her future. Monica's goals are to stay clean and sober and to become independent by getting a job and her own apartment. She did not work before her incarceration and has few job skills. She is thinking about going to the community college to become a licensed practical nurse. Most important, she wants to get her children back and become the mother she always wanted to be.

DISCUSSION

Monica's story is, unfortunately, like that of many poor women who become drug-involved and addicted. Her addiction and her recovery are further complicated by her criminal record and involvement with the criminal justice system. The connection between substance abuse and criminal behavior is well established, regardless of gender. However, substance abuse has a disproportionate impact on women.

In fact, it is women's substance abuse and the legal penalties associated with it that have fueled the surging numbers of women in the criminal justice system. Nearly one in three women serving time in state prisons reports committing the offense to obtain money to support a drug habit (Bloom, Owen, & Covington, 2003). Among convicted female jail inmates, 34.4 percent reported using drugs at the time of the offense, and 46.3 percent reported using both drugs and alcohol; about half described themselves as daily users (James, 2004).

Women in the criminal justice system also used drugs more than their male counterparts, on every measure of drug use in the month before and during the offense (Greenfeld & Snell, 1999; James, 2004). In fact, substance abuse and dependence are the most common psychiatric disorders among women in the criminal system. Epidemiological data indicate that the lifetime prevalence of substance abuse disorders among female jail detainees is slightly more than 70 percent, with 32.3 percent meeting the criteria for alcohol abuse or dependence and 63.6 percent meeting the criteria for drug abuse or dependence (Jordan, Schlenger, Fairbank, & Caddell, 1996; Teplin, Abram, & McClelland, 1996). Female jail detainees are almost nine times more likely to suffer from substance abuse or dependence than a comparison group of women in the general population (Jordan et al., 1996; Teplin et al., 1996).[1]

POLICY MATTERS

Drug-involved women who also have criminal justice involvement (reentering the community after incarceration, on probation or parole, or having a criminal record) face numerous challenges as they attempt to build lives that are free from drugs and crime—challenges that are further complicated by existing governmental policies. Thus, for social work practitioners in any setting, it is critical both to understand the prevalence of women's substance abuse and to be aware of the unintended negative consequences of U.S. policies enacted over the past 15 to 20 years that directly affect the ability of women like Monica to change their own lives.[2] Women who are striving to become drug-free and reunite with their children will need a variety of support, both emotional and concrete. Access to public welfare benefits that pay for food and other daily necessities is often critical to their ability to succeed in this endeavor. However, the federal Personal Responsibility and Work Opportunity Reconciliation Act of 1996 (P.L. 104-193), commonly referred to as welfare reform, imposed a lifetime ban on cash assistance (Temporary Assistance for Needy Families or TANF) and food stamp benefits (the Supplemental Nutrition Assistance Program) for people with felony drug convictions for conduct that took place after August 22, 1996. Although

---

[1]For additional information on the treatment needs of drug- and crime-involved individuals generally and women in particular, see Bloom, Owen, and Covington (2003) and Fletcher and Chandler (2007).

[2]Almost 6 percent of women in the United States met the criteria for drug dependence or drug abuse in 2010 (Substance Abuse and Mental Health Services Administration, 2010).

the act allowed each state to opt out of the ban, as of January, 2011, 10 states still maintained a complete ban on food stamp benefits and 11 states had a complete ban on TANF. Twenty-four states had modified but not eliminated the ban on food stamps and TANF, while only 15 and 13 states, respectively, had fully eliminated the ban on both benefits.

Safe, affordable, and stable housing is another essential element in a woman's ability to build a life that is both drug- and crime-free. Moreover, stable housing is often a prerequisite for regaining custody of children. Unfortunately, the Housing Opportunity Program Extension Act of 1996 (P.L. 104-120) (HOPE) establishes several ways in which women like Monica can lose their access to housing (both public, project-based housing and Housing Choice Vouchers or Section 8 housing) due to a drug conviction or drug use by the leaseholder, a housemate, or even a guest (Hirsch et al., 2002; Levi & Appel, 2003). Elements of the HOPE Act are often referred to as "one-strike" policies. These policies allow for the exclusion of prospective or current public housing tenants who have certain types of drug convictions, are using illegal drugs (even if they have no criminal record), or are viewed as a threat by the housing authority (for a full discussion of these policies, see Human Rights Watch, 2004). The effect of these policies has been to exclude a wide swath of needy people, including drug- and crime-involved women, from public housing (Hall, Golder, Conley, & Sawning, in press; Human Rights Watch, 2004).

Finally, low educational attainment and low job readiness are significant barriers to self-sufficiency for poor women generally, but present a particular risk for drug-involved women (Jayakody, Danziger, Seefeldt, & Pollack, 2004; Morgenstern et al., 2001). For example, among a sample of women receiving TANF, substance-abusing women were less likely to have attained a high school diploma or GED and were much more likely to report lower job readiness, as evidenced by a combination of low education and job skills, than non-substance-abusing women also receiving TANF (Morgenstern et al., 2001).

Unfortunately, as with welfare and housing benefits, there are governmental policies in place that make it difficult for drug- and crime-involved women to attain the education they need to help them find work and become self-sufficient. For example, in 1998, the Higher Education Act of 1965 (P.L. 89-329) was amended to prohibit anyone with a drug conviction from receiving federal financial aid for postsecondary education. Under the law, a student who was convicted of any offense involving the possession or sale of a controlled substance was not eligible to receive financial assistance during a period beginning on the conviction date; the period of ineligibility differed depending on the offense type and number of prior offenses.

In February 2006, the Deficit Reduction Act of 2005 (P.L. 109-171) partially repealed this ban; presently, only students who are convicted of a drug offense while in school and receiving federal financial assistance will be prohibited from receiving aid. Although this represents welcome and needed progress, the remaining restriction nevertheless decreases the number of people who can complete college. Moreover, a question about drug convictions remains on the Free Application for Financial Student Aid form—the gateway application for the majority of student financial aid, whether federal, state, or institutional—potentially deterring many previously drug- and crime-involved individuals from applying for financial aid because of the uncertainty about their eligibility, even in cases in which the offense occurred before their school enrollment (Hirsch et al., 2002; Levi & Appel, 2003).

SOCIAL WORK MATTERS

What can we do as social work practitioners to assist our clients who, like Monica, are facing difficult situations made even more challenging by short-sighted policies? Fortunately, there are a number of activities we can engage in that can "enhance [the] well-being and help meet the basic human needs" of drug- and crime-involved women (NASW, 2008, p. 1).

As direct practitioners we can educate and disseminate information—to our clients, our colleagues, and community-based organizations—about these policies and their potential impact on delivery of and access to services. It is critical for individuals in recovery from drug and crime involvement, and those that serve them, to have a clear and accurate understanding of their rights to access public programs and the limitations being placed on those rights by existing policies.

Furthermore, social work practitioners can use their knowledge of these policies to evaluate their own local context with respect to existing resources, unmet needs, and gaps in service provision. They can then work collectively with a variety of relevant stakeholders to develop and organize local resources to help address the challenges in daily living created by these policies. Finally, and perhaps most important, as social workers, we can advocate, and we can empower our clients to advocate for themselves, with local, state, and national lawmakers to eliminate these punitive policies and shift toward legislation that supports rehabilitation.[3]

DISCUSSION QUESTIONS

1. What resources exist to serve drug- and crime-involved women in your community? What service gaps might exist?

2. Identify the stakeholders within your local community that you would bring together to advocate at the local, state, or national level for policy changes as they affect drug- and crime-involved women. What types of advocacy work might you engage in to effect the needed policy changes at these different levels?

---

[3]Suggestions for rehabilitative policies can be found in Wahler, 2011.

3. Imagine that you are in a position to create a policy that focuses on rehabilitation for drug- and crime-involved women in your state. What actions would that policy specify? What are the intended outcomes of the policy you have created? Are there any unintended outcomes of your policy that you can predict?

REFERENCES

Bloom, B., Owen, B., & Covington, S. (2003). *Gender-responsive strategies: Research, practice, and guiding principles for women offenders.* Washington, DC: National Institute of Corrections.

Deficit Reduction Act of 2005, P.L. 109-171, 120 Stat. 4 (2006).

Fletcher, B. W., & Chandler, R. K. (2007). *Principles of drug abuse treatment for criminal justice populations: A research-based guide.* Bethesda, MD: National Institute on Drug Abuse.

Greenfeld, L. A., & Snell, T. L. (1999). *Women offenders* (National Criminal Justice Reference Service publication 175688). Washington, DC: Bureau of Justice Statistics.

Hall, M. T., Golder, S., Conley, C. L., & Sawning, S. (in press). Designing programming and interventions for women in the criminal justice system. *American Journal of Criminal Justice.*

Higher Education Act of 1965, P.L. 89-329, 79 Stat. 1219 (1965).

Hirsch, A. E., Dietrich, S. M., Landau, R., Schneider, P. D., Ackelsberg, I., Bernstein-Baker, J., & Hohenstein, J. (2002). *Every door closed: Barriers facing parents with criminal records.* Philadelphia and Washington, DC: Community Legal Services, Inc. & Center for Law and Social Policy.

Housing Opportunity Program Extension Act of 1996, P.L. 104-120, 110 Stat. 834 (1996).

Human Rights Watch. (2004). *No second chance: People with criminal records denied access to public housing.* New York: Author.

James, D. (2004). *Profile of jail inmates, 2002* (National Criminal Justice Reference Service publication 201932). Washington, DC: Bureau of Justice Statistics.

Jayakody, R., Danziger, S., Seefeldt, K., & Pollack, H. (2004). *Policy brief: Substance abuse and welfare reform.* Ann Arbor, MI: National Poverty Center.

Jordan, B. D., Schlenger, W., Fairbank, J., & Caddell, J. (1996). Prevalence of psychiatric disorders among incarcerated women. *Archives of General Psychiatry, 53,* 513–519.

Levi, R., & Appel, J. (2003). *Collateral consequences: Denial of basic social services based upon drug use.* New York: Office of Legal Affairs, Drug Policy Alliance.

Morgenstern, J., Riordan, A., McCrady, B. S., Blanchard, K., McVeigh, K. H., & Irwin, T. W. (2001). *Barriers to employability among women on TANF with a substance abuse problem.* Washington, DC: Administration for Children and Families.

National Association of Social Workers. (2008). *Code of ethics of the National Association of Social Workers.* Retrieved from http://www.socialworkers.org/pubs/code/code.asp

Personal Responsibility and Work Opportunity Reconciliation Act of 1996, P.L. 104-193, 110 Stat. 2105 (1996).

Substance Abuse and Mental Health Services Administration. (2010). Table 5.4B—Substance dependence or abuse in the past year among persons aged 12 or older, by demographic characteristics: Percentages, 2009 and 2010. In *National survey on drug use and health, 2009 and 2010.* Rockville, MD: Author. Retrieved from http://oas.samhsa.gov/NSDUH/2k10NSDUH/tabs/Sect5peTabs1to56.htm#Tab5.4A

Teplin, L., Abram, K., & McClelland, G. (1996). Prevalence of psychiatric disorders among incarcerated women. *Archives of General Psychiatry, 53,* 505–512.

Wahler, B. (2011). *Retribution or rehabilitation? Analyzing the conflicting goals of U.S. policies pertaining to drug felonies and their impact on women.* Manuscript submitted for publication.

CHAPTER 17

POLICY AND PRACTICES AFFECTING THOSE INVOLVED IN THE CRIMINAL JUSTICE SYSTEM

Sheryl Pimlott Kubiak and Gina Fedock

NARRATIVE

Mary is a 34-year-old woman convicted of possession of crack cocaine, which is a felony offense, and incarcerated in a midwestern prison with a sentence of two to four years. At the time of her incarceration, Mary was pregnant with her second child and, due to the length of her sentence, it was likely that the baby would be born during her prison term.

Although policies on birth during incarceration vary from state to state, most do not allow mother and child to remain together in prison nurseries. In fact, in most states there are no prison nurseries (Carlson, 2001, 2009; Enos, 2001). Mothers are sent to the hospital, often in chains, with an officer who is present during the labor and delivery. Once the mother has been medically cleared, she returns to prison and the baby is picked up by family members or someone from the child welfare system.

Mothers returning to prison without their infants grieve their loss and sometimes their choice of guardian for the child. Although women are often aware that the guardian lives in an unsuitable environment, they rationalize that this placement will be brief and it will be easier to resume custody from an informal guardian than if the child enters the formal child welfare system. Child welfare workers charged with assuring the safety and stability of the child may require a woman leaving prison to find safe housing and get a job before returning her child to her. These requirements are difficult for someone with a felony conviction, since many policies and practices impede success.

Mary's prior experience with the child welfare system resulted in the termination of her parental rights to her first child due to her drug addiction, and this experience informed her decision. She was adamant about not losing her rights to this child, but had no family or friends to whom she could entrust the baby's care and at one point considered giving guardianship to her landlord.

Luckily for Mary, at the time she was incarcerated, the state she lived in had a federally funded demonstration project that allowed her to enter a residential program that served as an alternative to incarceration and keep her baby with her. In addition to the federal funding, the program was also supported by the state department of corrections through the funding of the halfway house where the program was located.

Development of such a program had taken several years due to the need for changes in the department's administrative rules. These policy shifts allowed women with minimum sentences of two years or less for a nonviolent offense, and no serious mental illness, to be released from prison and remain in the residential program until they were eligible for parole. The program offered supportive services for mothers and babies, including treatment for mental health and substance use problems; parenting classes; classes to enhance writing, math, and job-seeking skills; and an on-site nursery (Kubiak, Young, Siefert, & Stewart, 2004).

Mary and her baby stayed in the program for six months, during which time she attended classes, treatment groups, and individual therapy and found a job. Mary's goals upon receiving parole and leaving the program were to find safe housing, maintain employment, and return to college. She found work in a fast food restaurant, the only place willing to hire her with a felony conviction, but on her wages she could not afford the safe housing she desired. She applied for Section 8 (a government housing subsidy) but was turned down due to her felony drug conviction. Lack of housing forced her to move in with a colleague who used drugs. The close proximity to her roommate's drug use tested Mary's resolve and she returned to using, which again endangered her parental status as well as her freedom, since drug use was prohibited by her parole conditions.

Her child's placement in foster care served as a wake-up call for Mary, and she began her quest to once again turn her life around so that she could regain custody. Eventually she qualified for a Habitat for Humanity house and felt stable enough to return to college. After meeting with an admissions coordinator, she felt hopeful that as a single mother she could find grants and loans to pay her tuition. However, once she filled out the formal application and reported the felony drug conviction, she learned she did not qualify for a federally supported school loan or Pell Grant. Mary put off her dreams for school and remains working in the fast food industry.

POLICY MATTERS

For a social worker working with Mary, understanding of the criminal justice system, and the implications of various policies related to criminal justice system involvement, are crucial for competent practice. Mary's experiences are similar to those of many others. Involvement in the criminal justice system can be life altering, affecting opportunities for housing, education, employment, and the welfare of one's children. Similarly, multiple policies related to conviction and incarceration directly affect social work practice with this population.

The Criminal Justice System and Women

Involvement in the criminal justice system has many stages, including arrest, arraignment, trial or plea bargaining, sentencing, and appeal. Criminal sanctions are determined at sentencing by the judge or the jury and can include fines, restitution, imprisonment (jail or prison depending on the severity of the offense), mandatory programming, and community supervision (which can include community service, mandatory rehabilitation, probation as an independent sentence, or parole after serving a prison sentence), and in some states, death.

In 2008, more than 1 million women were involved in the criminal justice system, including an estimated 737,814 on probation and 99,149 on parole (Bonczar & Glaze, 2009). Women account for nearly 7 percent of the population in state and federal prisons (Bonczar & Glaze, 2009). The increase in the number of women involved in the criminal justice system over the past 15 years can be largely attributed to changes in federal and state drug policy (the "war on drugs"), specifically tougher sentences for those involved in drug-related crimes. These policies had a particularly devastating effect on women, increasing the rate of conviction and incarceration faster than the rate for men (Harrison & Beck, 2006; Mauer & King, 2007). The number of non-Hispanic black women imprisoned for drug offenses increased more than eightfold after enactment of more punitive drug laws (Mauer & King, 2007).

Women involved across the continuum of the criminal justice system (convicted, incarcerated, on probation, or on parole) represent an especially vulnerable and marginalized population with multiple social work service needs. For example, they are likely to experience more mental health and substance use disorders than their male counterparts (Fedock, Fries, & Kubiak, 2011; James & Glaze, 2006) and other groups of women in the community, specifically those who have low incomes and those seeking treatment for mental health and substance use disorders (Kubiak, 2005; Kubiak & Arfken, 2006). Women involved with the criminal justice system have often experienced interpersonal and community violence and other traumatic life events (Pennell & Burke, 2003; Tusher & Cook, 2010).

Collateral Consequences Associated with Conviction

People convicted of a crime, whether or not their sentence includes incarceration, experience a social stigma that may limit their resources and opportunities. In addition to the direct consequences of a criminal conviction (such as confinement, the surveillance associated with probation or parole, and economic penalties like court fees and fines), they also face collateral consequences—indirect effects of the conviction that may impede, for example, their ability to vote, find a job, or qualify for government assistance.

Criminal records (including juvenile records) are often permanent and therefore have consequences throughout life. In particular, having a criminal record affects the ability to obtain basic needs such as food, clothing, housing, and steady employment (Freudenberg, Daniels, Crum, Perkins, & Richie, 2005; Green, Rockhill, & Furrer, 2007; Kubiak, Seifert, & Boyd, 2004; O'Brien & Young, 2006). Although these consequences can affect anyone with a conviction, those reentering the community may feel the effects more acutely.

For example, federally subsidized housing programs, including the Housing Choice Voucher Program (Section 8) and the Federal Public Housing Program, often deny housing to people with criminal convictions. Public housing agencies have the discretion to deny admission to prospective tenants who have been evicted from public housing because of drug-related criminal activity in the last three years, have engaged in a pattern of disruptive alcohol consumption or illegal drug use at any time in the past, or have engaged in any criminal activity that was drug-related, violent, or otherwise deemed a safety risk.

The Personal Responsibility and Work Opportunity Reconciliation Act of 1996 (P.L. 104-193) altered policies on financial assistance with a direct impact on people with drug convictions. Section 115 of the act, also known as the Gramm Amendment, directs states to deny assistance to people with felony drug convictions. This lifetime ban eliminates eligibility for Temporary Assistance for Needy Families for individuals convicted of a drug-related felony after August 22, 1996. Although some states choose to opt out of this clause, many women with drug convictions believe they are ineligible and do not apply (Kubiak, Siefert, & Boyd, 2004).

State employment laws and informal hiring practices also affect people with an arrest or criminal record (Samuels & Mukamal, 2004). People with a criminal conviction are banned from many employment opportunities, such as positions in nursing homes, day care centers, schools, and beauty salons. Even if women are able to find employment, it is often at low wages, and as a result, they may rely on informal employment or sex work (McLean, Robarge, & Sherman, 2006; van Olphen, Eliason, Freudenberg, & Barnes, 2009). However, informal employment excludes them from benefits such as Social Security and Medicare. There are also barriers to pursuing higher education due to state and local policies concerning criminal records (Samuels & Mukamal, 2004). Convictions involving possession or sale of a controlled substance can result in denial of federal financial aid.

Implications of Criminal Justice Involvement for Parenting

Parents with an arrest or those who are incarcerated have a substantially higher likelihood of interfacing with a child welfare system in comparison to the general population (Phillips & Dettlaff, 2009; Schirmer, Nellis, & Mauer, 2009). The majority of incarcerated women are parents of minor children; for example, 60 percent of women in state prisons are mothers of children under age 18 (Mumola, 2000). Whereas the majority of children of male prisoners are living with their mothers, only about a third of the children of incarcerated women are living with their fathers (Dallaire, 2007;

Mumola, 2000). Children are most often cared for by other family members when their mothers are incarcerated, but 10 percent are in foster care (Mumola, 2000). Moreover, due to the disproportionate representation of minorities in the criminal justice system, African American and Hispanic children are more likely to have an incarcerated parent than white American children (Mumola, 2000; Seymour & Wright, 2002).

The majority (60 percent) of mothers in prison are expected to serve more than 24 months (Mumola, 2000). The federal Adoption and Safe Families Act of 1997 (P.L. 105-89)(ASFA) requires the state to terminate parental rights when a child is in foster care for 15 months out of the most recent 22 months, unless a compelling reason exists not to do so. Women are required to show throughout incarceration that they are maintaining contact and being good parents in order to reunify with their children (Bates, Lawrence-Wills, & Hairston, 2001; Hairston, 1991). But maintaining contact with a child is difficult during incarceration. Many women are held in prisons that are between 100 and 500 miles from their children (Mumola, 2000). Over half of incarcerated women report never having a visit from their children, and one in three mothers report never speaking with their children by phone (Mumola, 2000). There are many barriers to incarcerated women's contact with their children. For example, calling their children's residence collect may not be possible if the adults at that residence refuse to accept collect calls or cannot afford them.

As many as 25 percent of female offenders are pregnant at prison intake or have delivered a baby within the past year (Knight & Plugge, 2005; Siefert & Pimlott, 2001; Wooldredge & Masters, 1993). Although medical services related to prenatal care and childbirth are available in most women's prisons, social work programs designed specifically for the psychological problems faced by pregnant and postpartum women, particularly those grieving the physical loss of their infants, are noticeably absent (Ferszt & Erickson-Owens, 2008; Wooldredge & Masters, 1993).

Concerns about child custody and termination of parental rights continue for women after release from incarceration as they face the collateral consequences described above. Under ASFA, states are encouraged to provide supportive services to help families stay together, yet such services are rarely available (Hunter, 2003). On reentry, many women lack the basic necessities they need to demonstrate that they are able to provide for their children. For example, lack of transportation might make it difficult to attend custody hearings, yet mothers who fail to appear risk negative repercussions.

SOCIAL WORK MATTERS

Understanding that state and federal policies have a direct impact on how a woman's criminal justice involvement will affect her ability to retain her parental rights, receive assistance for basic needs, and pursue an education is critical for any social worker working with women involved in the criminal justice system. Social workers are uniquely equipped to work in a variety of settings with clients who have criminal records, and each phase of the criminal justice continuum offers an opportunity for social work intervention. Understanding the multiple policies in existence, as well as their ramifications for their clients' lives, is crucial. Likewise, social work practice in the policy sector requires an awareness of how acutely policy affects community members.

DISCUSSION QUESTIONS

1. What type of policy advocacy would you focus on to improve Mary's life and opportunities?

2. How might Mary's child be affected by her limited opportunities?

3. Is it social policy or social stigma that most affects the likelihood of success for those convicted of criminal offenses?

REFERENCES

Adoption and Safe Families Act of 1997, P.L. 105-89, 111 Stat. 2115 (1997).

Bates, R., Lawrence-Wills, S., & Hairston, C. F. (2001). *Children and families of incarcerated parents: A view from the ground.* Chicago: University of Illinois at Chicago, Jane Addams College of Social Work, Jane Addams Center for Social Policy and Research.

Bonczar, T. P., & Glaze, L. E. (2009). *Probation and parole in the United States, 2008.* Washington, DC: Bureau of Justice Statistics.

Carlson, J. R. (2001). Prison nursery 2000: A five-year review of the prison nursery at the Nebraska Correction Center for Women. *Journal of Offender Rehabilitation, 33,* 75–97.

Carlson, J. R. (2009). Prison nurseries: A pathway to crime-free futures. *Corrections Compendium, 34*(1), 17–24.

Dallaire, D. H. (2007). Incarcerated mothers and fathers: A comparison of risks for children and families. *Family Relations, 56,* 440–453.

Enos, S. (2001). *Mothering from the inside.* Albany: State University of New York Press.

Fedock, G., Fries, L., & Kubiak, S. (2011, October). *Helping social workers understand service needs for incarcerated individuals: Exploring gender differences.* Paper presented at the annual meeting of the Council on Social Work Education, Atlanta.

Ferszt, G., & Erickson-Owens, D. (2008). Development of an educational/support group for pregnant women in prison. *Journal of Forensic Nursing, 4,* 55–63.

Freudenberg, N., Daniels, J., Crum, M., Perkins, T., & Richie, B. (2005). Coming home from jail: The social and health consequences of community reentry for women, male adolescents, and their families and communities. *American Journal of Public Health, 95,* 1725–1736.

Green, B. L., Rockhill, A. M., & Furrer, C. (2007). Does substance abuse treatment make a difference for child welfare case outcomes? A statewide longitudinal analysis. *Children and Youth Services Review, 29,* 460–473.

Hairston, C. F. (1991). Mothers in jail: Parent–child separation and jail visitation. *Affilia, 6,* 9–27.

Harrison, P. M., & Beck, A. J. (2006). *Prison and jail inmates at midyear 2005* (NCJ Publication No. 213133). Washington, DC: U.S. Department of Justice.

Hunter, T. N. (2003). Child welfare and alcohol and other drug treatment (AOD): Bridging the gap to comprehensive services. *Journal of Family Social Work, 7,* 63–73.

James, D. J., & Glaze, L. E. (2006). *Mental health problems of prison and jail inmates* (NCJ Publication No. 213600). Washington, DC: U.S. Department of Justice.

Knight, M., & Plugge, E. (2005). The outcomes of pregnancy among imprisoned women: A systematic review. *BJOG: An International Journal of Obstetrics and Gynecology, 112*, 1467–1474.

Kubiak, S. P. (2005). Cumulative adversity and multiple traumas of women of a particular social location. *American Journal of Orthopsychiatry, 75,* 451–465.

Kubiak, S., & Arfken, C. (2006). Beyond gender responsivity. *Women and Criminal Justice, 17*(2/3), 75–94.

Kubiak, S. P., Siefert, K., & Boyd, C. (2004). Empowerment and public policy: An exploration of the implications of Section 115 of the Personal Responsibility and Work Opportunity Act. *Journal of Community Psychology, 32*, 127–144.

Kubiak, S. P., Young, A., Siefert, K., & Stewart, A. (2004). Pregnant, substance abusing and incarcerated: Exploratory study of a comprehensive approach to treatment. *Families and Society, 85,* 177–186.

Mauer, M., & King, R. S. (2007). *Uneven justice: State rates of incarceration by race and ethnicity.* Washington, DC: The Sentencing Project.

McLean, R. L., Robarge, J., & Sherman, S. G. (2006). Release from jail: Moment of crisis or window of opportunity for female detainees? *Journal of Urban Health, 83*, 339–348.

Mumola, C. (2000). *Incarcerated parents and their children* (Bureau of Justice Statistics Special Report NCJ-182335). Washington, DC: Bureau of Justice Statistics.

OBrien, P., & Young, D. S. (2006). Challenges for formerly incarcerated women: A holistic approach to assessment. *Families in Society, 87,* 359–366.

Pennell, S., & Burke, C. (2003). *The incidence and prevalence of domestic violence victimization among female arrestees in San Diego County.* San Diego: San Diego Association of Governments.

Personal Responsibility and Work Opportunity Reconciliation Act of 1996, P.L. 104-193, 110 Stat. 2105 (1996).

Phillips, S. D., & Dettlaff, A. J. (2009). More than parents in prison: The broader overlap between criminal justice and child welfare systems. *Journal of Public Child Welfare, 3*, 3–22.

Samuels, P., & Mukamal, D. (2004). *After prison: Roadblocks to reentry. A report on state legal barriers facing people with criminal records.* New York: Legal Action Center.

Schirmer, S., Nellis, A., & Mauer, M. (2009). *Incarcerated parents and their children: Trends 1991–2007.* Washington, DC: The Sentencing Project.

Seymour, C. B., & Wright, L. E. (2002). *Working with children and families separated by incarceration: A handbook for child welfare agencies.* Washington, DC: Child Welfare League of America Press.

Siefert, K., & Pimlott, S. (2001). Improving pregnancy outcomes during imprisonment: A model residential care program. *Social Work, 46,* 125–135.

Tusher, C. P., & Cook, S. L. (2010). Comparing revictimization in two groups of marginalized women. *Journal of Interpersonal Violence, 25,* 1893–1911.

van Olphen, J., Eliason, M., Freudenberg, N., & Barnes, M. (2009). Nowhere to go: How stigma limits the options of female drug users after release from jail. *Substance Abuse Treatment, Prevention, and Policy, 4*(1), 1–10.

Wooldredge, J. D., & Masters, K. (1993). Confronting problems faced by pregnant inmates in state prisons. *Crime and Delinquency, 39,* 195–203.

CHAPTER 18

REFORMING CRIMINAL JUSTICE:

FROM PRACTICE TO POLICY

Frederic G. Reamer

I have spent much of my career working in criminal justice and correctional facilities. In addition to my duties as an academician, I have been a social worker in several prisons and, since 1992, a member of my state's parole board. I am passionate about preventing crime, assisting victims, and helping offenders address the issues in their lives that led them to commit serious crimes such as murder, rape, child molestation, burglary, embezzlement, fraud, automobile theft, and a wide range of drug- and alcohol-related offenses.

POLICY MATTERS

Social workers are uniquely positioned to appreciate the complex connection between direct practice (the delivery of services to individuals, families, and small groups) and broad public policy issues that affect clients' lives. The generalist perspective pioneered by social work more than a century ago, which recognizes the critically important role of clinical interventions, community-based interventions, advocacy, public policy, and research, is essential in our enduring efforts to understand why people commit crimes, how best to respond to offenders, and how to prevent crime (Poulin, 2009; Walsh, 2008).

We know, for example, that many offenders commit crimes because of their desperate efforts to cope with relentless poverty. Meaningful, constructive poverty-reduction efforts can translate into crime reduction. Other offenders commit crimes because of their drug addiction, persistent and severe mental illness, or difficulties with impulse control. Meaningful clinical intervention designed to reduce crime requires a deep understanding of complicated etiology that includes environmental factors (such as poverty, discrimination, and unaffordable housing) and individual factors such as addiction and mental illness (Conklin, 2009; Reamer, 2003; Siegel, 2008). A generalist perspective helps us grasp the complex individual and environmental factors that are correlated with crime and its prevention.

Because of our profound commitment to the generalist perspective, social workers understand that interventions focused on individual offenders, while critically important, will not address the broader, structural determinants of crime. Truly comprehensive and constructive efforts to prevent crime require simultaneous emphasis on individual offenders and their families, the communities in which they live, the organizations and agencies with which they have relationships and that serve them, and, especially, relevant public policies (especially in the form of statutes, regulations, and executive orders).

Social workers who have extensive experience in the criminal justice field fully understand the value of skilled clinical intervention, efforts to strengthen offenders' communities, organizational change designed to enhance the quality of social services, and enlightened public policies. The sad reality in many jurisdictions, however, is that the "system" falls far short in its efforts to rehabilitate offenders and prevent crime. Too often, funding is inadequate; personnel are not trained sufficiently; intervention approaches are misguided or not based on the best available empirical evidence; and public policies are shortsighted, antiquated, and replete with unintended consequences. The system is flawed, to be sure; yet I continue to believe that earnest and sustained social work efforts can improve it, especially when those efforts are rooted in a mature grasp of the rich connection between policy and practice. The following narrative provides an example.

NARRATIVE

As a member of the Rhode Island Parole Board, my statutorily defined duty is to preside over hearings for prison inmates who, by law, are eligible for parole. I also meet with crime victims who wish to share their thoughts and feelings about an inmate's potential release from prison. Prior to each parole hearing, I review copious prison records pertaining to the inmate's criminal record and recidivism (current and past offenses and incarceration), insight concerning his or her criminal conduct, participation in rehabilitation programs (such as substance abuse, anger management, and sex offender treatment), addictions (including drugs, alcohol, gambling, and sex), mental health and illness, family history and supports, employment history and prospects, education, and prison discipline. My duties also include approving discharge plans for those inmates who are released on parole. These may include some combination of electronic or GPS monitoring, home confinement, residential treatment, and outpatient counseling.

Over the years, during which I have presided over more than 20,000 parole board hearings, I have noticed a number of clear patterns that, in my view, must be addressed in a policy venue. Based on my personal experience and systematic review of relevant scholarly literature, it is evident that a very significant percentage of prison inmates are serving sentences that are connected, directly or indirectly, to their substance abuse, mental illness, or both (Re-entry Policy Council, 2005).

Various studies estimate that somewhere in the vicinity of 80 percent of prison inmates have struggled with substance abuse issues or are serving a sentence for a substance abuse–related offense—for example, possessing and selling heroin, assaulting a spouse with a deadly weapon while under the influence of narcotics, breaking into a home to steal items that can be sold for drugs, or killing an automobile passenger while driving under the influence of alcohol. In addition, researchers estimate that approximately 15 percent of the inmate population struggles with persistent and chronic mental illnesses, including schizophrenia, bipolar disorder, and dissociative disorders. Many inmates struggle with both substance abuse and mental illness, so-called co-occurring disorders (Hammett, Roberts, & Kennedy, 2002; Re-entry Policy Council, 2005).

As a social worker who seeks to understand the essential links between policy and practice, I feel obligated to address larger "systems" issues in addition to making decisions about individual offenders. I need to keep one eye focused on individual inmates (practice) and the other on broader structural and organizational issues that pertain to crime prevention (policy). Toward that end, I have participated in two protracted policy-related efforts to enhance the quality of crime prevention and services provided to offenders.

First, I have been involved in formal ongoing efforts to create and revise public policies that stipulate which inmates are eligible for parole (considering the nature of their offense and time served in prison) and criteria for parole release. Under my state's statute, the parole board is authorized to enact these policies). In my official capacity, I have participated in recent years in the drafting and revision of these policies, and in public hearings that provide opportunities for citizens and professionals to share their views about existing provisions and possible changes. Using my social work perspective and commitment to social work values, I have worked diligently to ensure that these policies take into consideration what we know about the causes of crime and constructive responses to it.

As a social worker, I have lobbied to ensure that comprehensive assessments of inmates prior to their parole hearings incorporate the information that social workers know as bio-psychosocial content, that is, information that includes clinical information (mental health and behavioral challenges) and, as well, important environmental information related to poverty, race, ethnicity, family, housing, employment, disabilities, and spirituality. As a result, the formal assessment protocols now used to generate information for parole board review are much more comprehensive than earlier versions. Because of these policy-change efforts, this protocol is now codified as a matter of administrative policy and statute.

My second policy-related effort arising out of my social work practice with offenders is ongoing and focuses explicitly on offenders who struggle with persistent and chronic mental illness. Over the years I have met hundreds of prison inmates who clearly are in prison for offenses that arise out of their mental illness. Typical examples include inmates diagnosed with bipolar disorder who stopped taking their medication while in the community, experienced a manic episode, and assaulted a neighbor with a knife during a dispute;

inmates who struggle with paranoid schizophrenia who consumed large quantities of alcohol and fired a handgun at passersby; and inmates who are suicidal who self-medicated with cocaine and robbed a convenience store while under its influence.

Prisons throughout the United States are filled with inmates who, were it not for their mental illness, would not be likely to commit serious crimes. I have interviewed many inmates with persistent and severe mental illness who did not get comprehensive mental health services in the community because of funding shortfalls, waiting lists, and other organizational impediments. My colleagues and I marvel at the number of inmates who are incarcerated because of crimes they committed while in the throes of a psychotic episode or other mental health crisis that might have been prevented.

As a result of my concern about this broader "systems" issue, I recently joined a statewide effort initiated by the chief judge of the state's district court and designed to create a streamlined, systematic protocol to identify people, as soon as possible after their arrest, who struggle with major mental illness; screen them for possible diversion out of the criminal court system and into the mental health system; and provide these individuals with comprehensive mental health services as an alternative to criminal prosecution and incarceration.

Ideally, this policy-driven strategy developed by an interdisciplinary task force will yield two critically important benefits. First and foremost, this structural change will increase the likelihood that mentally ill individuals who are charged with crimes will get the help and services they desperately need, and thus will prevent future crime. Mentally ill individuals who are incarcerated often struggle in prison because of the difficulty they have living with a large population of inmates whose behavior can be very challenging; mentally ill inmates are often victimized by predatory inmates. The stresses and strains of incarceration often exacerbate mental illness. Further, because of budgetary constraints, mentally ill inmates may not receive the neuroleptic and psychotropic medication that is most appropriate given their psychiatric diagnoses.

Second, this more enlightened policy strategy is likely to result in significant cost savings. Criminal justice and mental health professionals know quite well that the per diem and annual costs of incarceration far exceed the costs of high-quality community-based mental health services (for example, placement in a group home or supervised apartment with supportive services or referral for outpatient counseling).

SOCIAL WORK MATTERS

Many years ago, I chose to be a social worker because of the profession's deep-seated commitment to simultaneously enhancing the quality of life of individuals and addressing the broader environmental and policy issues that are closely connected to human suffering and its alleviation. For the first time in the history of social work in the United States, the current NASW *Code of Ethics* includes a mission statement that says, in no uncertain terms, that members of the profession are obligated to embrace social work's commitment to "enhance human well-being and help meet the basic needs of all people, with particular attention to the needs and empowerment of people who are vulnerable, oppressed, and living in poverty" (NASW, 2008, p. 1). In my view, social work is unique among the human service professions in its sustained commitment to this enlightened view concerning the need to focus simultaneously on individual well-being (practice) and broader structural and environmental issues that must be addressed to enhance individual well-being (policy). Throughout my career I have done my best to engage in both tasks and to understand the essential and complex connection between them. Indeed, that is what it means to be a social worker.

DISCUSSION QUESTIONS

1. Identify your primary social work interests (client population, field of practice, work setting). Provide examples of policy issues that have a direct connection to social work practice issues. In what ways are the practice and policy issues connected?

2. What specific policy issues would you like to address that are extensions of your social work practice interests? What specific steps can you take to become involved in policy efforts?

REFERENCES

Conklin, J. E. (2009). *Criminology* (10th ed.). Boston: Allyn & Bacon.

Hammett, T. M., Roberts, C., & Kennedy, S. (2002). Health-related issues in prisoner reentry. *Crime & Delinquency, 47*(3), 390–409.

National Association of Social Workers. (2008). *Code of ethics of the National Association of Social Workers.* Retrieved from http://www.socialworkers.org/pubs/code/code.asp

Poulin, J. (2009). *Strengths-based generalist practice* (3rd ed.). Belmont, CA: Brooks/Cole.

Reamer, F. G. (2003). *Criminal lessons: Case studies and commentary on crime and justice.* New York: Columbia University Press.

Re-entry Policy Council. (2005). *Report of the Re-entry Policy Council: Charting the safe and successful return of prisoners to the community.* New York: Council of State Governments.

Siegel, L. J. (2008). *Criminology* (10th ed.). Belmont, CA: Wadsworth.

Walsh, J. (2008). *Generalist social work practice.* Belmont, CA: Brooks/Cole.

CHAPTER 19

Social Workers as Expert Witnesses in Sexual Abuse Cases:

Educating and Advocating from the Witness Stand

Anne Hoffman

Policy Matters

The investigation and prosecution of child sexual abuse cases present daunting challenges for all of the professionals involved. In the last 30 years, significant advances have been made that have created a more child-friendly investigation process and a more enlightened judicial approach to the handling of child sexual abuse cases. However, with change come new challenges. The Supreme Court's 2004 *Crawford v. Washington* decision, which upheld the right of the accused to face his or her accuser and limited the exceptions to the hearsay rules, laid the groundwork in law for an expanding role for the investigating social workers in sexual abuse cases. This ruling disallowed the practice of social workers testifying in the stead of children under age 12 and forced prosecutors to put all victims on the stand, regardless of age or possibility of retraumatization. In response to these new demands, the role of the social worker in these cases has evolved into one of trained forensic interviewer, case manager, child protection worker, multidisciplinary team member, and expert witness.

Social Work Matters

Given the deep and lasting effects of the trauma suffered by sexual abuse victims, social workers have an ethical obligation to provide these children with support and protection, both through their traditional roles as child protection workers and case managers, and through newer avenues as highly trained forensic interviewers and expert witnesses (NASW, 2008). To be effective in these roles requires advanced training

123

specifically tailored to the skill sets social workers must develop to conduct and defend interviews of sexual abuse victims and to appear as expert witnesses to support the victim and to educate the jury from the witness stand.

Although investigating social workers have traditionally been charged with interviewing alleged victims of abuse as Child Protective Services staff, the role of specialized forensic interviewers is relatively new to the field (Veith, 2009). After several high-profile sexual abuse cases discredited the interviewing techniques used to gain disclosures from the alleged victims, specific interviewing protocols were developed by accredited organizations, along with training courses and materials for professionals conducting forensic interviews of victims of sexual abuse. These trainings include sections dedicated to testifying in court. Furthermore, there is now case law in support of forensic interviewers as expert witnesses using specific interview protocols (Veith, 2009). Also inherent in sexual abuse investigations, and the proceeding criminal prosecutions, are many issues that the social worker as an expert witness can address from the witness stand to support the child and to help the jury understand many of the complex clinical issues present in these cases.

Working with the prosecution, the social worker as expert witness may address many possible concerns the jury may have after a victim has testified, such as delayed disclosure, the child's affect on the stand, the child's risk-taking behaviors subsequent to the alleged abuse, the child's unsympathetic presentation in court, possible multiple psychological problems or diagnoses, or any other issues the prosecutor may determine need to be addressed and explained through the lens of the trauma suffered by the victim at the hands of the abuser.

In this context, the social worker as expert witness serves as an educator and advocate. A jury of laypeople cannot be expected to understand the effects of sexual abuse on a child and how that trauma manifests itself unless they receive a sound clinical explanation from a qualified expert. Therefore, it is the responsibility of the social worker to receive the training necessary to be that expert so that he or she can educate the jury.

Furthermore, having a social worker testify as an expert in the field of sexual abuse relieves the child from bearing the entire burden of proof in cases in which there is little or no physical evidence, no eyewitness, and no one else to corroborate the victim's statement. Many cases of sexual abuse come down to the "he said/she said" phenomenon: the victim's statement versus the defendant's denial, a child contradicting an adult. In these cases, the child victim and the state's case can benefit from the social worker's expert testimony (Arcaro, 2009).

The following case illustrates how expert witness testimony supported two victims in a child sexual abuse case by explaining and defending the forensic interview protocol. The testimony also involved educating the jury on issues of delayed disclosure and recantation and behaviors the victims displayed that the jurors said they would otherwise have found inconsistent with victims of sexual abuse. The mother's lack of support for her daughters was also a concern (personal communication with K. Knight, assistant state's attorney, Montgomery County State's Attorney's Office, Rockville, MD, March 21, 2001).

Narrative

Two sisters, ages 12 and 14, reported being sexually abused by their stepfather for three years. The abuse consisted of fondling, oral sex, and sexual intercourse, both vaginal and anal. The girls had delayed making a disclosure because they were afraid their mother would not believe them. Also, the apartment they shared with their mother, stepfather, and little brother was paid for by their stepfather, and their little brother was the son of their mother and stepfather.

The 14-year-old girl, Shantee, began drinking and skipping school just before her 13th birthday. Her grades dropped from As and Bs to Ds and Es. Her school counselor called her mother to discuss Shantee's absences and deteriorating school performance. Shantee's mother, Ms. Jones, complained that her daughter was disrespectful to her and to her husband. She said she had tried everything and was unable to communicate with her daughter. She said that she believed Shantee might benefit from some type of boarding school and that her younger daughter, Tya, was beginning to act out as well, and she did not want Shantee's influence to "ruin" Tya.

Over the course of the school year, Shantee's behavior continued to deteriorate. She was arrested for shoplifting and was caught smoking on school grounds. She was suspended for five days. Her mother asked for help, and the school counselor called the child welfare office seeking assistance.

The family received in-home services for the next four months. Both Tya and Shantee received mental health services from a trauma-trained therapist. During a session, Shantee made a reference to inappropriate touching by her stepfather. The therapist made a report to the in-home services social worker, who in turn made a report to the sexual abuse investigation unit. A sexual abuse investigation ensued.

Both girls were able to disclose the sexual abuse to the investigating social worker in detail in the process of a standardized forensic interview protocol. Both girls were sexually active at the time of the disclosure, so the findings reported from the physical examination were inconclusive. The girls both engaged in high-risk behaviors, including drinking, smoking, and skipping school. Shantee had an open case with the Department of Juvenile Services. Each of them had had multiple sexual partners by the time of the disclosure. Shantee had been reported as a runaway on three occasions. Their mother was extremely skeptical of their statements, and although she stated that she would support her daughters, she visited her husband in jail regularly and posted his bond when it was reduced to an amount within her means.

When the prosecutor in the case interviewed both victims, Shantee recanted. A determination was made to call the investigating social worker as an expert witness to defend the forensic interviews of the girls and to explain the delayed disclosures, the victims' risk-taking behaviors, possible reasons for the mother's lack of support, and the recantation.

On the stand, the social worker explained the RATAC interview protocol to the jury as a neutral, semistructured interview process that provided each child a framework to talk about what did or did not happen. The five steps of the protocol were explained to the jury, along with the foundation for the protocol itself. The social worker also explained the training received by the interviewers in the use of the protocol (National Prosecutor's Research Institute, 1999).

In the second part of the expert witness testimony, the social worker addressed the issues presented during the testimony of both victims. Both girls had testified with flat affect and blank, emotionless expressions. Neither child had expressed fear or anger at her stepfather, and both admitted remaining silent for more than three years both during the abuse and after it ceased. The girls also admitted to risk-taking behaviors including having multiple sexual partners, using drugs and alcohol, and truancy. Shantee also admitted to having recanted her disclosure, although she testified to the abuse under oath on the witness stand.

The social worker discussed the effects of trauma on victims of sexual abuse on the basis of both research and practice wisdom (Summit, 1983).[1] The victims' delayed disclosure, lack of affect, and risk-taking behaviors were explained as common phenomena associated with victims of chronic sexual abuse. When questioned about Shantee's recantation, the social worker explained the pressures on the child from her mother and the child's understanding of the family's financial dependence on her stepfather.

The jury found the stepfather guilty on all counts. Prosecutors poll jurors in any case in which an expert witness testifies so as to determine the efficacy and impact of the expert's testimony on the verdict. Juror feedback can be an invaluable tool for training multidisciplinary team members in sexual abuse cases. In this case, the prosecutor was told by individual jurors that the expert witness testimony provided by the social worker "made all the difference" regarding the verdict. Because of the information provided by the social worker, the jurors understood how the girls could testify about their experiences without showing emotion. They also told the prosecutor that they realized how Shantee could recant on the basis of the family's circumstances, even though they believed she had been sexually abused. Although neither girl initially appeared sympathetic to the jurors, listening to explanations about the effects of trauma on victims of sexual abuse helped them understand why the girls had responded the way they had, including their various risk-taking behaviors. The jurors told the prosecutor that they would not have reached a guilty verdict on the basis of the girls' testimony alone.

---

[1]A good source of information on these issues is the U.S. Department of Health and Human Services' Child Welfare Information Gateway (http://www.childwelfare.gov/).

DISCUSSION

These two children represent all of the victims of sexual abuse who have been processed through the legal system in this country. Fortunately, they had the benefit of a social worker trained as a forensic interviewer and an expert witness who was prepared to provide supporting testimony to defend the interview and to educate the jury regarding the multiple complicated clinical issues presented through the children's testimony. According to the jury in this case, had these children been left to speak for themselves without the support of the social worker's testimony, the outcome would not have been the guilty verdict the state sought and the victims deserved.

This case underscores the idea that social workers can no longer stay within the bounds of the traditional role of the child protection case manager. Advanced training in forensic interviewing is readily available, and it is the responsibility of child welfare agencies to ensure that their social workers receive this critical instruction. A child should not stand alone in a criminal proceeding. There is no better way to support a victim than to take the stand and testify as an expert to explain the forensic interview process and to educate the jury on the clinical issues surrounding sexual abuse cases.

What can individual social workers do? If local agencies lack training opportunities, social workers can advocate either to attend training or to bring trainers to the agency. Nothing can replace good training. There is also a wealth of information available through the Child Welfare League of America; the National Child Protection Training Center at Winona State University, Winona, Minnesota; the CornerHouse in Minneapolis, Wisconsin; NASW; and the American Professional Society on the Abuse of Children. All of these organizations have excellent Web sites full of information and links to additional resources. As an expert witness, the individual social worker can conduct sufficient research to support testimony on complex clinical issues. Remaining up to date on the latest information in the field is the responsibility of the witness. Do the research, read it, retain it, and use it.

Social workers must also stress the importance of practice wisdom and experience. In qualifying as an expert, be sure to speak to all facets of social work experience. Read the literature on qualifying as an expert. To provide expert witness testimony, the witness must possess the requisite "knowledge, skill, expertise, training or education in the area of inquiry" (Arcaro, 2009, p. 17). For an expert witness, it is critical to have a fully updated curriculum vitae listing all trainings attended and given, the dates of all expert witness testimony, and the areas of expertise in which testimony was provided.

If no one in the local agency has provided expert witness testimony before, be the first. Work with the agency attorney or the local prosecutor and advocate for both the child and the social work profession. Be prepared to explain how expert witness testimony will benefit the agency's case or the state's case. Point out the specific issues to be addressed, and outline the testimony that will provide the needed information and support for the child and the case. Present the research relevant to the argument, along with an up-to-date curriculum vitae.

If children can speak through the trauma of sexual abuse and its aftermath, surely social workers can support them by testifying as experts in an effort to educate the jury and to defend the forensic interview. Advocacy can take many forms. Expert witness testimony in sexual abuse cases may be one of the more specialized ways in which a social worker can stand up for children. It can also be one of the most effective. Seeing a child's face at the moment a guilty verdict is rendered can make all the effort seem worthwhile.

DISCUSSION QUESTIONS

1. How can a social worker testifying as an expert affect local policy concerning criminal trials of alleged sexual abusers?

2. What can social workers do to advocate for the training they need to become qualified forensic interviewers in order to defend those interviews on the stand?

REFERENCES

Arcaro, T. L. (2009). Child victims of sexual abuse and the law. *Michigan Child Welfare Law Journal*, *12*(3), 2–29.

Crawford v. Washington, 541 U.S. 36 (2004).

National Association of Social Workers. (2008). *Code of ethics of the National Association of Social Workers.* Washington, DC: NASW Press.

National Prosecutor's Research Institute. (1999). *Finding words: Interviewing children and preparing them for court.* San Diego: Author.

Summit, R. C. (1983). Child sexual abuse accommodation syndrome. *Child Abuse & Neglect, 7*, 177–193. Retrieved from http://www.secasa.com.au/index.php/workers/25/31

Veith, V. (2009). *The forensic interviewer at trial: Guidelines for the admission and scope of expert witness testimony concerning an investigative interview in a case of child abuse.* Retrieved from http://www.wmitchell.edu/lawreview/documents/8.Veith.pdf

DIRECT PRACTICE

CHAPTER 20

ALCOHOL ABUSE AND DEPENDENCE:

THE 7 PERCENT PROBLEM

Audrey L. Begun

THE SCOPE OF ALCOHOL DEPENDENCE

Alcohol dependence (also known as alcoholism or addiction to drinking alcohol) is generally characterized by alcohol craving; loss of control over drinking once started; physical dependence, identified by withdrawal symptoms when drinking stops; and developed tolerance, identified as needing to consume alcohol in increasing quantities to achieve the same outcomes (National Institute on Alcohol Abuse and Alcoholism, 2007). *Addiction* is unambiguously defined by the American Society of Addiction Medicine as a primary and chronic brain disorder, affecting and affected by both brain anatomy (structures) and physiology (functions), and as one in which excessive drinking is considered to be an outward manifestation of an underlying disease (American Society of Addiction Medicine, 2011).

With addiction, there is a persistent risk of relapse (hence the chronic aspect of the definition), negative physical and mental health consequences, and a relatively high co-occurrence of other problems, all coupled with significant possibilities for recovery. Debate exists as to whether alcohol abuse and alcohol dependence should be categorized as distinct disorders or as different points on a single continuum (Grove, McBride, & Slade, 2010).

Trends in the epidemiology of alcohol dependence across the United States have been tracked for a number of years. A national survey conducted in 2009 (Substance Abuse and Mental Health Services Administration, Office of Applied Studies [SAMHSA, OAS], 2010) indicated that 7.4 percent of the U.S. population aged 12 years and older (18.7 million individuals) meet diagnostic criteria for alcohol abuse or dependence, hence the "7 percent problem." Nevertheless, during 2009 only about 1.5 million received treatment for alcohol problems alone and 1.6 million for problems with alcohol combined with other drugs (SAMHSA, OAS, 2010). Most commonly, help was obtained through self-help groups, with far fewer individuals receiving specialty treatment in the form of outpatient or inpatient rehabilitation or from outpatient mental health service providers. The most common reason cited by individuals who self-identified as seeking treatment but not receiving it was not being able to afford the cost—not having health coverage, or having health coverage that did not cover the treatment (36.8 percent and 8.8 percent, respectively).

SOCIAL WORK MATTERS

These are important times for alcohol and other drug addiction research and practice. Many innovative intervention approaches have demonstrated efficacy and effectiveness in trials with many diverse populations (Mee-Lee, McClellan, & Miller, 2010). We have available a host of medical and behavioral health options to offer to clients struggling to overcome problems with alcohol. If one approach does not work, we have alternatives to offer. Important social justice questions arise, however, for social workers to consider and redress: To what extent does everyone in need have equal access to proven approaches? Where and why are there significant disparities between groups in access to treatment?

Social workers in all areas of practice need to develop their understanding of problems related to alcohol abuse and dependence. Alcohol-related problems are encountered in all types of populations that we serve and in all types of settings where we deliver services: schools, workplaces, child and family service agencies, medical centers, intimate partner violence programs (for victims and perpetrators), mental health programs, criminal justice institutions, housing programs, and many others (Amodeo, Fassler, & Griffin, 2002; Straussner, & Senreich, 2002; Sun, 2001). Whether or not they provide addiction treatment services, social workers are very often the first professionals encountered by individuals and families affected by alcohol problems (NASW, 2001).

Demonstration of the importance of integrating direct-practice social work with both an awareness of and ability to effect change at macro levels comes from one member of a population in triple jeopardy: women who are incarcerated and experiencing alcohol (or other drug) dependency problems.

Receiving indicated substance abuse treatment and mental health services while incarcerated, along with assured continuity of care during community reentry, are very near the top of the list of factors proven to contribute both to prisoners' community reentry success and to reducing recidivism (Begun, Rose, & LeBel, 2010; Golder et al., 2005). Social work matters in the lives of individuals with alcohol (and other drug) problems both in terms of direct services to this population and in terms of advocacy and other interventions at the family, group, institution, society, and global levels.

NARRATIVE AND DISCUSSION

Belinda is a 29-year-old woman serving her second jail sentence in a large midwestern community. She has not held steady employment since losing her last low-paying office reception job for being late and absent too often; she has lost other low-wage jobs before. Belinda describes herself as "mixed black and white" and has three minor-aged children staying with her mother. She was arrested and sentenced for selling marijuana and for child endangerment, since the delivery of drugs took place in her home while the children were sleeping. Belinda does not use illicit drugs herself but does drink alcohol daily, in risky quantities, and has illegally abused prescription drugs from time to time. She distributed the drugs for her boyfriend in order to pay her bills. Since her incarceration, she has lost her apartment lease, the landlord has disposed of her personal property, and her mother is seeking permanent guardianship of the children. Belinda's boyfriend remains in business.

●■●

Some scholars, after analyzing historical trends in arrest and incarceration rates, have concluded that the nation's "war on drugs" is a "war on women" in the way it is carried out, particularly on women of color, and they surmise that alcohol- and drug-related offenses among women cannot realistically be separated from the feminization of poverty, racism, sexism, and experiences of violent victimization (Belknap, 2001; Bush-Baskette, 1999; Chesney-Lind, 1997; Covington, 2006). Social workers have a responsibility to effect changes in policy, social institutions, and professional practices that promote social justice. This includes engaging in activities that help to reduce race, gender, age, mental health, disability, and other barriers to achieving employment that can support a family; securing safe, affordable, stable, and fair housing for individuals and families; and locating and paying for physical and behavioral health care as needed to promote healthy lives.

●■●

Belinda explained that in jail the only help for substance abuse problems is a once-a-month Alcoholics Anonymous (AA) meeting. The AA team is allowed by the jail administration to visit twice a month, dividing its time equally between men and women. Administrators acknowledge the ubiquity of alcohol and other drug problems among inmates but do not offer AA meetings more often because staff availability to move inmates to and from meetings is in short supply, as are suitable meeting rooms. Addiction practitioners in this community do some work with individuals in prison but do not work within the jails. They have expressed a belief that jail sentences are too unpredictable and short-term to effect the long-term changes needed for individuals to achieve sobriety.

●■●

This narrative demonstrates the importance of institutional policy for the delivery and receipt of services. In jails and prisons there may be a limited number of locations and time periods during which group interventions may be delivered while following protocols to ensure safety and security of inmates, staff, and service providers. The costs of delivering treatment services are borne by overburdened facility budgets. Furthermore, behavioral and physical health care costs may or may not be earmarked separately from general operating and other programming expenses. Even when treatment services are offered on a no- or low-cost basis by outside providers, the facility must provide security and space.

The narrative also demonstrates that our intervention practices are sometimes delivered without sufficient scrutiny of our underlying assumptions. Recent evidence has indicated that there is a significant benefit from an approach to alcohol abuse and dependence that involves screening, brief intervention, and referral to treatment—the treatment need not take place in the hospital emergency room or jail facility where the problems are identified in order to have a positive impact on outcomes (Begun, Rose, & LeBel, 2011; Begun, Rose, LeBel, & Teske-Young, 2009; Madras et al., 2009).

●■●

Belinda had a very high "positive" screening score of 31 on the Alcohol Use and Dependency Identification Test, in which a score of more than seven out of 40 indicates possible problem drinking patterns (Babor, Higgins-Biddle, Saunders, & Monteiro, 2001). She has sought treatment for her drinking problems in the past, but she was required to undergo a complete reassessment each time, which eroded her available eligibility dollars. This was required by county policy—the treatment provider could not be reimbursed for treatment without first conducting a standard evidence-based assessment protocol. Belinda found it difficult to attend the scheduled appointments because it meant taking time off from her hourly job, which she could not afford and which further jeopardized her vulnerable employment status.

Her most recent assessment resulted in Belinda being placed on a wait-list for treatment programs, with little hope of receiving care sooner than four months. While she waited, her only treatment option was free AA meetings. These were helpful to her in some ways, but amounted to undertreatment of her problem, and she was sometimes made uncomfortable by religious undertones in the meetings. Belinda said that the last time around she quit attending AA meetings because she "got tired of being hit on." She described the end of meetings in terms of running a gauntlet on the way to the parking lot, with men from the group "hittin' on you right and left." It just got too uncomfortable, and she did not know of any meetings for women only.

●■●

This narrative suggests that there are distinct inequities in the types of treatment that are available to different populations. Medications with demonstrated efficacy in assisting individuals to maintain sobriety by curbing cravings, reducing long-term withdrawal symptoms, and eliminating a "high" during relapse are not well disseminated to uninsured and institutionalized populations. Similarly, cognitive–behavioral therapy and other behavioral intervention programs with demonstrated efficacy are often difficult to afford. Although twelve-step programs have been helpful to millions around the world, reliance on this approach alone will fail many who struggle with alcohol addiction.

Another important factor for social workers to consider is the degree of fidelity with which an intervention program or protocol is delivered. It is not unusual for practitioners to drift from manualized treatment approaches. The resulting interventions may no longer represent what was originally tested by researchers or intended by policy and decision makers.

POLICY MATTERS

It is incumbent on social workers to advocate for policies and funding streams that will ensure that effective treatment services can be accessed by everyone in need. Accessibility is determined by "goodness of fit" characteristics, in conjunction with affordability, geography, and removal of physical barriers. Belinda's experiences highlight the importance of social work professionals attending to the entirety of a client's experiences with our programs. We need to pay attention to more than just what happens during our direct contact periods. Social workers need to address the cultural competence aspects of the services that are provided to clients, including competence across a broad range of cultural dimensions: race and ethnicity, gender, social class, sexual orientation, ability and disability, national origin and language, spirituality, and age.

DISCUSSION QUESTIONS

1. How do social workers begin to creatively and effectively address disparities in access to treatment services experienced by different populations?

2. How do social workers assess the differences between treatment failure related to an individual's efforts to change versus those attributable to contextual, systemic, and situational concerns?

REFERENCES

American Society of Addiction Medicine. (2011). *ASAM public policy statement: The definition of addiction.* Retrieved from http://www.asam.org/DefinitionofAddiction-LongVersion.html

Amodeo, M., Fassler, I., & Griffin, M. (2002). MSWs with and without long-term substance abuse training: Agency, community, and personal outcomes. *Substance Abuse, 23,* 3–16.

Babor, T. F., Higgins-Biddle, J. C., Saunders, J. B., & Monteiro, M. G. (2001). *AUDIT. The Alcohol Use Disorders Identification Test: Guidelines for use in primary care* (2nd ed.). Retrieved from http://whqlibdoc.who.int/hq/2001/WHO_MSD_MSB_01.6a.pdf

Begun, A. L., Rose, S. J., & LeBel, T. P. (2010). How jail partnerships can help women address substance abuse problems in preparing for community reentry. In S. Stojkovic (Ed.), *Managing special populations in jails and prisons, vol. 2* (pp. 1-2–1-29). Kingston, NJ: Civic Research Institute.

Begun, A. L., Rose, S. J., & LeBel, T. P. (2011). Intervening with women in jail around alcohol and substance abuse during preparation for community reentry. *Alcoholism Treatment Quarterly, 29,* 453–478.

Begun, A. L., Rose, S. J., LeBel, T. P., & Teske-Young, B. A. (2009). Implementing substance abuse screening and brief motivational intervention with women in jail. *Journal of Social Work Practice in the Addictions, 9*(1), 113–131.

Belknap, J. (2001). *The invisible woman: Gender, crime, and justice* (2nd ed.). Belmont, CA: Wadsworth/Thomson Learning.

Bush-Baskette, S. R. (1999). The "war on drugs" a war on women? In S. Cook & S. Davies (Eds.), *Harsh punishment: International experiences of women's imprisonment* (pp. 211–229). Boston: Northeastern University Press.

Chesney-Lind, M. (1997). *The female offender: Girls, women, and crime.* Thousand Oaks, CA: Sage Publications.

Covington, S. S. (2006). Challenges facing women released from prison. In R. Immarigeon (Ed.), *Women and girls in the criminal justice system: Policy issues and practice strategies* (pp. 44-1–44-11). Kingston, NJ: Civic Research Institute.

Golder, S., Ivanoff, A., Cloud, R. N., Besel, K. L., McKiernan, P., Bratt, E., & Bledsoe, L. K. (2005). Evidence-based practice with adults in jails and prisons: Strategies, practices, and future directions. *Best Practices in Mental Health: An International Journal, 1*(2), 100–132.

Grove, R., McBride, O., & Slade, T. (2010). Towards *DSM–V:* Exploring diagnostic thresholds for alcohol dependence and abuse. *Alcohol & Alcoholism, 45*(1), 45–52.

Madras, B. K., Compton, W. M., Avula, D., Stegbauer, T., Stein, J. B., & Clark, H. W. (2009). Screening, brief interventions, referral to treatment (SBIRT) for illicit drug and alcohol use at multiple healthcare sites: Comparison at intake and 6 months later. *Drug and Alcohol Dependence, 99*(1–3), 280–295.

Mee-Lee, D., McClellan, A. T., & Miller, S. D. (2010). What works in substance abuse and dependence treatment. In B. L. Duncan, S. D. Miller, B. E. Wampold, & M. A. Huble (Eds.), *The heart and soul of change: Delivering what works in therapy* (2nd ed, pp. 393–417). Washington, DC: American Psychological Association.

National Association of Social Workers. (2001). *Practice Research Network.* Retrieved from http://www.socialworkers.org/naswprn/substance.pdf

National Institute on Alcohol Abuse and Alcoholism. (2007). *What is alcoholism?* Retrieved from http://www.niaaa.nih.gov/FAQs/General-English/Pages/default.aspx#whatis

Substance Abuse and Mental Health Services Administration, Office of Applied Studies. (2010). *Results from the 2009 National Survey on Drug Use and Health: Volume I. Summary of national findings.* Retrieved from http://www.oas.samhsa.gov/NSDUH/2k9NSDUH/2k9Results.htm

Straussner, S.L.A., & Senreich, E. (2002). Educating social workers to work with individuals affected by substance use disorders. *Substance Abuse, 23*(3, Suppl.), 319–340.

Sun, A. (2001). Systematic barriers to the employment of social workers in alcohol and other drug treatment agencies: A statewide survey. *Journal of Social Work Practice in the Addictions, 1*(1), 11–24.

CHAPTER 21

IF I GO TO WORK, I WILL DIE:

THE IMPACT OF HEALTH POLICY ON DISABILITY RIGHTS

Romel Mackelprang

SOCIAL WORK MATTERS

The year was 1980. I was a young MSW and had just taken a job in the rehabilitation unit of a major hospital. My patients were people with severe neurological disabilities resulting from events such as spinal cord injury, stroke, and brain injury. My previous experience with disability was mostly limited to a cousin with Down syndrome, who was institutionalized until he died at age 16, and annual school field trips to tour the "mentally retarded" unit of the Utah State Training School. Because, at the time, individuals with severe intellectual disabilities were routinely placed in institutions such as this shortly after birth, these field trips were the primary exposure many students had to such individuals.

Graduate school in the late 1970s had taught me the importance of ethnic sensitivity and respect for women's rights. MSW students were also introduced to gay rights when a fellow student was "outed" and kicked out of his practicum because he was gay. He was concerned that the university's MSW program might try to expel him, but fortunately, his worries in that regard were unfounded (though it took some work to find a second practicum).

My MSW education taught me how Supreme Court decisions such as *Plessey v. Ferguson* (163 U.S. 537) and *Brown v. Board of Education of Topeka* (347 U.S. 483) shaped racial equality and how the 19th Amendment of the Constitution and Title IX of the Education Amendments of 1972 (P.L. 92-318) shaped women's rights. However, we were never exposed to the impacts of social policy on disability rights, such as the 1924 *Buck v. Bell* (274 U.S. 200) decision of the Supreme Court, which legitimized the forced sterilization of people with disabilities, and how similar eugenicist attitudes and policies set the stage for the Nazi T4 program, in which German hospitals were converted into extermination centers to kill between 75,000 and 200,000 people with disabilities (Garscha & Kuretsidis-Haider, 1997; Mackelprang & Salsgiver, 2009). Nor were we taught how the Rehabilitation Act of 1973 (93-112) provided protections for people with disabilities in employment and education. Fortunately, though my MSW program did not include content on disabilities and disability policy, it helped me develop critical thinking skills.

My experiences with one of my first patients, a 29-year-old married father of two young children who was paralyzed from the chest down forced me to rethink my beliefs. Before the automobile accident that had led to his spinal cord injury a year earlier, "John" had supported his family as a salesman, making enough money, he said, to live comfortably. Now, his family survived on his Social Security disability benefits, Supplemental Security Income, and Medicaid. When I observed that he was physically able to return to a sales job, he said that he would like nothing more than to work, but "If I go back to work, I will die." Work income would terminate his Medicaid, and his annual medical bills nearly equaled the income he would make. He said, "my condition doesn't stop me from working, the government does." About the same time, I worked with another patient who was forced to sell the family farm to pay medical bills.

Fast forward to the second decade of the 21st century. Though the Americans with Disabilities Act of 1990 (P.L. 101-336) outlaws discrimination against people with disabilities, these people face the same obstacles today as three decades ago. Unemployment and poverty remain very high among people with disabilities, as evidenced by 2011 U.S. Census Bureau data (DaNavas-Walt, Proctor, & Smith, 2011).

In 2010, 9.5 percent of householders ages 18 to 64 (8.8 million) reported having a disability. The median income of these households was $25,550 in 2010, compared with a median of $58,736 for households with a householder who did not report a disability (DaNavas-Walt et al., 2011).

The Census Bureau also reported that the poverty rate for people with disabilities is more than double that of those without disabilities, at 27.9 percent and 12.5 percent respectively. The story of a family with whom I became familiar as the chair of Washington State Independent Living Council illustrates that the programs that are intended to protect people with disabilities often limit their ability to fully participate in society.

NARRATIVE

In 2006, Jill and Boyd Lange and their young children, ages seven, nine, and 11, lived comfortable lives. When their youngest had started school, Jill had entered the workforce as a custodian at a local hospital. Boyd worked as an auto mechanic for a service station. Their combined income was about $70,000, and Jill's health insurance provided security. They lived in a mortgaged home and had two dependable automobiles and $20,000 in *savings for their children's education. Jill had been diagnosed with multiple sclerosis (MS) five years earlier, but her symptoms were minor.*

With little warning, Jill began to experience a significant exacerbation of symptoms. Within a few weeks, her eyesight seriously worsened, she experienced bladder control problems, and she needed to use a wheelchair for mobility. Her previous MS pattern of mild symptom relapse followed by remission evolved into secondary progressive MS, in which symptoms became more severe without significant remissions (National Multiple Sclerosis Society, n.d.).

Jill became unable to do custodial work, and her employer did not have another position for her, so, after her sick leave expired, she lost her job and applied for Supplemental Security Income. More important than the loss of income was the loss of her health insurance. Though Consolidated Omnibus Budget Reconciliation Act of 1985 (P.L. 99-272) regulations would have allowed her to keep her insurance, she would have had to pay the full premiums, which were exorbitant. She was forced to drop her policy, with its generous benefits for her family, and apply for Medicaid, which covered only her.

To meet the income means test for Supplemental Security Income, they had to "spend down" their children's college savings account to the $3,000 maximum. Then while lifting Jill, Boyd injured his back and had to change to a lower-paying job with the same employer. To pay for everyday family needs, as well as expenses their insurance did not cover the family's dental care and supplies for Jill that were considered nonmedical, Boyd found a minimum-wage second job as a parking attendant. Even so, their family income dropped well below $50,000, and they spent an average of nearly $1,000 monthly on uncovered family health expenses.

In four years, Jill's MS progressed to the point that she needed a power wheelchair for mobility and had started experiencing memory problems and mild confusion. The Langes could not afford a ramp to their home, so their church group pooled resources and built one. Their bathroom was not wheelchair accessible, so they improvised with a commode chair in the bedroom. Jill used a shower chair for washing, and Medicaid paid for an attendant to come into the home three times a week to help her with personal care tasks such as showering. Then Jill received notice that, because of state budget cuts, her attendant care was being reduced by more than 50 percent. Paratransit services were being cut as well, severely limiting her ability to get around in the community, volunteer with a local disability organization, and socialize with friends. Jill's children—now ages 11, 13, and 15—were increasingly being called on to care for her physical needs and to look after her safety. To add to the family problems, the 13-year-old was arrested for shoplifting and suspended from school for truancy.

Boyd's employer did not offer health insurance, and though he had been experiencing health problems he was unwilling to seek medical help. However, one day while at work at his mechanic's job, Boyd experienced chest pain and numbness in his left arm and was taken to the emergency room, where he was diagnosed with a mild heart attack. He was also diagnosed with serious high blood pressure. He refused to stay at the hospital for long, but his medical bills still amounted to more than $15,000.

Two weeks later, after Boyd told her they would have to file for bankruptcy, Jill attempted suicide by overdosing on her medications. She regurgitated many of the pills. When one of her children returned home to find her lethargic and sitting in her vomit, she was rushed to the hospital. Her stomach was pumped, and she was admitted to a medical unit and referred for a psychiatric consult. After five days in the hospital, she was stabilized medically and was no longer considered a danger to herself. Boyd's compromised cardiac health did not allow him to care for her, and due to state budget cuts, attendant care was severely limited, so she was discharged to a nursing facility.

POLICY MATTERS

In my work as a clinician, educator, and disability advocate, stories like the Lange family's are all too common. At the outset, after depleting assets, Jill qualified for Supplemental Security Income and Medicaid, but she lacked the work history that would have qualified her for Social Security Disability and Medicare). These four types of assistance are the result of a patchwork of laws including the 1935 Social Security Act (42 U.S.C.A. § 301 et seq.) and the Social Security Amendments of 1972 (P.L. 92-603). Assistance provided a safety net, but it also forced Jill and her family into dependence and eventually resulted in Jill's placement in a nursing facility. In some states, laws such as the Ticket to Work and Work Incentives Improvement Act of 1999 (P.L. 106-170) provide broader employment options, and the Deficit Reduction Act of 2005 (P.L. 109-171), which contains provisions known as "money follows the person," can encourage deinstitutionalization; however, because of lack of funding, the Lange's were unable to benefit from these federal policies.

In 2010, President Obama signed into law two legislative acts: the Patient Protection and Affordable Care Act (P.L. 111–148) and the Health Care and Education Reconciliation Act (P.L. 111–152), which together comprise what is referred to as the Affordable Care Act (ACA). ACA is intended to provide nearly universal access to affordable health care to U.S. citizens and contains provisions that allow states to provide increased community-based rather than institutional health care. Depending on how regulations are written and how the law is implemented in each state, ACA has the potential to greatly enhance the civil rights of people with disabilities in the United States, more so than any other law since the Americans with Disabilities Act of 1990 (P.L. 101-336), but individual states have great latitude on how to implement ACA. Thus, NASW, its state chapters, and individual social workers can advocate with the disability community to ensure that ACA meets its civil rights potential for people with disabilities and others. Effectiveness of ACA can be judged on criteria that include the following:

1. Access to health care should be available to all family members and to all members of society, whether through employment, insurance exchanges, or other means. People with disabilities like Jill should have the option to work without

losing medical coverage. Had Boyd had health care access, he would have been able to receive routine care rather than waiting until he had a heart attack to seek medical attention. The family would not have been forced into bankruptcy.

2. Health care should cover wellness care and provide resources to support living in the community rather than in institutions. Jill's at-home care, which cost less than $1,000 per month, was cut; however, Medicaid policies readily allow payment of more than $6,000 per month to keep her in a nursing facility. With the Lange's bankruptcy, the hospital and providers will likely write off the costs of caring for Boyd during his heart attack and pass these costs on to insurance companies and the public. According to Boyd's physician, preventive care would likely have averted the cascade of events from heart attack to suicide attempt and nursing facility placement. The indirect costs to Boyd, Jill, and their children are inestimable.

3. Health policies should promote family stability. In response to their inquiries, I had to inform Boyd and Jill (as well as innumerable married couples over the decades) that a divorce would solve many of their problems. If they divorced, Boyd could be compensated for providing Jill's attendant care rather than getting a second job, and he could save for their children's college education without worrying about resource limits.

The Langes provide one example of how social policies that affect millions constrict self-determination and the ability of people with disabilities to fully participate in society. Universal access to health care is truly a human rights issue, and contemporary arguments against universal access are spurious. Let's look at two of them. First, some argue that universal access to health care is socialism. But our government was built on a foundation, not only of individual rights, but of social responsibility to its members. If universal access policy is socialist, so are the U.S. highway system, the Federal Aviation Administration, the military, and federal education policies that require education for children up to age 18.

Another argument is that offering universal access to health care would be charity to the uninsured and we cannot afford it. The United States currently spends from 50 percent to more than 100 percent more per capita on health care than any other developed country, all of which provide universal health care. Yet our health indicators (such as life expectancy and infant mortality) are embarrassingly lower than those of other developed countries, and more than 50 million people in the United States are uninsured. Universal access would not expand charity; it would be an investment in a healthy society. Of more than 30 members, the United States and Mexico are the only OECD countries without policies on universal access to health care (Organisation for Economic Co-operation and Development, 2011).

A recent experience illustrated the irony of U.S. health policies. I led a group of students on a study-abroad experience in Ghana—which, although a poor country, has a policy of universal health care access. When one of my students became ill, she was able to see a health care provider and obtain antibiotics in Ghana. However, she observed that, because she was uninsured, she would not have sought medical help in the United States. Though our health care system is far superior to Ghana's, that country's social policies are more humane than those of the United States, one of the wealthiest countries in the world.

DISCUSSION QUESTIONS

1. How would decoupling health care access from employment and income influence the ability of people with disabilities to obtain and maintain gainful employment?

2. U.S. policy frames education for children ages five to 18 years as a social responsibility. However, we debate whether or not health care is an individual right, while other developed countries consider health care a societal responsibility. What are your thoughts?

3. Medicaid is generally considered a charity program for the poor. If it were reframed as a program investing in people with disabilities (similar to the way we define public education), how might it change the way Medicaid recipients are viewed?

REFERENCES

Americans with Disabilities Act of 1990, P.L. 101-336, 104 Stat. 327 (1990).

Brown v. Board of Education of Topeka, 347 U.S. 483 (1954).

Buck v. Bell, 274 U.S. 200 (1927).

Consolidated Omnibus Budget Reconciliation Act of 1985, P.L. 99-272, 100 Stat. 82 (1985).

Deficit Reduction Act of 2005, P.L. 109-171, 120 Stat. 4 (2006).

DeNavas-Walt, C., Proctor, B. D., & Smith, J. C. (2011). *Income, poverty, and health insurance coverage in the United States: 2010.* Washington, DC: U.S. Census Bureau.

Education Amendments of 1972, P.L. 92-318, 86 Stat. 235 (1972).

Garscha, W., & Kuretsidis-Haider, C. (1997, September). *War crimes trials in Austria.* Paper presented at the 21st annual conference of the German Studies Association, Washington, DC.

Health Care and Education Reconciliation Act, P.L. 111–152, 124 Stat. 1029 (2010).

Mackelprang, R. W., & Salsgiver, R. O. (2009). *Disability: A diversity model in human service practice.* Chicago: Lyceum Books.

National Multiple Sclerosis Society. (n.d.). *About MS.* Retrieved from http://www.nationalms society.org/about-multiple-sclerosis/index.aspx

Organisation for Economic Co-operation and Development. (2011). *OECD health data 2011.* Retrieved from http://www.oecd.org/document/16/0,3343,en_2649_34631_2085200_1_1_1_1,00.html

Patient Protection and Affordable Care Act, P.L. 111-148, 124 Stat. 1025 (2010).

Plessey v. Ferguson, 163 U.S. 537 (1896).

Rehabilitation Act of 1973, 93-112, 87 Stat. 355 (1973).

Social Security Act, 42 U.S.C.A. § 301 *et seq.,* 49 Stat. 620 (1935).

Social Security Amendments of 1972, P.L. 92-603, 86 Stat. 1329 (1972).

Ticket to Work and Work Incentives Improvement Act of 1999, P.L. 106-170, 113 Stat. 1860 (1999).

CHAPTER 22

SYNERGISTIC OPPORTUNITIES:

FAITH-BASED WORK, COMMUNITY COLLABORATIONS, AND INFLUENCING POLICY

Mayra Lopez-Humphreys

S ocial work and faith-based work have a complex relationship, though it has not always been this way. Communities of faith have historically played a key role in providing social services (Hall, 1990). Until the end of the 19th century, social work in the United States had its roots in faith-based work—that is, people motivated by religious reasons would often help the poor (Cnaan, Wineburg, & Boddie, 1999). As the field of social work strived to become an established profession in the late 20th century, the demands of scientific research influenced the profession's move toward empirical approaches, distancing itself from strong faith-based affiliations.

POLICY MATTERS

The tensions between social work and faith-based work continue to engender hostility and distrust, which have become increasingly notable since the enactment of section 104 of the Personal Responsibility and Work Opportunity Reconciliation Act of 1996 (P.L. 104-193), also known as "Charitable Choice provisions." Section 104 encourages states and localities to involve faith-based organizations and congregations in the provision of social services, while also protecting the religious character of an organization (Cnaan & Boddie, 2002). It has always been possible for religious organizations to receive public funds, but in the past, they were required to strictly separate their religious activities from their publicly funded programs.

In 2001, Charitable Choice provisions expanded under the presidency of George W. Bush. He signed executive orders that established the White House Office of

Faith-Based and Community Initiatives. The expansion created the opportunity for faith-based organizations and congregations to apply for contracts that would allow them to provide social services in several realms, including workforce development, mental health, and juvenile delinquency services. In 2009, President Barack Obama continued the investment in faith-based initiatives and established the White House Office of Faith-Based and Neighborhood Partnerships.

For many social workers, the enactment of policies encouraging the involvement of faith-based initiatives in the provision of social services raised concerns related to proselytizing and discriminating against clients and employees. Faith-based organizations are not a monolith; rather, their relationship to faith as it is expressed in practice takes on different forms (Working Group on Human Needs and Faith-Based Community Initiatives, 2003). At their best, faith-based organizations have embodied values and practices that are compatible and integrative with social work principles. At their worst, they have engaged in discriminatory practices and attitudes that have challenged and compromised the profession of social work. Research continues to affirm that when faith-based organizations are at their best, their partnerships with local communities are significant resources in addressing community needs and concerns (Owens & Smith, 2005). The following examples show how Charitable Choice provisions and the assets that exist within a faith-based organization have been leveraged, using deeply rooted local connections, to practice with community residents and address larger policy issues.

NARRATIVE

In 1998, as Charitable Choice provisions began to increase the involvement of faith-based organizations, a national research and evaluation institution Public/Private Ventures launched a 10-city demonstration project to evaluate the impact of involving churches in work with young offenders. Known as the National Faith-Based Initiative for High-Risk Youth, it drew its inspiration from what has been referred to as the Boston Miracle, a successful collaboration between police and clergy to reduce the rate of juvenile homicides (Berrien, McRoberts, & Winship, 2000).

In 1990, the number of homicides in Boston surged to 152. Many of these crimes were committed by young people who were increasingly engaged in gang-related drug and turf wars. The Boston Police Department adopted a strategy of community policing that targeted the worst offenders, while a group of African American ministers, calling themselves the Ten Point Coalition, engaged in aggressive street outreach, offering services and community-based interventions to get young people off the streets. The Boston Police Department and the clergy, who had often stood at odds over complaints of racial profiling and police harassment, eventually developed a strong collaborative relationship and by 1998, Boston's number of homicides had dramatically dropped to 34.

When Public/Private Ventures began its demonstration, it paid close attention to the informal social networks and interactions between volunteers and residents it believed were critical for successful engagement of young people:

[We] sought congregations with a significant percentage of members residing in the immediate neighborhood. Proximity makes it possible for volunteers to serve during formal program hours as well as informally through encounters on streets and playgrounds, in stores and on stoops. (Trulear, 2000, p. 2)

The idea was that small community churches in crime-plagued neighborhoods were more likely to attract volunteers. The presence of these volunteers on the same streets as the delinquent young people would provide stronger social networks than large "commuter" churches or traditional social service organizations. For this reason, Public/Private Ventures invested in New York City's various sites, which promised to deliver consistent, locally derived support and services for delinquent young people.

Linkages for Youth, Inc. (LFY) is a faith-based youth-serving organization in New York City that has leveraged the Charitable Choice provisions and built upon the success of the National Faith-Based Initiative for High-Risk Youth by developing a model that involves churches with young people who are found guilty of committing a delinquent act (that is, adjudicated youths)—with a focus on a narrowly bounded geographic community. LFY's mission is to empower indigenous faith- and community-based organizations to operate effective alternative-to-incarceration programs for youths. It seeks to invest in support systems within the neighborhoods in which the youths reside and to support local communities in taking responsibility for the supervision, support, accountability, and long-term development of their young people. LFY was formed with the deeply held conviction that effective work with young people requires that the residents of the neighborhoods where the young people live must be primary stakeholders in developing a sensible juvenile justice policy that furthers youth development and upholds community safety.

LFY provides direct services in one of the poorest urban counties in the United States and has worked steadfastly with rehabilitated, juvenile-system-involved youths by training them to serve as mentors and advocates for young people at risk of incarceration. It has also been able to convene grassroots faith-based community organizations on a regular basis in order to create strategies for advancing a community-driven juvenile justice reform agenda.

This consortium of organizations has shaped the formation of the Miriam Network, a group of clergy and community members committed to advocating for young people in the justice system. The Miriam Network educates communities, especially the members of faith-based organizations and congregations, by using biblical narratives as models for alleviating marginalization and exploitation in the context of juvenile justice reform. Members of the Miriam Network advocate for individual youths in the justice system, counsel and support parents whose children are in the justice system, educate their respective communities about juvenile justice reform, speak against policies and practices that are harmful to young people, and develop community-driven alternatives to incarceration.

LFY's Miriam Network has been instrumental in rallying members of the local faith community to become advocates for reducing youth incarceration. In 2011, faith-based organizations involved in the Miriam Network were successful in their advocacy efforts to close the Spofford Juvenile Detention Center in New York City. Such efforts have contributed to larger movement in New York City to close down underused, abuse-laden detention centers and redirect juvenile justice funds to local community programs that can directly help young people and families on an ongoing basis (Dwoskin, 2010). In addition, LFY has recently begun to train college students, through a partnership with a Christian college, on how to examine and interpret laws and policies that relate to or have an impact on adjudicated youths (such as the Juvenile Justice and Delinquency Prevention Reauthorization Act). They also learn how to mobilize their neighborhood faith-based organizations to support community-based alternatives to incarceration for youths.

SOCIAL WORK MATTERS

There is no debate that social services are moving toward privatization and the government is decentralizing its involvement in the provision of social services. Looking at these trends, social work practitioners at all levels are likely to engage with diverse faith-based organizations that are involved in social services and legislative advocacy. Equally important, Cnaan and Boddie (2001) emphasized that "the number of social workers working in or with faith-based organizations [will likely] increase. Hence, it is an imperative that social workers become well-versed in the Charitable Choice provision and its implications for education, practice, policy, and research" (p. 231).

Finding ways to collaborate with faith-based initiatives, while also maintaining one's social work values and ethics, is a vital skill for practitioners. At the same time, social workers in faith-based settings have the potential to inform the standards and procedure of service by ensuring the rights of recipients to refuse to participate in any religious activity while also facilitating an open space for recipients of faith in integrating their values and beliefs.

For disenfranchised, economically divested communities that are also often disproportionately made up of people of color, faith-based institutions can offer the opportunity to connect faith, empowerment, and justice with one's social identity (Gutierrez & Lewis, 1999). For example, many African Americans understand the success of the civil rights movement in the 1960s to be intrinsically connected to the organization and support that occurred within local churches. Working effectively with clients who express their faith as part of their identity means recognizing the strengths and resiliency that can be derived from that faith and the way these resources can also be integrated into the goals of the work.

It is important for social workers to remain aware of any tensions that exist between their personal and professional perspectives regarding faith-based initiatives and the way clients may experience faith-based work (Wood, 2002). Without such reflection, the potential for integration of faith-based organizations within policy advocacy can be diminished or altogether overlooked. When practitioners are able to identify ideological and philosophical tensions that may come with faith-based collaborations and develop a tolerance for such discomfort, they can begin to transcend ideological differences and identify common ground to address prevalent policy issues in urban neighborhoods.

Social environments form the dynamic terrain that informs how clients and social workers can together construct solutions to individual and systemic problems. The ecosystem perspective is a framework for understanding how fit and adaptation among varying systems are critical to the improvement of individuals and communities. This perspective views the client as part of an environmental system. This perspective examines the shared relationships between a system (for example, individual, family, community), others, and the social and the physical environment. It also is a model that will support social workers within faith-based organizations in linking individual needs to policy concerns. Tangenberg (2005) highlighted these opportunities, saying, "religious organizations are powerful social institutions that can motivate and sustain political action" (p. 200).

The ecosystem perspective can help social workers assess the role of spirituality and faith in the local community. Assessment can encompass the exploration of the ways faith organizations in the neighborhood are responding to social problems, the extent to which faith organizations are interested and involved in community collaborations, the level of influence and trust faith leaders have developed within the community, and the local policy concerns addressed by faith communities. For social workers proposing solutions and seeking support to address policy concerns and community needs, such information can provide useful opportunities and resources for collaboration with faith-based organizations and congregations.

DISCUSSION QUESTIONS

1. How can communities of faith contribute their resources to fostering more just, empowered, and thriving local neighborhoods?

2. As a neighborhood resident or emerging social worker, what do you see as needs in your community that can be linked to policy and local advocacy efforts?

REFERENCES

Berrien, J., McRoberts, O., & Winship, C. (2000). Religion and the Boston miracle: The effect of black ministry on youth violence. In M. Bane, B. Coffin, & R. Thiemann (Eds.), *Who will provide? The changing role of religion in American social welfare* (pp. 266–285). Boulder, CO: Westview Press.

Cnaan, R., & Boddie, S. (2001). Philadelphia census of congregations and their involvement in social service delivery. *Social Service Review, 75*, 559–580.

Cnaan, R., & Boddie, S. (2002). Charitable choice and faith-based welfare: A call for social work. *Social Work, 47*, 224–235.

Cnaan, R., Wineburg, R., & Boddie, S. (1999). *The newer deal: Social work and religion in partnership*. New York: Columbia University Press.

Dwoskin, E. (2010, August 4). Shutting upstate jails for city kids has made a fiery Bronx bureaucrat a host of enemies. *Village Voice, 55,* pp. 12–24.

Gutierrez, L., & Lewis, E. (1999). *Empowering women of color*. New York: Columbia University Press.

Hall, P. (1990). The history of religious philanthropy in America. In R. Wuthnow, V. Hodgkinson, & Associates (Eds.), *Faith and philanthropy in America* (pp. 38–62). San Francisco: Jossey-Bass.

Owens, M., & Smith, R. (2005). Congregations in low-income neighborhoods and the implications for social welfare policy research. *Nonprofit and Voluntary Sector Quarterly, 34*, 316–339.

Personal Responsibility and Work Opportunity Reconciliation Act of 1996, P.L. 104-193, 110 Stat. 2105 (1996).

Tangenberg, K. M. (2005). Faith-based human services initiatives: Considerations for social work practice and theory. *Social Work, 50,* 197–206.

Trulear, H. D. (2000). *Faith-based institutions and high-risk youth: First report to the field*. Philadelphia: Public/Private Ventures. Retrieved from http://www.ppv.org/ppv/publications/assets/24_publication.pdf

Wood, R. (2002). *Faith in action: Religion, race, and democratic organizing in America*. Chicago: University of Chicago Press.

Working Group on Human Needs and Faith-Based and Community Initiatives. (2003). *Harnessing civic and faith-based power to fight poverty*. Retrieved from http://www.community-wealth.org/_pdfs/articles-publications/anchors/book-sider-lynn.pdf

CHAPTER 23

SOCIAL WORK WITH VETERANS AND THEIR FAMILIES

Anthony M. Hassan and Joseph E. Chicas

The willingness with which our young people are likely to serve in any war, no matter how justified, shall be directly proportional to how they perceive the Veterans of earlier wars were treated and appreciated by their nation.

—George Washington

The war in Afghanistan is now the longest-running war in American history; it is being fought with a small, all-volunteer military made up of less than 1 percent of the United States population—service members who are looking for direction, inspired by a sense of patriotism, or want to continue a family tradition of military service. Whatever their reason for joining, they enter the ranks prepared to give their lives for their country.

Despite this heroic calling, they have undoubtedly grown weary after a decade of war. Men and women return to their homes, families, and communities with physical and psychological wounds and often little notice from other Americans. The transition from military to civilian life can be difficult and is not always negotiated successfully. There appears to be no end in sight to the ongoing stressors for our military personnel and their families. Today, tomorrow, and in the future, veterans and their families will cope with the mounting burden of repeated combat deployments and community reintegration challenges that, if not addressed, will jeopardize the continuation of our all-voluntary military force and our national security.

SOCIAL WORK MATTERS

Social work with veterans and their families is more critical today than ever before in our profession's history. Military social work's mission is akin to the primary mission of the social work profession: to enhance human well-being and help meet the basic human needs of all people, with particular attention to empowering and meeting the needs of military personnel and their families who are challenged and vulnerable. Fundamental to social work with service members, veterans, and their families is attention to the environmental forces that create, contribute to, and address life problems for military client systems. Social work with the military population is not only needed but also ethically responsible. This does not mean that social workers endorse war or aggression, but, rather, that they extend meaningful help to those who have been most affected by war. As is true of any field of practice, social work with the military involves mastery of content relating to social policies, specialized service delivery organizations, targeted clinical interventions, organizing, administrative practice skills, and knowledge of population characteristics.

NARRATIVE

Sergeant John Smith is a National Guard soldier. He recently returned home after a one-year deployment to Iraq, where he was a part of military efforts to disrupt terrorist operations. As a member of the Guard, he was not accustomed to being deployed to war. His military service prior to Operation Iraqi Freedom included monthly drills at the local base and support at statewide disasters. Since September 11, 2001, Sergeant Smith has been deployed to Iraq three times. His deployments ranged from nine to 17 months in length, with short periods in between that offered hardly enough time to adjust to civilian life in any meaningful way.

Sergeant Smith ran into significant financial hardship after his last deployment. When he returned to his economically depressed community, his employer could not offer him his old job back, because the company had downsized due to the poor economy, and thus Sergeant Smith was not protected by federal employment laws such as the Uniformed Services Employment and Reemployment Rights Act of 1994 (P.L. 103-353), which provides reemployment protection and other benefits for employees called into military service. Despite this setback, he was motivated to seek other opportunities for employment. He attended résumé workshops and job fairs and searched online for two months with no success. Few companies were hiring, and he struggled to translate his military experience and skills to fit civilian employers' needs. As time passed, he grew increasingly anxious and frustrated.

His friends and family began noticing changes in his mood and behavior. He started binge drinking and isolating himself from others. He was no longer the happy-go-lucky guy he was before he went to Iraq, and he was low in spirit and self-esteem. Sergeant Smith shared with a friend that being unemployed affected his sense of self-worth and left him feeling that he had no real sense of purpose. His family and friends were concerned about his well-being and strongly encouraged him to seek help.

Sergeant Smith agreed to get help and approached the U.S. Department of Veterans Affairs for support and treatment. Unfortunately, the nearest facility was 100 miles away from his home, making it difficult for him to keep his appointments. He reached out to a local community mental health agency for help, but became even more frustrated after he realized that the social worker was not familiar with military culture, which affected their therapeutic relationship. In addition, he was unable to locate a veteran-specific employment services organization that could help him translate his military experience into skill sets relevant to the local workforce. Eventually, his anxiety and frustration turned into anger, increasing hopelessness, and suicidal thoughts, which ultimately led to his hospitalization.

Discussion

Throughout the country, unemployment is a big challenge for National Guard members and reservists. The national unemployment rate was 9.1 percent in 2011, but it is 13.3 percent among all veterans and 14 percent among Guard members and reservists, with some returning units at 40 percent unemployment. The economic recession has led to significant job losses across all sectors. Guard members and reservists, like other veterans, face barriers to employment—such as the widespread media coverage of the mental health challenges faced by veterans, which has led to concerns among employers that veterans may not be able to do their job effectively because of problems such as traumatic brain injury or posttraumatic stress disorder (Little & Alenkin, 2011). But they face an additional challenge in that, unlike active duty military personnel, they have to frequently transition to and from civilian jobs (Foster, 2011). Frequent deployments, decreasing employment opportunities, and the veterans' mental health stigma put Guard members and reservists at serious risk for problems that can affect their transition from combat to civilian life (Riviere, Kendall-Robbins, McGurk, Castro, & Hoge, 2011).

There are a number of roles that social workers can and should embrace as they engage veterans such as Sergeant Smith. Working with veterans at an individual level begins with increasing military cultural competency. Cultural competency is always important in establishing a therapeutic alliance with the client. It is particularly important with veterans, given the stigma associated with their profession's warrior ethos and their reluctance to seek help. Their military rank, combat experience, and job specialty are important aspects of their identity, and social workers need to be able to assess how these factors interact or influence current and future behavior. In Sergeant Smith's case, a culturally responsive social worker was essential as he struggled to integrate his military and civilian experiences. Carefully inquiring about his experience in Iraq and recognizing the military cultural factors could be very helpful in assisting Sergeant Smith with finding the linkages between military and civilian life, connections that can facilitate the clinical process, whether it is therapy, case management, or a combination of both. To this end, social workers must continue to familiarize themselves with current literature and research and expand their knowledge of military culture and the interventions that are most effective in working with military personnel.

In addition, it is critical that social workers recognize that not all veterans struggle with traumatic brain injury or posttraumatic stress disorder, and that sometimes their main struggle is to achieve life goals related to the transition to civilian life. These goals can include going back to college, maintaining a job, having a child, or buying a home. Helping veterans achieve these goals is vital to their healthy transition to civilian life. As Sergeant Smith's case illustrates, failing to achieve his goal of employment had a direct impact on his mental health and daily functioning.

Policy Matters

The social work profession is also uniquely positioned to support veterans and military families at the organizational level. The combination of practitioner and agency-based capacity building is essential to respond to the growing number of veterans returning from war and adjusting to civilian and family life (Flynn & Hassan, 2010). Our profession is building this capacity in two important ways. First, we have launched a coordinated and formalized training process to increase the number of social workers prepared to work with veterans and their families. Specifically, the Council on Social Work Education's guidebook of military social work competencies (Council on Social Work Education, 2010) is helping to guide the formation of military social work courses and concentrations at civilian universities throughout the country. Second, we are developing professional training and the implementation of evidence-based practices within entire agencies that deliver care to veterans and their families. In Sergeant Smith's case, a significant challenge was finding a social worker who understood him and an agency that provided veteran-specific support. With the expansion of these training initiatives, we can ensure that we are adequately prepared to work with service members like Sergeant Smith and that we facilitate, and do not hinder, their attempts to access care.

It is unlikely that the health of veterans and their families, the quality of and access to care, or the need for qualified providers, will be adequately addressed without local, state, and federal agencies joining forces. Therefore, we as social workers need to bring together a diverse set of resources, identify new opportunities across the public and private sectors, and lay the foundation for a coordinated approach to supporting and engaging veterans and their families for many years to come. Community organizing is one of our key strengths because of our orientation to systemic change.

Social workers must invest in approaches that show the greatest promise for serving veterans and their families within their communities through local networks of care. This is essential for good community practice. One way of achieving this is through the development of initiatives to comprehensively address the needs of veterans and their family members. In other words, we need a community approach orchestrated by social workers that plays to the strengths of the community, including small, scalable clusters of stakeholders who have the resources and relationships in place to work well together. Social workers are a strong resource with the potential to bring together a comprehensive community response focused on advocacy, research, professional education and training, and partnerships. These types of initiatives can help guide practitioners, build community networks, inform policymakers, and identify broadly applicable and scalable translational research with promising real-world prevention interventions. The overall goal is for social workers to build new policy bridges that permit more effective and fiscally sound programs for the reintegration of veterans into civilian communities across the United States.

Advocacy and policy action on employment for veterans might include the development of a public awareness campaign that highlights positive images and strengths of veterans who are currently employed; lobbying to enhance work opportunity tax credits for employers of veterans, not as one-time credits but as quarterly credits for one year; advocating for a funding shift from employment preparation programs to peer-supported veterans' programs that emphasize mentorship and support for each aspect of employment, from résumé writing to apprenticeships; and promoting hiring fairs for veterans that go beyond collecting résumés and on-the-spot interviews (Little & Alenkin, 2011).

We must continuously search for solutions that incorporate individual, family, and community care that can support our veterans and their families beyond the services offered by traditional systems. Social work is the safety net for a civil society that is committed to supporting the brave men and women who wear the uniform in combat. They deserve our deepest gratitude and support.

Discussion Questions

1. Do you believe there are parallels between working with veterans and working with other types of clients? What are the similarities? What are some differences?

2. After reading this chapter, have your thoughts, feelings, assumptions, beliefs, values, or attitudes changed regarding working with veterans and military families? If so, how have they changed? If not, why do you think that is the case?

3. What were the strengths and limitations of the material covered in this chapter? What are the implications for you in your practice?

4. Can the all-volunteer force remain viable if returning veterans are seen as broken individuals? Please explain your answer.

References

Council on Social Work Education. (2010). *Advanced social work practice in military social work*. Retrieved from http://www.cswe.org/File.aspx?id=42466

Flynn, M., & Hassan, A. M. (2010). Unique challenges of war in Iraq and Afghanistan. *Journal of Social Work Education, 46,* 169–173.

Foster, M. E. (2011). Deployment and the citizen soldier: Need and resilience. *Medical Care, 49,* 301–312.

Little, R., & Alenkin, N. (2011). *Overcoming barriers to employment for veterans: Current trends and practical approaches.* Los Angeles: University of Southern California Center for Innovation and Research on Veterans and Military Families.

Riviere, L., Kendall-Robbins, A., McGurk, D., Castro, C., & Hoge, C. (2011). Coming home may hurt: Risk factors for mental ill health in U.S. reservists after deployment in Iraq. *The British Journal of Psychiatry, 198,* 136–142.

Uniformed Services Employment and Reemployment Rights Act of 1994, P.L. 103-353, 108 Stat. 3149 (1994).

CHAPTER 24

RESTORING PROTECTION FOR TORTURE SURVIVORS

S. Megan Berthold

NARRATIVE

One evening while on vacation, I received a call from the clinical director at the torture treatment center where I worked as a therapist. My client Chang, she informed me, was in the custody of the U.S. Border Patrol, detained when she had gone sightseeing to a U.S. city located too close to the border. They were threatening to deport her, as the U.S. Immigration and Customs Enforcement (ICE) officers' understanding was that her asylum case had been denied. Chang had been granted "withholding of removal" status by a U.S. immigration judge and had a copy of the judge's decision with her. Withholding of removal is an alternate form of legal relief allowing qualified individuals to remain legally in the United States.[1]

Chang repeatedly pleaded with the officers that she had legal status and told them that she was awaiting the decision of the Ninth Circuit Court of Appeals on the immigration judge's denial of her asylum. There was an error in ICE's computer system, which only contained the information that her asylum had been denied. The ICE officers also did not understand what withholding of removal meant. They continued to threaten to deport Chang and repeatedly denied her requests to call her attorney. Chang was finally allowed to contact our agency. My clinical director then telephoned Chang's lawyer, who was able to contact the detention center. Chang's lawyer eventually corrected the ICE officers' misunderstanding regarding withholding rulings, and Chang was released later that night.

Chang's story began when she was a student activist and a member of the opposition party fighting for democracy in a country ruled by a military dictatorship. Chang had been detained in a military prison on previous occasions after being arrested for protesting government policy. Her earlier offenses added fuel to her government's anger, and they detained

---

[1]Unlike asylum, withholding of removal does not permit the sponsorship of a spouse or minor children, nor does it allow a person to adjust his or her status later to that of permanent resident or U.S. citizen.

her again for over a year. During this detention, military officers repeatedly interrogated her about her involvement with the opposition party, demanding that she tell them about the activities of her friends and colleagues. Refusal led to brutal beatings with an iron rod while being threatened with death. There was no relief. Even while alone in her cell, she was forced to hear the screams of other political prisoners. Chang, still a virgin when she was first detained, was repeatedly gang raped, a gun held to her temple, her rapists ordering her not to tell anyone what they had done to her.

Sometime later, Chang managed to escape from her country and torturers, entering the United States alone and without family. She had one contact, a friend of her sister's named Judy, who offered her refuge. Chang understandably isolated herself from the world, secreted away in Judy's apartment month after month, fearful of the world and of men in particular, never feeling safe. Unable to speak to anybody, even to Judy, a kindly woman she had known since childhood, Chang became ever more isolated. Judy realized Chang required more help than she could offer as a friend, so she eventually located the torture treatment clinic where I practiced. Chang, she told me, was not eating, was desolate, suffered from panic attacks, and screamed when approached by anyone other than Judy. When I finally was able to communicate with Chang, I found her condition to be so bad that she even refused to meet with our medical director, who was a man.

Discussion

Survivors of state-sponsored torture flee their countries every day seeking safe haven and refuge. Those who find their way to the United States seeking asylum because of torture often face daunting challenges, including the endless fear of deportation.[2] Deportation often means deliverance back into the hands of the perpetrators with the real danger of further torture and even murder. Escape itself is dangerous, with many survivors unable to bring their children or other family members with them. In some cases, family members or close associates of the survivor are threatened, tortured, killed, "disappeared,"[3] or forced into hiding. These atrocities are perpetrated by

---

[2]Asylum seekers must demonstrate that they have been persecuted by the authorities in their country on the basis of at least one of five grounds: political opinion, religious beliefs or practices, nationality, race, or membership in a social group. For more information about asylum, see U.S. Citizenship and Immigration Services (2011a, 2011b).

[3]When people are "disappeared," they are kidnapped by the authorities or a rebel, guerilla, or militia group that the authorities cannot or will not protect them from. Their families, friends, and associates are unable to locate them. Months and years may go by with no news about them. Rarely, a person resurfaces, usually with evidence of abuse or torture. More commonly, a disappeared person is eventually assumed to be dead (murdered), although the lack of bodily remains and the uncertainty about the person's fate is agonizing for the loved ones left behind.

authorities seeking information or the location of survivors. Some survivors continue to remain in hiding even within U.S. borders, choosing to suffer alone, for fear of detection by their perpetrators or because they struggle to function in the larger world. This was the case for Chang.

POLICY MATTERS

The asylum officer who interviewed Chang initially referred her to court because she had not applied for asylum within her first year in the United States, as the law requires. There are exceptions to the requirement to apply for asylum within the first year. The immigration judge who heard her initial case denied her asylum for the same reason as the asylum officer (the "one-year rule"), despite ample psychological evidence and expert witness testimony on her inability to apply and testify on her own behalf within that time.

Asylum seekers initially have no benefits or rights in the United States. Like Chang, many rely on support from friends or associates. The Refugee Act of 1980 (P.L. 96-212) was landmark legislation designed to protect victims of persecution and provide for the effective resettlement of refugees to the United States. It added strength to America's obligation to protect refugees under the 1951 United Nations Convention and its 1967 Protocol Relating to the Status of Refugees.[4] Yet, in the more than three decades since this act was passed, the United States has not lived up to its obligations.

In 1996, the Illegal Immigration Reform and Responsibility Act (P.L. 104-208) was passed into law in the United States.[5] This law required that asylum seekers apply for asylum within one year of arrival in the United States. Those who do not meet the deadline are barred from being granted asylum, even if they are otherwise eligible and have been found to have a credible fear of future persecution. Thousands of asylum seekers with well-founded fears of persecution have been denied asylum and the protections that go along with it (Human Rights First, 2010a), sometimes without the

---

[4]The Convention Relating to the Status of Refugees, negotiated in 1951 (United Nations Convention, 1951), was designed to protect individuals persecuted in war-torn Europe prior to 1951 (the United States was not a signatory at that time). The United States signed and ratified the 1967 Protocol to the Convention (United Nations Protocol, 1967), which expanded the scope of the convention geographically and temporally and established a definition of the term "refugee." In 1980, the U.S. Congress enacted implementing legislation that brought U.S. laws into compliance with the Convention and Protocol. The Refugee Act of 1980 (P.L. 96-212) placed many of the substantive provisions of the Convention into U.S. asylum law; however, there are still gaps in the protections available for asylum seekers.

[5]The one-year filing deadline, passed in 1996, was not put into effect until 1997 and only began to serve as a bar to asylum with new cases filed in 1998.

full merits of their case being heard.[6] The one-year rule has proven ineffectual, causing increased costs and delays in the asylum system. Proponents of the deadline argued that it would help prevent fraud; however, it has prevented many with legitimate and credible claims from being able to receive asylum.[7]

Although exceptions to the one-year rule are allowed on the basis of changed or extraordinary circumstances,[8] it is often difficult to overcome this hurdle without official documentation, testimony from experts, and strong legal counsel.[9] Many torture survivors and other asylum applicants cannot afford to pay for attorneys or expert witnesses. Fortunately, Chang had a committed and effective attorney who saw her case through from start to finish on a pro-bono basis.

Another problem with the one-year rule is that there are disparities in how judges adjudicate this rule. In addition, many other disparities in the system exist, indicating a larger systemic problem. Independent reports, including one by the U.S. Government Accountability Office (GAO) (2008), document a number of disparities that affect an asylum seeker's chances of being granted asylum. Rates of asylum grants were

---

[6]Human Rights First (2010a) found that 53,400 applicants were denied asylum or had their cases delayed due to the one-year rule in the first 12 years since the deadline went into force, including survivors of torture and other forms of severe political, religious, and ethnic persecution. For example, an immigration judge denied the asylum case of an Eritrean woman who was sexually assaulted and otherwise tortured for being Christian because she missed the one-year filing deadline, despite the fact that the judge found her testimony to be compelling and credible (Human Rights First, 2010a, 2010b).

[7]Many other immigration reforms implemented since 1995 have provided effective ways to combat fraudulent claims (Human Rights First, 2010a).

[8]Examples of changed or extraordinary circumstances include changed country conditions resulting in increased risk of persecution, and severe physical or mental health problems that made it impossible to apply for asylum within the first year.

[9]Even when evidence of change or exceptional circumstances is presented, the one-year rule is not automatically waived (Human Rights First, 2010a). Asylum officers routinely refer applicants to immigration court when they have not filed in a timely manner. It is up to the judge whether to set aside the one-year rule. Many groups and individuals have advocated for the elimination of the one-year filing deadline. For example, Human Rights First (2008) presented recommendations to the incoming Obama administration. In 2009 the United Nations High Commissioner for Refugees joined 10 national nongovernmental organizations in sending letters to Secretary of Homeland Security Janet Napolitano and Attorney General Eric Holder recommending the elimination of the one-year filing deadline and other reforms to the asylum system and broader interpretation of the exception in the interim. Human Rights First submitted their recommendations to the UN Human Rights Council and to the US government for its annual human rights review. A submission to the UN Human Rights Council in April 2010 recommending the elimination of this deadline was sent by 18 national and 30 local refugee and migrant advocacy groups. A 2010 letter to members of the House of Representatives in support of the Restoring Protection to Victims of Persecution Act (HR 4800) was signed by 87 human rights, legal services, faith-based and refugee assistance organizations (including the nonprofit Program for Torture Victims, with which I was working) along with 81 individuals. For links to these letters and recommendations, see Human Rights First (n.d).

found to depend on such things as the city in which the applicant lived and the judge to which the case was assigned (the percentages of asylum denials ranged from 20 percent to 90 percent across judges), rather than on the merits of the case (GAO, 2008). Asylum applicants in San Francisco were 12 times as likely to be granted aslyum as those applying in Atlanta. The New York courts were 420 times more likely to grant asylum than courts in the rest of the United States. Asylum applicants who had an attorney had twice the chance of being granted asylum as those without legal representation. Other factors identified by the GAO that were associated with a higher chance of having one's asylum petition approved include being detained or having a male judge (male judges were 60 percent more likely to grant asylum than female judges). The GAO report included a strong recommendation to the Department of Justice's Executive Office for Immigration Review to identify judges who need further training in an effort to address these discrepancics.

Even if filed in a timely fashion, application for asylum is retraumatizing for most torture survivors. Like Chang, many survivors try hard to forget, but they must relive their traumas when they apply for asylum. Some of their experienccs are considered deeply stigmatizing or shameful in their cultures. Applicants frequently have difficulty testifying in front of an asylum officer or a court because their trauma has affected their ability to provide a linear, consistent, coherent account of their experiences (Brewin, 2007; Herlihy, Scragg, & Turner, 2002; Herlihy & Turner, 2006, 2007). Inconsistencies in their testimony often raise credibility concerns for the adjudicator, frequently resulting in a denial of asylum. Although there is an appeal mechanism, this can be an arduous, lengthy, and expensive process, one that not all survivors of torture or other forms of persecution can afford or endure.

●■●

Later on the evening Chang was detained by ICE, she called me, saying in a whisper, "they released me." With a trembling voice she shared with me the fear that filled her when uniformed male ICE officers began their interrogation. She found herself reliving past horrors as they informed her, "We're going to send you back—deport you. Your asylum was denied. We're sending you back!" She told me that the ICE officers put her into a small, dark, locked room and body searched her, including her breasts and groin. This created a flashback to the gang rape, solitary confinement, interrogation sessions, and threats she had endured as part of her year of torture in a military prison. It had taken several years of psychotherapy, medication, and treatment with an interdisciplinary team at my agency to bring her to the point where she was able to apply for asylum, work, and function in her daily life.

After her release from detention, Chang's retraumatization at the hands of the Border Patrol officers precipitated a sudden worsening of her psychological state. I provided crisis intervention, drawing on Chang's enormous strengths and resilient coping skills that she had employed over the previous several years to support her as she dealt with the setback.

•■■

Chang's case highlights the need for reform of the asylum law, including eliminating the one-year filing deadline and better and more uniform education of those who work in the immigration field. Appropriate standards and protocols for the treatment of detainees must be implemented to ensure that human rights remain protected. If the initial asylum officer had been able to rule on the merits of Chang's asylum case, she may have never had to go to court and she may have been able to reunite with her children five years sooner. Had the Border Patrol officers who detained Chang understood what her withholding-of-removal status meant, or even allowed her to call her attorney, she wouldn't have had to face further trauma at their hands. Policies affecting conduct by peace officers should be universally adopted to address the abuse of detainees and their rights, including illegal searches and denial of the right to counsel.

I have gained insights into the need for revised policies and laws from the struggles and obstacles faced by my clients and from what they have taught me as their therapist. Torture survivors themselves have led the way in many public education and advocacy efforts in this country and others, such as the campaigns led by the Torture Abolition and Survivor Support Coalition International (http://tassc.org). My colleagues and I have collaborated closely with torture survivors and staff from other torture treatment centers in the National Consortium of Torture Treatment Programs, legal representatives, nongovernmental organizations, other stakeholders, and like-minded legislators to support reform of the refugee and asylum law, including eliminating the one-year rule.

On the 30-year anniversary of the Refugee Act of 1980 (P.L. 96-212), Senator Patrick Leahy (D-VT) introduced the Refugee Protection Act of 2010 into Congress (S. 3113) with a bipartisan group of cosponsors to comprehensively reform U.S. refugee law.[10] The 111th session of Congress closed without passage of this legislation. On June 15, 2011, Senator Leahy and Representative Zoe Lofgren (D-CA) introduced a new version of the bill into the 112th Congress (S. 1202/H.R. 2185), titled the Refugee Protection Act of 2011. Among its many provisions, this act would ensure that the United States protects refugees and asylum seekers with bona fide claims, improve conditions of detention, protect family unity by allowing the reunification of migrant children separated from their families, and eliminate the one-year asylum filing deadline. At the time of writing, the chances of the Refugee Protection Act of 2011 passing in its entirety in the 112th Congress appeared slim, but there was hope that portions of this important legislation would be passed.

---

[10]This was a revised version of legislation Leahy introduced in the 106th and 107th Congresses to repeal some of the harshest parts of the 1996 Illegal Immigration Reform and Responsibility Act (P.L. 104-208).

SOCIAL WORK MATTERS

Over the years, I have been struck by the fact that many torture survivors were tortured because of their community organizing or advocacy work, and some were even working as social workers. Organizing women to fight for their rights has been seen as a threat by authorities in some societies. The courage, skill, determination, and resilience of these survivors in the face of severe obstacles has inspired me and helped to sustain me in this work, contributing even to my vicarious resilience. I have felt called to do more than provide clinical services. Often, an important and powerful part of the healing process for torture survivors can be reclaiming their voice as they reengage with political activism and reconnect with their pre-torture identity and role. Social workers can accompany survivors on this journey and have much to learn from survivor activists. As a clinical social worker providing psychotherapy and forensic services to torture survivors, I find it impossible to ignore the oppression and inequities they face.

What can social workers do about it? Providing clinical, forensic, and social services is often an important first step. Clinicians, however, sometimes feel that they are only scratching the surface and that their work with individual survivors does nothing to prevent further torture from occurring. Engaging in research with survivors can generate meaningful data that can be vital for advocacy efforts. Advocating for policy change at the local, national, and international levels informed by and grounded in knowledge from direct practice is important and needed. Clinical social workers can play a meaningful role in putting a human face on the need for reform, and some of their clients may also find participating in such social justice work to be therapeutic and meaningful.

The NASW (2008) *Code of Ethics,* which should permeate and inform all of our practice as social workers, stresses our responsibility to act in the face of injustice and discrimination. It is a call for social work practitioners to step outside of their usual role and engage in advocacy for system change and legislative reform. Fighting for social justice is one powerful pathway to healing the harm done by torture and other human rights violations (R. F. Mollica, 2006; R. G. Mollica, 2011).

NASW has been one of the leading voices in speaking out against the practice of torture in all forms, including against the U.S. government's use of torture. I urge social workers to join their colleagues in coalition with the National Consortium of Torture Treatment Programs, the International Rehabilitation Council for Victims of Torture, the National Religious Campaign Against Torture, Human Rights First, NASW, and other interdisciplinary professional, social, legal, and religious groups to speak out against torture, and to advocate for humane detention conditions and other policy and legislative change. Working on structural interventions and solutions that target the conditions and policies that led to or allowed the practice of torture in the first place is also in keeping with the mission and values we stand for as social workers.

●■●

Some months after Chang was released from detention, her attorney notified us that the U.S. attorney assigned to fight her asylum appeal had declined to pursue the matter and had convinced her supervisor to concede, stating that Chang was clearly qualified for asylum based on the record (and that the evidence presented regarding Chang's psychological inability to apply for asylum within one year of arriving in the United States was compelling). This cleared the way for her case to be sent back to federal immigration court, and her asylum was granted. Unlike some stories that don't end as happily, after many years separated from her two children, Chang was finally able to reunite with them in the United States.

Discussion Questions

1. In what ways can social workers get involved if they want to make a difference in the lives of torture survivors?

2. Is there a need for change in any policies or legislation related to refugees or asylum seekers in the United States? If so, what changes would you recommend and why? What strategy or strategies do you think would be most effective and feasible for achieving the change(s) you recommend?

References

Brewin, C. R. (2007). Autobiographical memory for trauma: Update on four controversies. *Memory, 15,* 227–248.

Herlihy, J., Scragg, P., & Turner, S. (2002). Discrepancies in autobiographical memories—Implications for the assessment of asylum seekers: Repeated interviews study. *BMJ, 324,* 324–327.

Herlihy, J., & Turner, S. (2006). Should discrepant accounts given by asylum seekers be taken as proof of deceit? *Torture, 16*(2), 81–92.

Herlihy, J., & Turner, S. (2007). Asylum claims and memory of trauma: Sharing our knowledge. *British Journal of Psychiatry: The Journal of Mental Science, 191,* 3–4.

Human Rights First. (2008). *How to repair the U.S. asylum system: Blueprint for the next administration.* New York: Author.

Human Rights First. (2010a). *The asylum filing deadline: Denying protection to the persecuted and undermining governmental efficiency.* New York: Author.

Human Rights First. (2010b). *Renewing U.S. commitment to refugee protection: Recommendations for reform on the 30th anniversary of the refugee act.* New York: Author.

Human Right First. (n.d.) *Reforms to the U.S. asylum and refugee systems.* New York: Author. Retrieved from http://www.humanrightsfirst.org/our-work/refugee-protection/reforms-to-the-u-s-asylum-and-refugee-systems

Illegal Immigration Reform and Immigrant Responsibility Act, P.L. 104-208, 110 Stat. 3009-546 (1996).

Mollica, R. F. (2006). *Healing invisible wounds.* Nashville, TN: Vanderbilt University Press.

Mollica, R. G. (2011, September 26). *Healing invisible wounds* [from SAMSHA Teleconference *Demystifying Trauma: Sharing Pathways to Healing and Wellness*]. Retrieved from http://www.promoteacceptance.samhsa.gov/teleconferences/archive/training/teleconference09262011.aspx

National Association of Social Workers. (2008). *Code of ethics of the National Association of Social Workers.* Washington, DC: NASW Press.

Refugee Act of 1980, P.L. 96-212, 94 Stat. 102 (1980).

United Nations Convention Relating to the Status of Refugees, July 28, 1951, 19 U.S.T. 6259, 189 U.N.T.S. 150.

United Nations Protocol Relating to the Status of Refugees, January 31, 1967, 19 U.S.T. 6223, 606 U.N.T.S. 267.

U.S. Citizenship and Immigration Services. (2011a). *Asylum.* Retrieved from http://www.uscis. gov/portal/site/uscis/menuitem.eb1d4c2a3e5b9ac89243c6a7543f6d1a/?vgnextoid=f39d3e4d7 7d73210VgnVCM100000082ca60aRCRD&vgnextchannel=f39d3e4d77d73210VgnVCM10 0000082ca60aRCRD

U.S. Citizenship and Immigration Services. (2011b). *Obtaining asylum in the United States.* Retrieved from http://www.uscis.gov/portal/site/uscis/menuitem.5af9bb95919f35e66f614176 543f6d1a/?vgnextoid=dab9f067e3183210VgnVCM100000082ca60aRCRD&vgnextchannel= f39d3e4d77d73210VgnVCM100000082ca60aRCRD

U.S. Government Accountability Office. (2008). *U.S. asylum system: Significant variation existed in asylum outcomes across immigration courts and judges: Report to congressional requesters.* Washington, DC: Author.

EDUCATION AND LOAN FORGIVENESS

CHAPTER 25

ENGAGING STUDENTS IN MACRO PRACTICE:

A SOCIAL PROJECT

Linda S. Moore

SOCIAL WORK MATTERS

Community intervention strategies can help social workers challenge unresponsive power structures in any area of practice. Many educators teach that the personal is political, and the person-in-environment principle of social work emphasizes affecting systems at all levels. However, students often are not comfortable using macro change strategies. Several studies of social work curriculums on both baccalaureate and master's levels indicate that little emphasis is placed on community intervention methodology (Haynes & Mickelson, 2000). If social action is ignored by educators, the profession and its clients will suffer.

The roots of professional social work are based in macro practice. During the Progressive Era, between 1890 and 1910, several social movements, many of which were led by social workers, emerged to advocate for services and policies to eliminate social injustice (Moore, in press). Settlement House and Charity Organization Society workers assessed the relationships of clients to their social environments and, on the basis of those assessments, used macro skills such as political advocacy and organization to promote social change (Bryan & Davis, 1990; Woods & Kennedy, 1922).

During the 1920s and 1930s, Bertha Capen Reynolds tried to unionize social workers and other workers. Her advocacy was not just political, but was based on the belief that by empowering clients we put them in charge of the intervention process (Reynolds, 1963). In the 1960s, social workers Whitney M. Young Jr. and Dorothy I. Height emphasized civil rights and social justice using macro strategies such as networking, demonstrations, and legislative efforts and undertook several organizational efforts such as Young's leadership in NASW.

Specht and Courtney (1995) argued in *Unfaithful Angels* that social workers should go back to their advocacy roots, because ignoring the importance of community strategies and advocacy that originated in the settlement movement and focusing too much on the individual in the quest for professionalism has weakened the profession. Social workers today are less vocal about issues that could be publically addressed than were Progressive Era reformers who brought about significant public awareness of oppression and discrimination. Today, we need to speak out and effect change (Haynes & Mickelson, 2000). The need for advocacy today is similar to the need during the Progressive Era. Once again, there are issues of immigration and global interaction, rights for disenfranchised populations, and the need to provide adequate resources for all citizens. As the nation experiences the Occupy movement, few will hear of social workers taking a leading role, despite the numbers of us who will join the demonstrations.

Although all baccalaureate students need to become comfortable with the common base of social work practice, most students link generalist skills with micro practice, specifically working with individuals and families. Many social work graduates are not choosing macro practice or are working with large organizations, organizing communities, developing programs, or working in planning and administration. According to NASW, only 1 percent of licensed social workers work 20 hours a week or more in community organization (Whitaker, Weismiller, & Clark, 2006). When the vast majority of undergraduate students prefer micro practice, preparing them to use macro strategies is challenging. Educators need to help students understand that the social environment has policy ramifications that may demand system change (Netting, Kettner, McMurtry, & Thomas, 2011) and that helping clients occurs on many levels using many skills. Instructional strategies that develop macro skills improve social work curriculums and enhance efforts to influence the policies that affect clients locally, nationally, and globally. Advocacy is a form of practice, and, when taught as a macro concept, it can promote social change.

Teaching community intervention helps students understand the basic tenets of macro practice, but allowing students to plan and carry out their own change projects is a more effective strategy. Eleanor Roosevelt (1958) argued that human rights begin where people are; in the case of our students, this often means that educators must engage them on their own campuses. Examples of student activities on the university campus include organizing or serving student groups focused on social justice, serving on university committees that make and evaluate policy, providing resources for disadvantaged groups, and informing appropriate officials about problems on the campus and providing alternatives to insensitive policies.

Teaching students how to interact with legislators, for example through a Student Day at the Legislature (Moore & Johnston, 2002), can enhance their understanding of the process of policy making and their role in advocating for clients and social justice. Rallies, marches, and other activities in support of certain issues are also tactics of advocacy, as is writing well-researched letters to policymakers advocating positions on issues. Swigonski (2011) suggested that we need to help students learn about their own world, looking at human rights in that world and how they are supported or violated. When students carry out a project, they learn to assess a community's problems and needs, work with community members to set goals, collect data, and do ongoing evaluation to determine that the project is effective (Moore & Dietz, 1999). If that project is on their own campus, it has an immediacy that can have a larger impact on them and ultimately help them better evaluate the worlds of their clients as they practice.

NARRATIVE

One specific example of advocacy occurred on a predominantly white private university campus where students in a generalist community practice class attempted to change university policy by making Martin Luther King Jr. Day an official university holiday. On November 2, 1983, President Reagan signed a bill establishing the birthday of Dr. King as a national holiday, to be celebrated on the third Monday of January, effective in 1986. It was not easy to pass the law. As with so many other civil rights laws and rulings, such as Brown v. Board of Education of Topeka *(347 U.S. 483), some states resisted and many argued its importance. Debates included King's significance compared to other national figures, charges that he had been a member of the Communist party, fears that the holiday was expected to make up for 300 years of slavery, and the cost of the holiday in overtime and vacation pay. In 2000, it was finally observed in all 50 states. However, some localities and schools still chose not to celebrate the holiday, thus the necessity for actions to challenge those decisions.*

This particular university did not recognize the holiday, and many students and faculty were frustrated by this. After administrative officials made public statements supporting increased diversity on campus, students believed recognizing Dr. King's birthday would indicate the administration's ability to "walk the walk." Class members believed that the entire campus should recognize the importance of the day and how it could affect the minority community within the university. The local school district and several local universities celebrated the holiday, so it appeared there was precedence for the action.

Students did the necessary research to learn about Dr. King and the political process that brought about recognition of his birthday; this preparation affirmed their desire to engage in the project. Through the assessment process, the class determined that many students, particularly students of color, supported the effort, as did most faculty members. They also found that most students of color, as well as staff on campus, felt excluded and marginalized by the lack of action; the debate about the holiday exacerbated these feelings.

A key issue was that most of the community was ignorant of the issue, a response from the majority culture reflecting the privilege it enjoyed. The biggest problem students determined, and the most surprising to them, was the lack of support from most administrative officials. This class was aware that it could try to force the issue using conflict strategies that would motivate the administration to act. They chose not to do so and, rather, tried to obtain community consensus as their strategy, despite knowing it would generate more subtle opposition than conflict strategies would (Haynes & Mickelson, 2000).

The students learned they had to be informed to respond to specious and erroneous arguments. They were told that Dr. King was more a local hero than a national or international leader. They were challenged with assumptions of his infidelity, his plagiarizing, his communist leanings, and other rumors. They were given incorrect information about accreditation standards regarding class meeting days and were told by administrative leaders that the holiday was unnecessary. They learned how to find the information that helped them argue their position and correct those who challenged them out of ignorance.

Students learned how to circumnavigate traditional structures and use informal mechanisms when they were refused help to access resources, voted down by the faculty senate, and discounted by other faculty and students. This was a key lesson on organizational and bureaucratic structure and how to work within it. Through these obstacles, students learned to nurture resources within and outside the university community, including faculty and student government support and the media.

Students experienced frustration and impatience with the pace of change and their perceived lack of support from the community. However, by remaining persistent, they were able to mobilize many student organizations, the student government association, several athletic teams, and many faculty. They were also able to gain support from important guest speakers visiting the university. Their efforts over a four-month period reflected community strategies, and they were successful. These strategies included representing community interests, linking community members to resources, emphasizing social justice, negotiating the political process, and teaching community members how to use their own power to enhance the community. Bertha Reynolds (1963) argued that social workers should work "at the crossroads of every life" (p. 3), listening to the voices of their clients. In this case, students listened to students of color and the many others who wanted greater cultural awareness on their campus.

The project helped students recognize the necessity of preparation, including informing themselves about an issue. Finding and effectively using resources was critical for success, as were determination, patience, and a sense of humor. The most important task was empowering the community to own the issue and take responsibility for its success. Collaboration was vital for this to occur. These are lessons class members all report using in professional practice. The passage of federal policy led them to take action to ensure that the policy was implemented where they lived and that their community benefitted from it. Although this project occurred in the 1990s, there is still great pride among the students who took part in it. The project remains the most successful of all social work student efforts on this campus and a model for community classes each year.

IMPLICATIONS

One of the most important outcomes from a successful project is that people begin to believe that they have power and can use it for positive change. Students often feel powerless in relation to faculty and administration and believe that they have little to say about policies that affect them daily. Changing this university policy led to continued efforts by students who accomplished many more policy changes at the university.

This class project led to increased recognition of diversity issues. Subsequent social work classes changed the university's antidiscrimination policy to prohibit discrimination based on sexual orientation; established an official university organization for students with disabilities and their supporters; established a recognized university organization for gay, lesbian, and bisexual students; formed an allies group to support sexual minorities; and influenced the administration to increase the number of social work faculty. Their efforts also led indirectly to the development of the University Council on Diversity and the establishment of a Community Scholars program providing financial aid for high-performing students in local high schools with significant dropout rates and low numbers of students who go on to college. It could also be argued that because these students raised awareness of diversity issues, their efforts led to increased hiring of minority faculty and staff, increased salary and benefits for all staff, and the availability of partner benefits.

POLICY MATTERS

Macro practice is about change. It can be initiated within an organization if there is a clear understanding of how it promotes a just world (Olson, 2011). Students in this example used their vision of a just university to promote concrete change that affected them, their social environment, and their practice, and this legacy lives on. As educators, we can give our students the gift of leaving such a legacy by helping them learn how macro practice can effect positive change in the lives of their clients. Kahn (2010) argued that community organizers must expect the impossible because they know how to be effective in what appear to be impossible situations: "We can never truly predict what human beings working together can accomplish and therefore we can never compromise with injustice" (p. 196). These students were told by several university official and faculty members they would never get university policy changed in four months, and yet they did. Educators can provide the spark to help students achieve this kind of success. The issues are all around us if we help students see them and are open to their vision.

DISCUSSION QUESTIONS

1. Can educators teach macro practice if they are not engaging in advocacy themselves? If so, what kinds of practice can they use for examples? If not, how do we get all faculty engaged in some form of advocacy efforts?

2. Is changing university policy a reasonable challenge for students compared with the kinds of policy issues they will face in their practice? If not, why not? If so, how?

REFERENCES

Brown v. Board of Education of Topeka, 347 U.S. 483 (1954).

Bryan, M.L.M., & Davis, A. F. (Eds.). (1990). *100 years at Hull House*. Bloomington: Indiana University Press.

Haynes, K. S., & Mickelson, J. S. (2000). *Affecting change*. Boston: Allyn & Bacon.

Kahn, S. (2010). *Creative community organizing*. San Francisco: Berrett-Koehler.

Moore, L. S. (in press). Women and the emergence of the NAACP. *Journal of Social Work Education*.

Moore, L. S., & Dietz, T. J. (1999). Four months to system change: Teaching baccalaureate students to affect policy. *Journal of Community Practice, 6,* 33–44.

Moore, L. S., & Johnston, L. (2002). Involving students in the legislative process. *Journal of Community Practice, 10,* 89–101.

Netting, F. E., Kettner, P. M., McMurtry, S. L., & Thomas, M. L. (2011). *Social work macro practice* (5th ed.). Upper Saddle River, NJ: Prentice-Hall.

Olson, J. (2011, October 22). Macro practice. [Electronic mailing list message.] Retrieved from http://BPD-L@listserv.iupui.edu

Reynolds, B. C. (1963). *An uncharted journey*. New York: Citadel Press.

Roosevelt, E. (1958, March 27). *In your hands*. Retrieved from http://www.udhr.org/history/inyour.htm

Specht, H., & Courtney, M. E. (1995). *Unfaithful angels: How social work has abandoned its mission*. New York: Free Press.

Swigonski, M. E. (2011). Claiming rights, righting wrongs: Educating students for human rights. *Journal of Baccalaureate Social Work, 16*(2), 1–16.

Whitaker, T., Weismiller, T., & Clark, E. (2006). *Assuring the sufficiency of a frontline workforce: A national study of licensed social workers*. Washington, DC: National Association of Social Workers.

Woods, R. A., & Kennedy, A. J. (1922). *The settlement horizon*. New York: Russell Sage Foundation.

CHAPTER 26

HELPING SOCIAL WORKERS HELP CLIENTS:

STUDENT LOAN FORGIVENESS

Sunny Harris Rome

POLICY MATTERS

From the mid-1980s until the mid-1990s, I was employed as a senior government relations associate with NASW's national office. In that capacity, I led the profession's lobbying efforts on issues including welfare reform, child welfare, education, civil rights, social services, and budget and appropriations. I was involved in all phases of the legislative process: enlisting sponsors and cosponsors for bills to advance social work interests, collaborating with like-minded organizations, testifying before Congress, meeting with legislators and their staff, and mobilizing other social workers to participate in the policy process. Although every issue that I worked on had important implications for clients, this chapter focuses on one issue in particular: student loan forgiveness. It serves as an excellent example of how policy affects practice.

NARRATIVE

I first became involved with loan forgiveness through my work on child welfare. NASW was one of approximately 80 organizations that participated in a coalition convened by the Children's Defense Fund and the Child Welfare League of America. Through weekly meetings that took place over several years, the coalition developed a comprehensive set of recommendations to improve federal policy for children involved in the child welfare, juvenile justice, and mental health systems. One of the many concerns that arose was the need for a stable cadre of qualified staff. At the time, child-serving agencies were challenged by an influx of families affected by homelessness, HIV infection, and a surging crack cocaine epidemic. Today, these agencies continue to struggle to meet the needs of families made vulnerable by the ailing economy as well as children entering care with increasingly complex emotional and behavioral problems. Recent estimates suggest that staff turnover rates in child welfare agencies average 20 percent to 40 percent annually (National Council on

Crime and Delinquency, 2006), and in some jurisdictions they are as high as 85 percent (Smith, 2004).

The lack of a stable workforce has direct and profound implications for clients. A 2003 study by the U.S. General Accounting Office concluded that child welfare agencies' difficulty in recruiting and retaining staff jeopardizes children's safety and permanency. As a consequence of high caseloads resulting from inadequate numbers of staff on the job, those who remain "have less time to establish relationships with children and their families, conduct frequent and meaningful home visits in order to assess children's safety, and make thoughtful and well-supported decisions regarding safe and stable permanent placements" (U.S. General Accounting Office, 2003, p. 19). Staff members with social work degrees are in particularly short supply. Nationally, fewer than 15 percent of child welfare agencies require their workers to have either a BSW or an MSW. Discouraged by low pay and high stress, the majority of social workers choose to enter other fields of practice.

As one approach to addressing these staffing challenges, our coalition proposed that students be entitled to have their loans forgiven if they choose child welfare work after graduation. A portion of the debt would be cancelled for each year of full-time employment, and after five years, the entire loan amount would be cancelled. This would provide a concrete incentive for social workers and others to enter the field and help to ensure that they stay on the job once hired. Loan forgiveness is a strategy that had already been used for teachers, active duty military, nurses, law enforcement officers, health professionals, and Peace Corps volunteers, among others. The promising nature of this strategy was reinforced by the results of a large-scale survey of BSW and MSW students, in which nearly 40 percent indicated that student loan forgiveness would make them more likely to enter the child welfare field (Rome, 1997).

Our target was the federal Perkins loan program, which at the time was the only program under which loans were provided directly to students rather than through a financial guarantor. The Perkins program is the oldest of the federal student loan programs, providing low-interest loans to both undergraduate and graduate students at more than 3,000 institutions of higher learning. NASW led the campaign to incorporate a new student loan forgiveness program into the Higher Education Act Amendments of 1992 (P.L. 102-325). The proposal we settled on entitled borrowers to have their Perkins loan debt gradually reduced and eventually cancelled if they worked full-time for a child or family service agency in a low-income community with children who were "low-income or at risk of abuse or neglect, have been abused or neglected, or have serious emotional, mental, or behavioral disturbances, reside in placements outside their homes, or are involved in the juvenile justice system" (P.L. 102-325, Section 469[b]). The scope of the provision reflected the coalition's focus on the children at the center of these systems, regardless of whether they happened to be receiving care because of child abuse, juvenile justice involvement, or mental health needs.

After organizing a small subset of the larger coalition, developing materials, courting allies, and mobilizing constituents from key districts, we succeeded in having the "family service agency" loan forgiveness provision introduced in the U.S. House of Representatives by George Miller (D-CA) and in the Senate by Christopher Dodd (D-CT). Despite a well-orchestrated lobbying effort, however, the provision was inexplicably dropped from the Senate bill at the last moment. We shifted our attention to getting the House bill passed and making sure that the loan forgiveness provision was incorporated in the conference commit-tee's final version of the Higher Education Act Amendments.

Meanwhile, a chance conversation with staff from the office of Rep. Scott Klug (R-WI) revealed that, at the urging of a single constituent, he had introduced a separate bill grant-ing loan forgiveness to professionals providing early intervention services to infants and toddlers with disabilities. Social workers were specifically included among those covered. This was a great illustration of the unpredictability of advocacy work. Numerous organiza-tions had invested countless hours to have the "family service agency" provision introduced, whereas a single call from a single constituent resulted in the introduction of the "early intervention" bill. It also underscored the importance of establishing a personal relation-ship with one's legislators. No professional lobbyist can replace the influence that regular constituents have with their elected representatives.

We decided, at this point, that it would be advantageous to lobby for both bills together. We contacted several key organizations in the disability community and reformulated our coalition, adding these groups to our members from child welfare, juvenile justice, and mental health organizations. This proved to be an important step as it resulted in a much more interesting variety of allies and a more effective lobbying campaign. Although social work students were potential beneficiaries of both provisions, the broader coalition allowed us to focus our arguments on meeting the needs of clients. Had NASW lobbied alone, we doubtless would have been accused of pursuing loan forgiveness strictly out of self-interest.

In fact, we had to make some careful strategy choices. For example, one of the key sena-tors whose support we desperately needed had indicated that, early in her career, she had sought a position as a child protective services worker only to be turned down because she lacked a social work degree. It seems she'd never quite gotten over this rejection, despite moving on to an illustrious career in the United States Senate. We made a point of having NASW keep a low profile with her office, while other advocates took the lead in seeking her support. This broader, more diverse coalition also made it possible to stress the wide array of graduates other than social workers who would be eligible for assistance. This included special education teachers, speech pathologists, audiologists, occupational therapists, physi-cal therapists, nurses, psychologists, nutritionists, and more.

Between the lobbying visits in Washington and the involvement of a targeted group of students and professionals from across the country, NASW and its allies were successful in getting both new loan forgiveness provisions passed and included in the final Higher Edu-cation Amendments of 1992. A few short years later, more than 1,000 students from over 400 schools had availed themselves of the new loan cancellation options. A follow-up study cast some doubt on the law's effectiveness in actually recruiting social workers into the tar-geted fields of practice but concluded that this was largely due to limitations in the Perkins program itself. Compared with other sources of federal financial aid, the program served *a relatively modest number of borrowers and provided much smaller loans (Rome, 2003). Real progress would depend on making loan forgiveness available under a wider range of programs. As it turns out, our success in creating these initial loan forgiveness opportunities was extremely important in laying the groundwork for ongoing efforts to expand loan forgiveness to larger numbers of social work professionals.*

SOCIAL WORK MATTERS

Today, students graduating with a BSW degree report an average loan debt of $18,609, those with an MSW degree owe an average of $26,777, and those with a doctorate in social work owe an average of $32,841 (NASW, 2008). NASW and others have persevered in promoting the creation of loan forgiveness options to help defray the costs of an education by reducing student debt. In addition to the Perkins provisions already discussed (which continue to be available), loan forgiveness is now available under additional federal loan programs. Clinical social workers may qualify for assistance in repaying student loans through the National Health Service Corps Loan Repayment Program. Doctoral social workers who devote at least 50 percent of their time to research may be eligible for assistance through the National Institutes of Health. Social workers in qualifying public service jobs (including many government and nonprofit agency positions) may be eligible to have their remaining loan debt canceled after 10 years of full-time employment (NASW, 2011; U.S. Department of Education, 2011; U.S. Department of Health and Human Services, 2011). The Higher Education Opportunity Act of 2008 (P.L. 110-315) created additional opportunities for social workers serving children, adolescents, and veterans; however, this program was not being funded at the time of this writing.

Bringing talented students into the social work field, and making it profitable for them to choose employment where the greatest needs exist, is a necessary element in providing for social work clients. Without the requisite qualified work force, client needs cannot be met. In addition to ongoing needs in child welfare, the aging of the American population is expected to result in an increased need for social workers in aging, health care, and disabilities. Specifically, the Bureau of Labor Statistics (2009) has projected that, between 2008 and 2018, employment will increase by 12 percent for child, family, and school social workers; 20 percent for mental health and substance abuse social workers; and 22 percent for medical and public health social workers. Compounding this increased demand is the fact that the social work workforce is significantly older than the workforce as a whole. We can expect a large number of retirements in the coming years, further diminishing our ability to meet growing client needs.

Policies that address workforce shortages have the potential to change client lives. Children who need protection from abuse, adolescents who need substance abuse treatment, adults who need therapy to address mental illness, and families who need help navigating the challenges of caring for an older adult all benefit from having properly trained and educated social workers available. Loan forgiveness is only one strategy to address staff recruitment and retention. Early success under the Perkins student loan program has enabled thousands of social work students to enter important fields of practice and has set the stage for other policies that we hope will make social work careers possible for thousands more.

DISCUSSION QUESTIONS

1. How would you go about persuading a policymaker that student loan forgiveness benefits clients, not just social workers?

2. What other kinds of policies can you suggest for addressing staff recruitment and retention concerns?

3. Using an agency with which you're familiar, provide an example of how the availability, or lack of availability, of qualified social work staff would be likely to affect clients.

REFERENCES

Bureau of Labor Statistics. (2009). Social workers. In *Occupational handbook 2010–11*. Washington, DC: Author. Retrieved from http://www.bls.gov/oco/ocos060.htm#outlook

Higher Education Act Amendments of 1992, P.L. 102-325, 106 Stat. 448 (1992).

Higher Education Opportunity Act, P.L. 110-315, 122 Stat. 3078 (2008).

National Association of Social Workers. (2008, February 5). *Web site to assist borrowers with student loan debt*. Retrieved from http://www.socialworkers.org/advocacy/updates/2008/020508.asp

National Association of Social Workers. (2011). *Federal student debt resources*. Retrieved from https://www.socialworkers.org/loanforgiveness/fedresources.asp?back=yes

National Council on Crime and Delinquency. (2006). *Relationship between staff turnover, child welfare system functioning, and recurrent child abuse*. Houston: Cornerstones for Kids.

Rome, S. H. (1997). The child welfare choice: An analysis of social work students' career plans. *Journal of Baccalaureate Social Work, 3*(1), 31–48.

Rome, S. H. (2003). Serving high-risk children: Recruiting through student loan forgiveness. *Children and Youth Services Review, 25*, 805–821.

Smith, B. D. (2004). Job retention in child welfare: Effects of perceived organizational support, supervisor support, and intrinsic job value. *Children and Youth Services Review, 27*, 153–169.

U.S. Department of Education. (2011). *Public service loan forgiveness*. Retrieved from http://studentaid.ed.gov/PORTALSWebApp/students/english/PSF.jsp

U.S. Department of Health and Human Services. (2011). *National Health Service Corps loan repayment*. Retrieved from http://nhsc.hrsa.gov/loanrepayment/

U.S. General Accounting Office. (2003). *Child welfare: HHS could play a greater role in helping child welfare agencies recruit and retain staff*. Washington, DC: Author.

CHAPTER 27

WE CAN HELP YOU (BUYER BEWARE):

CAN A POOR STUDENT GET AN EDUCATION?

James J. Kelly

One of the first things I learned as a beginning social worker is that policies crafted by legislators to help people sometimes have the opposite result. Too often, the message conveyed to people in need is "We can help you (buyer beware)."

NARRATIVE

This became clear to me when, as a young man, I began my career as a caseworker in Memphis, Tennessee. Mr. and Mrs. Charles were my first clients. When Mr. Charles mangled his hand working the Mississippi barges, the couple was suddenly unable to pay the rent and feed their 10 children. My job was to help Mr. and Mrs. Charles apply for two programs: Aid to Families with Dependent Children (AFDC), which provides monthly cash, and the Women, Infants, and Children (WIC) program, which provides basic food items.

We soon ran into a snag. In the course of working with this couple, I learned that Mrs. Charles was pregnant. According to rigid rules governing the aid programs, and because this was a first-time application, we would have to wait until the new baby's arrival before the family could be certified for AFDC and WIC benefits. For the application, we chose a delivery date for the new baby on the basis of what a medical intern had told Mrs. Charles in one of her prenatal care visits to the local charity hospital.

As any social worker who has worked with families will know, things do not always go as planned. Mrs. Charles's due date passed and she had yet to deliver her baby. Had the intern erred? Did Mrs. Charles deliberately misunderstand the expected date in hopes of getting early benefits? Had I acted unethically by encouraging the couple to submit an application with an incorrect date of birth? Unfortunately, because of rigid eligibility rules, the missed delivery date jeopardized the start of WIC and AFDC benefits to this needy family. I recall thinking, "These social welfare policies are supposed to help people in need. But, in reality, the policies lack the flexibility to work in a real-life situation."

POLICY MATTERS

My understanding of the "we can help you (buyer beware)" nature of social welfare policies has served me well over the years. Currently, as president of a small private college, I still see the effects of rigid policies—policies that are designed to help the needy often fail to do so. Now my clients are college students, and my goal is to help as many of them as possible to get a quality education. Although I am not in a social work agency, I still see myself as a social worker. As a higher education administrator, I engage in macro practice, and I use my clinical social work skills to help students reach their goal of successfully completing college.

The greatest challenge I face in helping students is the "we can help you (buyer beware)" dilemma. This time it is because of rigid government policies about providing financial support for needy students, and again I find myself feeling overwhelmed by the difficulty of the task.

Although our college is located in a wealthy area, over 90 percent of our 650 students receive financial assistance. Students represent the spectrum of the socioeconomic scale, ranging from poverty to great wealth. The challenge for the poor students is to complete four years of college with financial assistance that is scarcely enough to get them through. To survive, these students struggle to adapt. They move off campus because their federal and state assistance is not enough to cover the cost of dormitory living. I have known students who work three part-time jobs but have no money at the end of the month to buy food. To help, the college provides free lunches for all students several times a month. This allows students to get healthy meals without shame or stigma. It also gives them a common dining experience, with attendant social support from faculty and fellow students. However, these meals are inadequate to deal with the students' problem. Just as elementary and middle school teachers see students falling asleep in their classes—unable to pay attention because they are tired, hungry, and frustrated—I see many of these same obstacles as we educate the future leaders of our country.

A vital part of my job is to advocate for these students. I advocate for financial aid and other student support programs that are sufficient to enable students to fully engage in learning. As a social worker, I am aware of the historical basis for helping people to succeed in the face of poverty. The first social workers emerged from the group of women who began entering colleges in large numbers in the United States in the latter part of the 19th century (Jimenez, 2010). At the same time, university faculty expanded the social sciences, which led to an emerging interest in new solutions to old social problems such as poverty. The idea that providing financial support to poor people could help them to achieve social and economic success became the basis for the nation's policies regarding financial assistance to college students.

THE PITFALLS OF STUDENT LOANS

Many people think that government-funded student loans and grants are a "magic bullet" for college students. Although most students in need are able to obtain federal and private loans and grants, when it comes to repayment they are at the mercy of the economic cycle.

Students accrue large debts they that may be unable to pay off after graduation because of their inability to find well-paying work. Due to financial problems, some students are forced to leave college or to cut back to less than half-time enrollment. Current loan contracts require that students in these circumstances begin repayment within six months, an impossible task for any student unable to find well-paying work. Even students who are able to continue full-time study are often so discouraged by the prospect of long years of repayment that they lessen their debt load by taking on more part-time work. This places enormous pressure on them and jeopardizes their college success.

There is a great need for personal financial literacy regarding student loans. Students need to understand that government-based student loans are, with rare exception, forever obligations; these loans are not wiped out in the event of personal bankruptcy. Because parents often cosign on private educational loans, these debts have been known to pursue the family even after the death of a student.

Once again, I see a "we can help you (buyer beware)" dilemma: Although the government offers financial aid to support a college education, the amount of aid is insufficient. Predictably, when students drop out of college or fail as a result, politicians have yet another argument for cutting student loan programs. A student loan policy that was truly humane would provide students with the support they need to succeed and loans that are significantly reduced through participation in public service programs after graduation. Students could then complete their studies with less financial and emotional stress and face an easier road as they launch their working careers.

On October 26, 2011, President Obama announced his plan to reduce student debt, and it is a step in the right direction. According to Field (2011),

> under Mr. Obama's plan, current students who have both direct loans and bank-based guaranteed loans will get an interest-rate reduction if they consolidate into the government's direct-loan program. Roughly 5.8 million students could qualify for the benefit, the White House estimates.
>
> The president is also accelerating a reduction in the maximum percentage of discretionary income that borrowers in income-based loan-repayment plans pay, from 15 percent to 10 percent. That cut was scheduled to take effect in 2014, but Mr. Obama's plan moves it up two years.

As Field went on to say, this will help current students if their debt falls into certain categories, but it will not help those who have graduated and are saddled with large debt. In fact, their interest rate is about to double. Only Congress can reverse this devastating change and fully tackle the entire student debt crisis.

SOCIAL WORK MATTERS

The social work profession has advocated for supporting student success through the Dorothy I. Height and Whitney M. Young, Jr. Social Work Reinvestment Act, which would provide grant funding for students on the front end of their education. In addition, NASW has advocated for the College Cost Reduction Act, the Higher Education Act Reauthorization, and the National Health Service Corps Loan Repayment program, all of which address loan forgiveness or repayment. As a society, we must urge Congress to change bankruptcy laws to include student loan forgiveness.

We should allow college graduates to pay off their loans via public service by signing up for the Peace Corps, the Job Corps, or military service or by working as social workers in underserved neighborhoods or for underrepresented populations.

A well-educated population is essential to the restoration of our flagging economy. It is time for our legislators to offer viable debt financing, repayment, and retirement alternatives that provide motivation and hope.

DISCUSSION QUESTIONS

1. What policy changes could positively affect the success rate of college students who come from poor families?

2. How can social workers advocate for policy changes in student financial assistance programs?

3. What factors contribute to the perpetuation of inadequate student support policies in the United States?

REFERENCES

Field, K. (2011, October 26). Obama's student-loan plan scores political points but offers limited relief. *Chronicle of Higher Education.* Retrieved from http://chronicle.com/article/Loan-Plan-Scores-Political/129551/

Jimenez, J. (2010). *Social policy and social change: Toward the creation of social and economic justice.* Thousand Oaks, CA: Sage Publications.

EQUALITY AND SOCIAL JUSTICE

CHAPTER 28

LOVE, MONEY, DEATH, AND TAXES:
WHY MARRIAGE EQUALITY MATTERS

Jeane W. Anastas

Marriage is not just a social tradition; it is also a legal and financial institution. Marriage represents a commitment and celebration of love, and—as a public, state-regulated relationship—it confers many rights and imposes many responsibilities on those who choose to marry. Although cohabitation without marriage, divorce, remarriage, and childbearing and parenting outside of marriage are all becoming more common, marriage remains an aspiration for most people in intimate relationships. Same-sex marriage, however, is currently legal in only a few states and the District of Columbia (National Gay and Lesbian Task Force, 2011), and the federal Defense of Marriage Act (P.L. 104-199) (DOMA) requires that the federal government and all of its agencies and programs recognize only marriages between a man and a woman. The United States is one of only four Western democracies that does not recognize same-sex marriages or domestic partnerships (Weeks, 2008).

Marriage is normally thought of as a personal matter, and weddings are events designed to celebrate love and commitment for a lifetime going forward. Many couples choose to marry at the point that they have decided to begin "forming a family," because partners in a marriage take responsibility not only for each other's care and well-being but also for any child of that marriage, by birth or adoption.

POLICY MATTERS

Federal social policies are generally "pro marriage" (Lind, 2004). For example, the Temporary Assistance for Needy Families program contains a Healthy Marriage Initiative that encourages states to "support healthy marriage activities"; while arguing for the benefits of two-parent families for children, however, it limits this support to those in marriages the federal government recognizes (Administration for Children and Families, U.S. Department of Health and Human Services, 2011). Although not all within the lesbian, gay, bisexual, and transgender (LGBT) community think marriage is something to aspire to, in the United States issues surrounding illness and inheritance encountered by gay men with AIDS and the increase in childbearing and childrearing among lesbians (and, in the case of the latter, gay men) have fueled efforts to legalize same-sex marriage (Weeks, 2008).

In 1997 and again in 2004, the U.S. General Accounting Office (GAO) issued reports on federal laws in which "marital status is a factor in determining or receiving benefits, rights, and privileges" (GAO, 2004, p. 1) to identify the reach of DOMA. In 1997, the report identified 1,049 of these, and in 2003 that number had grown to 1,138. Those affecting the most people were in the categories of Social Security and related programs, including housing and food stamps; veteran, service member, and federal civilian employee benefits; taxation; immigration; and employment benefits more generally.

SOCIAL WORK MATTERS

The social work profession calls for equal rights for LGBT people in all areas, including marriage for those who choose it (NASW, 2009). In addition, many of the provisions about marriage enumerated by the GAO affect programs at the core of the social safety net and relate to concerns that the social work profession has had since its inception.

Why does marriage equality matter to social work? Using my own life situation, this chapter illustrates why this issue is relevant to social work practice in aging, health care, and child and family services as well as for those serving LGBT clients and communities and those who make advancing human and civil rights a focus of their practice.

NARRATIVE

When same-sex marriage became legal in Massachusetts through a state Supreme Court decision, my life partner J. and I had been living together for 25 years. Together, we had been providing for three children from my previous traditional marriage, we owned a home, and we had balanced two professional careers. However, health problems had by then forced J. into early retirement, and we wanted to take whatever steps we could to address access to affordable health insurance, to have unquestioned access to each other during a serious illness, and to provide for each other through inheritance in the ways that we intended.

Although the town clerk in our small rural community felt "personally uncomfortable" issuing us a marriage license, at her suggestion we went to City Hall in nearby Northampton and received a license to marry for "Party A" and "Party B" (not "husband" and "wife," as on previous forms). On July 3, 2004, we were married by a justice of the peace on the patio of our home in the company of our grown children, their spouses, and our closest friends.

Why did we marry? Our first reason was an intangible one: We wanted to be part of making gay and lesbian relationships visible. We also wanted to put to rest the ideas that the legalization of same-sex marriages would somehow weaken traditional ones. Our marriage would become part of our state's vital statistics; our relationship would be seen and counted. Perhaps we were also seeking the greater sense of social inclusion that can result from marriage recognition (Badgett, 2011; Rothblum, Balsam, & Solomon, 2011).

Our relationship, and especially J.'s role as a coparent to our children, had at times been marginalized. To illustrate, one of our children suffered an acute and life-threatening illness when a college student, one that required risky emergency surgery. When we all gathered in the hospital emergency room to hear the diagnosis and the treatment plan, the noncustodial father was included by the physician in the meeting but J.'s presence in the discussion was questioned. Would it have made a difference if she could have been introduced as my wife? To their credit, once they got to know us all, the medical team did not make this mistake again, although that moment was painful in the middle of what was already a difficult time. (Most important, our son ultimately made a full recovery.) No caring "coparent" should be excluded from the ability to be there for a sick child. However, the hospital had no legal obligation to allow J. to visit our son during the many days he was in intensive care, nor would they have needed to do so if the patient had been me.

Prior to the opportunity to marry, J. and I had gone to the trouble and the expense of crafting legal documents, like reciprocal durable power of attorney documents and health care proxies, to ensure our access to each other when hospitalized and to establish our right to make medical decisions or take financial actions for one another when needed. By getting married, we would not need this special paperwork to exercise these rights and responsibilities for one another in Massachusetts or any other state that might recognize the marriage, as New York (our other state of residence) now does.

DISCUSSION

Because of DOMA, however, no one in a same-sex marriage in the United States currently enjoys "marriage equality." In the summer of 2011, the Justice Department decided not to defend DOMA in the federal courts, although other parties may choose to do so. In addition, there is currently legislation before Congress seeking to repeal DOMA, known as the Respect for Marriage Act (S.598/H.R.1116), which President Obama supports.

Why is this change needed? Here are some of the most important inequities that gay and lesbian married couples face under DOMA:

Social Security benefits are provided to surviving spouses who are 60 and over when a covered spouse dies. A spouse also has the choice to collect a benefit in retirement that is based on his or her own earnings history or that of the spouse. These benefits are not allowed to those in same-sex marriages. In addition, the Internal Revenue Service taxes retirement plan proceeds and other assets that go to a surviving partner who is not in a federally recognized marriage.

In our case, J. had to retire early due to ill health and, hence, collected a reduced Social Security check. If I die before she does, she will not be able to access the larger monthly benefit that would accrue to her as my widow, although a husband of mine would. Participants in all federal retirement systems, including those related to military service, cannot provide for same-sex partners or spouses either. In addition, if J. and I still had minor children, they could not receive benefits through the Social Security system as a result of her retirement, death, or disability unless she had legally adopted them, which is not possible in many states. Although most think of Social Security as a system that supports older people, about 4.4 million children in the United States also currently receive benefits (Social Security Administration, 2011). On the basis of U.S. Census data, it is estimated that there are at least 250,000 children being reared in same-sex households (Carey, 2011), and the effects of DOMA on access to Social Security benefits is only one way in which they currently enjoy fewer economic and social protections than do children whose parents are in traditional marriages.

Domestic partner employment benefits are taxed (Badgett, 2007). I am fortunate that my employer offers domestic partner benefits. Especially before J. was eligible for Medicare (retired but under the age of 65), the ability to provide health insurance coverage for J. when she no longer had any of her own through employment was essential. However, I pay income tax on the value of those benefits; those in marriages recognized by the federal government do not. This reduces our ability to save for our needs in old age, among other things. This inequity is just one of many that, despite the myth of affluence (Badgett, 2001), leave gay and lesbian people, on average, with fewer economic resources than others, with problems of poverty being especially acute for younger lesbians, transgender people, children in households headed by same-sex couples, and lesbian couples over 65 years of age (Half in Ten, 2011).

These are only some of the inequities imposed by DOMA; others affect such well-known programs as the Consolidated Omnibus Budget Reconciliation Act of 1985 (P.L. 99-272); the Family and Medical Leave Act of 1994 (P.L. 103-3); and provisions for the economic support of dependent children in the income tax code, such as head of household tax status and the child tax credit if the person in the household with income is not the biological or adoptive parent of the child. Children of parents in traditional marriages can automatically benefit from the resources of both parents; children of those in same-sex marriages or domestic partnerships often cannot.

Even if DOMA were to be repealed or found unconstitutional, there are currently 29 states with constitutional amendments and an additional 12 that have laws that limit the recognition of marriages in similar ways (Human Rights Campaign, 2010). Because states have long had the right to define who can and cannot marry, more work would likely have to be done to make marriage and related state-level benefits accessible to all same-sex couples who decide to marry.

Not everyone approves of same-sex relationships or parenting, and gay marriage is not a cause embraced by all in the gay community (LaSala, 2007). Nevertheless, polls show that the majority of Americans support equal inheritance rights, employment benefits rights, access to earned Social Security benefits, and hospital visitation rights for same-sex couples (Carey, 2011). However, federal and state barriers to marriage equality are not the only important issue facing LGBT people. Although some states and localities provide them, there are no federal civil rights protections in place for LGBT people. Nor is there any federal law with respect to protection from workplace discrimination, although one has long been proposed (the Employment Non-Discrimination Act [H.R. 1397/S. 811, 2011]), despite the fact that workplace rights for LGBT people have widespread public support. There are important health inequalities facing LGBT people, including young people (Gay and Lesbian Medical Association, 2001; Human Rights Campaign, 2011). The drive for marriage equality, however, has gained some momentum and deserves our best advocacy efforts. Meanwhile, many, like J. and me, are "voting with our feet for the ordinary virtues of care, love, mutual responsibility," and "the importance of being ordinary" (Weeks, 2008, p. 792).

DISCUSSION QUESTIONS

1. Is marriage equality the most important priority for advocacy on behalf of LGBT people? Why or why not?

2. What constitutes a couple? What constitutes a family? How could your definition be incorporated into policy?

3. What effect does the recognition of "gay marriage" have on people who do not identify as gay, lesbian, or bisexual? Are these positive or negative?

REFERENCES

Administration for Children and Families, U.S. Department of Health and Human Services. (2010). *ACF healthy marriage initiative.* Retrieved from http://www.acf.hhs.gov/healthy marriage/about/factsheets_hm_matters.html

Badgett, M.V.L. (2001). *Money, myths, and change: The economic lives of lesbians and gay men.* Chicago: University of Chicago Press.

Badgett, M.V.L. (2007). *Unequal taxes on equal benefits: The taxation of domestic partner benefits.* Retrieved from http://www.hrc.org/resources/entry/the-williams-institute-center-for-american-progress

Badgett, M.L.V. (2011). Social inclusion and the value of marriage equality in Massachusetts and the Netherlands. *Journal of Social Issues, 67,* 316–334.

Carey, R. (2011, July 20). *Written testimony submitted to the Committee on the Judiciary, U. S. Senate.* Retrieved from http://thetaskforce.org/downloads/release_materials/final_tf_doma_testimony_7_20%20_11.pdf

Consolidated Omnibus Budget Reconciliation Act of 1985, P.L. 99-272, 100 Stat. 82 (1986).

Defense of Marriage Act, P.L. 104-199, 110 Stat. 2419 (1996).

Family and Medical Leave Act of 1994, P.L. 103-3, 107 Stat. 6 (1993).

Gay and Lesbian Medical Association. (2001). *Healthy people 2010: A companion document for LGBT health.* San Francisco, CA: Author. Retrieved from http://www.glma.org/_data/n_0001/resources/live/HealthyCompanionDoc3.pdf

Half in Ten. (2011, October). *Restoring shared prosperity: Strategies to cut poverty and expand economic growth.* Retrieved from http://halfinten.org/uploads/support_files/restoring-shared-prosperity-2010.pdf

Human Rights Campaign. (2010, January). *Statewide marriage prohibitions.* Retrieved from http://www.hrc.org/files/assets/resources/marriage_prohibitions_2009%281%29.pdf

Human Rights Campaign. (2011). *Issue: Health.* Retrieved from http://www.hrc.org/issues/health

LaSala, M.C. (2007). Too many eggs in the wrong basket: A queer critique of the same-sex marriage movement [Commentary]. *Social Work, 52,* 181–183.

Lind, A. (2004). Legislating the family: Heterosexist bias in social welfare policy frameworks. *Journal of Sociology & Social Welfare, 31*(4), 21–35.

National Association of Social Workers. (2009). Lesbian, gay, and bisexual issues. In *Social work speaks: National Association of Social Workers policy statements, 2009–2012* (8th ed., pp. 218–222). Washington, DC: NASW Press.

National Gay and Lesbian Task Force. (2011, June 28). *Relationship recognition for same-sex couples in the U.S.* Retrieved from http://thetaskforce.org/downloads/reports/issue_maps/rel_recog_6_28_11.pdf

Rothblum, E. D., Balsam, B.K.B., & Solomon, S. E. (2011). The longest "legal" U.S. same-sex couples reflect on their relationships. *Journal of Social Issues, 67,* 302–315.

Social Security Administration. (2011, June). *Benefits for children* (Publication No. 05-10085 ICN 468550). Retrieved from http://ssa.gov/pubs/10085.html

U.S. General Accounting Office. (2004). *Defense of Marriage Act: Update to prior report.* Retrieved fromhttp://www.gao.gov/new.items/d04353r.pdf

Weeks, J. (2008). Regulation, resistance, recognition. *Sexualities, 11,* 787–792.

CHAPTER 29

INEQUALITY, SOCIAL WELFARE POLICY, AND SOCIAL WORK

Vicki Lens and Irwin Garfinkel

Income inequality in the United States peaked in the 1920s, just before the stock market crash, and then decreased for the next half century, most dramatically during the Great Depression and World War II. A similar trend occurred in other advanced industrialized or rich nations in Western Europe. In the past 30 years, inequality has increased in nearly all rich nations, especially in the United States. Indeed, the share of income of the top 1 percent of the population, as reported in tax returns in 2007, was nearly as great it was in 1928 (Saez, 2009).

Among families with children, the richest one-fifth of the population earns about 10 times as much as the poorest one-fifth (Garfinkel, Rainwater, & Smeeding, 2010). Welfare state programs, which include all public health, education, and welfare programs, in combination with the taxes required to finance them, reduce inequality. The richest quintile of families pay more in taxes than they receive in benefits, while the poorest quintile receive more in benefits than they pay in taxes, narrowing the ratio of top to bottom from 10 to 3 (Garfinkel et al., 2010). Welfare state programs also reduce economic insecurity and poverty and promote human development. Unfortunately, the U.S. welfare state is less adequate than that of many other rich nations. As is illustrated vividly in the case below, the United States falls short in reducing insecurity and poverty and in promoting human development for those at the bottom of the economic ladder.

NARRATIVE

Ellie is a 22-year-old African American woman who became pregnant at 20 years old. She had hoped to marry the father of her child, but he abandoned her shortly after learning she was pregnant. Ellie has been unable to locate him to obtain child support. Although she worked in a variety of jobs, Ellie lost her employment when she became pregnant and was then unable to pay her rent. Proud of her ability to support herself until then, she avoided seeking help from the Department of Social Services (DSS) and even slept in her car. But then, as she explained, "the car died on me. I didn't have that, so I had no other choice" but to apply for welfare. The DSS placed Ellie in a homeless shelter, and after two months, she was able to find housing for her and her newborn son.

Housing choices were scarce for Ellie, as there was very little affordable housing in the suburban county she lived in. She rented an apartment in the basement of a private home, but after a year the landlord decided he "didn't want to deal with social services anymore," as he wanted to collect rent for the apartment "off the books." The DSS told her they would not help her pay her rent or moving expenses unless she was formally evicted, so she was unable to look for alternative housing until she was served with an eviction notice, three days before Christmas. Ellie and her son, then a year old, stayed with a friend for a few weeks but were forced to leave when the DSS was too slow in paying her rent there. She ended up homeless once again, and DSS placed her and her son in a shelter nearly 50 miles away from her family and support system. After a few more weeks, DSS finally processed the paperwork for a new apartment she had found.

Ellie may now lose this apartment because she recently returned to work full time, making her ineligible for welfare but leaving her without enough money to pay all expenses. Ellie has substantial work experience, especially in telemarketing and retail sales. As she explained, "I'm not the type that's going to sit at home. You know, I was the only person in the shelter with a résumé. When you have a newborn, the first six months you are at home every day with the baby. But then after that I was like, you know, staying basically at the poverty level, I couldn't take it anymore, so I got a part-time job right down the street." Ellie made $400 a month working as a telemarketer.

A family of two in the county where Ellie lives receives $712 a month in Temporary Assistance for Needy Families (TANF) benefits, the federal welfare program for low-income families. Ellie receives only $602, because some of her work income is subtracted from her grant. Because she had been homeless, Ellie also received a special supplemental grant of $552 from the county for housing, which—together with the $602 grant, her earnings, Supplemental Nutrition Assistance Program benefits (also known as food stamps), Medicaid, and child care benefits enabled her to afford the $1,000-a-month rent for her apartment.

After Ellie's life was unsettled by the birth of her son, her abandonment by his father, eviction, and homelessness, she regained her footing and created a stable life for her son and herself. Then she decided to return to work full time, having found a job on her own as a telemarketer making $12.50 an hour, or $438 a week. Ellie's new job, however, leaves her ineligible for welfare benefits, including the special housing supplement she was receiving, and day care, all of which she still needs to make ends meet. As Ellie explains, she comes home each month with $1,883 before taxes, out of which "I'm supposed to pay $1,000 for rent, plus child care, which is $250 a week, myself. So that's $2,000 a month right there." She is also no longer eligible for food stamps and has lost her child care subsidy. She will be losing her Medicaid, and her employer does not offer health insurance.

Ellie wants to continue working. She says, "They want us to work, I want to work. Give me a little help. I'm 22, I'm still young, I've still got the opportunity to make all my dreams come true." She tried talking to her caseworker at the DSS, telling him "you're expecting me to work, and pay my rent on my own, but you're gonna cut off my day care? How am I supposed to work?" He told her, "Well, you know you're making excess income, you only have one kid, you should pay your bills yourself." Ellie asked for help to attend school or a training program so can she could earn more income but was informed that there was no money in the budget for that and her only option was to work. As she explains her choices, she can go back to working part time and remain eligible for welfare, or she can do the seemingly impossible and work two full-time jobs, the only way she will ever make enough money to support herself and her son.

POLICY MATTERS

There are many people like Ellie who live on the edge between welfare dependency and a fragile self-sufficiency. They teeter between the two because of gaping holes in both our economic system and our social safety net. As Ellie's case shows, economic and social stability require employment that pays a living wage, secure and stable housing, access to health care, and supports that allow parents to properly care for their children, including day care when they are working or time at home when the children are very young. It also requires a welfare bureaucracy that intercedes quickly and efficiently when needs arise.

Basically, all of these elements are missing, beginning at birth. The United States is the only rich nation without a national paid parental leave program (Garfinkel et al., 2010). Research shows that Ellie's decision to stay home for the first six months of her child's life was the right one for her child's long-term development (Majumdar, Piasecki, Raskin, & Waldroup, 2008). Welfare benefits helped her to achieve that, but at barely adequate levels. TANF permits an exemption from the work rules, which requires welfare participants to engage in work activities in exchange for their benefits, for only three months within the first year of a child's life.

Ellie has faced additional obstacles since she returned to work. Even though she earns $12.50 an hour, 72 percent more than the minimum wage of $7.25, she is still unable to pay all her expenses, even working full time. The earned income tax credit and the child tax credit help Ellie by increasing her annual income by $2,070, or about $172.50 per month, but Ellie can get the money only once a year in her income tax refund (Eamon, Wu, & Zhang, 2009). The child tax credit is very close economically to a universal child allowance, which every other rich nation has, except that child allowances arrive every month, when they are needed.

Ellie's position is especially precarious because she is a single parent and cannot rely on another wage earner to help cover the family's expenses. Although most poor single mothers like Ellie now establish paternity and legal entitlement to child support, the fathers of their children often pay very low or irregular amounts of child support because their incomes are so sporadic (Sinkewitz & Garfinkel, 2009). If the United States had a child support assurance system that guaranteed a minimum payment to each parent legally entitled to private child support, as is the case in the Scandinavian nations, Ellie and her son would be more economically secure (Garfinkel & Nepomnyaschy, 2009).

One of the major reasons that Ellie cannot stretch her income to cover her family's needs is the lack of affordable housing. The median rent for a two-bedroom apartment in the suburb where Ellie lives is $1,760, which is basically her entire monthly salary. Ellie could turn to public housing programs, which would lower her rent considerably and likely prevent another bout of homelessness, but such programs are scarce. There are two primary federal housing programs—public housing, which is owned and operated by the government, and the Section 8 program (also referred to as the Housing Choice Voucher program), which provides vouchers to subsidize rentals in the private housing market and limits the amount of rent a family must pay to 30 percent of its monthly adjusted income (U.S. Department of Housing and Urban Development, 2010).

To be eligible for Section 8, a family's income must not exceed 50 percent of the median income in the county where they live. The median income in Ellie's county of residence is $82,984; Ellie's annual income of $22,776 puts her well below the median; thus, she would be eligible for Section 8. There is no public housing in the county where Ellie lives, although if she lived in a county with such housing, she would likely be eligible for it. However, the high demand and low supply of public and Section 8 housing means long wait lists. Only about 25 percent to 30 percent of those who are eligible for housing subsidies receive them (Olsen, 2007). If the federal government provided sufficient funding through either public housing or Section 8 vouchers to assist all of those who are eligible, as it does for food stamps, a big part of Ellie's problems would be solved.

Child care costs are another large expenditure for Ellie. The cost of full-time day care can range from $4,000 to more than $13,000 a year, depending on the geographic location (National Association of Child Care Resources and Referral Agencies, 2010). When she was receiving public assistance, Ellie's child care was funded through the federal Child Care and Development Block Grant, which provides funding to states to help parents pay for child care, either in the home or in a child care center. States can also use funds from their TANF block grant to pay for child care. However, now that Ellie is no longer eligible for public assistance, she must pay for child care herself. If the United States provided universal child care as do Sweden, Denmark, and France, or fully funded entitlements to income-tested child care as do the Netherlands, Canada, and New Zealand, more of Ellie's problems would be solved (Garfinkel, Rainwater, & Smeeding, 2006).

Ellie is also no longer eligible for Medicaid because her annual income of $22,776 exceeds the 2011 income cap of $13,400 for a family of two. Her son, however, will continue to be eligible for Medicaid, because the income cap is set higher for children than for parents. Her employer does not provide health insurance, and Ellie cannot afford the cost of private health insurance. If Ellie lived in any other rich nation, she and her son would be covered by a national health insurance system (Garfinkel et al., 2010).

Ellie will eventually benefit from the federal Patient Protection and Affordable Care Act of 2010 (P.L. 111-148), and will receive a tax credit to help her purchase health insurance through an affordable insurance exchange, which is a private market mechanism set up by the law for individuals who do not have employer-based health care (Koh & Sebelius, 2010). The tax credit will be available to people with incomes between 100 percent and 400 percent of the poverty line. Ellie's income is well within these guidelines, but these benefits will not go into effect until 2014. Ellie is also no longer eligible for food stamps as her income is more than $4,000 over the gross income limit for a family of two in 2011, which is set at $18,204.

In sum, Ellie is part of the population most affected by income inequality and gaping holes in the American welfare state—the working poor. She earns too little money to pay for her basic needs but too much to qualify for help from most government programs. She will likely cycle between welfare and work, between homeless shelters and inadequate housing, as she struggles to provide for her son and herself.

SOCIAL WORK MATTERS

There are some steps a social work practitioner can take to help an individual like Ellie—including making sure she is getting all of the government benefits she is entitled to, especially if she loses her job. A social work practitioner might look for community college or vocational education programs, along with tuition assistance programs to enable Ellie to increase her skills and earn more income. He or she might also help Ellie put together a plan to reduce her housing and day care costs by looking for cheaper housing, such as a shared living arrangement, and more affordable day care. A social worker could also refer Ellie to nonprofit social service agencies that can provide emergency rental payments, food, day care, and other assistance.

However, a social worker will probably run into many of the same roadblocks that Ellie has already dealt with. Policy changes are clearly needed, although addressing inequality is extremely challenging. Although the United States led the world in the provision of mass public education throughout most of the 19th and 20th centuries, we have always been less generous when it comes to cash and in-kind assistance to the poor, and we have been laggards in the development of social insurance programs (Garfinkel et al., 2010). Still, progress is possible, and social workers have played an important role in advocating for programs to reduce economic insecurity and inequality. If the United States had paid parental leave, national health insurance, child allowances, child support assurance, fully funded child care and housing subsidy programs, and a more generous TANF program, Ellie's life would be far more economically secure, and her child's chances of flourishing educationally, economically, physically, and emotionally would be much higher.

There are many venues for social work practitioners to make their views known and to advocate for these changes in policy. Legislative bodies routinely hold hearings on various government programs, especially when they are coming up for reauthorization. Social workers can ask to testify, or submit written statements, using stories such as Ellie's to expose the gaps and flaws in our welfare state. State and federal agencies responsible for implementing social policies are required to solicit opinions from the public when issuing new rules and regulations. Social workers can respond by providing information about the effects of social policies and suggesting regulatory changes that make benefits more accessible. Social workers can also enter the public debate by writing letters to the editor and op-ed pieces or responding to others' blogs or writing their own. As social workers, we are well positioned to educate others about the daily struggles of our clients and what policy changes would help them most.

DISCUSSION QUESTIONS

1. If you were a policymaker, what sort of child support assurance program would you create, and what checks, balances, and regulations would you incorporate to make this program flourish?

2. What public assistance programs, in addition to those listed in the article, could Ellie benefit from?

3. Given the challenges involved in bringing about policy change, especially large-scale change, to what policy changes would you give the highest priority?

4. What do you think is the best way to approach an advocacy campaign on behalf of people with challenges like Ellie's? How would you frame the issues? To whom would you direct your arguments, and how?

REFERENCES

Eamon, M. K., Wu, C., & Zhang, S. (2009). Effectiveness and limitations of the earned income tax credit for reducing child poverty in the United States. *Children and Youth Services Review, 31*(8), 919–926.

Garfinkel, I., & Nepomnyaschy, L. (2009). Assuring child support: A reassessment in honor of Alfred Kahn. In S. B. Kamerman, S. Phipps, & A. Ben-Arieh (Eds.), *From child welfare to child well-being: An international perspective on knowledge in the service of making policy* (pp. 231–254). New York: Springer.

Garfinkel, I., Rainwater, L., & Smeeding, T. (2006). A re-examination of welfare states and inequality in rich nations: How in-kind transfers and indirect taxes change the story. *Journal of Policy Analysis and Management, 25,* 897–919.

Garfinkel, I., Rainwater, L., & Smeeding, T. (2010). *Wealth and welfare states: Is America a laggard or leader?* New York: Oxford University Press.

Koh, H. K., & Sebelius, K. G. (2010). Promoting prevention through the Affordable Care Act. *New England Journal of Medicine, 363,* 1296–1299.

Majumdar, N., Piasecki, M., Raskin, J., & Waldroup, W. (2008). Effects of experience on brain development. In A. Guerrero & M. Piasecki (Eds.), *Problem-based behavioral science and psychiatry* (pp. 31–47). New York: Springer.

National Association of Child Care Resources and Referral Agencies. (2010). *Parents and the high cost of child care* (NACCRRA Publication No. 937-0702). Arlington, VA: Author.

Olsen, E. O. (2007). *Promoting homeownership among low-income households* (Opportunity and Ownership Project Report No. 2). Washington, DC: Urban Institute.

Patient Protection and Affordable Care Act of 2010, P.L. 111-148, 124 Stat. 1025 (2010).

Saez, E. (2009). *Striking it richer: The evolution of top incomes in the United States.* Berkeley, CA: University of California Berkeley, Institute for Research on Labor and Employment.

Sinkewicz, M., & Garfinkel, I. (2009). Unwed fathers' ability to pay child support: New estimates accounting for multiple-partner fertility. *Demography, 46,* 247–263.

U.S. Department of Housing and Urban Development. (2010). *Fact sheet for HUD assisted residents* (HUD Publication No. 7787). Washington, DC: U.S. Government Printing Office.

CHAPTER 30

HOUSING:

A BASIC HUMAN RIGHT

Adrienne Walnoha and Tracy Soska

I n his final State of the Union address, on January 11, 1944, Franklin D. Roosevelt introduced to America a "Second Bill of Rights"—economic rights that included a "right of every family to a decent home." In 2011, the rate of homeownership is at the lowest level since 1998, with 66.5 percent of American households owning their home. The National Low Income Housing Coalition (2010) noted that America's foreclosure crisis has taken its toll on both homeowners and renters, with 40 percent of those affected by the crisis being renters, who often had no idea the home they were renting was in foreclosure proceedings. In this economic climate of recession, alarming foreclosure rates, and high rates of unemployment, social workers serve more and more individuals and families for whom housing is the most pressing need and often beyond their financial ability (Soska, 2008).

The National Low Income Housing Coalition (2010) report *Out of Reach* calculated the amount of money a household must earn to afford a rental unit at an area's fair market rent, which is based on the generally accepted affordability standard of paying no more than 30 percent of one's income for housing. From these calculations, the hourly wage a worker must earn to afford the fair market rent for a two-bedroom home was derived. The result of this calculation—called the "housing wage"—was, for example, $16.09 per hour for Pennsylvania (National Low Income Housing Coalition, 2010), but the minimum wage for Pennsylvania is $7.25 per hour (MinimumWage.org, 2011). Given the housing wage in Pennsylvania, for example, a person would need to work more than 80 hours per week at a minimum-wage job just to afford housing.

Although many service providers, including social workers, might see homelessness as a function of behavioral health issues, one must consider the impact of economic issues. Economic costs do not end at the individual level. Research conducted by the Coalition for the Homeless (2011) in New York City showed that to shelter a family for a year in a traditional homeless system costs about $38,000, whereas rental assistance, used to subsidize otherwise unaffordable rental rates, can be provided at the drastically reduced cost of $7,700.

These dollar figures do not speak to the emotional, social, educational, and physical costs of experiencing homelessness. Thus, although homelessness remains primarily an economic issue, it is often exacerbated by behavioral health and social issues. We must be especially mindful of this economic context and demand legislation and policies that support an ample supply of safe, decent, and affordable housing.

NARRATIVE

In Amelia's experience, housing policies, both local and national, created barriers to her family's recovery from homelessness. Amelia was working but had been homeless for two years. She had been married to an abusive alcoholic with whom she had two children. The abuse had shattered her sense of self, and she was clinically depressed. She knew she needed to get out of the relationship for the sake of her children (one boy and one girl). She took them first to a hotel she described as seedy, where people sometimes stayed by the hour, and they witnessed violence and drug use.

Amelia tried her best to get into a housing program. However, she was working full time and was not seen as having any type of disability. Shelters would not take her, as she had money for the hotel from her job. In addition, Amelia had a teenage son, and most local shelters would not accept teenage boys—an informal policy stemming from the belief that most battered women are battered by men, and having a young man in the facility might pose a safety and treatment risk.

Transitional and permanent housing programs didn't see her as having need. The staff questioned why a mother with a full-time job was homeless. However, what they didn't take into consideration was that Amelia had gone from place to place for two years. She had applied for subsidized housing and had been on waiting lists for over a year. None of these providers knew that she went to work late almost every day and had not actually completed her work in months. She was expecting to be fired any day when her employer discovered this.

She had relentlessly pursued housing supports and talked about this with her children. When program after program turned her down, she struggled to explain to them why. She said that she had to start showing them copies of her applications and denials so they would believe she was trying. She was also humiliated by the fact that she had to take her children with her at times to apply for services. The experiences included a visit to the public assistance office, where an armed guard at the door prompted her children to inquire if she had done something wrong.

Amelia's parents also blamed her for the situation and refused to help her. They felt she could have tried harder to keep her marriage together, and if she would have just stayed with her husband, none of this would have happened. Both Amelia and her children needed counseling to process their feelings about becoming homeless and staying homeless for so long. Therapy for the family had been ongoing and one of the most critical supports through their homeless journey.

Amelia submitted an application to Community Human Service's Families United Program in Pittsburgh, along with a four-page letter pleading her case. The Families United staff read her story and contacted her immediately. This was a woman doing everything she could and having doors repeatedly shut in her face. She was literally begging for help, and her shame showed in her words. The program accepted her and immediately began supporting her transition to permanent housing, where she resides to this day. Now, she works temporary jobs when she can, because her mental health treatment has progressed slowly and is emotionally exhausting. She acts as a volunteer for Community Human Services and serves as a motivational speaker. She volunteers at her son's school and with his sports teams. Her daughter just graduated from high school and is heading to college. The agency is working with Amelia to repair her credit in hopes that she will be able to buy a home, and she hopes to return to full-time work once her psychiatric medications have been stabilized.

POLICY MATTERS

Many systems and policies came into play to shape Amelia's journey through homelessness. Some systems and policies magnified her problems, and others helped in her recovery. The limitations of housing policies, systems, and programs are particularly acute and of concern in this case.

Housing providers themselves can present challenges. The homeless shelter system is designed to provide short-term accommodation. Typically it is not designed or funded to address treatment needs, serve atypical or large family configurations, house men and women together, or support individuals who appear able to provide for themselves. Many shelter facilities have limited space and cannot accommodate families with children, especially male teenagers. Those who do have space and serve families often have restrictions related to family size and composition. Amelia's case is a perfect example of how services are often not designed or funded to serve the variety of people who need them.

Another barrier to rehousing homeless individuals and families is the nature of the rental market. It is difficult to recruit private landlords to rent to individuals who have credit issues or poor rental records and are relying on an agency to subsidize their rent. Landlords are skeptical about whether participants will be able to care for their housing, will not invite troubled guests to visit, and will keep up with their portion of the rent. Stereotypes of homeless people are another concern. Frequently, one of the first questions landlords ask is whether the homeless clients are drug addicted or have a criminal record. Often the units individuals can afford to lease on the market are less attractive, small, outdated, in poor condition, and in less desirable neighborhoods. This also applies to subsidized properties.

The need for affordable housing vastly outstrips the supply, and people often pay significantly more for their housing—up to 50 percent of total income (National Low Income Housing Coalition, 2010). Affordable properties often take only the most financially attractive applicants or require so much paperwork that homeless individuals and families frequently give up on the process. For example, they may require a mailing address to which they can mail application updates and requests for additional information, and they often require a personal visit to the office. However, most shelter stays are limited 30 days and thus do not provide a stable mailing address. And getting to an office during office hours, without money and with one's belongings and children in tow, can incredibly difficult.

Finally, private and subsidized properties have many restrictions related to criminal history. Amelia had been named in a domestic dispute charge with her husband. She had also written bad checks while trying to keep her family housed in hotels. This resulted in several denials for housing, which created an even greater sense of hopelessness.

Service professionals can also make the road more difficult. Some judged Amelia on her appearance and showed limited insight into the causes of homelessness. Many individuals who are homeless do work, but there is a common misconception of staff working in the homeless and entitlement program service systems that if individuals experiencing homelessness are employed, they should not need financial assistance. Many landlords assume that someone who has been involved with the criminal justice system cannot be a good tenant or neighbor.

The processes to apply for entitlements are in themselves a barrier for people who desperately need and are qualified for those benefits, especially those experiencing mental health issues. Amelia felt powerless to help herself partly because she was ashamed to ask for services, which also speaks to the stigma still attached to mental illness and accessing social services.

In the end, master's-level social workers at Community Human Service were able to see through the surface to the heart of Amelia's struggles. They were able to give her and her family what they needed the most—a home. From that home, she could address her treatment needs, provide her children with a stable environment, keep them in the same school with peers with whom they could build relationships, and begin to heal.

SOCIAL WORK MATTERS

Amelia's struggle to get services sheds light on many of the flaws in the U.S. housing system. It should compel us as social workers to advocate for the preservation of existing affordable housing, the construction of new affordable housing, and a recalculation of fair market rents on the basis of area median income and the assumption that tenants should not pay more than 30 percent of their income for housing costs. It also provides us with critical insight into the costs of homelessness in our country.

In cities like New York, rental subsidies to make housing affordable cost the state and federal government 20 percent of what it would cost to provide shelter directly. With these savings, communities could create and maintain affordable housing and provide services to those who so desperately need them. In addition, when individuals and families can access affordable housing, they have more ability to access employment, primary and behavioral health care, and education and to build social capital and supports. It is the role and responsibility of social workers to ensure that decision-makers in local, state, and national government understand our nation's real housing crisis and the widespread need for affordable housing for those experiencing homelessness and poverty. On every level and for every issue, social workers create the space in which people in need can have a voice and the systems on which they depend can be held accountable for their basic human right—to have a home.

DISCUSSION QUESTIONS

1. How much do you or your family pay for housing, and how does this amount compare to the affordable housing standard of 30 percent of income or less?

2. Is affordable housing an issue in your area? If so, what are populations that you perceive as facing the most difficult housing challenges?

3. In his final state of the union address, Franklin Delano Roosevelt presented to the country a "Second Bill of Rights"—economic rights that included a "right of every family to a decent home." In reflection on this case, why have we in America yet to make adequate housing a basic human right?

REFERENCES

Coalition for the Homeless. (2011). *Rental assistance program.* Retrieved from http://www.coalitionforthehomeless.org/programs/rental-assistance-program

Minimum-Wage.org. (2011). *Pennsylvania minimum wage 2011, 2012.* Retrieved from http://www.minimum-wage.org/states.asp?state=Pennsylvania

National Low Income Housing Coalition. (2010). *Out of reach 2010.* Retrieved from http://www.nlihc.org/oor/oor2010

Soska, T. (2008.) Housing. In T. Mizrahi & L. Davis (Eds.), *Encyclopedia of social work* (20th ed.) (pp. 388–395). Washington, DC: NASW Press and Oxford University Press.

CHAPTER 31

IMMIGRATION:
LINKING POLICY TO PRACTICE

Mark Lusk

A mong the most contentious issues of the day is the debate about immigration. Seemingly irreconcilable positions at each end of the spectrum give the impression that a democratic solution to the polarized debate may be beyond reach. Yet the immigration debate of today is but another manifestation of the historic American oscillation between nativism and democratic inclusiveness that has shaped our country since its founding. Over the past two decades, immigration policy has been a particularly divisive subject that has sharply divided political parties and stalled any meaningful discussions about immigration reform and a path to citizenship for the more than 12 million undocumented immigrants who presently reside in the United States.

In this chapter, I link contemporary immigration policy to practice. Despite the xenophobic context in which immigration law and policy is enforced, there remains much that can be done to work effectively on behalf of immigrants, whether they are documented or not. I very briefly summarize immigration policy; identify some policy areas that provide windows to citizenship; and discuss how social workers, by working with attorneys and community activists, can advance the human rights of immigrants.

As has happened many times before in American history, the contemporary generation of immigrants is being used as a political football to whip up nativist hysteria and distract people from the more fundamental issues affecting our economy. In 1882, the Chinese Exclusion Act was passed to counter the "Yellow Scare" of a supposed deluge of "un-American" Chinese people invading our shores, when in fact Chinese laborers had arrived in the country legally, providing extremely low-cost, expendable, and exploitable labor to build the Union Pacific railway and to work on other hazardous projects on which many died. Today the same rhetoric—that groups of foreigners pose a risk to the safety, welfare, and culture of America—is invoked to castigate and demonize other groups of people who are here to take on difficult, low-paying, and dangerous jobs. The group that is most selectively demonized is made up of Hispanics, primarily those from Mexico.

In immigration debates, the more things change, the more they stay the same. During the Irish Potato Famine of 1845 to 1851, many thousands of displaced Irish families immigrated to America. Often, for lack of resources, they indentured themselves to hard physical labor to pay back the cost of the Atlantic passage. Anti-Irish hysteria was such that Irish-born Catholic immigrants were at the very bottom of the ethnic hierarchy, comparable to the freed African American slaves whose neighborhoods they shared. Oddly, the Irish were somehow considered to be non-white.

During the U.S. Mexican War of 1846 to 1848, American troops occupied Veracruz, and the bluecoat Army invaded Mexico City. On Mexico's defeat, the United States took possession of two-thirds of Mexican soil under the 1848 Treaty of Guadalupe Hidalgo—territory that includes present-day New Mexico, Arizona, California, and adjacent lands. The Gadsden Purchase of 1853 resolved a U.S.–Mexico border dispute concerning a major swath of territory in southern Arizona and New Mexico.

About a century later, Japanese American citizens lost their jobs, had their land and property confiscated, and were imprisoned in internment camps. Some 120,000 were imprisoned due solely because of their national origin. A few decades ago, we were worried about the Mariel Boat People from Cuba, who purportedly had been let out of Fidel Castro's prisons and were no more than "common criminals," even though it was widely known that Castro's prisons were full of political prisoners whose only offenses had been to seek greater freedom. And a decade earlier, Americans were at great pains to "assimilate" the many Vietnamese and Hmong refugees who had left Indochina in the wake of our failed two-decade-long military engagement in southeast Asia.

POLICY MATTERS

So the course of current events is grounded in history, a history of Manifest Destiny over North America and the Monroe Doctrine, which treated all of Latin America as our rightful backyard. The pendulum, which has periodically swung from democratic inclusion to nativist exclusion, is now is firmly at the apex of its rightward cyclic swing. The last effort to regularize the status of Mexicans in the United States since the Bracero Program of the 1940s and 50s occurred under the administration of President Ronald Reagan, who signed a sweeping immigration reform bill into law—the Immigration Reform and Control Act of 1986 (P.L. 99-238). That bill was jointly sponsored by Republicans and Democrats in Congress. Times have changed. The United States grants legal permanent residency to a little over one million people per year (Monger & Yankay, 2011). Lawful immigration from Mexico to the United States is severely restricted. About 140,000 Mexicans are able to immigrate to the United States per year (Monger & Yankay, 2011). Their pathway is primarily petitions by Mexican Americans holding citizenship to provide lawful admission to immediate family members ("family-sponsored immigrants"). Another key avenue is employment-based preferences for work in targeted areas of the labor market.

Although about one-tenth of all immigrants in the United States are granted refugee visas or political asylum, it is very rare for Mexicans to obtain such visas as they require proof of persecution or serious harm due to religion, ethnicity, political affiliation, or other criteria as defined in the Refugee Act of 1980 (P.L. 96-120). In El Paso, Texas, federal immigration judges deny over 83 percent of asylum cases from Mexico and Central America (Aguilar, 2011).

NARRATIVE: THE MEXICAN NATIONAL CRISIS

During the past five years, Mexico has been in a state of profound crisis as a result of a war declared by President Felipe Calderon on the Mexican drug cartels. The president has sent thousands of troops to the border region to combat organized crime. The result has been an abject failure that has backfired completely. Once kept at bay by massive bribes of government officials, the cartels are now in open combat with each other and with the government (Campbell, 2009). The result has been widespread mayhem and chaos. Since Calderon was elected, at least 60,420 Mexicans have been murdered (Hernandez, 2011).

As a result of the widespread violence and crime in Mexico, some 230,000 Mexicans have fled, at least half emigrating to the United States—often without documentation, effectively becoming a new group of refugees (Rice, 2011). As many as half of those refugees are believed to reside in greater El Paso, where they can blend in with the 82 percent Hispanic majority population.

The thousands of Mexicans who have fled to the United States during the past few years to escape death threats, extortion, property confiscation, and torture have little or no recourse to be granted asylum and must reside here on an undocumented basis with continual threat of deportation. My own ongoing interviews of Mexican refugees reveal that their greatest fear is apprehension and deportation by U.S. immigration authorities— deportation to what they believe will be their certain death.

SOCIAL WORK MATTERS

Although the situation that confronts refugees in the U.S.–Mexico border region is dire, organizations and individual leaders, including social workers, have come together to provide an array of services, advocacy, and legal remedies for Mexican refugees. I have been involved with that community for over four years as an activist and volunteer. Although it is unlikely that federal immigration policy will fundamentally change in the near term, social workers and attorneys can work to promote social justice for Mexican refugees and victims of violence. In most cities and large communities in which there is a substantial population of immigrants, there is an array of nongovernmental organizations (NGOs) that serve them. Found not only in border cities like El Paso, these agencies—from Portland, Oregon, to Providence, Rhode Island—provide assistance of all kinds to immigrants, both documented and not. NGOs include faith-based organizations that provide food, housing assistance, and sanctuary as well as counseling and shelter for victims of domestic violence. Also among them are nonprofit civil rights law firms.

Community leaders, well aware that there are no government benefits that accrue to unauthorized immigrants, have joined hands across the nation to reach out and provide shelter, sanctuary, legal aid, health care, and public advocacy to this population. In El Paso, for example, none of the NGOs that serve immigrants in the region ask for immigration documents as a condition of receiving services. Providers are concerned with the humanitarian issues that confront the population by working to promote social justice for people who have fled countries such as Guatemala, Honduras, and Mexico due to political and racial persecution. I have been involved in this since I was a postdoctoral fellow at the University of Arizona and participated in the Sanctuary Movement, which sheltered refugees from the U.S.-supported civil wars in Central America. Advocacy on behalf of immigrants, especially those who have been "criminalized" by the nation's xenophobic immigration laws, goes to the roots of social work and the Settlement House movement. And, as argued by Cleaveland (2011), it is central to the mission of contemporary American social work.

Two agencies in El Paso represent the best examples of how we can put policy into practice with immigrants: the Paso del Norte Civil Rights Project and Border Interfaith. The Paso del Norte Civil Rights Project was founded in 2006 by Gabriela Garcia. In time, the small El Paso satellite office of the Texas Civil Rights Project in Austin appointed staff attorneys, paralegals, and social work interns to work for civil rights in the region. The project provides pro bono legal services to residents of west Texas and southern New Mexico. Services include legal representation in both state and federal courts for victims of civil rights violations either by government agents or corporations. Also included is representation for victims of domestic violence and other crimes in immigration courts through the Violence Against Women Act of 2000 (P.L. 106-386), known as VAWA (Paso del Norte Civil Rights Project, 2012). In addition, the agency runs an economic justice program that focuses on recovering wages for workers whose employers do not pay them ("wage theft") or who violate their rights as defined by U.S. labor law. It is important to know that United States civil rights and labor laws also protect noncitizen immigrants, and the Paso del Norte Project aggressively prosecutes those who would deny immigrants their civil rights.

Paso del Norte has successfully litigated several Americans with Disabilities Act of 1990 (P.L. 101-336) cases. It settled a racial profiling suit involving the El Paso Sheriff's Department, requiring it to respect American immigration law. The project expanded VAWA services to 20 counties in the El Paso region. The project successfully settled a case involving the unlawful tasering of members of vulnerable groups in a suit stemming from an electronic assault by city police on a man undergoing from a diabetic seizure. The agency has also obtained numerous "T" and "U" visas, providing legal residency for numerous people who had, respectively, been trafficked and sold or been victims of severe crimes such as rape (Paso del Norte Civil Rights Project, 2012). Current immigration law permits persons who have been trafficked to be granted residency with the T Visa. The U Visa can grant immigration to individuals who petition for protection after being victims of qualifying criminal activity.

The second noteworthy project that puts policy into practice is Border Interfaith of El Paso. This group, founded in 1999, comprises members of Catholic, Protestant, and Jewish congregations and the local teacher's union. Border Interfaith is a member of the Industrial Areas Foundation (IAF), a national community action network founded by the late Saul Alinsky. The IAF is aimed at combating social injustice, and poverty, through grassroots organization (Stout, 2010). Border Interfaith, like its parent organization, attacks local-level powerlessness by registering voters, holding informational meetings for voters, convening candidate forums in which politicians answer specific questions "yes" or "no," and holding politicians responsible at public accountability sessions. In El Paso, elected officials have suddenly gained a new interest in previously ignored low-income sectors of the city as Border Interfaith has helped to organize those communities. Several exurban colonias—unincorporated residential areas inhabited by immigrants—have obtained residential water supply, electricity, and telephone service only after Border Interfaith and colonia residents pressured elected officials to provide what, under current policy, was their due. This is an excellent example of translating policy to practice through the democratic process.

In sum, new Americans, as well as those migrants whose legal status is not secure, deserve fair and equitable treatment. Although current immigration law provides few protections, NGOs staffed by attorneys, social workers, clergy, and volunteers can democratically press for change and justice under existing labor and civil rights laws.

DISCUSSION QUESTIONS

1. Describe the immigration debate in the Unites States. Which perspective on immigration is ascendant?

2. Is grassroots activism a realistic mechanism for changing current immigration policy? If so, how? If not, what could be an alternative strategy?

3. Why is immigration an issue for social workers?

4. What would an ideal immigration policy look like?

REFERENCES

Aguilar, J. (2011, July 30). Analysis reveals asylum records of judges. *New York Times*, Retrieved from http://www.nytimes.com/2011/07/31/us/31ttasylum.html?pagewanted=all

Americans with Disabilities Act of 1990, P.L. 101-336, 104 Stat. 327 (1990).

Campbell, H. (2009). *Drug war zone: Frontline dispatches from the streets of El Paso and Juarez*. Austin: University of Texas Press.

Cleaveland, C. (2011). We are not criminals: Social work advocacy and unauthorized migrants. *Social Work, 55,* 74–81.

Hernandez, E. M. (2011, December 12). En cinco años del Calderonismo, suman ya 60 mil 420 asesinados [In five years of the Calderonismo, the death toll totals 60,420]. *El Diario de El Paso,* p. B1.

Immigration Reform and Control Act of 1986, P.L. 99-238, 100 Stat. 3359 (1986).

Monger, R., & Yankay, J. (2011). *U.S. legal permanent residents, 2010: Annual flow report.* Washington, DC: Department of Homeland Security.

Paso del Norte Civil Rights Project. (2012). *Paso del Norte Civil Rights Project.* Retrieved from http://www.texascivilrightsproject.org/?page_id=480

Refugee Act of 1980, P.L. 96-120, 94 Stat. 102 (1980).

Rice, A. (2011, July 28). Life on the line. *New York Times.* Retrieved from http://www.nytimes.com/2011/07/31/magazine/life-on-the-line-between-el-paso-and-juarez.html?pagewanted=all

Stout, J. (2010). *Blessed are the organized: Grassroots democracy in America.* Princeton, NJ: Princeton University Press.

Violence Against Women Act of 2000, P.L. 106-386, 114 Stat. 1491 (2000).

CHAPTER 32

HELPING LOW-INCOME FAMILIES OBTAIN ECONOMIC SECURITY:

THE VALUE OF LOCAL PARTNERSHIPS

Trina R. Williams Shanks

SOCIAL WORK MATTERS

Helping low-income families receiving public assistance to find and maintain stable employment at a decent wage is a major challenge. The challenge became more urgent with the passage of the Personal Responsibility and Work Opportunity Reconciliation Act (P.L. 104-193) in August 1996 as the federal cash assistance program shifted from Aid to Families with Dependent Children to Temporary Assistance for Needy Families (TANF). With the addition of lifetime time limits and mandatory work rules, monetary support for families raising children is no longer an entitlement. Recently, the increased unemployment that has resulted from the 2007 to 2009 recession makes finding stable work and maintaining economic security even more challenging. A strategic mix of partnerships and collaborations at the local level can often help low-income families to navigate economic barriers and pitfalls that are particularly daunting in a difficult economy. This chapter recounts my role in helping to create a program that offers such a niche of opportunity in an often-shifting political landscape.

NARRATIVE

In the mid-1990s, two churches in Nashville created a strategic plan to open a community center through which they could serve residents in their surrounding neighborhoods. Their intention was to provide low-income households access to services that would help support their families as they attempted to make the transition from welfare to work. The plan was quite ambitious and included purchasing a centrally located building, coordinating pro bono medical, dental, and mental health services and offering a space for meetings and child-centered activities. In the summer of 1997, the nonprofit organization Christian Community Services started by these two congregations (one predominantly African American and the other predominantly white) invited me to work on a temporary contract to help them implement portions of the plan to get the project started.

My first several weeks were spent in strategic meetings with parties ranging from the mayor to leaders of local human service organizations to members of the two congregations. These conversations allowed me to become familiar with a range of perspectives and what relevant stakeholders were willing to contribute to the effort. One thing was very clear: although many were pleased that the two congregations wanted to become more involved in assisting economically vulnerable families, no one was ready to sign a six-figure check to purchase the building and fund the original vision fully.

Once the board reaffirmed that I was not expected to work full time on fundraising, we agreed to launch a pilot to create an on-site family mentoring program. We asked for referrals of low-income families either receiving TANF or living in public housing who were struggling and might benefit from a network of support provided by the two congregations. We made it clear that we could not guarantee jobs and would not be a typical workforce development program, but that we would commit to supporting the individuals as long as they needed.

Eight families had agreed to participate when we launched the program in fall 1997. Although most were single mothers with young children trying to cope with the new expectations and work requirements that came with cash assistance, our initial group was quite diverse. Two had recently completed drug rehabilitation and were trying to assume the daily responsibilities of living sober. One was diagnosed with a serious mental illness, and a few others exhibited potential signs of depression. Another was married and living independently, but her partner had been incarcerated, so she also was raising young children alone.

Each of these families was assigned a mentor, either an individual or a couple from one of the sponsoring congregations, who committed to work with them in the pilot program for three months. We had a weekly meeting that lasted about two hours—including a prepared dinner, the children attending an age-appropriate tutoring or activity session, and the adults attended a life-skills session along with their mentors. There were a few additional activities, but the main expectation was that mentors would meet with their assigned families independent of these scheduled sessions two to three times during the quarter to get to know one another and discuss any existing issues more in depth. For some participants, the main engagement occurred during the scheduled weekly meetings and the interactions that took place within the group. Others rarely attended because of work and other commitments, but they built strong relationships with their mentors and stayed connected to the program, sometimes by sending their children to events. A few withdrew and didn't actively participate.

Several participants started telling their friends and families about the program and asking whether others could enroll. The official response was that others could attend the weekly sessions as long as they weren't disruptive, but they wouldn't be assigned a mentor until the next quarter began. Thus, we had a core group, plus a following that shifted from week to week, comprising participant guests and volunteers who took turns helping to prepare and serve meals, lead the children's sessions, and provide transportation.

Although the program started out with little formal structure, a few interesting things developed naturally. Participants who attended the weekly sessions regularly appreciated the guest speakers and life-skills topics, but often ended up counseling one another and providing information amongst themselves. Volunteers who worked with the young people began to investigate educational requirements and often worked alongside parents to advocate for the children at their schools to ensure that they received what they needed to make academic progress.

Individual breakthroughs sometimes occurred through these new relationships. One mentor was able to help a participant apply for and obtain a job with flexible hours in his organization. Another participant finally got her driver's license restored after her mentors went with her to court and helped her work through the paperwork and secure fine reductions. A group of volunteers went thrift store shopping with participants and helped them pick out outfits that looked nice and would be appropriate for a job interview. Two participants attended our board retreat, as the first quarter ended and we made decisions on how to continue the program, and provided wonderful insights as to how the program might be improved. One of the most important developments, however, was that we gained an inside view of public housing just as major changes were about to occur.

Our initial group was quite diverse. They lived throughout the city in settings that ranged from Section 8 rentals to four different public housing developments. This not only made providing transportation difficult, it also prevented the program from having a strong presence in any one community. And given that participants faced very different issues, it was hard to organize a set of life lessons that would be relevant to everyone (the session on managing finances received the most positive evaluation).

One participant stayed in a public housing complex that had been selected for renovation as part of the first HOPE VI program grant in the city.[1] She expressed concern to me about what would happen to the residents who were being relocated as the old buildings were torn down and new ones were built. This led to a series of conversations with local housing

---

[1]HOPE VI stands for Housing Opportunities for People Everywhere, which was launched in 1992. Its aim is to help severely distressed public-housing communities with revitalization efforts that include advanced physical improvements, management improvements, social and community services to address resident needs, and more mixed-income settings (see Popkin et al., 2004; U.S. Department of Housing and Urban Development, n.d.).

authority staff and eventually with the developers and architects who designed plans for the public housing renovation, during which a new vision for our program emerged.

We continued to run the quarter-by-quarter family mentoring program, and several of the initial eight families remained engaged (some agreeing to become peer mentors). Our nonprofit went on to negotiate a memorandum of understanding with the local housing authority. Our organization would pay to have additional space built into the new HOPE VI community center, where the program would then be housed. Although already participating families and referrals were welcome to reenroll, our focus would shift to recruiting families as they entered the new housing development, with the goal of working with them as they articulated their long-term goals and put together five-year self-sufficiency plans. In addition, the program introduced an Individual Development Account (IDA) program, which provided matched savings incentives that participants could use for asset development—specifically, education, starting a business, or buying a new home.

Once our vision became clearer and we found a real niche, the program could begin to ask more of participants. Rather than continuing to talk generally about financial management, we developed a structured financial education program that eventually linked participants to sound advice and real monetary resources. In order to qualify, participants had to be working and could not miss more than two classes. They received individualized guidance on their self-sufficiency plans as well as an educational agreement for their children. Not everyone who entered the new public housing area was interested in participating in our program, but a steady stream of residents (about one-third) did choose to enroll. Many have obtained support and resources to reach their goals of education, business ownership, and home ownership and are no longer on public assistance.[2]

POLICY MATTERS

As mentioned earlier, the passage of the Personal Responsibility and Work Opportunity Reconciliation Act and the conversation on helping low-income families make the transition from welfare to work was part of the backdrop that informed this project. Similarly, the HOPE VI program, administered by the federal Department of Housing and Urban Development (HUD), created circumstances that matched well with our program strengths. Residents had access to high-quality affordable housing in a mixed-income setting. When they enrolled, they were enthusiastic and focused on making a new start. A natural community was formed in specific geographic areas. In fact, based on the complementarity between the evolving work and the federal program, the two congregations went on to establish partnerships with two other HOPE VI developments located near their church buildings.

---

[2]For a more detailed summary of the theoretical model undergirding the program and statistics on its progress through 2009, see Williams Shanks, Boddie, and Rice (2010).

As a researcher in the area of asset building,[3] I am particularly excited about a lesser-known opportunity offered through HUD—the Family Self-Sufficiency (FSS) Program (Notice of Availability, 2011a, 2011b).[4] The FSS program was first established by the Cranston-Gonzalez National Affordable Housing Act (P.L. 101-625) in 1990 as a strategy for helping families who are receiving public assistance to become financially self-sustaining. The FSS program has two components: a five-year contract designed with a case manager to outline goals moving the household toward financial independence and the establishment of an escrow savings account.

Residents of public housing pay 30 percent of their total income in rent. To eliminate disincentives to employment, if household income increases, any additional rent collected based on the increase goes into the escrow account. Once the household fulfills its contract, moving out of public housing and not receiving public cash assistance for 12 months, the full amount of the savings in the escrow account is transferred to the head of household.

Some note that the FSS program, although a sound policy, has limited participation (Cramer, 2004; Rohe & Kleit, 1999; Sard, 2001). The federal government subsidizes the escrowed rent increases but does not pay the local housing authority for additional staff to run the program or provide the necessary case management. Thus, our program made a natural partner. Our staff provides case management, and volunteer mentors can offer more individualized support. Through such partnerships, all the major components of the FSS program are met. By offering a network of support and resources, our program provided a buffer that encouraged participants not to allow temporary setbacks to deter their progress. By establishing emergency savings accounts in addition to the HUD escrow account, participants acquired resources to handle unexpected expenses. When they finally do leave public housing, participants are in a better position to manage successfully on their own. Community action agencies and other local organizations that run IDA programs could also be recruited to partner with the local housing authority to start FSS programs by offering case management and supportive services.

---

[3]Asset building refers to strategies that increase financial and tangible assets such as savings, homes, and businesses. It is based on the assumption that social welfare should be discussed not only in terms of income and consumption but also in terms of the development of long-term resources for individuals, families, and communities. One well-known example of this approach is the IDA; other examples include Child Development Accounts (also called Child Savings Accounts), eliminating asset limits in public benefits, and emphasizing saving rather than credit in financial practices. See the Center for Social Development Web site (http://csd.wustl.edu/AssetBuilding/Pages/default.aspx) for research reports as well as national and international examples.

[4]Although there is no strong experimental evidence of outcomes, a recent evaluation of the program by HUD found that program participants are more likely than nonparticipants to earn higher incomes and remain employed (de Silva, Wijewardena, Wood, & Kaul, 2011).

Although I now study and develop new policy ideas that offer more structural and universal approaches to providing greater economic security to low-income families and their children, working with this project made it clear that being engaged with and knowledgeable about existing policies and programs that affect low-income families is also beneficial. Working with existing programs, it is possible to knit together strategic partnerships and collaborations that can provide a better transitional safety net until the political moment arrives when more progressive policy change is possible. Such a creative partnership between policy and local practice can make any government investment more effective.

DISCUSSION QUESTIONS

1. How did the passage of the Personal Responsibility and Work Opportunity Reconciliation Act influence the economic security of low-income households with children?

2. Describe some of the ways that Christian Community Services assisted low-income families and how did the program change after establishing a partnership with the local housing authority?

3. What is asset building, and how are policies and programs that help low-income families generate long-term financial resources distinct from other forms of assistance?

4. What is the Family Self-Sufficiency Program, and what are some of the reasons that it has had limited participation?

REFERENCES

Cramer, R. (2004, October). Family self-sufficiency program: An asset-building opportunity. *Shelterforce Magazine, 137*. Retrieved from http://www.nhi.org/online/issues/137/FSS.html

Cranston-Gonzalez National Affordable Housing Act, P.L. 101-625, 104 Stat. 4079 (1990).

de Silva, L., Wijewardena, I., Wood, M., & Kaul, B. (2011). *Evaluation of the Family Self-Sufficiency Program: Prospective study.* Retrieved from http://www.huduser.org/portal/publications/affhsg/eval_fssp.html

Family Self-Sufficiency Act of 2011, HR 34, 112th Cong., 1st Sess. (2011).

Notice of Availability: Notice of Funding Availability (NOFA) for HUD's Fiscal Year (FY) 2011 Housing Choice Voucher Family Self-Sufficiency Program. (2011a, April 29). Retrieved from https://www.federalregister.gov/articles/2011/04/29/2011-10501/notice-of-availability-notice-of-funding-availability-nofa-for-huds-fiscal-year-fy-2011-housing

Notice of Availability: Notice of Funding Availability (NOFA) for HUD's Fiscal Year (FY) 2011 Public and Indian Housing Family Self-Sufficiency Program Under the Resident Opportunity and Self-Sufficiency (ROSS) Program. (2011b, April 29). Retrieved from https://www.federalregister.gov/articles/2011/04/29/2011-10462/notice-of-availability-notice-of-funding-availability-nofa-for-huds-fiscal-year-fy-2011-public-and

Personal Responsibility and Work Opportunity Reconciliation Act of 1996, P.L. 104-193, 110 Stat. 2105 (1996).

Popkin, S. J., Katz, B., Cunningham, M. K., Brown, K. D., Gustafson, J., & Turner, M. A. (2004). *A decade of HOPE VI: Research findings and policy challenges*. Retrieved from http://www.urban.org/publications/411002.html

Rohe, W. M., & Kleit, R. G. (1999). Housing, welfare reform, and self-sufficiency: An assessment of the Family Self-Sufficiency Program. *Housing Policy Debate, 10,* 333–369.

Sard, B. (2001). *The Family Self-Sufficiency Program: HUD's best kept secret for promoting employment and asset growth*. Retrieved from http://www.cbpp.org/cms?fa=view&id=174

U.S. Department of Housing and Urban Development. (n.d.) *About Hope VI*. Retrieved from http://portal.hud.gov/hudportal/HUD?src=/program_offices/public_indian_housing/programs/ph/hope6/about

Williams Shanks, T. R., Boddie, S. C., & Rice, S. (2010). Family-centered, community-based asset building: A strategic use of individual development accounts. *Journal of Community Practice, 18*(1), 94–117.

FINANCES

CHAPTER 33

FINANCIAL SOCIAL WORK

Reeta Wolfsohn

More and more Americans are experiencing some form of financial crisis and are concerned about whether they can hold on to their homes; send their children to college; survive soaring gasoline, utility, and food prices; or ever retire. Their concerns have merit, as approximately 2.6 million people slipped into poverty in the United States in 2010, and 46.2 million Americans were living below the official poverty line, which is the highest number in the 52 years that the U.S. Census Bureau has been publishing these statistics. Among the middle class, median household incomes in 2010 fell to levels last seen in 1997. Minorities were hit hardest. Blacks experienced the highest poverty rate at 27.4 percent, and the rate among Hispanics rose to 26.6 percent. Among whites, 9.9 percent lived in poverty. Additionally, 16.4 million children (22 percent) were living in poverty in 2010, which is the highest number since 1962, and 1.5 million children were homeless (DeNavas-Walt, Proctor, & Smith, 2011).

In October 2011, 46.2 million Americans relied on the federal government's food stamp program, which was a 6 percent increase in one year (U.S. Department of Agriculture, 2011), and 52 million adults were uninsured in 2010 (DeNava-Walt et al., 2011). Overwhelmed and ill prepared for their changing financial circumstances, these men and women need new knowledge and skills for coping with the ever declining availability of services and support systems and their ever growing need for help.

> I am remembering my professor of social welfare policy in my MSW program asking us on the first day of class, "How many of you have had a course in economics?" and shaking his head sadly when only one or two of us could say "yes." His point was that macroeconomic policy affects the distribution of income, wealth and other social goods, not to mention the funding of social, health and human services. (Anastas, 2011)

After spending 14 years establishing and working in the field of financial social work, I know money is the number one stressor in people's lives; the number one cause of divorce; and a driving force behind domestic violence, child and elder abuse, and crime. Declining economic conditions contribute to a burgeoning need for client programs and services, even as the availability of both is constantly diminishing. The result is an escalation in the severity, degree, and extent of clients making their way through the remaining social service systems.

Regardless of the type of social work practiced, the presenting problem, the setting, or the population, financial problems and stress are part of most people's lives and need to be understood, addressed, and managed. Clients experiencing domestic violence, divorce, homelessness, job or health care loss, mental illness, depression, suicidal ideation, or addiction too often lose their sense of self and self-worth because they are out of control and out of touch with their money and lack the financial knowledge or money management skills to take it back.

Money is foundational to every stage of the lifecycle, from the cost of having, raising, and educating a child to paying for end-of-life health care and funeral expenses. Yet, more than a decade into the 21st century, most U.S. youths complete high school without learning the basics of money management (Bernard, 2011), although their futures depend on their avoiding debt and building assets. The absence of financial education in schools contributes to a consumerist culture and debt-encumbered society. Without the skills and the tools needed to make sound financial decisions, or the process and the context from which to make them, many clients receiving social work services are vulnerable to predatory lenders and financial scams and more easily tempted by the lure of illicit easy-money schemes. These choices can quickly create a downward spiral from which it is difficult to escape.

Financial behavioral change is an unlikely priority for men and women who don't know the long-term consequences of payday loans, bankruptcy, foreclosure, rent-to-own arrangements, late payments, bad checks, loan defaults, or cosigning for someone else's loan. Persistent financial problems are unavoidable for anyone who doesn't understand that a credit score affects everyone's ability to get a job, a car, a loan, a credit card, a home, or insurance, or that a poor credit score increases the cost of everything.[1]

NARRATIVE

This example demonstrates how fragile financial security is for many families.

Karen, a 57-year-old woman working in the financial industry, and her husband, Paul, 61, have four children: a 23-year-old son who has graduated from college; a 20-year-old daughter in college; a 17-year-old son, a high school junior who wants to be a doctor; and a 14-year-old son who isn't thinking beyond his next exam. Both parents had excellent college educations and want the same for their children.

---

[1]For more on credit scores, see Marquit (2010).

Until four years ago, they were on track with most of their financial goals: college savings, retirement funds, and home ownership. Then Paul was laid off from his high-paying executive position, which had provided the family's health insurance. Unable to find a new job, he started a consulting business, which always seemed to be about to get off the ground but never did.

Since then, they've spent all of their college and retirement funds, have increased their credit card debt by over $61,000, and have taken out over 100 thousand dollars in loans for their two older children's educations. They have taken out additional school loans in their children's names, which their children don't know about or realize they will be responsible for paying. Their home is about to be foreclosed.

The financial stress and pressure has both parents clinically depressed, with Paul unable to sleep and Karen unable to eat and fighting tears at work all day. Without medical coverage, they have been neglecting these physical and emotional problems.

They finally acknowledged the need for each to generate more income and began aggressive job searches, accepting they might have to relocate, or perhaps live in different cities from each other. They continue to try to avoid bankruptcy and delay foreclosure to keep from further damaging their FICO scores and jeopardizing Karen's ability to find a new job in finance. (A FICO score is a credit score developed by the Fair Isaac Corporation in the late 1950s. It is the most widely used measure of creditworthiness [see Foust & Pressman, 2008].)

They also came to realize they could no longer protect their children from the reality of the family's dire financial circumstances. After learning the details, their oldest son is angry about the student loans he feels saddled with. Their daughter found a part-time job on campus to defray some of her school expenses. The son who is in high school is struggling to excel academically and to successfully compete in two sports, with the hope of a scholarship.

The future for each family member is tenuous, but moving from deceit to honesty and inactive or reactive to proactive financial behavior has reduced some of their guilt and shame, and it has contributed to a degree of hopefulness and of positive feelings about their financial future.

SOCIAL WORK MATTERS

Financial social work is a behavioral model that moves clients beyond basic needs with a psychosocial, multidisciplinary approach focused on the thoughts, feelings, and attitudes that determine each person's relationship to and behavior with money. It expands self-awareness and sense of self; provides financial knowledge; helps clients integrate better decision making and self-assessment into their daily lives; and engages clients with ongoing motivation, validation, and support. These are the basic requirements of sustainable, long-term financial behavioral change.

Stabilizing clients who present with a broad spectrum of physical, emotional, safety, mental health, and financial needs is a practitioner's necessary first step, but it addresses the symptoms and not the causes. Unfortunately, this effort often fails to eliminate the potential for recidivism because the financial component of clients' lives, the foundation of their current circumstances and a constant threat to emotional stability, is most often not attended to. That is when, where, and why financial social work is most needed.

POLICY MATTERS

The current political climate makes passage of laws addressing the health and financial well-being of Americans difficult to pass but easy to systematically dismantle. One example is the Patient Protection and Affordable Care Act of 2010 (P.L. 111-148); another is the Credit Card Accountability Responsibility and Disclosure Act of 2009 (P.L. 111-24). Both have been challenged and changed, in an effort to limit their ability to help Americans with financial problems and without access to health care. Unfortunately, a law to reduce the potential for people to have a second chance at a better financial future easily passed and went unchallenged: the Bankruptcy Abuse Prevention and Consumer Protection Act of 2005 (P.L. 109-8). The Credit Card Accountability Responsibility and Disclosure Act established the Consumer Financial Protection Bureau and included funding to make it the first major government agency to combat consumer abuses in the marketplace. But before it went into effect, on July 21, 2011, H.R. 1315, the Consumer Financial Protection Safety and Soundness Improvement Act of 2011, legislation weakening the Consumer Financial Protection Bureau, was passed.

There is an important role for financial social work in advocating for laws that help social work clients and against those that do not. These laws affect the lives of social workers as much as the lives of their clients, making advocacy and activism beneficial personally and professionally and financial social work relevant to all areas of practice. Speaking up and speaking out on behalf of those who can't, or who have not tradition-ally done so for themselves, is foundational to all social work practice.

Social workers have the education, training, and experience to help people modify their behavior. As positive financial role models and knowledgeable financial resources and referral sources, they also have greater potential for engaging clients in financial behavioral change by providing money-management tools and skills, financial boundaries, help, hope, and encouragement, which expand self-awareness and contribute to improved financial circumstances. As the recent recession and all that has followed demonstrate, the economy affects everyone, but especially the lives of the middle class and those living in poverty, making financial social work practice and advocacy germane to social workers and social work client populations regardless of the state of the economy.

DISCUSSION QUESTIONS

1. How could financial social work benefit your particular client population?

2. What are three specific advantages financial social work advocacy could provide for social workers, their clients, and the social work profession?

3. How could your agency, organization, or practice integrate financial social work into client services?

REFERENCES

Anastas, J. (2011). It's the economy . . . once again. *NASW News, 56*(8). Retrieved from.http://www.socialworkers.org/pubs/news/2011/09/its-the-economy.asp

Bankruptcy Abuse Prevention and Consumer Protection Act of 2005, P.L. 109-8, 119 Stat. 23 (2005).

Bernard, T. S. (2010, April 9). Working financial literacy in with the three R's. *New York Times*. Retrieved from http://www.nytimes.com/2010/04/10/your-money/10money.html

Credit Card Accountability Responsibility and Disclosure Act of 2009, P.L. 111-24, 123 Stat. 1734 (2009).

DeNavas-Walt, C., Proctor, B. D., & Smith, J. C. 2011. *Income, poverty, and health insurance coverage in the United States: 2010*. Retrieved from http://www.census.gov/prod/2011pubs/p60-239.pdf

Foust, D., & Pressman, A. (2008, February 8). Credit scores—Not so magic numbers. *Bloomberg Businessweek*. Retrieved from http://www.businessweek.com/magazine/content/08_07/b4071038384407.htm

Marquit, M. (2010, October 6). Why a good credit rating is important even if you don't use credit. *Moolanomy*. Retrieved from http://www.moolanomy.com/3770/why-a-good-credit-rating-is-important-even-if-you-dont-use-credit-mmarquit01/

Patient Protection and Affordable Care Act of 2010, P.L. 111-148, 124 Stat. 119 (2010).

U.S. Department of Agriculture (2011). *Food and nutrition service*. Retrieved from http://www.fns.usda.gov/pd/snapmain.htm

GOVERNMENT PROGRAMS

CHAPTER 34

ADVENTURES IN WORKFARE POLICY

Leon H. Ginsberg

POLICY MATTERS

The outlook for social welfare programs and the social work profession that supported them did not look good in 1981 when Ronald Reagan took office as president of the United States. He replaced Jimmy Carter, who served as president from 1977 to 1981, and whose proposed Better Jobs and Income program had failed in Congress. The Carter plan promised a guaranteed minimum income for American families. It was only a slight modification of the Family Assistance Program introduced by President Richard Nixon, who served from 1969 until, facing impeachment, he resigned in 1974. Nixon proposed and saw the passage of the Supplemental Security Income program, the remnants of his Family Assistance Program, which would have also guaranteed a minimum income to all American individuals, couples, and families. Congress refused to adopt Nixon's program, which would have supported families, ended the federal–state Aid to Families with Dependent Children (AFDC) program, which dated to the Social Security Act (42 USCA § 1305) of 1935, and would administer all financial assistance through the Social Security Administration. Supplemental Security Income federalized the adult categories of Aid to the Blind, Aid to the Disabled, and Aid to the Aged, which had been administered by states in the same way as AFDC but now were incorporated in the federal program.

Reagan, who had been governor of California, was noted for his conservative position on social issues, including social welfare. When he announced his domestic program in 1981, he presented a clear break from the Nixon and Carter guaranteed-income proposals. Instead, he proposed significant reductions in social welfare, including the AFDC program, the Supplemental Nutrition Assistance Program (food stamps), and Social Security.

Although the two preceding presidents had announced their support for a program that could take assistance for the poor out of the politics of state legislatures, Reagan embarked on a totally different approach. At the center of his policies was a proposed

25 percent tax reduction, with the savings to individuals expected to stimulate the economy; a general decrease in the size and scope of government; and reductions in welfare (AFDC), food stamps, school meals, Medicare, and Medicaid (Hauenstein Center for Presidential Studies, n.d.). These reductions would have detrimental effects on many social work clients, especially those with low incomes, who often depend on these programs for their basic financial support, nutrition, and health care. Many social agencies that provided child and family services, mental health, and care for the aging and ill received some of their support from federal funds. Reducing them would reduce the ability of such programs to provide services.

SOCIAL WORK MATTERS

A retrospective social work view of the Reagan policies in the NASW *Encyclopedia of Social Work* (Abramovitz, 1996) characterized the Reagan program as making low-income people choose unpaid work instead of welfare as part of an attack on the welfare state. One could hardly predict that a Reagan policy proposal could save the AFDC program in at least one and probably several other states.

NARRATIVE

At the time Reagan was elected, I was serving as commissioner of the West Virginia Depart-ment of Welfare, later renamed the Department of Human Services. I was appointed to the position in 1977 by Governor John D. Rockefeller IV.

President Carter was also elected in 1976, and relations between the state and federal governments were close and in concert with one another. Joseph Califano, who served at the beginning of the Carter presidency as secretary of the Department of Health, Education, and Welfare,[1] held hearings on welfare reform and appointed task forces to make recom-mendations on an overhaul of the system. I served on some of those task forces, along with representatives from other states, officials of the Department of Labor, theoreticians from the Brookings Institution, and others.

The proposal, developed over several months, essentially fine-tuned the Family Assistance Plan. It would combine food stamps, financial assistance, work improvement programs such as the Work Incentive program, and Medicaid for low-income people. But the plan did not pass Congress. Of course, those of us who worked on the proposal were disappointed. I recall discussing the result with a Brookings Institution economist, Henry Aaron. We won-dered how the current, unreformed system would fare in Congress and thought it would be lucky to receive a handful of votes.

---

[1]The name of the department was changed to the Department of Human Services when the Depart-ment of Education was created.

The failure of the Better Jobs and Income program can be attributed to opposition from several directions. For some, it was too generous and would institutionalize support for low-income families. Many in the general public and in Congress believed that recipients of welfare were lacking in industry. The belief that "welfare queens" lived lavishly on assistance payments had some currency (Zucchino, 1997). Others thought the program was insufficiently generous and would actually lower benefits for the poor in some states. The Carter proposal made efforts to balance the concerns of those who were skeptical about assistance with the needs of low-income families, but it failed.

Reagan and his running mate, George H. W. Bush, carried all but a few states—Georgia, Hawaii, Maryland, Minnesota, Rhode Island, West Virginia, and the District of Columbia—in 1980. President Reagan's welfare reform and other economic measures were contained in the Omnibus Budget Reconciliation Act of 1981 (P.L. 97-35). One of the hallmarks of that legislation was the creation of nine block grants to replace some of 50 categorical programs that the federal government had sponsored with the states. Part of the concept was to reduce the detailed reporting and compliance required by the states for their accountability to the federal government. The nine block grants included grants for social services, preventive health and health services, and community services. The plan was to reduce overall funding by 20 percent and to allow some exchanges of funds among the block grants.

When officials from the federal Department of Health and Human Services wanted to present their plan to the West Virginia Department of Human Services and its constituents—including clients, local social services offices, and voluntary programs that received some of their funding through the department—I arranged for a meeting on the campus of Glenville State College, rather than in a more urban center, which would involve extensive media coverage of what would be a potential crisis in the provision of services to clients and their families.

AFDC was not included in a block grant. However, additional restrictions were placed on it to reduce its size and encourage recipients to seek employment. The Reagan administration did not intend to propose a guaranteed income. One of the changes in the program was the elimination of the permanent work incentive, which allowed working parents receiving AFDC to keep one-third of every dollar they earned above the AFDC grant without any reduction in the grant. Instead, the reform legislation limited the funds that recipients could retain above the AFDC grant amount to the first four months of their earnings after beginning to receive AFDC grants. States could no longer allow clients to retain the amount of a standard work allowance, which would help them pay for the costs of holding a job and the actual cost of child care to make it possible for parents to work in lieu of staying home with their children.

Also in 1981, Congress gave the states authority to design and evaluate their own work experience programs, which included funding for job searches, work relief (which became known as Community Work Experience Programs, or CWEP), and the subsidization of a job with AFDC grants (Moffit & Wolf, 1987).

Under this background of welfare restrictions and federal cost-cutting, I was faced with both implementing the Reagan changes and providing the maximum possible assistance to the low-income citizens of West Virginia. The Reagan initiatives were popular with many voters, with the state legislature, and with some of the governor's staff. With the choice of reducing or eliminating some assistance programs or instituting a work program, which would satisfy federal officials, the state legislature, and the state executive branch, we implemented the program.

We proposed a West Virginia CWEP program, which we called Workfare; the Reagan officials approved our plan, and we implemented it. It was well regarded by the legislature and the governor's office, and it saved assistance for large numbers of clients, especially men in high-unemployment areas. The jobs that were created were almost always for the purposes of providing essential services, rather than simply occupying the time of the participants in order to provide them with financial support. There were not many non-CWEP jobs available in the state, even for skilled people. Unemployment was high. So AFDC was often the only alternative for those who had exhausted their unemployment benefits. One town used clients as armed law enforcement officers. Another deployed them to assist with flight control in its small airport. Other clients worked as aides in hospitals and other health care facilities. Many worked for the Department of Highways.

I was astonished when major media outlets began coming to West Virginia to study our work experience innovations. People magazine sent reporters and a photographer and ran an extensive story. The Wall Street Journal carried a front-page story on the program. ABC, CBS, and NBC all covered the welfare-employed on their national newscasts. A British television news program, a version of 60 Minutes, sent a team to West Virginia. I was interviewed by a radio news reporter from Australia during the commuting hours in Sydney. Obviously, there was interest in workfare all over the world.

DISCUSSION

Of course, not everything about workfare programs is perfect. Some clients find them demeaning, and some call workfare unpaid labor. But in West Virginia in the 1980s, CWEP had the unusual quality of appealing to public officials as well as clients. It saved assistance for thousands of clients who might otherwise have lost their benefits.

Ironically, West Virginia, one of the few states that did not support President Reagan's election in 1980, was often cited by Reagan welfare officials as an example of the effectiveness of their policies.

Since the 1980s, an increasing number of states have instituted welfare-to-work programs. At the federal level, these programs were included in the 1996 Personal Responsibility and Work Opportunity Reconciliation Act (P.L. 104-193) proposed by President Bill Clinton and passed by Congress. The U.S. assistance program now functions under a new name, as AFDC has become Temporary Assistance for Needy Families.

CONCLUSION

In the late 20th century, public assistance policies were changed more significantly than ever since the passage of the Social Security Act in 1935. One of the most important of those changes was a revision in the ideas about work requirements for recipients. In its original conceptualization, Aid to Dependent Children, which became AFDC, was to make it possible for mothers to stay at home to rear their children—so they would not have to work. As times changed and as more women, including those with children, began to be employed, public attitudes changed. When men became eligible for AFDC as well, the idea that clients should work and work for their assistance grants became popular with elected officials and the public.

This chapter suggests that the development of workfare in one state helped save the assistance benefits for disadvantaged clients. Although initially a controversial, experimental idea, work requirements have become the standard throughout the United States and have become part of the character of state–federal public assistance.

DISCUSSION QUESTIONS

1. The chapter states that unemployment was high in West Virginia at the time the work program was introduced. Would the introduction of work requirements have been more or less controversial in a state with low unemployment and a stronger economy?

2. Some social workers suggest that political awareness and involvement must be part of the knowledge and efforts of all social workers. Is political awareness and involvement optional or should it be a focus of social workers?

3. In the era described in this chapter, media coverage of issues such as poverty, public assistance, and social welfare policy, was extensive. Is there more or less media attention to these issues now? If there are differences, speculate about some of the reasons for the changes.

4. Discuss the impact of reductions in federal funding for human services on clients, social workers, and social agencies, as described in this chapter.

REFERENCES

Abramovitz, M. (1996). Aid to Families with Dependent Children. In R. L. Edwards (Ed.), *Encyclopedia of social work* (19th ed., Vol. 1, pp. 183–194). Washington, DC: NASW Press.

Hauenstein Center for Presidential Studies. (n.d.). *Reaganomics.* Retrieved from http://www.gvsu.edu/hauenstein/reaganomics-40.htm

Moffitt, R., & Wolf, D. A. (1987). The effect of the 1981 Omnibus Budget Reconciliation Act on welfare recipients and work incentives. *Social Service Review, 61*(2), 247–260.

Omnibus Budget Reconciliation Act of 1981, P.L. 97-35, 95 Stat. 357 (1981).

Personal Responsibility and Work Opportunity Reconciliation Act of 1996, P.L. 104-193, 110 Stat. 2105 (1996).

Social Security Act, 42 USCA § 1305, 49 Stat. 620 (1935).

Zucchino, D. (1997) *Myth of the welfare queen*. New York: Touchstone.

CHAPTER 35

SOCIAL WORKERS ADVOCATING FOR SOCIAL SECURITY

Stephen H. Gorin

POLICY MATTERS

Social Security is the nation's fundamental social welfare program. Its beneficiaries include older adults, people with disabilities, and survivors of deceased workers, many of them children. Social Security also provides support to military veterans and their families (Olsen & O'Leary, 2011).

Social Security benefits provide a key source of support to many recipients. Without them, the poverty rate for older adults would approach 50 percent; two-thirds of older adults "rely on Social Security benefits for most of their income" (Strengthen Social Security, 2011). Social Security benefits are particularly important to residents of rural areas and small cities, and in some cases, they are crucial to the success of local businesses (J. Stallman, economist at University of Missouri, cited in Bishop & Gallardo, 2011).

Despite its importance, Social Security has long faced opposition (Altman, 2005). Alf Landon (1936), the Republican candidate for president in 1936, described the legislation as "unjust and stupidly drafted." In recent decades, opposition to the program, at least in its current form, has accelerated. In 2005, President George W. Bush tried to partially privatize the program, arguing that younger workers could gain a better return by investing part of their payroll deduction in stocks and bonds (Weller, 2005). Although this proposal was eventually defeated, opposition to the program remains.

In the wake of the recession that began in 2007, and concern about growing federal debt, politicians in both parties have called for cuts to Social Security (Montgomery, 2011; Ruffing & Van de Water, 2011). Yet, as the U.S. Congressional Budget Office (2011) noted, the Social Security Trust Funds are solvent through 2038, after which the program will still be able to meet around 20 percent of its obligations. As many experts acknowledge, fixing Social Security will not be a difficult task (Reno & Lavery,

2009). On the other hand, reducing "benefit levels for future generations" would result in "a relatively lower standard of living for most of the elderly and disabled population" (Goss, 2011, p. 7). Polling data have generally found widespread opposition, particularly among older voters, to cutting Social Security (Greenberg, Carville, Seifert, & Walker, 2011; Strengthen Social Security, 2012).

NARRATIVE

In response to concern about efforts to cut Social Security benefits, an organization called Social Security Works, with funding from Atlantic Philanthropies, convened a broad-based coalition called Strengthen Social Security (http://strengthensocialsecurity.org) aimed at defending and strengthening this vital program. The codirectors of this effort are Eric Kingson, a professor of social work at Syracuse University and an acknowledged expert on Social Security, and Nancy Altman, also a leading expert and assistant to Alan Greenspan during his tenure as chair of the commission that developed the 1983 amendments to Social Security. NASW is a member of this coalition.

In a further effort to build opposition to efforts to cut Social Security, Social Security Works, Atlantic Philanthropies, and the Center for Community Change funded a campaign to raise Social Security as an issue in the 2012 New Hampshire presidential primary. The key organizations in this effort were the New Hampshire Citizens Alliance, a broadly based advocacy group devoted to social and economic justice, and the Granite State Organizing Project, a coalition of religious and labor organizations. The New Hampshire chapter of NASW also joined the coalition. I, as executive director, played a leading role in the coalition and served as a resource for information about Social Security. Other community, advocacy, and religious organizations in the coalition included Every Child Matters, the Alliance for Retired Americans, and the National Committee to Preserve Social Security and Medicare.

Coalition members and allies engaged in a range of activities. Central among these was following the presidential candidates and asking them to pledge to oppose any effort to cut Social Security benefits. Since New Hampshire residents expect presidential candidates to engage in "retail politics," such as meeting voters and soliciting their opinions, approaching candidates was not difficult. Coalition supporters attended town meetings, press conferences, and house parties and in some instances approached candidates on the street as they were campaigning.

The coalition also used the media in this effort. Members released data and reports, many obtained from Social Security Works, demonstrating the importance of Social Security to all generations, not just older adults. They participated in radio interviews and wrote letters to the editor and op-ed columns. In my role as NASW–New Hampshire executive director, I arranged interviews and debated on New Hampshire Public Radio. I also wrote and coauthored op-ed columns that were printed in several newspapers and spoke at several senior centers. Although the presidential candidates, most of whom were Republicans, did not always agree on the importance of preserving the program in its current form, most of them did address the issue.

SOCIAL WORK MATTERS

Social workers, and individuals with connections to our profession, have a long history of involvement with Social Security. In a real sense, we were present at the creation of this vital program. Social Work pioneers such as Grace Abbot, Eveline Burns, Wilbur J. Cohen, Harry Hopkins, and Frances Perkins played leading roles in the development of the program. Cohen, whom John F. Kennedy called Mr. Social Security, was perhaps the nation's leading expert on the program, and Charles Schottland, another pioneer, served as commissioner of Social Security. In 2008, NASW's Delegate Assembly urged social workers to advocate for "the preservation and integrity of social security" (NASW, 2009).

How can we do this? To begin with, social workers practicing with individuals who rely on Social Security can work with colleagues to offer first-hand evidence of the importance of the program to their clients. Personal contact, through meetings, letters, and telephone calls, often has a significant impact on legislators and their votes. Although Social Security is a federal program, advocates can also lobby state legislators to enact resolutions calling on Congress and the president to protect the integrity of this program.

NASW chapters and social workers can also help organize and participate in coalitions to defend and strengthen Social Security. Social workers can support candidates committed to addressing the program in a manner consistent with the values of our profession (Reno & Lavery, 2009). Social workers might also consider running for local or federal office on a platform of defending and strengthening Social Security.

Social workers have a critical stake in preserving and strengthening this vital program. As a near-universal program, Social Security is our nation's fundamental form of social insurance; anything that threatens it poses a threat not only to our clients on Social Security but also to a wide range of other programs and services and the people who benefit from them. In addition, many members of our profession are themselves approaching retirement age and will soon need Social Security benefits (Social Work Policy Institute, 2011). Many are also women, who often live longer than men and "have a greater chance of exhausting other sources of income" (U.S. Social Security Administration, 2011). By participating in the effort to defend Social Security, we advocate not only for our clients but for our colleagues and ourselves as well.

DISCUSSION QUESTIONS

1. Historically, what role have social workers played in advocating for Social Security?

2. Can the organizing effort described in the Narrative be replicated in your area? What groups might be involved?

REFERENCES

Altman, N. J. (2005). *The battle for Social Security: From FDR's vision to Bush's gamble.* Hoboken, NJ: John Wiley & Sons.

Bishop, B., & Gallardo, R. (2011, October 31). Rural counties more dependent on Social Security. *Daily Yonder.* Retrieved from http://www.dailyyonder.com/rural-more-dependent-social-security/2011/10/29/3578

Goss, S. C. (2011, June 23). *Testimony by Stephen C. Goss, chief actuary, Social Security Administration to the House Committee on Ways and Means Subcommittee on Social Security.* Retrieved from http://waysandmeans.house.gov/UploadedFiles/Goss_Testimony.pdf

Greenberg, S., Carville, J., Seifert, E., & Walker, D. (2011, November 10). Seizing the new progressive common ground. *Democracy Corps.* Retrieved from http://www.democracycorps.com/wp-content/files/Common-Ground-Memo-FINAL1.pdf

Landon, A. (1936). *"I will not promise the moon": Alf Landon opposes the Social Security Act, 1936.* Retrieved from http://historymatters.gmu.edu/d/8128

Montgomery, L. (2011, July 6). In debt talks, Obama offers Social Security cuts. *Washington Post.* Retrieved from http://www.washingtonpost.com/business/economy/in-debt-talks-obama-offers-social-security-cuts/2011/07/06/gIQA2sFO1H_story.html

National Association of Social Workers. (1999). Aging and wellness. In *Social work speaks: National Association of Social Workers policy statements, 2009–2012* (pp. 14–21). Washington, DC: NASW Press.

Olsen, A., & O'Leary, S. (2011). Military veterans and Social Security: 2010 update. *Social Security Bulletin, 71*(2). Retrieved from http://www.ssa.gov/policy/docs/ssb/v71n2/v71n2p1.html

Reno, V. P., & Lavery, J. (2009, October). *Fixing Social Security: Adequate benefits, adequate financing.* Retrieved from http://www.socialsecuritymatters.org/Get_the_Facts_files/Fixing%20Social%20Security.pdf

Ruffing, K., & Van de Water, P. N. (2011, January 11). *Social Security benefits are modest: Policymakers have only limited room to reduce benefits without causing hardship.* Retrieved from http://www.cbpp.org/cms/index.cfm?fa=view&id=3368

Social Work Policy Institute. (2011). *Investing in the social work workforce.* Retrieved from http://www.socialworkpolicy.org/wp-content/uploads/2011/10/SWPI-Inv-in-the-Wrkforce-Final-Report.pdf

Strengthen Social Security. (2011). *Social Security FAQ.* Retrieved from http://strengthensocialsecurity.org/social-security-faq#e

Strengthen Social Security. (2012). *Polling.* Retrieved from http://strengthensocialsecurity.org/resources/polling.

U.S. Congressional Budget Office. (2011, August). *CBO's 2011 long-term projections for Social Security: Additional information.* Retrieved from http://www.cbo.gov/ftpdocs/123xx/doc12375/08-05-Long-TermSocialSecurityProjections.pdf

U.S. Social Security Administration. (2011). *Social Security is important to women.* Retrieved from http://www.ssa.gov/pressoffice/factsheets/women.htm

Weller, C. E. (2005, May 5). *Primer on President Bush's "plan" for Social Security privatization.* Retrieved from http://www.americanprogress.org/issues/2005/05/b668125.html

Health

CHAPTER 36

CANCER POLICY CAN MEAN LIFE OR DEATH

Elizabeth J. Clark

POLICY MATTERS

The debate surrounding the cost and use of health care remains central to many of the budgetary issues we are facing as a nation. We repeatedly hear how we can no longer afford to care for all of our citizens and that our two signature health programs—Medicare and Medicaid—will not be viable in the future.

With great hope, we watched the passage of the Patient Protection and Affordable Care Act (P.L. 111-148) (ACA) in 2010. Many of us in the social work profession were disappointed that reform did not go further, that a single-payer system did not make the cut (Gorin, 2009). Equally disappointing have been the attempts to repeal the advances that were codified in federal law. The ACA was a beginning, but much more change is needed. One area that requires additional attention is the prevention and treatment of cancer.

The World Health Organization (2011) has indicated that cancer has the distinction of being a leading cause of death across the globe. Also, cancer is primarily a disease of the elderly, and as the baby boomers age, the prevalence of cancer will be greater than ever before.

Probably no area of health care is more susceptible to disparities and inequities than oncology. We know that different racial and ethnic groups, people in certain geographic areas, and those who are uninsured are diagnosed with cancer at later stages. They also may be unable to get the cancer treatments they need. This means that their chances of cure or control of the disease are, as a result, diminished (National Cancer Institute, 2011).

Regardless of practice setting, all social workers interact with clients and family members who have cancer. Whether in hospitals, community agencies, schools, prisons, or private practice, cancer has become a part of our professional lives and of the American landscape. One in two men and one in three women will be diagnosed with cancer. This translates into over 1.5 million individuals receiving a cancer diagnosis each year (American Cancer Society, 2010). As a result, social workers need to have a basic understanding of the disease and its impact on individuals and society. Also, as social workers, we have an ethical responsibility to be part of the policy discussions and policy outcomes that will apply to our clients.

Each day in our country, policy decisions are made that affect cancer prevention, cancer treatment, and the health of people living with a cancer diagnosis. These policy decisions cover many areas, and we see the results of these changes at doctors' offices, at hospitals, at pharmacies, at health care agencies, and at the workplace. They may occur at the organizational, the community, the state, or the national level. Regardless of the level of the policy decision, the final impact is always personal.

NARRATIVE

The following example shows how health care policies affect one couple who were planning an early retirement that is now derailed by cancer:

Mr. Troy is an electrician for a large airplane manufacturing plant. He feels lucky to have had steady and good-paying work for over 30 years. He and his wife have been careful with money over the course of their marriage, and they were planning to take an early retirement. They want to move closer to their grandchildren, and they hope to do some traveling to visit some national parks.

Mr. Troy can draw on his company pension without penalty at age 62. His wife, who is a year younger, is a part-time secretary at a small local business. She does not have a pension or health insurance. Mr. Troy carries her on his company's insurance. Maintaining health insurance coverage has been their one barrier to early retirement. They have been trying to find a way to fill the insurance gap between Mr. Troy's leaving work and being eligible for Medicare at age 65.

Six months before his 62nd birthday, Mr. Troy begins having some urinary problems. He goes for a checkup, and his doctor notices that his prostate-specific antigen test is higher than normal. Further tests confirm that Mr. Troy has prostate cancer. The cancer has been caught fairly early, and his doctor feels that no immediate treatment is needed. Instead, they will engage in what is referred to as "watchful waiting." The doctor will keep a close eye on the cancer, and if there are any changes, cancer therapy will be started.

Although Mr. Troy's daily life hasn't changed too much, his plans for the future and for early retirement have changed dramatically. They have been put on hold. Mr. Troy now had a history of cancer, a "preexisting condition" in insurance jargon.

He and his wife have been reviewing applications for buying private insurance to fill the gap if they retired early. Each application asks about a history of cancer, some require the applicant to be cancer free for at least 12 months before being eligible, and many request a five-year period. Mr. Troy is not yet receiving any treatment for his prostate cancer, but with watchful waiting, he will never be considered cancer free.

The Troys note that all of the newspapers have touted the health care reform bill and the fact that preexisting conditions would no longer prohibit people from getting insurance. On further checking, they are disappointed to find that the preexisting condition mandate does not begin until 2014.

The Troys have also read about the extension of COBRA (formally the Consolidated Omnibus Budget Reconciliation Act of 1985 [P.L. 99-272]) under "Obamacare," and they think maybe that would help them with the insurance gap. COBRA requires employers to offer group medical coverage to employees and their dependents who otherwise would lose their group coverage due to individual circumstances. Continuation of coverage must be offered regardless of any health condition, such as cancer.

It is timely that Mr. Troy's employer is offering a refresher session on his company's benefits, and Mr. Troy attended. He had always been happy with his excellent health care coverage. He knew he regularly paid a small part of the monthly cost to cover both himself and his wife, but he was shocked to learn that under COBRA you pay the full cost of the insurance premium plus a 2 percent administrative fee. The monthly cost for the family policy would be over $2,600, a prohibitive amount for the Troys. Not only that, even with the recently mandated extension, Mr. Troy could only get COBRA for 18 months after leaving employment. It is another dead end.

Other options seem nonexistent. The Troys certainly can't go without insurance. Mrs. Troy could try to find a full-time job with benefits, but she does not have a college degree, and jobs are scarce in their town. Also, that would mean that Mrs. Troy would still need to work until age 65 to maintain her own insurance. The easiest solution is to give up the idea of early retirement.

The Troys biggest worry now is that Mr. Troy's cancer might get worse. If he couldn't work at all, they would have no choice but to pay for COBRA.

DISCUSSION

Many couples, like the Troys, enjoy good health and good insurance coverage during their working lives. Things go smoothly until an accident or an illness occurs, or until a policy change sets off a sequence of negative events. For example, at the organizational level, a company may decide that they can no longer afford to provide health care benefits for their employees or for their employees' family members. Or they may adopt a new health care plan that limits coverage and increases out-of-pocket expenses. In the recent recession, many companies have reduced staffing, leaving previous employees uncovered. To complicate matters, small companies with fewer than 50 employees are not required to offer Family and Medical Leave Act of 1994 (P.L. 103-3) benefits, and people who must be out for an extended time for surgery or other treatments may lose their jobs and, subsequently, their insurance coverage (U.S. Department of Labor, 2011a, 2011b).

Some organizations provide lifetime insurance benefits at group policy rates for individuals who retire from their company. As health care premiums increase, these costs are being transferred to the retiree. Worse yet, some companies have decided to discontinue this benefit for future retirees (Society for Human Resource Management, 2011). This means that individuals will no longer be able to use their previous employer's group insurance as a secondary insurance to Medicare to pick up expenses, such as deductibles, for which Medicare does not pay. Also, the retired individual, who is often on a fixed income, will need to absorb all out-of-pocket health costs or purchase a Medigap policy. For people with cancer, a Medigap policy may be essential. It is important to note that in the six-month period immediately following enrollment in Medicare Part B, people 65 and older cannot be denied Medigap insurance because of health status or history.

Other problems can occur with changes in the types of treatment provided under existing insurance policies. For example, health insurance companies, including Medicare plans, may change their drug formularies, and patients may no longer be able to get the drugs they have been using or that their health care team has recommended. Other times, the insurance carrier or a government agency may decide that a cancer medication is no longer cost-effective. For example, a controversy arose recently when Medicare stated that it would not always reimburse for a Food and Drug Administration–approved prostate cancer medication. Although Medicare covers the routine cost of clinical trials, many private insurers do not. New and effective treatments may take years to be covered, and clinical trial expenses may be excluded as nonstandard treatment. Frequently, the best cancer therapy may be the standard therapy plus a new medication that is still in a clinical trial phase. If the trial is not covered, the person with cancer will be unable to get the optimal care recommended.

Some treatments, such as blood and bone marrow transplants for specific cancer diagnoses, are only available to those who can afford to pay for them. Other treatments are available only in some geographic areas. If a hospital, clinic, or doctor's practice closes in a particular community, a patient must have sufficient resources to be able to travel to a center where the care is still offered. People with cancer undergoing an allogeneic bone marrow transplant (using donor marrow) must travel to a medical center that performs such transplants, for example. Add to this the fact that the average length of stay in a medical center after the transplant is 100 days. The insurance costs are high, and the costs for family members to accompany their loved ones and be available for support are not covered by insurance.

These caveats may seem to invoke worst-case scenarios, but they are actually quite common. We do not need to look far to see the impact of policy decisions for people with cancer.

SOCIAL WORK MATTERS

As social work practitioners, we can help clients dealing with cancer in a variety of ways. We can offer psychosocial support and counseling to help them adapt to their diagnosis and the changes in their lives. We can provide patient education materials and skills training to help them become savvy consumers and self-advocates. We can function as patient navigators and case managers to help them get through the maze of health care appointments and tests that they need. We can point them to resources such as medication assistance programs and community services, and we can encourage them to seek legal counsel when they face a system roadblock that seems insurmountable. These are important and comprehensive social work services, and oncology social workers do an outstanding job of providing such services to thousands of cancer patients each day. Yet we cannot stop there.

As social work advocates and activists, there is more that we can, and must, do. We can follow and weigh in on proposed social policy issues and regulations that will have a negative impact on our clients with cancer. We can join social workers and other health care colleagues to propose alternatives to bad policy and to advocate for positive change. It does not take much time or great effort to make a phone call to a legislator or administrator, to write a letter to an editor, or respond to a blog. Take every opportunity to attend town hall meetings or participate in community events to object to closings of local health programs or to bring awareness to gaps in available cancer care services. Be a part of the dialogue and deliberations about how health resources are allocated.

If possible, consider assuming a leadership position within organizations when one becomes available, and think about running for an elected office or working for a candidate who believes that the provision of care for people with cancer is essential and just. Make sure that the social work perspective and social work voice are both present in the debate.

Decisions made today will have long-term consequences, not just for your practice, your agency, or your community, but for your clients and even your own family. It will take years to undo some of the measures being put in place. Many people with cancer cannot wait that long.

DISCUSSION QUESTIONS

1. Can an individual social worker really have any impact on national policy?

2. When we discuss oncology social work, we generally think of work with the person with cancer and his or her family members. Do most agencies or health care settings get involved with policy?

REFERENCES

American Cancer Society. (2010). *Cancer facts and figures 2010.* Retrieved from http://www.cancer. org/acs/groups/content/@epidemiologysurveilance/documents/document/acspc-026238.pdf

Consolidated Omnibus Budget Reconciliation Act of 1985 (COBRA), P.L. 99-272, 100 Stat. 82 (1986).

Family and Medical Leave Act of 1994, P.L. 103-3, 107 Stat. 6 (1993).

Gorin, S. H. (2009) Health care reform: The importance of a public option [Editorial]. *Health & Social Work, 34,* 83–85.

National Cancer Institute. (2011) *Cancer health disparities.* Retrieved from www.cancer.gov/cancertopics/types/disparities

Patient Protection and Affordable Care Act, P.L. 111-148, 119–124 Stat. 1025 (2010).

Society for Human Resources Management. (2011). *Build a bridge to health exchanges for early retirees.* Retrieved from http://www.shrm.org/hrdisciplines/benefits/Articles/Pages/Exchanges-Retirees.aspx

U.S. Department of Labor. (2011a). *Compliance assistance.* Retrieved from http://www.dol.gov/ebsa/compliance_assistance.html

U.S. Department of Labor. (2011b). *Employment law guide.* Retrieved from http://www.dol.gov/compliance/guide/fmla.htm

World Health Organization. (2011). *Cancer.* Retrieved from http://www.who.intl/cancer

CHAPTER 37

The Relationship of Practice, Policy, and Research in Breast Cancer Disparities

Sarah Gehlert

Although I primarily identify as a researcher, the nature of my work in health disparities of necessity blurs the lines between research, practice, and policy. I could not possibly understand what determines the breast cancer outcomes of African American women, my research focus, without hearing the voices of individual women, their families, and other members of their communities. Likewise, developing a fully articulated multilevel model of the determinants of the disparity between the breast cancer mortality rates of African American and white women requires knowledge of the health, mental health, and other needs of African American women and the services available to them. It also requires knowledge about the local, state, and federal policies that influence their health. Social workers agree without hesitation that good practice requires taking a holistic view of a situation. I would argue that a holistic perspective is equally important for social work research. The lessons that I learned from eight years as a health social work practitioner have served me well as a researcher.

Policy Matters

Practice and policy influence my research in two main ways. First, they form important parts of the multilevel framework that I use to conceptualize what drives cancer disparities. They also keep me ever mindful of the need to shape practice and policy to decrease disparities. Existing practices and policies about breast cancer affect who receives breast cancer treatment and how this treatment is delivered. Therefore, these practices and policies are important determinants of breast cancer disparities between African American and white women. As such, they shape how I conceptualize and conduct my research, and are part of a multilevel framework of cancer determinants that my colleagues and I have developed to guide our research (Warnecke et al., 2008). According to the framework, cancer disparity determinants occur in three constellations: (1) distal determinants, which include population-level social conditions embedded in shared social norms; (2) intermediate determinants, which include the more immediate social and physical contexts and social relationships in which the distal effects are experienced; and (3) proximal determinants, which include biological, genetic, and individual-level factors such as health behavior. For example, the Centers for Disease Control and Prevention's Breast and Cervical Cancer Early Detection Program would be considered a distal determinant, and local health departments' prevention practices would be considered intermediate determinants.

In addition to being part of the holistic frame of reference for my work, practice and policy shape my research by keeping me mindful that eliminating disparities depends on translating research into solutions. Although disparities researchers have become adept at documenting and measuring health disparities and understanding their determinants, we have been remarkably unsuccessful at eliminating health disparities at the population level (Gehlert & Colditz, 2011). We have generated knowledge without equal attention to converting that knowledge into solutions to health and other social problems.

AFRICAN AMERICAN WOMEN AND BREAST CANCER

My reasons for focusing on African American women with breast cancer are twofold. First of all, the subtype of breast cancer experienced by many African American women differs from that seen among the majority of white women in fundamental ways—principally, age at onset, trajectory, and survivorship. Although African American women are less likely to develop breast cancer than white women, they are much more likely to die from the disease. Breast cancer tends to occur at a younger age among African American women. According to Newman (2005), 30 percent to 40 percent of African American breast cancer patients in the United States are younger than 50 years of age, compared with 10 percent of white breast cancer patients. W. F. Anderson, Rosenberg, Menashe, Mitani, and Pfeiffer (2008) refer to this as a crossover effect, in which breast cancer incidence is higher among African American women under 40 years of age than among white women in the same age group, yet lower among African American women 40 years of age or older.

Likewise, women of West African ancestry are overrepresented among those with the basalar subtype of breast cancer (which is closely related to the so-called triple negative breast cancer), which not only occurs earlier in life than other subtypes, but is more lethal and aggressive (Hudis & Gianni, 2011). According to data from the Surveillance Epidemiology and End Results system, 23.4 per 100,000 white women die from the disease each year, compared to 32.4 per 100,000 African American women (Alterkruse et al., 2010). It is estimated that African American women are on the whole 37 percent more likely to die from breast cancer than white women. Likewise, the five-year relative survival rate for white women is 90 percent, compared with 77 percent for African American women (American Cancer Society, 2009).

The second reason that I focus my research on breast cancer among African American women is that fewer evidence-based psychosocial interventions are available for African American women than for white women. This largely is due to our lack of knowledge about the characteristics and needs of African American women with the disease, especially those with the basalar or triple negative subtype (Newman, 2005). Earlier onset and more aggressive course almost certainly require a different approach to treatment and likely affect women's coping with the disease.

We have been less successful at designing and testing interventions for African American women than we have for white women of moderate and high socioeconomic status. Recently, B. Anderson et al. (2010) published the results of one of the only psychosocial clinical trials for breast cancer survivors. They were able to demonstrate increased survival time after a group-administered cognitive–behavioral intervention for women with breast cancer, yet none of the women in the study was African American. Support and self-help groups are much more readily available to women with breast cancer than are psychotherapeutic techniques or approaches and have demonstrated utility (Daste & Rose, 2005), yet these groups are much more likely to be found in predominantly white neighborhoods than those that are predominantly African American.

TRANSLATING RESEARCH INTO SOLUTIONS

The notion that the African American–white disparity in mortality may largely be due to social factors is supported by markedly different African American and white mortality differences across major cities in the United States. According to Ansell et al. (2009), from 2002 to 2005, the disparity in mortality between African American and white women in Chicago was on average twice that of the United States as a whole and five times that of New York City. It is clear, however, that these social factors interact.

Two large transdisciplinary projects focusing on social determinants of racial and ethnic differences in breast cancer in Chicago, one at the University of Chicago and the other at the University of Illinois at Chicago (UIC), were undertaken as part of a federally funded initiative to ameliorate health disparities. Over time, the two projects informed one another's science and collaborated to change policy. Among other things, the UIC team found that later stage of breast cancer at diagnosis, which is associated with poorer outcomes, is more common among women living in census tracts in which higher percentages of residents live below the federal poverty line

(Campbell et al., 2009). Other Chicago investigators working at the same time (Whitman, Ansell, Orsi, & Francois, 2011) found higher mortality among African American women living in Chicago to be associated with poorer quality of mammography in medically underserved areas.

The project at the University of Chicago used a full multilevel model to understand how factors in women's social environments contribute to the African American–white disparity in breast cancer mortality. The transdisciplinary team of social, behavioral, clinical, and biological/genetic researchers (directed by me) investigated various levels of the model, from the cellular to the societal. All were committed to investigating social influences but focused on a different aspect of the cells-to-society chain to understand factors that are influenced by and influence women's social environments. Specifically, the team used a multilevel model to identify pathways linking community-level experiences to biological changes that are associated with the more lethal and aggressive basalar subtype of breast cancer.

In the shared model, dilapidated housing, crime, and fractured communities engender isolation and depression among African American women and, in so doing, alter stress-hormone response (Gehlert et al., 2007). The investigation was prompted by observations in the team's animal models of the effects of social isolation and stress that indicated a series of complex genetic interactions after which breast cancer developed. We have been able to connect factors in the social environments of women to changes in hormone expression (Gehlert, Mininger, & Cipriano-Steffens, 2010) and currently are designing neighborhood-level interventions that we expect also to produce downstream proximal-level changes (Gehlert, Mininger, Sohmer, & Berg, 2008).

Narrative

The following example shows how social factors at the distal and intermediate levels interact with biology to affect the outcomes of a woman's breast cancer:

Ms. Harris is a 30-year-old African American woman who recently was diagnosed with breast cancer. She lives in the predominantly African American neighborhood in which her family has lived for generations. Because there were no large medical centers near her neighborhood, she made an appointment at a nearby community health clinic to get her routine mammogram. The limited availability of appointments for mammography and the misconception that Ms. Harris was at low risk due to her younger age meant that she was given an appointment six months after her initial call. The clinic had only one overworked mammographer, who was unable to read her mammogram for four months, at which time Ms. Harris was called in to see a physician. At the time of her surgery, Ms. Harris's basalar subtype of breast cancer was advanced, and her prognosis is poor.

DISCUSSION

Clearly, although research to illuminate the determinants of African American–white disparities in breast cancer mortality is essential, it cannot change the situations of women like Ms. Harris without a concomitant change in policy. Both the University of Chicago and UIC centers used community-based participatory research approaches aimed at producing policy change in addition to research findings. By working with community partners and presenting research results through both community and scientific channels, the two groups were able to inform a variety of audiences about racial disparities in breast cancer in Chicago and some of their social determinants.

Their work with community partners helped nurture the development of the Metropolitan Chicago Breast Cancer Mortality Task Force, a consortium of investigators, policymakers, and community stakeholders that had initially organized around the work of Whitman and Ansell (Ansell et al., 2009; Whitman, Ansell, Orsi, & Francois, 2011). The task force was the impetus for the enactment of Illinois's 2009 Breast Cancer Disparities Act (P.L. 95-1045), which incentivizes community clinics to improve the quality of their mammography by reimbursing them at the Medicare rate (three times higher in Illinois than the alternative, the Medicaid rate) and eliminates copayments for women on Medicaid who are diagnosed with breast cancer.

SOCIAL WORK MATTERS

The question of whether social work's purpose is to provide material and psychological aid to individuals and families who are currently suffering or to reform the conditions that cause suffering has existed since at least the 1890s. Too often, social work practitioners and academic researchers have chosen to focus on one side of the question to the exclusion of the other. Arguably, although practitioners have begun to value evidence-based practice, researchers have remained firmly in the camp of gathering data to foster change, too often undertaken by others. I hold that, at a time when we are beginning to see bridging between disciplines to enhance outcomes, we should encourage bridging between practitioners and researchers within our own discipline. It is very difficult for me to imagine doing research without carefully considering practice and policy. Research, practice, and policy are inextricably bound in my work on breast cancer mortality disparities between African American and white women.

DISCUSSION QUESTIONS

1. What is the present consensus, if any, on whether the mission of social work is to provide material and psychological aid to individuals and families who are currently suffering or to reform the conditions that cause suffering? Has it changed over time?

2. Who do you think should be primarily responsible for initiating policy change? What are the roles, if any, of practitioners and researchers in producing change?

REFERENCES

Alterkruse, S. F., Kosary, C. L., Krapcho, M., Neyman, N., Aminou, E., Waldron, W., et al. (2010). *SEER breast cancer statistics, 1975–2010.* Bethesda, MD: National Cancer Institute.

American Cancer Society. (2009). *Breast cancer facts and figures 2009–2010.* Retrieved from http://www.cancer.org/Research/CancerFactsFigures/BreastCancerFactsFigures/breast-cancer-facts--figures-2009-2010

Anderson, B., Thornton, L. M., Shapiro, C. L., Farrar, W. N., Mundy, B. L., Yang, H.-C., & Carson, W. E., III. (2010). Behavioral, immune, and health benefits after recurrence for psychological intervention participants. *Clinical Cancer Research, 16,* 3270–3277.

Anderson, W. F., Rosenberg, P. S., Menashe, I., Mitani, A., & Pfeiffer, R. M. (2008). Age-related crossover in breast cancer incidence rates between black and white ethnic groups. *Journal of the National Cancer Institute, 100,* 1804–1814.

Ansell, D., Grabler, P., Whitman, S., Ferrans, C., Burgess-Bishop, J., Murray, L. R., et al. (2009). A community effort to reduce the black/white breast cancer mortality disparity in Chicago. *Cancer Causes and Control, 20,* 1681–1688.

Campbell, R. T., Li, X., Dolecek, T. A., Barrett, R. E., Weaver, K. E., & Warnecke, R. B. (2009). Economic, racial and ethnic disparities in breast cancer in the US: Towards a more comprehensive model. *Health & Place, 15,* 870–879.

Daste, B. M., & Rose, S. R. (2005). Group work with cancer patients. In G. L. Grief & P. H. Ephross (Eds.), *Group work with populations at risk* (pp. 15–30). New York: Oxford University Press.

Gehlert, S., & Colditz, G. (2011). Cancer disparities: Unmet challenges in the elimination of disparities. *Cancer Epidemiology, Biomarkers, and Prevention, 20,* 1809–1814.

Gehlert, S., Mininger, C., & Cipriano-Steffens, C. M. (2010). Placing biology in breast cancer research. In L. Burton, S. P. Kemp, M. Leung, S. A. Matthews, & D. Takeuchi (Eds.), *Communities, neighborhoods, and health: Expanding the boundaries of place* (pp. 57–72). New York: Springer.

Gehlert, S., Mininger, C., Sohmer, D., & Berg, K. (2008). (Not so) gently down the stream: Choosing interventions to ameliorate health disparities. *Health & Social Work, 33,* 163–167.

Gehlert, S., Rebbeck, T., Lurie, N., Warnecke, R., Paskett, E., Goodwin, J., et al. (2007). *Cells to society: Overcoming health disparities.* Bethesda, MD: National Cancer Institute, U.S. Department of Health and Human Services.

Hudis, C. A., & Gianni, L. (2011). Triple-negative breast cancer: An unmet medical need. *Oncologist, 16*(10), 1–11.

Newman, L. A. (2005). Breast cancer in African American women. *Oncologist, 10*(1), 1–14.

Warnecke, R. B., Oh, A., Breen, N., Gehlert, S., Paskett, E., Tucker, K. L., et al. (2008). Approaching health disparities from a population perspective: The National Institutes of Health Centers for Population Health and Health Disparities. *American Journal of Public Health, 98,* 1608–1615.

Whitman, S., Ansell, D., Orsi, J., & Francois, T. (2011). The racial disparity in breast cancer mortality. *Journal of Community Health, 36,* 588–596.

CHAPTER 38

PSYCHOSOCIAL ISSUES IN LIFE-LIMITING ILLNESS:

CONTINUITY OF CARE

Katherine Walsh

POLICY MATTERS

I have been a practicing social worker for 33 years, the first 13 in acute and chronic health care settings and the last 20 in home-based health and hospice care private practice, and teaching. Beginning as a case manager in a chronic care facility in the late 1970s, my professional social work roles have included clinical social worker in an urban comprehensive cancer center and a small community hospital; visiting nurse social worker; psychosocial services director in a hospice program; professor of social work overseeing students in a wide variety of practice settings; and, for the past 22 years, therapist in private practice specializing in illness, trauma, and loss.

Social work services to medically ill clients are reimbursed through different mechanisms in the current health care system. Hospitals, skilled nursing facilities, and hospices are expected to provide them as part of the daily rate charged to Medicare, Medicaid, and other insurers. For outpatient clinics, private practices, and visiting nurse/home care services, they are billed for separately, usually under a *Diagnostic and Statistical Manual of Mental Disorders* (4th ed.) (*DSM–IV*) diagnosis (American Psychiatric Association, 1994). Therefore, an individual undergoing cancer or cardiac treatment in the hospital, as well as their family members, can receive social work intervention to relieve anxiety or depression and facilitate adjustment to the illness without a *DSM–IV* diagnosis, while the same patient and family at home, receiving treatment in an outpatient setting can only receive social work intervention if their insurance approves the services, based on a *DSM–IV* diagnosis. The result of this policy is that psychosocial care is fragmented and is not equally available or accessible to all patients and families who may need it; depending on geographic location and their individual insurance carrier. Acute, fragmented care is favored by this policy over coordinated, prevention-oriented, and community-based care.

In addition, medical services are favored over mental health and psychosocial services, and there is no reimbursement for either collateral contacts with interdisciplinary colleagues or advocacy activities that are essential to client health and mental health at all stages of a serious or life-threatening illness.

These restrictive policies have made it essential for social workers to advocate through a variety of channels to ensure client access to psychosocial services across the illness continuum. As a practitioner, I teach clients the skills they need to advocate for themselves, often using the Cancer Survival Toolbox, a free self-advocacy training program created collaboratively by cancer survivors, oncology social workers, and nurses (National Coalition for Cancer Survivorship, 2011). I also advocate on the behalf of clients in local forums, such as provider meetings with insurers, and in national forums like the President's Cancer Panel. As a member of the board of directors and eventually as president of the Association of Oncology Social Work, I promoted the work of our legislative advocacy committee and brought the social work perspective to organizations such as the National Patient Advocacy Foundation, National Coalition for Cancer Survivorship, Leukemia and Lymphoma Society, and C-Change—all organizations advocating for policies to improve care for people with cancer.

As a program director for hospice and a member of the medical advisory boards of the American Cancer Society and Cancer Connection (a local grassroots organization), I have created programs to address unmet needs of individuals and families who are members of underserved populations. As a professor, I help students make the link between practice and policy and promote membership in NASW as a first step to participating in the advocacy efforts of the profession. Yet with all these activities, I still have to carry out advocacy interventions and educate clients about self-advocacy every day in my practice.

SOCIAL WORK MATTERS

> The Institute of Medicine Report on Improving Palliative Care and Cancer underscored the importance of addressing both physical and psychosocial symptoms and has been essential in the development and utilization of best practice guidelines and standards. "These standards require expert assessment and intervention by an interdisciplinary team in order to develop and implement comprehensive treatment plans that address the complex factors that contribute to physical and psychosocial distress." (Meier & Beresford, 2008, p. 182)

This quotation, written by palliative care physicians, underscores the importance of the interdisciplinary team, which in hospital- or home-based medical programs often includes physicians, nurses, social workers, rehabilitation specialists, and sometimes spiritual counselors. Social workers are employed on interdisciplinary teams in these settings because they are equipped to assess clinical disorders such as major depression, generalized anxiety disorder, acute stress disorder, and posttraumatic stress disorder, and also because "quality clinical social work care attends to a range of biological, psychological and social issues that patients, families and children (dealing with serious illness) regularly face" (Berzoff & Silverman, 2004, p. 266).

These issues often present early in the illness continuum, sometimes at the time of diagnosis if not before, and may require intervention intermittently, if not continuously, during the acute, palliative care, and end-of-life phases.

The National Quality Forum recognized the importance of ongoing management of psychological reactions in its preferred practices for palliative care. One of 38 preferred practices is to "assess and manage the psychological reactions of patients and families (including stress, anticipatory grief, and coping) in a regular, ongoing fashion in order to address emotional and functional impairment and loss" (National Quality Forum, 2006).

The Forum also noted that coordination of care is a "significant element in the provision of optimal care for complex, chronic diseases such as cancer" but that "follow-up of families of patients who have died demonstrate that 15 to 21 percent of these families believe there were significant problems with the coordination of care" (National Quality Forum, 2006).

Depending on reimbursement policies, social work services may or may not be available at different points along the continuum. Social work services are not billable but, rather, are provided as part of the day rate for hospitals, skilled nursing facilities, and inpatient palliative care and hospice programs. Because these programs and facilities do not receive specified reimbursement, social work services are often limited to risk screening and assessment or discharge planning, even when depression, anxiety, and family adjustment to illness are identified problems, which they are in about one-third of patients diagnosed with cancer.

Counseling services, the primary intervention to treat these psychosocial problems, are limited by sheer numbers of cases the (often solitary) social worker carries. I often receive referrals to my psychotherapy practice, from social work colleagues in medical and hospice settings, of clients who they have assessed to have significant psychosocial distress. I use a variety of evidence-based models of intervention, including cognitive–behavioral therapy and family therapy, that can prevent or ameliorate psychosocial distress and prevent acute hospitalizations as well as complicated grief reactions in surviving family members.

NARRATIVE

The following case is an example of a life-limiting illness that requires psychosocial intervention—over its entire course, including during the palliative care phase—that is often unavailable in our fragmented system, due to restrictive policies.

Effrosini is a 52-year-old married woman who immigrated to the United States with her husband when they were in their early 20s for her husband to attend graduate school. Her extended family lives in Greece. She has a son, 24, who lives and works in Colorado, and a daughter, 15, in high school. She has worked in the restaurant industry for many years, and her husband is a consultant who travels for work. She was referred for counseling by the social worker in the large urban comprehensive cancer center, 90 miles from the semirural community in which she lives, where she was diagnosed with liver cancer.

Her situation is like that of many clients living far from the facility where the diagnosis and treatment recommendations were made. She receives treatment in a private oncologist's office in her home town, where no psychosocial services are provided. She expressed a great deal of distress on learning of her diagnosis because of the uncertain survival associated with it, and she and her husband came to the initial therapy session together, saying they were shocked by the diagnosis and frightened about the prognosis, and asked for help in managing anxiety as well as with family adjustment issues.

After three joint sessions focused on Effrosini's and her family members' adjustment to the diagnosis, Effrosini attended individual sessions, and we began cognitive–behavioral therapy to help her with anxiety, depressed mood, and the physical side effects of chemotherapy, which she received both in the oncologist's office and through a portable pump she wore at home and at work. After eight weekly sessions in which she mastered several cognitive behavioral techniques, she was experiencing less anxiety and sessions were reduced to once a month and focused largely on managing the ongoing stresses of illness—including concerns about how her illness was affecting her elderly mother and a mentally ill sister as well as her husband and children. She preferred not to attend a support group that met in her area, saying that her energy was very low in the evenings, when the group met.

She used the therapy very effectively and—although determined to work, exercise, eat healthily, and think positively—often used the sessions to deal with her sadness and fears about her cancer, crying appropriately and expressing concern about the future, including seeing her daughter get to college. After about 10 months, her chemotherapy was modified due to tumor progression, and her anxiety understandably increased. Six months later the regimen was altered again, due to unavailability of one of the chemotherapy agents. I recommended that she get in touch with a national advocacy organization to learn about collective action that she might participate in to influence this drug shortage. Although greatly distressed that she was unable to continue with the chemotherapy agent, Effrosini felt some empowerment from taking collective action with others.

With the change in chemotherapy came increased symptoms—including nausea, some jaundice, and intense fatigue—which impeded her ability to work, eat, exercise, and socialize in the way she had been able to until then. Her level of distress fluctuated in accordance with these symptoms, and she wept during therapy sessions, stating repeatedly, "I love my life, and I just want to live it." She was especially concerned about disrupting her daughter's high school experience and preparation for college and deliberated over whether to ask her son to move closer to home from Colorado. She struggled with depression but found it helpful to continue working as much as she was able, even though it required her to rest much more each day.

Collaboration with her oncologist and general practitioner were required to coordinate antidepressant and antianxiety medication, and we resumed weekly counseling sessions. One day she called to say that her daughter had had a "meltdown," and following this, we held a family session with her daughter and husband. I made a referral to the school adjustment counselor and made myself available to her daughter and the family for additional counseling. Effrosini and I also taught her daughter and husband the breathing, progressive muscle relaxation, and guided imagery exercises she had learned in her cognitive–behavioral therapy, and they practiced daily together.

All of this took place while Effrosini was undergoing active treatment and working and before she was eligible for Visiting Nurses Association palliative care or hospice services. Approximately three months later, a consultation with the comprehensive cancer center resulted in the recommendation to cease chemotherapy treatments, and hospice care was initiated. The hospice social worker and I were then able to collaborate in providing for both her and her family's psychosocial and bereavement needs. Following Effrosini's death, her husband participated in individual grief counseling with me before he was ready to enter a hospice bereavement support group.

CONCLUSION

Due in part to my existing relationships with many of the other community providers, desired outcomes were achieved with Effrosini and her family, but my ability to provide effective services throughout the illness continuum required significant time and effort in collateral contacts that were not reimbursed. This care could be provided, in part, because this family had resources that not all families have. The co-pays for her therapy sessions, for example, and transportation to various providers were manageable for her because of her income status and family support system, but a major problem with the current health care system is that this kind of care is not routinely affordable or accessible for those with more limited income and in communities with fewer resources.

DISCUSSION QUESTIONS

1. What advocacy efforts do you think are necessary to ensure adequate psychosocial services for patients and families across the continuum of care in serious and chronic illness?

2. How can social workers in medical settings work together to improve reimbursement for mental health services to medically ill clients with significant psychosocial distress?

REFERENCES

American Psychiatric Association. (1994). *Diagnostic and statistical manual of mental disorders* (4th ed.). Washington, DC: Author.

Berzoff, J., & Silverman, P. (2004). *Living with dying: A handbook for end-of-life care health professionals.* New York: Columbia University Press.

Meier, D. E., & Beresford, L. (2008). Social workers advocate for a seat at the palliative care table. *Journal of Palliative Medicine, 11*(1), 10–14. doi:10.1089/jpm.2008.9996

National Coalition for Cancer Survivorship. (2011). *Cancer survival toolbox.* Retrieved from http://www.canceradvocacy.org/toolbox/

National Quality Forum. (2006). *A national framework and preferred practices for palliative and hospice care quality.* Retrieved from http://www.qualityforum.org/Publications/2006/12/A_National_Framework_and_Preferred_Practices_for_Palliative_and_Hospice_Care_Quality.aspx

CHAPTER 39

DOMESTIC VIOLENCE, WOMEN'S HEALTH, AND THE POWER OF SOCIAL WORK

Tricia B. Bent Goodley

NARRATIVE

Madeline could only describe her situation as "complicated." With her two children in tow, she started out by saying that she was tired and that she couldn't take it anymore. Her story unfolded before me.

We had been working together for more than three months due to a report from her children's school of educational neglect. Her older daughter was repeatedly truant, and her younger daughter was constantly fighting with other children. She talked about trying to make ends meet and not having enough food. Her husband lost his job working in a factory six years ago. She was later terminated from her job. She said that she had often been late or absent from work due to medical issues. She had missing teeth and said that she could not complete her dental work because she lost her health insurance.

Although she had high blood pressure and had suffered a minor stroke, she said that medication for her depression was her priority. Unfortunately, she took that medication only sporadically, when she had enough money. She often missed her appointments and was increasingly forgetful. Her children said that she often blacked out "for no reason." Madeline blamed the medication and the stress of trying to deal with her children's behavior.

However, on this day, she had a different story. She said that she was being physically abused, that it all began after her husband lost his job, and that she needed to stay in a shelter long enough for her family to send for her and the children. Madeline said that she had tried to get a protective order three years before, but the order was denied because she didn't look like a victim of domestic violence and there was no criminal record of the abuse. She never went to the court again.

As her husband became more violent, the abuse became more visible to others at her job. They became uncomfortable with her bruises, missing teeth, lacerations, and broken arm. Her ability to arrive on time and do her job was compromised by the abuse. Although people at her job knew about the abuse, there was no workplace policy in place that would allow

her to request or receive assistance. She said that she didn't even know what domestic vio-
lence was until she went to the hospital for the broken arm and saw a poster with a picture
of someone who looked like her. However, the possibility of domestic violence was not further
explored by the emergency room staff, and so she did not provide additional information.

Madeline went on to explain that her older daughter was truant because she was afraid
she would come home and find her mother dead, so she stayed home and watched after her.
Madeline expressed great concern for her and for her younger daughter, who she felt was
acting out because she was angry. Madeline went on to talk about her chronic headaches,
forgetfulness, memory loss, and, at times, inability to put words together. She said that
her husband had repeatedly choked her and hit her on the head. She said that the doctor
never asked her if her symptoms could have been caused by abuse. Madeline didn't know
what to do.

I asked her what finally led her to tell me what was happening. She said that over the
years she had been infected with sexually transmitted diseases by her husband. However, her
most recent visit to the emergency room revealed that she was HIV positive.

DISCUSSION

Madeline was absolutely correct: Her story was complicated. Women's health issues
are often complicated and riddled with the blunt realities that women face from day to
day, from economic problems to caregiving responsibilities that compete with self-care.

As a social worker, I have had an opportunity to see both how policy intersects with
these complex issues and the power of social work to bring healing and possibility into
people's lives (Bent-Goodley, 2011). Madeline's story is an example of how policy and
practice are linked and how we, as social workers, can provide someone like her with
healing and hope.

Domestic violence is very much a women's health issue. Madeline's experience is
not unique. Over five million women seek medical assistance annually due to domestic violence (National Center for Injury Prevention and Control, 2003). Women
who experience abuse are 50 percent to 70 percent more likely to have other health
issues—such as chronic diseases, arthritis, headaches and migraines, chronic pain,
stroke, urinary tract and vaginal infections, pelvic inflammatory disease, gastrointesti-
nal problems, depression, anxiety, and stress-related issues—than women who are not
abused (Breiding, Black, & Ryan, 2008; Campbell et al., 2002; Wuest et al., 2008).

The link between HIV and domestic violence is also quite startling, as survivors of
domestic violence are at increased risk of becoming HIV-infected due to forced sex
and inability to negotiate safer sex practices (Bent-Goodley, 2007; Lichtenstein, 2006;
Rountree, Goldbach, Bent-Goodley, & Bagwell, 2011). Nearly one-half of survivors
have lost consciousness during a domestic violence incident (Banks, 2007). In a recent
study examining the treatment of survivors in emergency rooms, it was found that
nearly three out of four women were not identified as domestic violence survivors even

though they had made police reports of domestic violence within a week of seeking medical treatment (Rhodes et al., 2011). Almost 20 percent of abused women report having a partner who prevented them from receiving medical treatment, compared with 2 percent of all women (McCloskey et al., 2007). The same study found that survivors were more likely to get help for intimate partner violence when they were given information from their medical care provider.

POLICY MATTERS

When I think about Madeline's needs, the link between policy and practice and the role of social workers seems obvious. The Violence Against Women Act (P.L. 103-322) was passed in 1994 and was reauthorized in 2000 and 2005, and it was up for reauthorization at the time of this writing. This law has provided federal leadership on addressing violence against women. Although it primarily addresses legal and criminal issues related to domestic violence, it also expanded support services for survivors of violence. As it relates to women's health, it increased funding for primary prevention and emphasized the importance of providing culturally competent care and reaching underserved populations. These services were crucial for Madeline because they furthered her ability to access culturally competent services and promoted her safety and health.

The Family Violence Prevention and Services Act (P.L. 98-457) was enacted as part of the Child Abuse Amendments of 1984 (P.L. 98-457) and is the largest source of funding for shelters and emergency services for survivors of domestic violence. This law makes it possible for over 70,000 women to receive shelter services daily, yet over 9,000 women are still left without such services due to lack of resources (National Network to End Domestic Violence, 2011). Madeline relied on these services to keep her and her children safe and ensure that their most immediate health and other needs were met.

The Patient Protection and Affordable Care Act of 2010 (P.L. 111-148), often referred to as the Affordable Care Act, was signed into law on March 23, 2010. This historic legislation is groundbreaking in its protections and expansions of services and resources for vulnerable people. It also includes provisions for domestic violence that are important for someone such as Madeline. It prohibits health insurance companies from imposing restrictions on coverage of preexisting conditions associated with domestic violence. This provision is particularly important for Madeline because of the long-term consequences of her traumatic brain injury and her stroke. The Affordable Care Act includes other important provisions, such as the Maternal, Infant, and Early Childhood Home Visitation Program, the Pregnancy Prevention Fund, the Head Start Initiative, and the Defending Childhood Initiative. The Maternal, Infant, and Early Childhood Home Visitation Program provides coordinated and comprehensive services to communities identified as at risk of domestic violence. The at-risk classification includes communities with a high prevalence of domestic violence.

Home visitation would have helped Madeline identify supports and advocates early in the stages of the violence.

The Pregnancy Prevention Fund will provide support to women who are pregnant and survivors of domestic violence, and the Head Start program will be given support to offer curricula that prevent and respond to domestic violence. The Defending Childhood Initiative's support for child witnesses of domestic violence will provide crucial support for Madeline's two daughters. In addition, the institution of patient navigators or people designated to guide patients as part of the Affordable Care Act will provide Madeline with an advocate who can help her access the health care system in a way that meets her health needs and empowers her simultaneously.

Although macro-level policy is important and sets a national tone, policies at the local level—administrative and judicial—also have an important impact on domestic violence survivors' health and well-being. Workplace policies are needed to help survivors of domestic violence negotiate sick time and attend to legal and medical issues associated with the violence without penalty or fear of loss of employment. Employers have identified domestic violence as a major issue for the workplace. Despite this, many employers lack policies and procedures for addressing it.

More than one-third (37 percent) of survivors have experienced a negative impact on work performance, such as being late, missing work days, and losing opportunities for promotion and career advancement. Survivors have reported missing eight million work days annually, and for at least 50 percent they have reported losing a job because of domestic violence (National Center for Injury Prevention and Control, 2003). The loss of a job can be devastating for a survivor, because it forces her to rely more heavily on the perpetrator and it limits her mobility and choices. It can also result in the loss of health insurance.

The Security and Financial Empowerment Act (S.1740) was introduced in October 2009 at the national level to help provide guidance for these types of issues for employers. If passed, it will allow survivors to take off time during the work day without penalty for medical attention, safety planning, and obtaining legal support. Employers would also be required to put safety measures in place for survivors of domestic violence, and the law would ensure that unemployment insurance was consistently available to survivors across all states. This law can make an important contribution; however, employers can also generate their own policies to ensure that these provisions are in place, that employees are aware of signs of violence and stalking, and that survivors know where they can turn within the institution for help. Madeline needed this type of support, but it was unavailable from her employer.

Judges and magistrates also play a major role in the daily lives of survivors. Although there is no uniform policy that governs the roles of judges, state and local governments should be held accountable for their treatment of survivors. The judge who heard Madeline's case didn't believe that she "looked like a victim" and, thus, did not help her. Such statements, unfortunately, are not unique to her story. Not having this support created additional stress and heightened risk for Madeline. It also made her feel that her problem was insignificant. Thus, judges and magistrates are powerful and important to the health of survivors. The action or lack of action of a judge or magistrate can have detrimental or life-saving consequences. The judge's lack of action compounded Madeline's problem and resulted in her staying in an unsafe and unhealthy situation. Therefore, requiring training and monitoring judicial performance through administrative policies and protocols can improve survivor health and safety.

Health screenings and assessments are very important. Having policies and procedures in all medical settings can help health care workers to identify and help survivors. Madeline made multiple trips to the emergency room. She went to the dentist for cracked and lost teeth. She also suffered a traumatic brain injury. Her husband did not allow her to go to the doctor's office unaccompanied, and no one ever thought to ask if she was experiencing abuse. The doctors never thought to meet with her without her husband, and, as a consequence, they missed opportunities to help her. Madeline's health was compromised in many ways over the years: poor oral health, sexually transmitted diseases, stroke, depression, and traumatic brain injury. Thus, administrative policies are key to supporting the health of survivors and must take place in addition to macro-level policy making.

SOCIAL WORK MATTERS

The policies described above have provided social workers with a means of helping women as they try to address the complicated issues of domestic violence in their lives. As social workers, we make use of the resources sanctioned or created as a result of policies, and we advocate for policies that would better support survivors. Social workers are uniquely equipped to provide both the direct service and the advocacy needed to help women become empowered and to secure the resources they need to rebuild their lives. As a profession, we are particularly suited because of our training to connect policy and practice in specific ways to advance the needs of our clients. The power of social work is ultimately centered in our ability to help our clients empower themselves and build a better life for themselves and generations to come. We are well positioned to meet this call to action.

DISCUSSION QUESTIONS

1. What role can social workers play to advance domestic violence policies that empower survivors of domestic violence?

2. What advantage do social workers bring to the policy process because of our combined clinical and macro-level training?

References

Banks, M. (2007). Overlooked but critical: Traumatic brain injury as a consequence of interpersonal violence. *Trauma, Violence & Abuse, 8,* 290–298.

Bent-Goodley, T. B. (2007). Health disparities and violence against women. *Trauma, Violence & Abuse, 8,* 90–104.

Bent-Goodley, T. B. (2011). *The ultimate betrayal: A renewed look at intimate partner violence.* Washington, DC: NASW Press.

Breiding, M. J., Black, M. C., & Ryan, G. W. (2008). Prevalence and risk factors of intimate partner violence in eighteen U.S. states/territories, 2005. *American Journal of Preventive Medicine, 34,* 112–118.

Campbell, J., Jones, A. S., Dienemann, J., Kub, J., Schollenberger, J., O'Campo, P., Gielen, A., & Wynne, C. (2002). Intimate partner violence and physical health consequences. *Archives of Internal Medicine, 162,* 1157–1164.

Child Abuse Amendments of 1984, P.L. 98-457, 98 Stat. 1749 (1984).

Family Violence Prevention and Services Act, P.L. 98-457, 98 Stat. 1757 (1984).

Lichtenstein, B. (2006). Domestic violence in barriers to health care for HIV-positive women. *AIDS Patient Care & STDs, 20,* 122–132.

McCloskey, L. A., Williams, C. M., Lichter, E., Gerber, M., Ganz, M. L. & Sege, R. (2007). Abused women disclose partner interference with health care: An unrecognized form of battering. *Journal of General Internal Medicine, 22,* 1067–1072.

National Center for Injury Prevention and Control. (2003). *Costs of intimate partner violence against women in the United States.* Atlanta: Author.

National Network to End Domestic Violence. (2011). *Domestic violence counts 2010: A 24-hour census of domestic violence shelters and services across the United States.* Washington, DC: Author.

Patient Protection and Affordable Care Act of 2010, P.L. 111-148, 124 Stat. 119 (2010).

Rhodes, K. V., Kothari, C. L., Dichter, M., Cerulli, C., Wiley, J., & Marcus, S. (2011). Intimate partner violence identification and response: Time for a change in strategy. *Journal of General Internal Medicine, 26,* 894–899.

Rountree, M. A., Goldbach, J., Bent-Goodley, T., & Bagwell, M. (2011). HIV/AIDS knowledge and prevention programming in domestic violence shelters: How are we doing? *Journal of HIV/AIDS & Social Services, 10,* 42–54.

Violence Against Women Act of 1994, P.L. 103-322, 108 Stat. 1902 (1994).

Wuest, J., Merritt-Gray, M., Ford-Gilboe, M., Lent, B., Varcoe, C., & Campbell, J. C. (2008). Chronic pain in women survivors of intimate partner violence. *Journal of Pain, 9,* 1049–1057.

CHAPTER 40

END-OF-LIFE, PALLIATIVE, AND HOSPICE CARE

Karen Bullock and Jodi Hall

End-of-life care refers to multidimensional assessment and interventions provided to assist individuals, their families, and members of their social support network as they approach death. This care may include palliative or hospice care. One may receive palliative care in a hospice setting, long-term care facility, hospital, or at home. Whether sudden or expected, the end of a person's life is a unique experience that can have a significant impact on the individual, her or his family system, and the family legacy; those who survive the experience will share their experiences with others, and those shared experiences will inform future end-of-life care decisions.

Practitioners across disciplines are often faced with a moral conundrum when providing end-of-life and palliative care, because professional boundaries, practice standards of care, and individualized goals of care may seem to conflict with one another. Social workers are trained to "start where the client is" and allow for self-determination in the helping relationship. Moreover, in keeping with the profession's social justice commitment, it is necessary to consider the client's culture and unique end-of-life-care wishes and preferences if we are to provide optimal care. To this end, NASW (2004) has developed *Standards for Social Work Practice in Palliative and End-of-Life Care* to ensure that social workers continue to acquire and incorporate values, skills, and knowledge that are consistent with our code of ethics to meet the needs of our clients and patients along the continuum of illness and in interdisciplinary care settings.

POLICY MATTERS

In addition to standards for practice, those of us with expertise in end-of-life, palliative, and hospice care have a great appreciation for the policies that have helped to shape and advance care options. One in particular is the Patient Self-Determination Act (P.L. 101-508) (PSDA), which gave individuals the right to facilitate their own health care decisions, refuse treatment, and make their care decision known in advance.

Congress passed this law as an amendment to the Omnibus Budget Reconciliation Act of 1990 (P.L. 101-508). It became effective in 1991 and required many Medicare and Medicaid providers (hospitals, nursing homes, hospice programs, home health agencies, and HMOs) to give adult individuals, at the time of inpatient admission or enrollment, certain information about their rights under state laws governing advance directives—including the right to participate in and direct their own health care decisions, the right to accept or refuse medical or surgical treatment, and the right to prepare an advance directive—and about the provider's policies that govern the exercise of these rights. The act also prohibits institutions from discriminating against a patient who does not have an advance directive. Furthermore, it requires institutions to document patient information and provide the option of advance care planning and an advance directive.

The law explicitly states that individuals have the right to make decisions regarding their care, including accepting or refusing specific options, and to make these preferences known in an advance directive. It also requires health care facilities and agencies to discuss advance health care directives with a patient at the point of admission to a care facility.

This law was a noble attempt to guarantee that patients will receive the care that they feel is optimal and culturally appropriate. However, those of us in social work recognized the need to explore the connection between social welfare policy and clinical practice (Humphreys et al., 1993) years before there were systematic assessments of the effectiveness of written directives in the care of seriously ill hospitalized patients (Teno et al., 1997), because we recognized that different interpretations of policy can result in practices that don't necessarily produce intended outcomes. A perfect example is the rally of support for hospice care as the gold standard of care for patients at the end of life.

Hospice is a philosophy of care that takes a team-oriented approach to addressing symptom management and the emotional, psychosocial, and spiritual needs of a patient and family members. In the 1970s, when it was established as a care model in the United States, hospice care was not directed at hospitalized patients. The PSDA has been instrumental in the implementation of policies that have improved care that patients at the end of life receive in hospital. Most people in the United States still die in hospitals, and hospice care is most often provided in the home of the patient, a family member's home, or a nursing home (National Hospice and Palliative Care Organization [NHPCO], 2011). Therefore, such policies are an important point of focus as the cost of health care, especially hospital care, continues to soar in our turbulent economy.

Patients of any age, religion, race, or illness may be eligible to receive hospice and palliative care. Yet individuals of racial and ethnic minority groups tend to underutilize this care, with less than 20 percent representation among hospice beneficiaries (NHPCO, 2011). The care is covered under Medicare and Medicaid and by most private insurance plans, HMOs, and other managed care organizations.

Palliative care extends this philosophy of care to patients who are not at the end of life but who could benefit from receiving this care earlier in their illness or disease process. No specific therapy or intervention that is deemed beneficial to the patient is excluded (NHPCO, 2011). Needs are continually assessed, and treatment options are explored and evaluated in the context of the patient's values, symptoms, and goals of care. Social workers agree that such care, when it is provided in a holistic model and helps a patient to live and die with dignity, is consistent with our mission of social justice (Altilio & Otis-Green, 2011).

Practitioners who provide end-of-life care are often faced with the challenge of how best to meet the needs of an increasingly diverse U.S. population. Policies that are intended to improve care for the dying may actually create barriers to a good death when consideration isn't given to cultural distinctions (Bullock, 2011). The following is an example of how one family was affected by the implementation of a policy that stemmed from the PSDA.

NARRATIVE

A 62-year-old African American woman with a diagnosis of advanced stage IV ovarian cancer received surgery and has been receiving chemotherapy up until this particular clinical social work assessment. She has bowel obstructions and cannot eat and is presently on total parenteral nutrition, which is a method of supplying all nutritional needs intravenously, at home and in the hospital. She has a urinary tract infection and is taking antibiotics. She also has significant abdominal, back, and leg pain.

Her life expectancy is limited, probably less than three months. Her oncologist states there is no additional cancer treatment that will help her and that hospice and palliative care is "all that we can offer" at this stage.

The patient is alert and oriented and able to make decisions. She is an elementary school teacher and worked until two months ago. She is proud of her career and her life accomplishments. She is unmarried and told the social worker that her daughter would be making the health care decisions on her (the patient's) behalf. The patient lost her mother to lung cancer nine months before this clinical encounter. She has two sons, who are unmarried and have moved in with her over the last three months. She has a brother, who is the oldest of the siblings and lives less than five miles away. The number of family members involved in the decision making was a concern for the treatment team. However, it is consistent with the norm for the family's culture.

The social worker called for a palliative care consult, noting that the patient is in severe pain and that her brother has been screaming at her and telling her she would become an addict if she took the morphine. He has told the nurses that they are forbidden to give her any morphine and that she was not to have any more Ativan, a medication used to relieve anxiety, or other psychiatric medications because they were making her "dopey" and she needed to be alert to continue fighting.

The patient has been documented as saying that she is not ready to give up and wants to talk to the oncologist again about whether or not she can take one more round of chemotherapy. She does not want to give up the total parenteral nutrition and wants to go home so she can be in her community with her church family. When asked about her pain and whether she is getting enough pain medication at home, she states it is okay. When asked directly about whether her brother is withholding adequate pain and antianxiety medications from her at home, she says, "Oh, he gives it to me . . . when he thinks I need it." When asked if this is acceptable to her, she says, "I trust that he's going to do what's right. He is not yelling. He just talks like that." She then says, "He does the best he can to help me."

Members of the palliative care consult team invoke the PSDA and explain to the patient that she had the right to make an autonomous decision on the course of her care, without her brother or sons and daughter, and that she is mentally capable of doing so. A discussion about how the patient's care may become a burden to the family is initiated and concludes with a recommendation that she consider an inpatient hospice unit. Advance care planning is suggested, with an emphasis on completing an advance directive while there is still time.

The social worker, who has worked extensively with African Americans, concludes that the patient is, at this point, attempting to comply with care recommendations. Shortly thereafter, the patient agrees to the inpatient admission but tells the clinical team that she is afraid to tell her brother that is what she wants. The social worker is identified as the team member who is best suited to assist the patient and family with this challenge.

The social worker meets the patient's brother, who states that he recently lost his mother to lung cancer and lost his father when he was in high school. He took care of his little sister (the patient) and put her through college and then took care of his mother when she was ill. He is not ready to give up the fight and lose his only living sibling, his sister. He says that his sister was misdiagnosed for months and that her cancer could have been cured if not for the ignorance of her physicians. He also blames his sister for not telling him about her symptoms earlier as he could have made sure she had early treatment. He is hostile and extremely angry.

He has a written record of every treatment date and time and every medication that she has taken. One pain doctor told him that she had a toxic level of Ativan in her system. (This was six months ago, when she was home and took an amount that made her unable to function.) Therefore, he does not want her to receive any Ativan. He believes it is more important for her to be awake and alert so that she can "fight this" than to "give up" and take pain and anxiety drugs. He claims to understand that she will die of this cancer, but he believes she has a lot of quality time left.

SOCIAL WORK MATTERS

Fortunately, end-of-life, palliative, and hospice care take a team-oriented approach that includes social workers, because our training equips us with in-depth knowledge about working with ethnic, cultural, and economic diversity; family and support networks; multidimensional symptom management; bereavement; trauma in interdisciplinary practice; interventions across the life cycle; and systems interventions that address the fragmentation, gaps, and insufficiency in the U.S. health care system. These are critical areas for policy revisions and implementation of change in palliative and end-of-life care.

Social workers are prepared to analyze, influence, and advocate at local, state, and federal levels for policy changes that can lead to improvements in the care of patients across the care continuum. It is important for policies to be based on social work research in end-of-life, palliative, and hospice care to address many of the previously overlooked issues surrounding gaps in services, especially for underrepresented populations of diverse ethnicities, cultures, economic conditions, life styles, family types, and functioning.

DISCUSSION QUESTIONS

1. What are the implications of applying policies without flexibility and consideration for cultural differences?

2. What are some steps that can be taken to revise policies to meet the needs of a more diverse client and patient constituency?

REFERENCES

Altilio, T., & Otis-Green, S. (2011). *Oxford textbook of palliative social work*. New York: Oxford University Press.

Bullock, K. (2011). The influence of culture on end-of-life decision making. *Journal of Social Work in End-of-Life & Palliative Care*, 7(1), 83–98.

Humphreys, N. A., Deans Lake, S., Demont, P., Hollidge, C. Mangiardi, P., Nol, J., Rudd, J., Stalker, C., & Twomey, J. (1993). Integrating policy and practice: The contribution of clinical social work. *Smith College Studies in Social Work, 63*, 177–185.

National Association of Social Workers. (2004). *Standards for social work practice in palliative and end-of-life care*. Washington, DC: Author.

National Hospice and Palliative Care Organization. (2011). *Caring connections: Palliative care*. Retrieved from http://www.caringinfo.org/i4a/pages/index.cfm?pageid=3354

Omnibus Budget Reconciliation Act of 1990, P.L. 101-508, 104 Stat. 1388 (1990).

Patient Self-Determination Act, P.L. 101-508, 104 Stat. 1399-115 (1990).

Teno, J., Lynn, J., Wenger, N., Phillips, R. S., Murphy, D. P., Connors, A. F., Jr., et al. (1997). Advance directives for seriously ill hospitalized patients: Effectiveness with the Patient Self-Determination Act and the SUPPORT intervention. *Journal of the American Geriatrics Society, 45*, 500–507.

CHAPTER 41

ALZHEIMER'S DISEASE AND RELATED DEMENTIAS:
COMPLEX FAMILY CARE

Lisa P. Gwyther and Jessica L. Katz

SOCIAL WORK MATTERS

No social work professional will go through his or her career without being personally or professionally affected by Alzheimer's or related dementing diseases. Social work, as a central professional discipline, is included in almost every media report about the aging of baby boomers, the effects of the economic downturn and the loss of safety nets for this generation, and the urgent need to "retool" the health care workforce for an aging America (Institute of Medicine of the National Academies, 2008).

The number of people over the age of 65 will double to more than 80 million during the next 40 years (Vincent & Velkoff, 2010). The greatest risk factor for dementia remains advancing age. There are currently more than 5 million people in the United States with Alzheimer's disease, the most common cause of dementia, cared for by 15 million family caregivers (Alzheimer's Association, 2011a). In a recent poll, Alzheimer's was named as the second most feared common chronic condition of late life, after cancer (Blendon et al., 2011). Regardless of practice setting, every social worker should expect to have clients, family members, or friends who have some form of dementia or who care for family members with this condition. Alzheimer's is a common chronic progressive condition of late life; the fifth leading cause of death in people over 65; and catastrophic in its costs and conflicts for individuals, families, and society (Alzheimer's Association, 2011a).

Family caregivers are on the front lines of Alzheimer's care. It has been estimated that family caregivers provide 80 percent of at-home Alzheimer's care and spend an average of 40 hours a week providing direct care and supervision (Alzheimer's Association, 2011a; Alzheimer's Association & National Alliance for Caregiving, 2004). In 2009, family members' unpaid personal care was valued at $450 billion (AARP Public Policy Institute, 2011). Alzheimer's families provide exceptionally challenging, physically intimate, and emotionally wrenching care; respond to disruptive behavioral and psychiatric symptoms (such as wandering, paranoia, and agitation); and face progressive and variable functional declines, a long bereavement process, and tough ethical decisions. As helping professionals, it is imperative that social workers become better educated about dementia and its individual, family, community, and societal outcomes to effectively support clients. We must advocate for and practice giving back control to families dealing with dementia so that they can make their own decisions about what services will meet their unique needs. At a minimum, we have a responsibility to offer dementia-capable guidance even if we will never practice in a dementia-specific setting.

The Duke Aging Center Family Support Program has been a state-level, state-funded first-responder clearinghouse and technical assistance center for individuals, families, and professionals with questions about dementia recognition, diagnosis, care, services, research, and policy for over 25 years. In 1984, the Administration on Aging encouraged all state aging services to begin to identify and serve families affected by Alzheimer's disease. At that time in North Carolina, the Duke Family Support Program had taken a lead with the national Alzheimer's Association and with state foundation support to mobilize community support group programs. A contract from the North Carolina Department of Health and Human Services Division of Aging expanded access and information from the Duke Family Support Program throughout the state. The program started with one, and then two, social workers working with people with Alzheimer's disease and their families who participated in the first Alzheimer's disease and family care research studies. At that time, families were eager to meet and learn from others and from engaged research and clinical professionals. The first monthly support group for Alzheimer's families began meeting at Duke in 1979 and has continued to meet monthly ever since. The group has an open, revolving membership and is facilitated by two Duke social workers.

NARRATIVE AND DISCUSSION

Mr. H was attending his second Duke Family Support Program meeting when we met. He is a 78-year-old retired traveling evangelist. He and his wife, who is 80, have been married for 56 years. About eight years before, he began to observe changes in his wife. While working as a retail sales clerk one summer, she came home from work complaining that her coworkers told her she was getting disorganized. He noted that items in their house and files on the computer began to disappear. She was becoming uncharacteristically repetitive, and she began substituting general descriptive nouns for names (for example, "that place" instead of "the grocery store").

Their family physician diagnosed her with Alzheimer's disease. Mr. H had never suspected the diagnosis and describes feeling like he "had just been hit by a baseball bat." He tried to maintain normal aspects of their shared life, which included continuing to travel for his work. He said he had known that it was time to retire three years before when his wife ran out of a hotel in the middle of the night. As he described it, being a caregiver became his new full-time job.

At first, Mr. H said, he had no idea how to respond to his wife. He had little patience with her behavior and was frustrated with both her and the disease. Neither their family physician nor the neurologist they consulted gave them much guidance on how to live with her disability. Mr. H decided it was his responsibility to educate himself about the disease and the skills required to be his wife's caregiver. He attended community lectures, gathered materials from the Internet, and read books on the disease. At the encouragement of a friend from church, he began to attend our monthly caregiver support group. He hoped that the group participants would provide him with support and that the group itself would be a forum to educate others.

●■●

It is not uncommon for families to leave appointments with health care professionals with little guidance and few expectations about what happens next. They may be forced to "piece together appropriate next steps" (Alzheimer's Association, 2011b). The search for answers and guidance often leads families to seek out support groups. Most families delay attending support groups, often because they are unsure about the diagnosis or feel disloyal seeking help without the participation or consent of the impaired person. Online information can be overwhelming, contradictory, and irrelevant to immediate personal concerns.

Duke's early research comparing family caregivers who did and did not attend support groups (before there was online information) found that support group participants knew more about the disease and more about relevant services than nonparticipants but that this knowledge was not sufficient to overcome other barriers to timely and appropriate service use (Gwyther, 1998). Current research testing interventions to support Alzheimer's family caregivers tends to find minimal effects from support groups on caregiver stress, burden, or depression, often because families do not attend regularly or often enough to achieve a sustained benefit. Yet many families describe their first successful support group meeting as an "aha—you, too" moment of immediate identification as they find themselves forging a common bond with strangers experiencing a similar situation.

●■●

The Hs rely on Social Security as their primary source of income. Mr. H describes them as "challenged financially" but says he has learned to find necessary additional funds. They have four daughters, all of whom provide varying levels of financial, emotional, and instrumental support. Yet only one daughter lives nearby, and all the daughters are limited by time and distance as well as skills and understanding of the impact of their mother's illness on her and her husband's routines.

Mr. H is grateful for assistance from their church, including meal preparation, a house to rent, and spiritual support. He attributes his resilience in the face of such adversity to his strong faith and his equally strong community of faith. In addition, he appreciates that his local Department of Social Services pays for 10 hours a week of in-home personal care, but this is not respite for him. Because they cannot afford the $65-a-day fee for adult day health services, they are currently on the waiting list for a subsidy for Mrs. H to attend the five-day-a-week program. Ideally, Mr. H would like more help in his home. He may not necessarily prefer or need the respite offered by a 40-hour-a-week adult day program, but he does not want to institutionalize his wife, nor can they afford additional private in-home respite services.

●■●

Caregivers like Mr. H often desire more control of the professional care and resources available to them. There is a clear need for more flexible, consumer-directed services for dementia family caregivers. Consumer-directed services offer family caregivers more control, with guidance and support in selecting appropriate, timely, culturally acceptable, and affordable services based on perceived needs and preferences (Masters, 2006).

As an example, North Carolina's Project CARE (Caregiver Alternatives to Running on Empty) provides dementia-specific, consumer-directed, flexible, and tailored respite services up to an annual cap per family and with the expert guidance of a local consultant to families in slightly less than half of all North Carolina counties. Consumer-directed services have been shown to help families extend the time they are able to provide care in their homes (Masters, 2006). Because of its focus on client control and decision-making, consumer-directed service honors self-determination, a value all social workers are obligated to uphold.

The issue for Mr. H and other Alzheimer's family caregivers is that there is no system of long-term services and supports. Aging and community-based services are fragmented and inadequately linked to the health care system; they focus exclusively on an elder's financial status or impairments in noncognitive activities of daily living when determining eligibility; and they are not sufficiently person- or family-centered. There are no uniformly available respite services from the national Family Caregiver Support Program. Many Alzheimer's families find traditional aging services unprepared to handle the unique behavioral and communication issues of their impaired family members. Families ask us why they can't choose to be the paid "provider" in a consumer-directed system similar to the successful Medicaid Cash and Counseling demonstrations in several states. Cash and Counseling has assisted many families by providing "beneficiaries with a monthly allowance to arrange their supportive services and hire workers as they see fit" (Foster, Brown, Phillips & Carlson, 2005, p. 474), including hiring friends or family. In general, the issue for many well-intentioned family caregivers is that the service nonsystem uses family care up first rather than supporting the family caregiver. The serious physical and mental health consequences of ignoring the needs of current family caregivers will jeopardize the health care system for years to come.

● ■ ●

Often, Mrs. H does not recognize her husband, becomes acutely confused, and wanders outside if Mr. H doesn't watch her constantly. This constant vigilance is a major predictor of negative health consequences for Mr. H. He is concerned about his wife's safety and over-whelmed by her need for constant supervision and reassurance. He admits he could benefit from more time for himself and for running errands. Unfortunately, there are no dementia-specific or dementia-capable family-centered respite services in his area like North Carolina Project CARE.

Mr. H acknowledges concern about the future and the quality of care his wife would receive should something happen to him. He is currently exploring options available to her. He assumes his daughters may not be able to care for their mother in their own homes. He realizes that Mrs. H may need, and qualify for, Medicaid-funded full-time personal care, offered only in long-term care facilities. Yet he is not comfortable with the variable quality of the care received by residents with dementia in such facilities.

Mr. H believes that changes need to be made to the system of care for people with Alzheimer's because, as he noted, facility staff are not always knowledgeable about how to work with people with dementia. He is firm in saying he does not want his wife to be aban-doned to "babysitters" but, rather, insists on trained, compassionate caregivers. He is right-fully proud of how he has learned to improve the quality and effectiveness of his care for her through his active research. His initial fear, confusion, and anxiety have been replaced with courage, acceptance of the challenge, confidence, hope, and purpose. His focus has shifted from just managing his wife's Alzheimer's symptoms to helping her use her remaining skills. Still, he wonders how he can assure the transfer of those hard-won understandings to others who will care for her.

POLICY MATTERS

It is unfortunate that caregivers like Mr. H must worry about care quality and the lack of dementia-capable services. This is a common source of anxiety among family care-givers who turn to the Duke Family Support Program. Enhancing the quality of pro-fessional care provided to people with dementia is among the top four goals of a recent major federal policy initiative, the National Alzheimer's Project Act (P.L. 111-375) (NAPA) (U.S. Department of Health and Human Services, 2012). NAPA aims to create and maintain a strategic national plan to overcome Alzheimer's disease, includ-ing improving the coordination and evaluation of research and services. Signed into law by President Obama in January 2011, NAPA was the first legislation specifically geared toward Alzheimer's disease, which the Alzheimer's Association (2011c) deemed a victory. Due to the unprecedented number of older adults confronting Alzheimer's or Alzheimer's family care, public policy must address a national system of person- and family-centered dementia-capable long-term services and supports. A dementia-capable system of care will rely on social workers and other health care professionals with the knowledge and skills necessary to work with people with Alzheimer's and to support their family caregivers.

All older adults, including those with dementia, deserve quality care from professionals when their family members need help in providing care. With the expansion of the Lifespan Respite Act (H.R. 6350) and the National Family Caregiver Support Program (Older Americans Act Amendments of 2000 [P.L. 106-501]), and the proposed Health Outcomes, Planning, and Education for Alzheimer's Act (S. 738), extension of loan forgiveness to social workers and other professionals through the Caring for an Aging America Act (S. 1095), and the Alzheimer's Breakthrough Act (H.R. 6350), policy is moving in the right direction. Still, there are no current policies that are geared specifically toward the unique needs of Alzheimer's caregivers. Social workers witness first-hand the physical, financial, and emotional toll of Alzheimer's family care as well as the frustration and helplessness expressed by clients in the all-too-frequent "no-care zone."

It is our duty to serve such vulnerable populations. Social workers must take the lead in advocating with and for Alzheimer's families for better training and coordination of health and social service professionals, better reimbursement for dementia-specific expertise and guidance, and expanded equity and access to dementia-capable social work professionals wherever families face these tough care issues.

DISCUSSION QUESTIONS

1. What might you do to enhance dementia-capable practice in your agency?
2. What policy changes are needed related to Alzheimer's and family care?
3. What can social workers do to advocate for Alzheimer's policies on the local, state, and national levels?

REFERENCES

AARP Public Policy Institute. (2011). *Valuing the invaluable: The economic value of caregiving in 2009* [Data file]. Retrieved from assets.aarp.org/rgcenter/ppi/ltc/fs229-ltc.pdf

Alzheimer's Association. (2011a). *2011 Alzheimer's disease facts and figures* [Data file]. Retrieved from www.alz.org/downloads/Facts_Figures_2011.pdf

Alzheimer's Association. (2011b). *Alzheimer's from the frontlines: Challenges a national Alzheimer's plan must address* [Data file]. Retrieved from www.alz.org/documents_custom/napareport.pdf

Alzheimer's Association. (2011c). *National Alzheimer's Project Act (NAPA)*. Retrieved from http://www.kintera.org/site/pp.asp?c=mmKXLbP8E&b=5829219

Alzheimer's Association, & National Alliance for Caregiving. (2004). *Families care: Alzheimer's caregiving in the United States* [Data file]. Retrieved from www.alz.org/national/documents/report_familiescare.pdf

Alzheimer's Breakthrough Act of 2009, H.R. 6350, 111th Cong. (2009).

Blendon, R. J., Georges, J., Benson, J. M., Wikler, E. M., Weldon, K. J., Baumgart, M., et al. (2011, July). *Key findings from a five-country survey of public attitudes about Alzheimer's disease.* Poster session presented at International Conference on Alzheimer's Disease, Paris.

Caring for an Aging America Act, S. 1095, 112th Cong. (2011).

Foster, L., Brown, R., Phillips, B., & Carlson, B. L. (2005). Easing the burden of caregiving: The impact of consumer direction on primary informal caregivers in Arkansas. *Gerontologist, 45,* 474–485.

Gwyther, L. P. (1998). Social issues of the Alzheimer's patient and family. *American Journal of Medicine, 104*(4, Suppl. 1), 17S–21S.

Health Outcomes, Planning, and Education for Alzheimer's Act, S. 738, 112th Cong. (2011).

Institute of Medicine of the National Academies. (2008). *Retooling for an aging America: Building the healthcare workforce.* Washington, DC: National Academies Press.

Lifespan Respite Care Authorization Act of 2010, H.R. 6350, 111th Cong. (2010).

Masters, J. L. (2006). The benefits of consumer-directed services for caregivers of persons with Alzheimer's disease. *Families in Society: The Journal of Contemporary Social Services, 87,* 583–589.

National Alzheimer's Project Act, P.L. 111-375, 124 Stat. 1400 (2011).

Older Americans Act Amendments of 2000, P.L. 106-501, 114 Stat. 2226 (2000).

U.S. Department of Health and Human Services (2012). *Draft framework for the national plan to address Alzheimer's disease.* Retrieved from http://aspe.hhs.gov/daltcp/napa/Framework-Draft.pdf

Vincent, G. K., & Velkoff, V. A. (2010). *The next four decades: The older population in the United States 2010 to 2050* [Data file]. Retrieved from http://www.census.gov/prod/2010pubs/p25-1138.pdf

CHAPTER 42

HEALTH CARE REFORM AND THE ROLE OF SOCIAL WORK

Robyn Golden and Melissa Frey

POLICY MATTERS

Care coordination is a vital service for older adults, people with chronic conditions and those with medical situations made complex by psychosocial and environmental factors. These needs can be readily met by social workers, as they are members of a profession familiar with the "person-in-environment" framework and skilled in navigating complex systems. The Patient Protection and Affordable Care Act (P.L. 111-148) acknowledged the need for care coordination in its provisions but failed to recognize the potential role of social workers in meeting these requirements. Social workers are at risk of being left out of care coordination due to the lack of concrete roles for them within health care reform's provisions, despite their demonstrated value in effectively and efficiently providing health care–related services. Social workers must advocate on behalf of their clients and the profession to secure care coordination for those who need it and to ensure that social work receives a recognized role in providing these services.

Care coordination is a useful tool for helping patients with complex health needs to navigate a large and complex health care system. Care coordination seeks to provide seamless transitions from one care setting to another through the use of qualified health care professionals who provide individual care plans for patients in need (National Priorities Partnership, 2008). It is believed that patient-centered plans can help ensure that unnecessary health care spending will be controlled, patients will have better access to needed care, and the burden on patients and their families to find continuous care on their own will be reduced.

Although not everyone requires formal care coordination services, they can be particularly useful for a subset of patients with heightened risk for adverse events or for getting lost in the system. For example, those with multiple chronic conditions requiring care from specialists may find the health care system particularly complicated to navigate. Self-management tasks, such as keeping track of appointments or taking medications, become more and more complicated as more care providers are introduced into the patient's circle of care.

The need for care coordination for this population will only intensify in the coming years. In 2005, one out of every two American adults had at least one chronic illness, and this number is expected to grow exponentially over the next 10 years (Centers for Disease Control and Prevention, 2010).

Other people who could benefit from care coordination include those with insufficient social or economic resources, limited or no insurance, and low levels of health literacy and any other people with nonmedical factors diverting energy and attention from their health care tasks.

SOCIAL WORK MATTERS

Many issues experienced by patients who can benefit from care coordination can be readily addressed by social workers. Older adults seeing multiple providers, those with chronic conditions, and those with nonmedical issues complicating their medical care could all benefit from the services social workers can provide as case managers, therapists, and advocates. Social workers can educate patients regarding their benefit options and application processes and can help them complete the corresponding benefit applications. Beyond the role of case managers, social workers can provide the emotional support that patients need while they undergo the cumbersome and arduous process of identifying and applying for resources. Social workers can also research appropriate referrals and advocate for increasing access to care. They can then increase access to care for individual patients by explaining the available resources and options. These key social work care coordination roles are critical to bridging gaps in medical settings.

NARRATIVE

An example of the role of social work in care coordination can be seen in the following case study. The client is a woman with multiple needs, medical and nonmedical, that can be addressed using social work skills and knowledge.

Josefina is a Latina woman who was forced to retire after an injury at work left her disabled. Since the loss of her job, Josefina no longer has a source of income to pay for housing for herself and her adult dependent child. As a result, she moved in with one of her other children. There are 10 people living under the same small roof, with extremely limited resources for food and other necessities.

Like many of her family members, she came to the United States to seek better opportunities. She made the move later in life and supported her children as a single mother after leaving an abusive marriage. This move has left her with no significant savings.

As a 62-year-old woman, Josefina does not yet qualify for Medicare, and she has no insurance. She has an extremely difficult time paying the sliding-scale fees required at her federally qualified health center and cannot afford her medications. She has numerous medical problems, including diabetes, hypertension, high cholesterol, and arthritis. She needs advanced dental care and was recently diagnosed with depression and anxiety. She is overwhelmed by her medical problems and is unsure where to begin dealing with them.

In addition to her own physical and mental health concerns, Josefina is constantly concerned about taking care of her adult dependent child, who has his own significant medical problems. Josefina speaks of the excessive costs incurred from his medical care and limited options for Medicaid providers. In addition, Josefina speaks limited English. She often gets medical and benefit information in the mail, most of which is in English.

Josefina was eager to apply for disability benefits. She spent months collecting all of the paperwork, with a social worker helping her through the process and translating documents as needed. She found providers slow to return her paperwork, if they did at all. Nonetheless, she was not discouraged and filed the application. After waiting months for a response, she learned that she was denied the benefit. She is planning to apply again and is hopeful that perhaps next time her application will be approved.

Josefina has heard of health care reform on the news and wonders if it will help her and her family pay for any of the medications and medical services they need. She would like to receive treatment for her depression but cannot afford even sliding-scale fees and has difficulty finding a provider who speaks Spanish. Josefina fights a daily battle to support her family and herself and never loses hope that perhaps even one of her many needs will be met soon.

DISCUSSION

Josefina's situation is complex but quite common to members of her generation. Many patients face multiple challenges at once, including finding specialty medical providers, serving as a caregiver for a family member, applying for public benefits, and paying for medications. Those with chronic conditions often see providers or seek help from different organizations, government offices, and community agencies that do not communicate with each other. Patients with multiple chronic conditions can see up to 16 physicians annually (Bodenheimer, 2008). Without assistance from professionals such as social workers, who can use their training to coordinate all of these tasks, people with complex health problems can become lost while trying to navigate the large and complex health care system, resulting in poor health outcomes and a reduced quality of life.

Care coordination is a recognized area of improvement through health care reform, especially for Medicare and some Medicaid beneficiaries (Feinberg & Reamy, 2011). Although there are other people who could benefit from care coordination but do not fit into this classification, including the underinsured and uninsured and those not yet eligible for Medicare, many of these patients will have greater access to services through practice-level, patient-centered medical home initiatives. The *patient-centered medical home* is defined as "a health care setting that facilitates partnerships between individual patients, and their personal physicians, and when appropriate, the patient's family. . . . Care is facilitated by registries, information technology, health information exchange, and other means to assure that patients get the indicated care when and where they need and want it in a culturally and linguistically appropriate manner" (American Osteopathic Association, n.d.). Outpatient medical homes will also provide an infrastructure for long-term coordination, which will complement the transitional care coordination that will be offered on an acute basis as patients move from one care setting to another (P.L. 111-148, § 3026).

Increased support for care coordination through medical homes and transitional care, coupled with additional incentives for more integrated care through bundled payments and accountable care organizations, will lay the groundwork for widespread delivery of these services. However, at present, social workers are not included as part of this foundation. The lack of a concrete or reimbursable role for social workers in the health care reform provisions will reduce the likelihood that members of the profession will be hired to fill care coordination positions. As a result, social workers face the stark reality of being left out of this important development in health care, which would be a disservice to patients in need of coordinated care. That is, unless we as profession speak up.

As we advocate for our clients, we must also advocate for ourselves and our colleagues. Social workers have long served in the role of coordinating patient care, though this service has historically not been reimbursable under insurance policies. As the health care climate continues to change and funding, especially from government sources, is cut, valuable nonbillable services risk being lost. Unless we fight for our inclusion in care coordination provision through medical home and care transition initiatives, social work services will continue to be cut. Now is the time for social workers to advocate for the value and provision of our core skills by urging that care coordination become a reimbursable and fully accessible service to those who require it.

DISCUSSION QUESTIONS

1. Can you think of a specific case that may have been adversely affected by a lack of care coordination?

2. How can social workers advocate for their role in care coordination and inclusion in health care reform?

REFERENCES

American Osteopathic Association. (n.d.). *Patient-centered medical home.* Retrieved from http://www.osteopathic.org/inside-aoa/development/practice-mgt/Pages/patient-centered-medical-home.aspx

Bodenheimer, T. (2008). Coordinating care—A perilous journey through the health care system. *New England Journal of Medicine, 358,* 1064–1071.

Centers for Disease Control and Prevention. (2010). *Chronic disease prevention and health promotion.* Retrieved from http://www.cdc.gov/chronicdisease/stats/index.htm

Feinberg, L., & Reamy, A. M. (2011). *Health reform law creates new opportunities to better recognize and support family caregivers.* Retrieved from http://www.aarp.org/relationships/caregiving/info-10-2011/Health-Reform-Law-Creates-New-Opportunities-to-Better-Recognize-and-Support-Family-Caregivers.html

National Priorities Partnership. (2008). *National priorities and goals: Aligning our efforts.* Retrieved from http://www.nationalprioritiespartnership.org/uploadedFiles/NPP/08-253-NQF Report Lo[6].pdf

Patient Protection and Affordable Care Act, 111-148, 124 Stat. 119 (2010).

HIV/AIDS

CHAPTER 43

THAT'S WHAT FRIENDS ARE FOR:

30 YEARS OF HIV/AIDS ADVOCACY

Gary Bailey

> *First is to SEE the problem or situation lived by clients. Second is to ANALYZE the factors (personal, cultural, institutional) that contribute to the problem. Third is to ACT to change the problem or situation.*
>
> —Dawn Belkin-Martinez

The most recent World AIDS Day, December 1, 2011, marked the 30th anniversary of the global HIV/AIDS epidemic. It is hard to believe that there is now an entire generation of individuals worldwide who do not remember when these seven letters—HIV/AIDS—were not a part of their collective consciousness. The 2011 theme for World AIDS Day was "Getting to Zero: Zero New HIV Infections. Zero Discrimination. Zero AIDS-related Deaths" (World Health Organization, 2011).

I became involved in the fight against HIV/AIDS after the deaths of three friends in the late 1980s. One was a 30-year-old man who had immigrated to the United States from Ireland and had enormous success in the hospitality business in Boston. He contracted *Pneumocystis carinii* pneumonia and was dead within six days of his diagnosis. A second friend, from high school, who was in his late 20s and living in Boston, was diagnosed with AIDS, and I remember going to visit him at a local teaching hospital and finding that his meal tray had been left on the floor outside of his room because the staff would not go into his room for fear of catching "it." He was also abandoned by his other friends and family members. I remember having to "suit up," as if I were entering the most highly infectious place on the planet, just to sit by the side of his bed. The third was also a very close friend in his early 30s and someone whom I had known for a number of years before he developed toxoplasmosis. Toxoplasmosis is found in humans worldwide and in many species of animals and birds. Cats are the definitive host of the parasite. Human infection may result from carelessly handling cat litter, which can lead to accidental consumption of infectious particles. What was not known at the time was that toxoplasmosis also affects people who have weakened immune systems. I remember sleeping on the floor of this friend's hospital room as part of a rotating group of friends because he was afraid to be alone (Toxoplasmosis, 2011).

It was during this period that I realized I had to do something more than what I had been doing. Helping one person and one friend at a time, though not unimportant, was not enough to deal with the almost weekly news of friends' illnesses and subsequent deaths and funerals. It was then that I became engaged, both personally and professionally, at local and national levels, as I continue to be at the international level. NASW, then and now, along with countless social work practitioners, helped to develop systems and responses to the impact that this epidemic had and was having on many different communities of which I was and am a part.

For over 20 years, I have been actively involved with the AIDS Action Committee, Inc. (AAC), located in Boston. AAC is New England's oldest and largest AIDS service organization. I served as chair of the board of directors for six years. In June 2010, I had the distinction of being among 25 individuals honored by this important organization as someone "whose contributions to the fight against AIDS over the last two-and-a-half decades have been invaluable in the care for those affected by HIV/AIDS and to prevent new infections" (see http://action.aac.org/site/PageServer?pagename=25years_about). Sadly, 30 years later, there is still so very much for all us to do.

Since it was first described in 1981, HIV/AIDS has claimed millions of lives across the globe. On June 5, 1981, the Centers for Disease Control and Prevention's (CDC) *Morbidity and Mortality Weekly Report* (*MMWR*) published news of *Pneumocystis carinii* pneumonia in five previously healthy young men in Los Angeles; two had died. This report was later acknowledged as the first published scientific account of what would become known as HIV (human immunodeficiency virus) and AIDS (acquired immunodeficiency syndrome).

In the United States, the CDC (2011) has estimated that 1,178,350 people were living with HIV at the end of 2008, with 594,496 having died from AIDS since 1981. At this 30-year mark, efforts are being accelerated under the national HIV/AIDS strategy of the United States, with goals of reducing the number of people who become infected with HIV, increasing access to care, optimizing health outcomes for people living with HIV, and reducing HIV-related health disparities (White House Office of National AIDS Policy, 2010). According to UNAIDS (2011), in 2010, globally, there were 2.7 million new HIV infections, 1.8 million people died of AIDS-related illnesses, and an estimated 34 million people were living with HIV and year's end (AIDS & HIV Around the World, n.d.).

Initially, HIV/AIDS was viewed as a problem that affected men; MSM (men who have sex with men); and, most specifically, white gay men. As a result of this preconception, the harm that HIV/AIDS was also doing to women around the world was largely overlooked. Yet today, nearly half of all adults living with HIV around the world are women. Around 76 percent of women living with HIV are in sub-Saharan Africa. Among young people living with HIV in this region, three in every four are female (Women, HIV and AIDS, n.d.).

Disparities continue to abound. In my home state of Massachusetts, African Americans account for more than 25 percent of HIV/AIDS cases while making up only about 5 percent of the state's total population. AIDS is the leading cause of death among African American men and women ages 25 to 44 in the United States. Most HIV-positive women have been infected with HIV through heterosexual sex. Physically, women are more susceptible than men to HIV infection through heterosexual sex, and this fact alone means that special attention must be paid to protecting them if they are not to be disproportionately affected by the epidemic (Bailey, 2010b). Data from the CDC show that among teens, girls accounted for more than half of new HIV infections reported in 2001. Globally, women make up 60 percent of 15- through 24-year-olds who are HIV positive. Many millions of children around the world have already been orphaned by AIDS and become themselves easy prey to the virus. Michel Sidibé, executive director of UNAIDS, has stated that "this epidemic unfortunately remains an epidemic of women" (UN News Service, 2010).

POLICY MATTERS

The following example shows how strategy and advocacy affected a positive outcome for changes in legislation in Massachusetts in terms of helping prevent new cases of HIV/AIDS through intravenous drug use (IDU). This was a piece of legislation that I had been actively involved with during my tenure as chair of the AAC board. IDU and needle sharing created a sense of discomfort in many communities and, truthfully, also created discomfort among some HIV/AIDS treatment providers. Access to treatment was an issue that competed with creation of programs and services that would prevent new infections and increased deaths. (I thank my colleagues at the AAC, particularly executive director Rebecca Haag for her assistance in developing this case and for her unwavering leadership on this issue.)

NARRATIVE

In 2005, the need for, and benefit of, increased access to clean needles was clear. The rate of HIV infection related to injection drug use hovered around 40 percent among all people living with HIV/AIDS in Massachusetts, and Massachusetts was one of only three states in the nation in which it was illegal to purchase a syringe in a pharmacy without a prescription. To reduce the rate of new infections, the AAC set as its number one priority the passage of legislation to repeal the requirement for a prescription to purchase hypodermic needles and syringes in pharmacies.

Believing that then-governor Mitt Romney would veto the plan, the goal was to have the legislation pass both the state Senate and House of Representatives by veto-proof margins. In Massachusetts, that means support of two-thirds of the present and voting members in each chamber.

To achieve this goal, the AAC formed and chaired the Massachusetts Pharmacy Access Campaign, a coalition of groups committed to removing the prescription requirement for needle sales. Campaign members included representatives from all stakeholder groups: AIDS service organizations, law enforcement, the pharmacy community, the substance abuse recovery community, and many other public health and community-based organizations.

The campaign produced a briefing packet with fact sheets, copies of supportive editorials, and various supporting documents that outlined the basics of the bill. These packets were distributed to all members of the legislature. As the campaign progressed, staff developed additional educational materials to address concerns, such as adequate disposal systems.

The AAC maintained and monitored detailed lists of all state legislators to track votes and ensure that key, influential legislators had been contacted or visited by constituents in their district. This required increasing the constituent capacity in each legislative district through phone banks, e-mail, and individual phone calls.

Several bills proposing removing the prescription requirement were filed, and in May 2005, the Joint Committee on Public Health held a hearing on these bills. The campaign presented more than five hours of testimony from people living with HIV; people with a history of injection drug use; pharmacists; public health officials; law enforcement officials; substance abuse and health care providers; social workers; academics; and local officials, including two of the state's district attorneys.

As a result of this successful hearing, several bills were consolidated into one (H.4176) and reported out of committee favorably in June. By October 2005, campaign members had visited or communicated with all of the 160 members of the House of Representatives. By November, the House leadership was encouraged by the level of support (90 of 160 members) and agreed to bring the legislation to the floor for a vote and to seek a larger majority. The House passed the pharmacy access bill by a 115 to 37 vote, a veto-proof majority.

The bill then went to the Massachusetts Senate for action. The campaign worked with key senators and staff to outline the benefits of the legislation and to formulate a strategy. In early February 2006, the coalition sponsored a legislative briefing, hosted by the Senate chair of the Joint Committee on Public Health, to educate members of the Senate on the issues, and it supplemented this hearing with individual meetings.

The Senate amended the bill to include an expanded disposal system provision and additional criminal penalties for using a spent needle as a weapon. A vote on the bill was delayed by procedural maneuvers by a single senator. However, because of support from the Senate president's office, the bill was finally passed by the Senate in late June 2006.

Governor Romney vetoed the legislation over the Fourth of July weekend, but on July 14, 2006, the Massachusetts Senate and House of Representatives enacted the legislation over the governor's veto. The decriminalization provision of the law became effective immediately. Pharmacies were authorized to begin sales on September 18, 2006 (Bailey, 2010a).

SOCIAL WORK MATTERS

The International Federation of Social Workers' (Tomaszewski et al., 2006) International policy on HIV/AIDS states the following in its introduction:

> HIV/AIDS is a global pandemic that affects individuals, families, and entire communities around the world and has profound social and economic implications. In 2004, the pandemic killed an estimated 3 million people, and an additional 40 million were living with the infection. The epidemic primarily affects the world's poorest people in countries with the greatest gender inequities, disparities in income, and access to productive resources. HIV/AIDS is primarily a heterosexual epidemic in developing countries, yet sex between men remains a critical aspect of the epidemic in middle and high-income countries. (However an estimated one-third of new infections now occur by heterosexual contact in these countries). Often caregivers, families, and friends encounter the same stigma and prejudice as those they care for endure. The everyday psychosocial issues for persons living with or affected by HIV/AIDS are compounded by poverty, homelessness, addictions, unsanitary living conditions, war and trauma, discrimination, and societal indifference.
>
> The demographics behind HIV/AIDS are as diverse as the world in which we live and work, calling for a range of responses from the social work profession. The eradication of HIV/AIDS represents one of humanity's greatest challenges, one that requires cooperation and comprehensive collaboration between scientific disciplines, governments, social institutions, the media, the social work and health care professions, and the general public.
>
> Social workers, by virtue of their training, their commitment to human rights, and the fact that they are uniquely placed within a wide variety of health and welfare settings, can play a very effective role in the global effort to address the HIV/AIDS epidemic.

I (Bailey, 2010a) have highlighted some of what has been learned over the past 30 years in the fight against HIV/AIDS and how social workers and other individuals working in combating this epidemic can become more effective:

- Appreciate the role of the social worker as a change agent.
- Develop and understand one's own values and strengths as an advocate and social activist within the context of one's work.

- Gain an understanding of case-to-cause advocacy, and learn how individuals can intervene in systems to create positive change.
- Recognize the effects of racism, heterosexism, ageism, ableism, and other forms of oppression.
- Develop understanding of social action at various levels: personal, cultural, and institutional.
- Develop knowledge of the role and responsibility of government entities in meeting the basic human needs of individuals and families.
- Understand the role of advocacy in influencing policy outcomes.
- Understand the role of advocacy in influencing resource allocation decisions within social institutions. (p. 173)

In their article "Advocacy" in the *Encyclopedia of Social Work*, Schneider, Lester, and Ochieng (2008) state that "social work advocates fought for basic human rights and social justice for oppressed, vulnerable, and displaced populations" (p. 61). What is it that we can do as a global social work community? We can continue the work begun 30 years ago in response to this epidemic. We can continue to fight to ensure that people have access to much needed information about prevention and that access to treatment be guaranteed globally.

DISCUSSION QUESTIONS

1. Can an individual social worker really have an impact on policy at the local, state, and national levels?

2. How does the concept of "politics of the personal" relate to an issue such as HIV/ AIDS?

REFERENCES

AIDS & HIV around the world. (n.d.). Retrieved from http://www.avert.org/aroundworld.htm

Bailey, G. (2010a). HIV-related political and legislative intervention. In C. Poindexter (Ed.), *Handbook of HIV and social work: Principles, practice, and populations* (pp. 173–182). New York: John Wiley & Sons.

Bailey, G. (2010b, December 1). *IFSW – open letter of president Gary Bailey – World AIDS Day 2010.* Retrieved from http://www.socialworkblog.org/practice-and-professional-development/2010/12/ifsw-open-letter-of-president-gary-bailey-world-aids-day-2010/

Centers for Disease Control and Prevention. (1981, June 5). *Pneumocystis* pneumonia—Los Angeles. *Morbidity and Mortality Weekly Report, 30,* 250–252.

Centers for Disease Control and Prevention. (2011, June 3). Thirty years of HIV—1981 to 2011. *Morbidity and Mortality Weekly Report, 60,* 689.

Schneider, R. L., Lester, L., & Ochieng, J. (2008). Advocacy. In T. Mizrahi & L. E. Davis (Eds.-in-Chief), *Encyclopedia of social work* (20th ed., Vol. 1, pp. 61–65). Washington, DC, and New York: NASW Press & Oxford University Press.

Tomaszewski, E. P., Gronningsaeter, A., Hall, N., Paul, S., Wilson, M., & López, L. (2006). *International policy on HIV/AIDS*. Retrieved from http://www.ifsw.org/p38001031.html

Toxoplasmosis. (2009, December 1). Retrieved from http://www.ncbi.nlm.nih.gov/pubmedhealth/PMH0001661/

UNAIDS. (2011, November 21). *Nearly 50% of people who are eligible for antiretroviral therapy now have access to lifesaving treatment* [Press release]. Retrieved from http://www.unaids.org/en/resources/presscentre/pressreleaseandstatementarchive/2011/november/20111121wad2011report/

UN News Service. (2010, June 9). Noting progress to date, ban urges greater efforts against HIV/AIDS. *UN News Centre*. Retrieved from http://www.un.org/apps/news/story.asp?NewsID=34977&Cr=aids&Cr1

White House Office of National AIDS Policy. (2010). *National HIV/AIDS strategy for the United States*. Retrieved http://www.whitehouse.gov/sites/default/files/uploads/NHAS.pdf

Women, HIV and AIDS. (n.d.). Retrieved from http://www.avert.org/women-hiv-aids.htm#content Table0

World Health Organization. (2011). *World AIDS day*. Retrieved from http://www.who.int/mediacentre/events/annual/world_aids_day/en/index.html

CHAPTER 44

MANAGING THE HIV CARE SYSTEM:
SOCIAL WORKERS AS CLIENT NAVIGATORS AND POLICY ADVOCATES

Evelyn P. Tomaszewski

SOCIAL WORK MATTERS

HIV/AIDS continues to challenge the nation's health, economic, and social systems. For social workers on the frontlines, our values, beliefs, and practice standards have guided us as we dedicate our efforts to meet the competing and evolving needs of people living with and affected by HIV/AIDS. Our profession's response to HIV/AIDS requires a diverse range of social work skills, across all fields of practice, whether we work as a mental health or behavioral health clinicians, advocates, researchers, policymakers, or educators.

Social workers address biomedical, psychosocial, and spiritual concerns at the micro, macro, or mezzo level of practice. Working with clients who have a life-changing illness such as HIV/AIDS requires an ability to talk with them and their families about complex personal issues such sexuality, end-of-life and death concerns, religious and spiritual beliefs, and relationships. HIV/AIDS has necessitated open discussions with colleagues and policymakers about historically taboo topics such as sexual orientation and gender identity, sex work, adolescent sexuality, and substance use.

Three decades ago, our nation's response to HIV/AIDS was slow, and the negative impact on clients and communities was profound. Despite expanded services, education about HIV/AIDS, and the move toward integrating HIV care into all health services, stigmatizing attitudes still exist. Studies show that a large percentage of Americans still voice discomfort with working with a person with HIV or AIDS (Henry J. Kaiser Family Foundation, 2011). Thus, 30 years into the HIV/AIDS pandemic, combating stigma and discrimination remains an important task for all social workers.

The commitment of the social work profession to culturally competent practice requires an understanding of the implications and role of racism, homophobia and heterosexism, class conflict and poverty, and ageism on clients, programs, and policies (NASW, 2012). The social work profession has responded and must continue to respond to these individual and systemic challenges through advocacy within communities, agencies, and state and federal government.

Social workers must negotiate the seemingly disjointed aspects of care across a wide spectrum of economic contexts, social and cultural communities, political climates, and health care systems. Social work skills are critical as we work to ensure continuity of care for people living with HIV/AIDS. Medical case management is the starting and sustaining point of many HIV/AIDS services programs and clinics and is a role often carried out by social workers. Case managers must address psychosocial supports, adherence counseling, risk and harm reduction, and health education to clients across the lifespan (Ka'opua, Giddens, & Tomaszewski, 2008).

Working with clients with HIV/AIDS and co-occurring diagnoses also requires an understanding of the biomedical complexities of HIV and AIDS—defining clinical conditions, and of the impact of a mental health diagnosis and substance use on the client's health and well-being. People with HIV experience depression and anxiety and a range of psychosocial concerns as they adjust to the impact of the diagnosis and face the difficulties of living with a chronic life-threatening illness. These range from concern about a shortened life expectancy and the loss of social support to how a child, partner, or friend will react to learning of their HIV diagnosis.

Mental health disorders, including substance use disorders, are documented to affect both risk taking behaviors and help seeking behavior or uptake of services for HIV/AIDS. Research demonstrates that case management improves client adherence to both HIV/AIDS medications (antiretroviral treatments) and other recommended mental health and wellness treatments (World Health Organization, 2008).

NARRATIVE

The following narrative highlights the effect of case management and access to HIV/AIDS care and treatment on a client's overall well-being.

About a year ago, when Susan was seeing a new gynecologist, she noted on her intake form that for some months she had been feeling tired, waking up at night all sweaty, and feeling achy. She assumed she was in early menopause. After talking with her new doctor, she was offered a range of tests, including one for HIV. While taken aback, she agreed to the tests. Susan was shocked to learn that she was HIV positive. She was so embarrassed by the diagnosis that she did not return to her doctor and for months was concerned that her colleagues would find out and would judge her or respond negatively. She did tell her sister, Elena. Susan has not told her 10-year-old son, Joe, why she has been sick, and she has sworn her sister to secrecy.

Susan's worries and lack of energy led to her missing a lot of work, and about four months ago she lost her job. She decided that she couldn't afford to keep her health insurance current by paying the premiums herself. Susan and her son have moved in with her sister temporarily.

Elena encouraged her to go to the local HIV/AIDS program, and about two months ago she had her intake visit at the Open Doors Clinic, where she met with the medical staff and was assigned a medical case manager. She has seen her medical case manager, a social worker named Jill, a couple of times. They talked about her health, her worries about housing, and how seeing the doctor will help her to stay healthier. Susan cannot believe she is talking about all this and finds herself admitting she is anxious about her future and worries about caring for her son. She also just feels low on many days. Jill helped Susan to better understand what HIV does to her body and how some of her physical symptoms could be a result of the virus or other life stressors. Jill also gave Susan information about the AIDS Drug Assistance Program (ADAP) and arranged for her to speak with someone about housing through the Housing Opportunities for Persons with AIDS program.

Susan also met with a social worker at the community mental health center (CMHC) for what Jill called a full mental health assessment. Susan has discussed her concerns about her parenting ability, her extended family, and her health. The CMHC social worker helped Susan to understand how her anger has created stress on her body, the impact of depression on her overall health, and different ways of coping with her anxiety. And although the time is not right just yet, Susan is beginning to talk about when and how she will tell Joe about her health.

Recently, while in the lobby of the Open Doors Clinic, Susan heard some clients making plans to attend an upcoming town hall meeting for the National HIV/AIDS Strategy. Although Susan isn't on HIV medicines yet due to the cost, she met a woman last week who told her she had to go on a waiting list for her medications. Susan plans to talk to Jill about how to attend the town hall meeting.

POLICY MATTERS

Susan's diagnosis of HIV means that she can access a range of services through programs funded by the Ryan White Comprehensive AIDS Resources Emergency Act (P.L. 101-381) (RWCA). Enacted in 1990, the RWCA has been amended and reauthorized four times, most recently in 2009. The program's resources have been modified over time to address new and emerging needs of people living with HIV (Health Resources and Services Administration, 2011).

The RWCA provides comprehensive funding for health care, treatment, and support services in U.S. states and territories. It is intended to meet the needs of people who are uninsured, underinsured, or have no other source of health coverage. For Susan, her job loss meant the end of her affordable health insurance. Having access to a clinic funded through the RWCA provided Susan with core medical services that are specific to her health needs and most likely would not otherwise be available to her in her community. The RWCA outlines how funds can ensure clients can access substance abuse outpatient care, mental health services, home- and community-based health care services, and early intervention services. Each state and territory has the final decision on defining the behavioral health aspects of core medical services. In Susan's state, the RWCA-funded clinics are not required to use these funds for mental health treatment. Fortunately, a network of mental health services is funded through other sources, so Susan can see a social worker at a community mental health center. However, for many clients in certain parts of the United States, the limited funding for services, or lack of integration of services, for people with mental health and substance use disorders, HIV/AIDS and related physical, psychological, and social problems creates an additional serious barrier to treatment for HIV/AIDS.

Through RWCA funds, clients have access to ADAP, with the caveat that each state and territory can determine eligibility for the ADAP program with regard to both the income level that determines eligibility and coverage for specific HIV medications. As Susan overheard another client say, she lives in one of the states that have ADAP waiting lists (there are currently 10). Susan is concerned that when she needs HIV/AIDS antiretroviral treatments, she may also have to go on a waiting list. For another 17 states and Puerto Rico, various cost containment measures reduce the number of drugs that are covered.

RWCA funds can be used for a range of nonmedical services, including transportation, housing, outreach, and legal services. Legal services are particularly critical as some clients lose their jobs due to actions taken by employers that are based on an employee's HIV or AIDS status.

Despite the major improvements in care and treatment through RWCA-funded programs, the policies and laws have not translated to fully integrated services. To address the disconnect between policies, resources, and practice, the White House National HIV/AIDS Strategy (NHAS) was conceived (Office of National AIDS Policy, 2010). Through social media, town hall meetings, and Webinars, community and service providers, including social workers, provided testimony on the needs, challenges, and necessary changes to better integrate HIV care. Susan's approach to a life-changing illness is to take part in the advocacy efforts necessary to keep the NHAS responsive to the needs of people living with or affected by HIV/AIDS.

The increase in testing for HIV/AIDS means more people know their health status and can access treatment. This additional need has stretched the resources of RWCA programs and has resulted in an increasing number of states limiting access to ADAP medications. It is critical that social workers advocate for additional ADAP resources and for sufficient funds to both expand HIV services and sustain those services that are so much a part of the community.

Social workers can take action to support the goals of the National HIV/AIDS Strategy. First, we can work to reduce new HIV infections by addressing at-risk behaviors with clients through support and education (including comprehensive sexuality education), and incorporate evidence-based mental health and substance abuse prevention and treatment into our clinical and case management programs. Second, we can work to increase access to care and improved health outcomes by voicing support for RWCA programs and other federal and state HIV programs, including provider training and education programs. Because of our understanding of the unique biopsychosocial–spiritual effects of living with HIV/AIDS and skills in assessment and treatment for clients with co-occurring health and behavioral health conditions, we can also identify gaps in essential care and services and advocate for resources at the local, state, and federal levels. Third, social workers can address and reduce health disparities for people at risk of or living with HIV/AIDS by building collaborative relationships across agencies and program areas and ensuring culturally competent services to all clients.

Social workers need to learn about the NHAS Federal Implementation Plan, which outlines how federal agencies currently funding HIV-related services can be culturally relevant and client-centered and build current and future community capacity. An example is working to ensure that federal and state agencies implement policies and funding that use professional case management and clinical social work services to ensure improved health outcomes. Finally, social workers must insist that the newly created health care system, and its state-specific variations, include integration of RWCA services so that people living with HIV or AIDS continue to receive the care they need and deserve.

Clearly, social workers have been, and continue to be, leaders in program planning and policy advocacy as well as translating knowledge of HIV/AIDS and related social welfare needs into practice solutions. Staying current with HIV/AIDS issues allows us to advocate for our clients, provide feedback and guidance to public officials, and professionally negotiate the systems in which we practice.

DISCUSSION QUESTIONS

1. What is the role of the social worker in sustaining and delivering the mandates set forth in the RWCA and the National HIV/AIDS Strategy?

2. How are social work core values, such as addressing issues of gender, cultural differences, poverty, and stigma addressed in the NHAS?

3. How can we ensure that social work professionals stay current in the biomedical and psychosocial aspects of living with HIV/AIDS and co-occurring diagnoses?

REFERENCES

Health Resources and Services Administration. (2011). *Ryan White HIV/AIDS program*. Retrieved from http://hab.hrsa.gov/

Henry J. Kaiser Family Foundation. (2011). *HIV/AIDS at 30: A public opinion perspective*. Retrieved from http://www.kff.org/kaiserpolls/upload/8186.pdf

Ka'opua, L., Giddens, B., & Tomaszewski, E. (2008). Case management for persons with HIV/AIDS. In A. Roberts & G. Greene (Eds.), *Social workers' desk reference* (pp. 801–807). New York: Oxford University Press.

National Association of Social Workers. (2012). *HIV/AIDS stigma: Making the connection to discrimination and prejudice.* Retrieved from http://www.socialworkers.org/practice/hiv_aids/siteInfo/facts.asp

Office of National AIDS Policy. (2010). *National HIV/AIDS strategy.* Washington, DC: Author. Retrieved from http://www.whitehouse.gov/administration/eop/onap/nhas

Ryan White Comprehensive AIDS Resources Emergency Act of 1990, P.L. 101-381, 104 Stat. 576 (1990).

World Health Organization. (2008). *HIV/AIDS and mental health: Report by the secretariat.* Retrieved from http://apps.who.int/gb/ebwha/pdf_files/EB124/B124_6-en.pdf

PARITY

CHAPTER 45

PARITY FOR MENTAL HEALTH AND SUBSTANCE USE DISORDERS

Peter J. Delany and Joseph J. Shields

Millions of people living in America suffer from mental and substance use disorders, yet only a small percentage of these individuals are able to obtain treatment. Of the 7.1 million people age 12 or older who met the criteria for dependence on or abuse of illicit drugs, only 974,000 (13.7 percent) reported having received treatment in the past year. For the more than 17.9 million people who suffer from alcohol dependence, the percentage and number receiving treatment is somewhat lower (7.7 percent or 1.4 million) (Substance Abuse and Mental Health Services Administration [SAMHSA], 2010). The majority of people age 18 years and older who suffer from serious mental illness (60.8 percent), report receiving some form of treatment for their condition (SAMHSA, 2011). Adult women were more likely than adult men to report having received treatment in the past year—63.8 percent and 54.5 percent respectively (SAMHSA, 2011). These numbers have remained fairly consistent since 1990.

The most cited reason for not receiving treatment for a substance use disorder, among those who met the criteria and perceived a need for treatment, was lack of health coverage or ability to afford the cost of care (38.1 percent). Another 7.4 percent indicated that they had health insurance, but it did not cover the cost of treatment (SAMHSA, 2011). Among adults 18 or older who identified a need for mental health treatment but reported not receiving treatment in the past year, 42.5 percent indicated that they could not afford the cost of treatment, whereas another 7.2 percent indicated that their health insurance did not cover mental health treatment or counseling, and 10.2 percent indicated that their health insurance did not pay enough for mental health treatment or counseling (SAMHSA, 2010).

Social Work Matters

In October 2008, the Paul Wellstone and Pete Domenici Mental Health Parity and Addiction Equity Act (P.L. 110-343) (MHPAEA) was signed into law. The MHPAEA supplemented the Mental Health Parity Act of 1996 (P.L. 104-204) and extended its provisions to substance use disorders. As a result, group health and health insurance issuers that offer mental health and substance abuse services are required to provide benefits that are no more restrictive than medical or surgical benefits with respect to aggregate lifetime and annual dollar limits. Further, the MHPAEA mandates that group health plans and health insurance issuers guarantee that the predominant financial requirements (copayments and deductibles) and treatment limitations (number of visits) for medical and surgical benefits apply to benefits for mental health and substance use disorders.

With the passage of the Patient Protection and Affordable Care Act (P.L. 111-148) (ACA) in 2010, there are new opportunities to change the way substance use and mental health services are financed and delivered. Barry and Huskamp (2011) noted that key provisions within the ACA have the potential to address serious challenges of access to and coordination of care that have negatively affected the quality of life for vulnerable populations. They noted that provisions such as the expansion of Medicaid, employer mandates to offer insurance, and the creation of health insurance exchanges with subsidies to people with low incomes are expected to increase coverage for 3.7 million people with serious mental illness who currently are uninsured (Barry & Huskamp, 2011).

It is clear that the lack or limitations of health insurance benefits for mental health and substance use disorders have kept millions of Americans from receiving treatments that can reduce the burden of those disorders and improve their lives and those of their families and the communities in which they live. Though the MHPAEA does not require the provision of such benefits, it is designed to eliminate inequalities in the provision of benefits that have kept many individuals from seeking or receiving treatment services. The goal is to improve access to care for those who suffer from these chronic conditions in much the same way that Americans with other chronic health conditions—such as diabetes, hypertension, and asthma—have access to care. The passage of the MHPAEA and the ACA are important steps in that they emphasize the need to expand coverage to those in need of services and enhance the quality of care through better coordination of services.

Narrative

The following example outlines how a focus on a policy of improving access to care can affect one individual with depression and substance use.

Mrs. Johnson is a bus driver and a classroom aide for a medium-sized school district where she has been working for 20 years. She and her husband, who works as a janitor and handyman at their church, live modestly and are very involved in their church and community. Mrs. Johnson loves working at the school and is well respected by parents and teachers for her work with the children. Through the school system, she was able to purchase basic health insurance for herself and her husband. Because of the low copayments, she was able to take advantage of the Preferred Provider Organization (PPO) option. For the past 10 years she has been under the care of a doctor for problems with high blood pressure and Type II diabetes.

Nine months ago, Mrs. Johnson was informed that because of budget cuts, her hours as a classroom aide would be reduced by half, with a corresponding reduction in pay and benefits. She will now have to pay more for her health insurance, which places a substantial burden on her and her husband. To reduce the cost, she switched from the PPO plan to a health maintenance organization (HMO) plan.

Recently, Mrs. Johnson was seen in the emergency room of a local hospital; her insulin levels were found to be dangerously low, and her blood pressure was dangerously high. Doctors were able to stabilize Mrs. Johnson's medical condition and released her after several days, with a recommendation to follow up with her primary care physician to review the adequacy of her medications and possibly develop a new treatment plan.

Mr. Johnson took Mrs. Johnson to the HMO clinic. Because this was a meeting with a new doctor, Mrs. Johnson asked that her husband be present during the examination. After briefly reviewing Mrs. Johnson's medical history, the doctor prescribed a new blood pressure medication and adjusted her insulin dosage. He advised her to return to the clinic in three months for a follow-up evaluation.

Before leaving the office, Mr. Johnson told the doctor that his wife had become increasingly sad over the reduction of her work hours and increasingly hopeless about their economic situation. She also appeared to lose interest in church activities and had been negligent in monitoring her diabetes. He said that she had begun drinking regularly, and he often found empty bottles in the recycling bin when he came home. After confirming the information with Mrs. Johnson, the doctor decided to prescribe an antidepressant. He told her that there was little that they could do about her drinking and advised her to stop drinking on her own or join an Alcoholics Anonymous (AA) group.

In the weeks following the clinic visit, Mrs. Johnson's drinking increased, as did her depression. One morning after she had stayed up late drinking many glasses of wine, a friend at her school bus driving job confronted her about her work performance and her drinking. She admitted to her friend that she had a drinking problem. She told him that she had seen a doctor at the HMO clinic who prescribed a medication for depression and told her to attend AA meetings for her drinking. The friend told her that her behavior had to change immediately or she most likely would lose her bus driving position. He told her that she should contact the school system's employee assistance program (EAP) for help.

Afraid of losing her job, Mrs. Johnson immediately called the EAP office and was able to get an appointment with Mr. Gonzales, a social worker. She was quite anxious when she arrived at the EAP office, but Mr. Gonzales reassured her and asked her to tell him what prompted her to make an appointment. She told him about losing her classroom aide hours and how this loss had affected the way she felt and that she had begun drinking more than she should.

He asked her how often she drank, and she responded, "just about every day." He then asked her how much she normally drank at a time, and she responded, "a couple of glasses of wine." He asked, "by a couple do you mean two, three, four, or more than four glasses?" She said that on most days it was a bottle of wine, which normally amounts to five glasses. He asked her whether she had sought professional help for her sad feelings and drinking. She told him that she had visited the HMO clinic and told the doctor about her sad feelings and that he had given her a prescription for her depression but told her that the only thing that he could do about her drinking was to encourage her to stop or join an AA group. She said that in the three weeks since the visit to the clinic she had stopped taking the medication because it made her feel funny but had continued drinking.

The social worker told Mrs. Johnson that the doctor's advice was inappropriate but that many doctors downplay alcohol problems because they view alcoholism as personal failure and not a medical problem. He assured Mrs. Johnson that help was available and that he would help her to access it. He also informed her that new federal legislation will eventually require parity for substance use and mental health services and that although the provision does not become mandatory until 2014, her insurance company had already implemented it. While Mrs. Johnson was in his office, he asked her to call the behavioral health division of the HMO and make an appointment to meet with one of the counselors. She told the receptionist about her situation and said that the EAP social worker had referred her, and she was able to get an appointment for the next afternoon.

When she arrived at the HMO, she met with a psychiatrist who conducted an intensive evaluation. As a result of this evaluation, he made a change in her medications and then scheduled her to meet with a clinical social worker who would help her find the services that would best help her with her drinking problem. Mrs. Johnson met with Ms. Boyd, the social worker, who talked with her about her drinking problem and her home and work situation. They decided together that Mrs. Johnson might be best served in an outpatient treatment program. The HMO offered a number of different outpatient treatment programs—an intensive program that ran Mondays through Fridays for six hours a session as well as a number of traditional outpatient programs with two-hour sessions. They decided that because she needed to keep her job, the intensive program would not work for her but that a program that ran on Monday through Thursday evenings for two hours would best meet her needs. It was also the program that Ms. Boyd worked in as an addictions social worker.

Mrs. Johnson joined the outpatient treatment program and participated four evenings a week. She was also able to have a one-hour session each week with Ms. Boyd, and she met with the psychiatrist every six weeks to review her medications. At the advice of Ms.

Boyd, she began attending AA meetings regularly. After six months of outpatient treat-ment, Mrs. Johnson decided that she was strong enough to discontinue the treatment, but she maintained her involvement in AA. Although her economic situation has not changed, she has a much more optimistic outlook. She has stopped drinking completely. She has reconnected with her church community and has remained active in AA. Because of her alcohol abstinence, her blood pressure and blood sugar levels have stabilized, making her a healthier person.

DISCUSSION

Because of the economic downturn, it is not unusual for individuals from all eco-nomic levels to move from being fully employed to being underemployed or unem-ployed, which has a significant impact on both a person's economic and emotional life. Mrs. Johnson was fortunate in that there was an option to switch to an HMO plan that included behavioral health services as part of the benefits package. If this had not been not available, Mrs. Johnson could have elected to continue her cur-rent health insurance under the Consolidated Omnibus Budget Reconciliation Act (P.L. 99-272) (COBRA), which gives workers and families who lose their group health benefits through changes in employment status the right to continue the benefits for a set period of time. However, individuals normally have to pay the entire premium to stay enrolled. In some cases, individuals who cannot afford the premium may be eligible for reductions in premiums through COBRA Continuation Assistance under the American Recovery and Reinvestment Act of 2009 (P.L. 111-5).

The case of Mrs. Johnson is complex in that it involves the management of several chronic health conditions at the same time—diabetes, depression, and alcoholism. Success for the individual patient, the employer, and the insurance company hinges on coordinating care so that better health and functioning are attained and costs are kept in check. In this case, having a knowledgeable EAP social worker involved to initiate the appropriate care and having a trained addictions social worker to help Mrs. Johnson establish and coordinate a care plan within the current insurance environ-ment were critical for addressing her health care needs, reducing health care costs, and enhancing her productivity as a school system employee.

POLICY MATTERS

As the health care environment continues to change, it is important that social workers have an understanding of laws and related policies. In recent years, a num-ber of laws like the MHPAEA and the ACA have been passed. Most people know in general that the new laws might affect their health care, but they don't always know the specifics of the laws and how these laws have given them new rights as health care consumers.

Mrs. Johnson's story introduced two social workers who had different responsibilities. The EAP social worker functioned as a resource for Mrs. Johnson. To be effective in his role, he had to have the knowledge and skills to conduct a brief assessment and know what services were appropriate and available. He knew immediately that the doctor who told Mrs. Johnson that there was no help for her drinking problem outside of AA was mistaken, and that Mrs. Johnson had a right to receive substance abuse services. His knowledge of the MHPAEA and of the health insurance plans offered by the school system allowed Mrs. Johnson to access the appropriate services.

The second social worker functioned in a different role. When first meeting Mrs. Johnson, she had to assess the nature and extent of her problems and determine how these problems were affecting her family, work, social relationships, and responsibilities. She then worked with Mrs. Johnson to create a care plan that was appropriate to address her condition, fit her unique circumstances, and was cost effective for the insurance carrier and the school system. She also served as Mrs. Johnson's counselor during the treatment process.

Social workers have a unique role to play in the behavioral health arena. Beside their clinical role in implementing interventions that address mental health and substance use disorders, they also need to be aware of the federal and state policies that affect the kind, quality, and frequency of services. It is important to know what services clients are entitled to receive. It is also important that social workers know the services that are available in various insurance plans and work with clients to create appropriate and cost-effective treatment plans.

Discussion Questions

1. How can social workers prepare themselves for the changes in the way behavioral health services are delivered and financed?

2. There is increased emphasis on integrating behavioral health services across health care settings and a special emphasis on preventing substance use and mental disorders. How can the profession of social work influence the expanded role of prevention and management of chronic health conditions?

References

American Recovery and Reinvestment Act of 2009, P.L. 111-5, 123 Stat. 115 (2009).

Barry, C. L., & Huskamp, H. A. (2011). Moving beyond parity—Mental health and addiction care. *New England Journal of Medicine, 365,* 973–975.

Consolidated Omnibus Budget Reconciliation Act of 1985, P.L. 99-272, 100 Stat. 82 (1986).

Mental Health Parity Act of 1996, P.L. 104-204, 110 Stat. 2944 (1996).

Patient Protection and Affordable Care Act of 2010, P.L. 111-148, 124 Stat. 119 (2010).

Paul Wellstone and Pete Domenici Mental Health Parity and Addiction Equity Act, P.L. 110-343, 122 Stat. 3765 (2008).

Substance Abuse and Mental Health Services Administration. (2010). *Results from the 2009 National Survey on Drug Use and Health: Mental health detailed tables.* Retrieved from http://oas.samhsa. gov/NSDUH/2k9NSDUH/MH/tabs/TOC.htm

Substance Abuse and Mental Health Services Administration. (2011). *Results from the 2010 National Survey on Drug Use and Health: Summary of national findings* (NSDUH Series H-41, HHS Publication No. [SMA] 11-4658). Rockville, MD: Author.

CHAPTER 46

POLICY, PRACTICE, AND PARITY:

CLINICAL SOCIAL WORK ADVOCACY IN WASHINGTON STATE

Laura W. Groshong

POLICY MATTERS

In 1997, there was a growing awareness of the imbalance between medical/surgical coverage and mental health coverage in most insurance plans. This awareness led to a desire on the part of clinical social workers and other mental health professionals to require insurers to cover mental health treatment as fully as—or "at parity" with—medical services. Social workers are well aware of the way that mental disorders interfere with a client's ability to meet basic needs; clinical social workers were thus in the forefront of the groups that promoted mental health parity at the state level and nationally. Many plans still did not cover outpatient mental health treatment or did so in only a very limited way. After eight years of coalition building, education of the public and legislators, and building bridges to the business community, Washington state finally passed a mental health parity law in 2005. This bill influenced the passage of a 2008 federal law requiring coverage of mental health treatment at parity with medical/surgical treatment, the 2008 Paul Wellstone and Pete Domenici Mental Health and Addictions Equality Act (P.L. 110-343).

A groundbreaking work on the imbalance in coverage for mental health treatment (Miller, 1994) was followed by more attention to the issue. In 1999, the U.S. surgeon general issued a position paper, *Mental Health: A Report of the Surgeon General,* on the importance of mental health treatment for overall health care (U.S. Department of Health and Human Services, 1999). It received little attention at the time, but it brought focus to the issue of the disparity between medical and mental health treatment. States took a variety of steps toward mental health parity—for example, by mandating mental health coverage for serious mental illnesses, or in insurance plans offered by larger companies, or for state employees, or by limiting out-of-pocket expenses. But even today, few states require true mental health parity.

NARRATIVE

A small interdisciplinary group of lobbyists and mental health clinicians met in 1998 in Seattle, Washington, to discuss their concerns about the coverage of mental health benefits. There had been ongoing problems with private insurers who were trying to control mental health treatment when benefits were used up and patients wanted to pay privately. There was also an accusation by one insurer, Regence BlueShield, that clinicians were rewriting their records when audited; it claimed the right to seize hard drives without notice to prevent this practice. Some insurers tried to limit which providers could be allowed to provide mental health treatment. In short, there were numerous attempts by insurers to limit access to mental health treatment, which convinced clinicians that it was time to take a stand on how mental health treatment was covered in Washington state.

There were some obstacles to overcome in building the coalition that would eventually help create the strongest state mental health parity law in the country. First, members had different ideas about the form that the parity law should take. Given the conflicts with insurers, some feared that pushing for a comprehensive parity law would backfire by creating stronger opposition from insurers. Others believed that because insurers would attack whatever they did, it was better to aim high. There were also tensions between different mental health disciplines, which were still fighting to be included as providers covered by insurance panels. (Until 2001, clinical social workers were certified but not licensed in Washington state. Certification is a lesser form of regulation than licensure, providing obstacles to disciplines that opposed inclusion of clinical social workers as providers.)

During the course of the campaign to achieve mental health parity, several unanticipated events helped us along. First, Washington state insurance commissioner Deborah Senn established a rule in 1998 that required insurers to include professionals from every licensed or certified health care group as covered providers for mental health treatment. This helped calm the turf wars that had interfered with the ability of mental health professionals from different disciplines to work together.

Second, Commissioner Senn held a public hearing in 1999 to call attention to the lack of adequate mental health coverage. Ninety people attended, and the state legislature took notice. The first mental health parity bill was presented in 2000. Though it would be five years before the bill finally passed, the effort had begun.

Third, the Washington Coalition for Insurance Parity (WCIP) grew and became more effective. In 2002, Randy Revelle, a former King County executive who had struggled with bipolar disorder for 15 years, became the chair of WCIP. His organizational, networking, and fundraising skills were essential to the success of the parity bill in 2005. Once Revelle became involved, there was no question of what level of parity would be sought: It would be all or nothing.

The composition of the coalition began to change as well. Several consumers joined the coalition board, along with some insurance agents (notably Seth Corry, who pushed to give individual plans mental health parity) and representatives of hospitals, medical groups, and outpatient clinics. By 2005, there were 142 groups supporting WCIP, which raised over $150,000 for a media campaign and brochures to educate the public about the importance of mental health treatment.

I was honored to represent clinical social work in the WCIP effort on behalf of the Washington State Society for Clinical Social Work and the Washington State Coalition of Mental Health Professionals and Consumers. In addition, I formed links with five psychoanalytic groups that also supported the effort. I believe that the systems understanding that I was able to provide helped the process of the monthly WCIP board meetings.

DISCUSSION

There were several major keys to successful passage of mental health parity legislation in Washington state. The first was the crafting of a message that would appeal to the public and to employers. Our message that access to mental health treatment saves money and cuts absenteeism drew on several major studies to make the following points:

- Absenteeism due to stress has increased threefold, from 6 percent to 19 percent from 1980 to 1988. Stress, which often appears clinically as anxiety or depression, is very responsive to mental health treatment (Goldman & Taube, 1988).
- Of outpatient psychotherapy patients, 85 percent are seen for 15 visits or fewer and show significant improvement.
- For every dollar spent on outpatient mental health treatment, four dollars are saved on inpatient mental health treatment (Stewart, Ricci, Chee, Hahn, & Morganstein, 2003).
- Clinical depression costs American businesses nearly $29 billion a year in lost productivity and absenteeism (Sederer & Clemens, 2002).

SOCIAL WORK MATTERS

The persistence of a core group of leaders—including Lucy Homans, Betty Schwieterman, Eleanor Owen, Seth Corry, and me—was a crucial component of the effort. The five of us, who were members of the WCIP board from 1998 to 2010, had a history together and an understanding of the issues that arose again and again as legislators and insurance commissioners changed. We built an alliance with physicians so that psychotherapy was considered as important as medication in treatment of many mental health disorders. Ties with consumer groups, such as the National Association for Mental Illness and the National Coalition of Mental Health Professionals and Consumers, were also important in establishing a broad base of support for mental health coverage. Communication with hospitals, drug companies, and community mental health clinics contributed to the ultimate success of the parity bill.

The framing of mental health disorders as a spectrum—that is, explaining that there were many types of mental disorders that required a variety of treatment methods—was critical to passing a comprehensive bill. Many states had passed parity laws that only covered "serious" mental illness or psychotic disorders that frequently required hospitalization. WCIP pointed out the importance of treating chronic disorders that did not inhibit basic functioning, such as personality disorders and dissociative disorders, and argued against excluding Axis II disorders (disorders that include characterological difficulties but not necessarily cognitive difficulties). WCIP also pointed out that restricting mental health coverage was fundamentally unfair and that untreated mental disorders led to higher levels of medical difficulties. The push from insurers to see all treatment as connected to acute disorders, such as adjustment disorders or episodes of chronic disorders, was a difficult battle that was eventually won.

The 2005 bill that passed was not our first or second choice. It would only apply parity to companies with 50 or more employees. It would take six years to fully implement, starting with equal copayments for non–Employee Retirement Income Security Act (ERISA) plans—that is, self-insured plans that were developed by companies themselves, not by an insurer—moving to equal annual and lifetime limits by 2008, and finally to mandated coverage of almost all diagnoses in the *Diagnostic and Statistical Manual of Mental Disorders* (4th ed., text rev.) (American Psychiatric Association, 2000). Our persistence resulted in a broadening of the parity law to include small businesses and individual plans in 2008. A parallel move toward mental health parity on the national level was not as ambitious as the Washington state effort but resulted in a mandated offering for all ERISA plans, which took effect in 2009, and equal copayments for mental health and medical services, which will be phased into Medicare by 2014. With these federal laws, the vast majority of insurance plans will be required to cover mental health benefits at parity with medical/surgical benefits.

The value of building coalitions, in this case the Washington Coalition for Insurance Parity, in legislative campaigns is illustrated by the passage of the Washington state mental health parity law, an effort that took eight years to pass legislatively.

The major keys to the WCIP's success included forming a broad enough coalition to present a consistent message and generate widespread support for mental health parity; persistence during the six years that it took to make the campaign viable; the framing of insurance coverage across the range of mental health disorders; and the phasing in of mental health parity laws over five years to avoid the opposition that immediate implementation would have generated.

DISCUSSION QUESTIONS

1. What is mental health parity, and how does it affect clinical social workers?

2. Who wrote the national position paper that called attention to the inadequate coverage of mental health disorders, and what was the name of the paper?

3. Name three of the four major reasons that mental health parity is good for overall health and cuts costs.

4. What is the Washington Coalition for Insurance Parity?

5. What is an ERISA insurance plan?

6. Does mental health parity support social work values?

REFERENCES

American Psychiatric Association. (2000). *Diagnostic and statistical manual of mental disorders* (4th ed., text rev.). Washington, DC: Author.

Goldman, H., & Taube, C. (1988). High users of outpatient mental health services, II: Implications for practice and policy. *American Journal of Psychiatry, 145,* 24–28.

Miller, I. (1994). *What managed care is doing to outpatient mental health: A look behind the veil of secrecy.* Boulder, CO: Boulder Psychotherapists' Press.

Paul Wellstone and Pete Domenici Mental Health and Addictions Equality Act, P.L. 110-343, 122 Stat. 3765 (2008).

Sederer, L. I., & Clemens, N. A. (2002). Economic grand rounds: The business case for high-quality mental health care. *Psychiatric Services, 53*(2). Retrieved from http://psychiatryonline. org/article.aspx?articleid=87021

Stewart, W. F., Ricci J. A., Chee, E., Hahn, S. R., & Morganstein, D. (2003). Cost of lost productive work time among US workers with depression. *JAMA, 289,* 2218.

U.S. Department of Health and Human Services. (1999). *Mental health: A report of the surgeon general.* Washington, DC: U.S. Public Health Service.

RESEARCH

CHAPTER 47

SOCIAL WORK RESEARCH MATTERS

Joan Levy Zlotnik

SOCIAL WORK MATTERS

Armed with a recent social work PhD, which I earned in mid-career, and 12 years of work in national social work organizations, I became the executive director of the Institute for the Advancement of Social Work Research (IASWR) in 2000. As the fifth executive director in the seven years of IASWR's existence, I had my work cut out for me. I was tasked with promoting social work research, supporting capacity building within social work education programs, and strengthening federal support and funding for social work research. Spurred by a report by the Task Force on Social Work Research (1991), which was funded by the National Institute of Mental Health (NIMH), IASWR was created as a nonprofit organization, supported by NASW and four social work education organizations—the Council on Social Work Education, the Association of Baccalaureate Social Work Program Directors, the Group for the Advancement of Doctoral Education, and the National Association of Deans and Directors of Schools of Social Work. In 2000, they were joined by a sixth supporting organization, the Society for Social Work and Research.

One key part of IASWR's role was to demonstrate the importance and relevance of social work research to addressing social and health problems faced by our nation. Demonstrating relevance to decision makers was essential if we were to be successful in increasing the funding for social work research and improving the training of social work researchers. We also sought broader use of social work research findings in the development of policies and evidence-based practices. IASWR also worked to make sure that social workers were included on federal advisory boards and other groups working on issues of significance to social work practice.

One immediate task was to come up with a comprehensive definition that describes the depth and breadth of social work research. The resulting definition promulgated by IASWR incorporates the definition developed by the Task Force on Social Work Research and adds to it.

Social work research involves the study of preventive interventions, treatment of acute psychosocial problems, care and rehabilitation of individuals with severe, chronic difficulties, community development interventions, organizational administration, and the effects of social policy actions on the practice of social work (Task Force on Social Work Research, 1991, p. 1). Social work research may cover the entire lifespan, and may be focused at clinical and services and policy issues, focusing on individual, family, group, community, or organizational levels of intervention and analysis. It is primarily conducted by persons educated in the field of social work, that is, holding BSW, MSW, and/or DSW/PhD degrees, or who hold faculty positions in accredited social work education programs. Social work research is customarily conducted under university and/or community-based institutional auspices such as hospitals, prisons, social services and community development organizations or through professional, policy or research entities. (IASWR, 2009, p. 2)

Beyond promulgating a definition, we also needed to have real-world examples of the types of issues that social work research addresses. For example, qualitative and quantitative research by social workers adds to our understanding of the difficulty that a person with severe mental illness has in adhering to a regime of medication, the psychosocial factors that must be considered when an elderly wife is dealing with her husband's advancing Alzheimer's disease, and the organizational factors in public social service agencies that contribute to high rates of staff turnover. It helps us find ways to decrease the isolation of a young mother so as to reduce the risk of child maltreatment and to enhance job readiness skills so that a person can obtain and retain a job.

The following narrative offers a case example and then describes a social work research project that was aimed at ameliorating such situations. It identifies the contributions of social work research, both to addressing the psychosocial needs of people receiving health care services and to clarifying the important roles that social workers can fulfill within the health care delivery system.

Narrative

Across our communities, each day women are screened for breast and cervical cancer. In most cases nothing is found, and the women go about their daily business until their next Pap smear or mammogram is scheduled. In other instances, the result of the screening is positive, and this news is accompanied by a recommendation for medical follow-up. Such was the situation of Maria Ramirez, a 41-year-old woman living in Los Angeles County. She had been in the United States since she was 18, but she spoke little English. After lengthy hesitation, she finally went to a doctor for a physical, followed by an initial mammogram, which she found extremely uncomfortable.

She was told that a small abnormality had been spotted in the mammogram, and she was encouraged to monitor it by having another test in six months. But Maria did not have the money for the second test. She was concerned after being told that something might be wrong with her, so she did talk with some people in her community, but she took no action. A lot of other things were happening in Maria's family. She and her husband both lost their jobs in a restaurant kitchen. Maria also cared for her aging mother and two of her grandchildren and a nephew during the day, so she was extremely busy. Despite their limited means, Maria and her husband regularly saved money to send home to their families. Unfortunately, all of this ended when advanced breast cancer was diagnosed. Maria died eight years after her initial screening.

DISCUSSION

Was there an intervention that might have helped when Maria was told that her mammogram was positive? What role might social workers play?

To answer these and similar questions, social work researcher Kathleen Ell of the University of Southern California School of Social Work created Project SAFe (Screening Adherence Follow-up Program) and tested it in several settings (Ell, Vourlekis, Lee, & Xie, 2007). Project SAFe has been recognized as an evidence-based program by the National Cancer Institute (2010) and highlighted in the Institute of Medicine's (2008) report on addressing psychosocial needs for people with cancer, *Cancer Care for the Whole Patient.* Project SAFe is a case management intervention. It uses trained members of the community (patient navigators) who are supervised by a licensed clinical social worker to follow up with low-income women, many of them women of color, who have had a positive breast cancer screen. Social workers were also available to provide supportive and mental health services to the women. This type of intervention has been replicated in several communities and has been applied to people who are at high risk for diabetes and do not have regular access to health care. It has also been found to be cost-effective.

POLICY MATTERS

This is but one example of a growing body of social work research that is making a difference in the lives of vulnerable adults and children. Examples of the recent outcomes of social work research can be found in numerous journal articles and reports, including a December 2008 special issue of *Social Work Research* and a September 2010 special issue of *Research on Social Work Practice.* One of the hallmarks of much social work research is its relevance to practice, and in many instances the strong practice experience of the researchers themselves is reflected in the studies that they undertake.

Building funding support for social work research and the training of social work researchers over the past two decades did not happen by chance. Policymakers, advocates, and thought leaders played key roles in increasing investments in social work research (McRoy, Flanzer, & Zlotnik, 2012). After the Task Force on Social Work Research report, NIMH's National Advisory Mental Health Council reviewed the report's recommendations and directed NIMH to implement them. This meant that NIMH invested money in the enterprise of social work research. This included funding support to get both IASWR and the Society for Social Work and Research off the ground and the funding of a special competition to create social work research development centers in schools of social work.

Beyond the seven schools that received funding from NIMH, National Institute on Drug Abuse (NIDA) also launched a social work research initiative, ultimately funding eight research centers. In addition, Congress included in the reports that accompany appropriations bills language that encourage social work research, suggesting that the National Institutes of Health (NIH), the Centers for Disease Control and Prevention, the Department of Defense, and the Agency for Healthcare Research and Quality support social work researchers (Zlotnik & Solt, 2008). In 2003, spurred on by advocacy from social work organizations, through the Action Network for Social Work Education and Research, Congress asked NIH to create a plan of action for social work research. The *NIH Plan for Social Work Research* (NIH, 2003) recognized the relevance of social work research across all of NIH and presented nine recommendations that were implemented under the leadership of the Office of Behavioral and Social Sciences Research at NIH. A Social Work Research Working Group representing the Office of Behavioral and Social Sciences Research, NIMH, NIDA, the National Institute on Aging, the National Cancer Institute, the National Institute on Alcohol Abuse and Alcoholism, and several other institutes and offices worked closely with IASWR and the Society for Social Work and Research to implement the recommendations.

IASWR met regularly with NIH staff, participated in several coalitions (especially the Coalition to Advance Health through Behavioral and Social Sciences Research), recommended leading social work researchers for advisory boards and working groups, pointed out examples of social work research to federal stakeholders, and kept the social work field informed about funding opportunities through a weekly e-mail alert (Zlotnik, Biegel, & Solt, 2002; Zlotnik & Solt, 2006, 2008). In addition, technical assistance was provided to help social work faculty who had substantial knowledge about clinical practices and social work interventions to transform their social work knowledge and research questions into fundable research proposals.

As these efforts occurred, recognition of social work research and researchers has also increased. Research in areas like child welfare, health disparities, working with people with serious and persistent mental illness, and dissemination and implementation is carried out by social work researchers. They undertake complex studies, often with both a qualitative and a quantitative component, that try to determine which interventions work best for whom and under what conditions (see Boston College Graduate School of Social Work, n.d.; IASWR, 2009).

There are many unanswered questions about what the most effective psychosocial interventions are, yet progress is being made and social work research is steadily growing. This progress is not occurring in isolation: policymaker support and advocacy by the profession have been critical to making it a reality.

Discussion Questions

1. What practice questions do you have that could be answered by social work research?

2. What role might you take as a practitioner to support federal legislation that would build social work research capacity?

References

Boston College Graduate School of Social Work. (n.d.). *Social work NIH grant directory.* Retrieved from http://www.bc.edu/swnihdirectory

Ell, K., Vourlekis, B., Lee, P.-J., & Xie, B. (2007). Patient navigation and case management following an abnormal mammogram: A randomized clinical trial. *Preventive Medicine, 44,* 26–33.

Institute for the Advancement of Social Work Research. (2009). *Directory of social work research grants awarded by the National Institutes of Health: 1993–2009.* Retrieved from http://www. socialworkpolicy.org/publications/iaswr-publications/iaswr-directory-of-funded-research.html

Institute of Medicine. (2008). *Cancer care for the whole patient: Meeting psychosocial health needs.* Washington, DC: National Academies Press.

McRoy, R., Flanzer, J., & Zlotnik, J. L. (2012). *Building research capacity and infrastructure.* New York: Oxford University Press.

National Cancer Institute. (2010). *Research-tested intervention programs.* Retrieved from http://rtips. cancer.gov/rtips/programDetails.do?programId=307723

National Institutes of Health. (2003). *NIH plan for social work research.* Retrieved from http://obssr. od.nih.gov/pdf/SWR_Report.pdf

Task Force on Social Work Research. (1991). *Building social work knowledge for effective services and policies: A plan for research development: A report of the Task Force on Social Work Research.* Retrieved from http://www.socialworkpolicy.org/publications/iaswr-publications/building-social-work-knowledge-for-effective-services-and-policies-a-plan-for-research-development-a-report-of-the-task-force-on-social-work-research-november-1991.html

Zlotnik, J. L., Biegel, D. E., & Solt, B. E. (2002). The Institute for the Advancement of Social Work Research: Strengthening social work research in practice and policy. *Research on Social Work Practice, 12,* 318–337.

Zlotnik, J. L., & Solt, B. E. (2006). The Institute for the Advancement of Social Work Research: Working to increase our practice and policy evidence base. *Research on Social Work Practice, 16,* 534–539.

Zlotnik, J. L., & Solt, B. E. (2008). Developing research infrastructure: The Institute for the Advancement of Social Work Research. *Social Work Research, 32,* 201.

Social Work Matters:
The Power of Linking Policy and Practice
READING GUIDE

OVERVIEW

The narratives of professional social workers found in this book are based on experiences that are complex and profound. Social workers develop strong voices because they see firsthand the devastating effects of poverty, abuse, addiction, illness, mental health issues, and other significant challenges. Research stems from these challenges and the work undertaken to overcome them, and as a result best practices are established.

A majority of social workers tackle these weighty and important situations practicing directly with clients, determining how to achieve successful outcomes on an individual basis. These social workers can produce further positive effects on the health and well-being of their clients and communities through advocacy. Social workers with practice experience make excellent advocates because they understand clearly the challenges facing their clients, including their presenting problems, environmental factors, and strengths that can be used to help them. Social workers understand how organizational policy, state regulations, and federal law can help or hinder their clients in their pursuit of better lives. Social workers have acquired resources for clients, organized communities for causes, and coordinated grassroots advocacy campaigns. They have played significant roles in enacting important state and federal legislation into law, including Social Security, civil and women's rights, and Medicare and Medicaid.

The following learning objectives, policy questions, and additional resources should serve as a resource for readers of *Social Work Matters: The Power of Linking Policy and Practice.*

LEARNING OBJECTIVES

- Understand the different kinds of legislation and policies (organizational, local, state, and federal) and why they are important to the profession of social work and the clients served by social workers.

319

- Name various "actors" involved in the policy-making process, including professional social workers, and the roles that they play.
- Identify the social, legal, economic, political, and ethical realities that can affect the policy process.
- List some of the milestones that our nation has reached in terms of creating and maintaining the social safety net and determine what role social workers have played in achieving those milestones.
- Recognize what constitutes a success in policy making. Does it only include the passage of legislation in full?
- Realize why compromise is often used in the policy-making process. What would compromise look like in a current policy discussion?
- Familiarize yourself with different state and national coalitions and community partnerships. Why are they important to the policy making process?
- Identify strategies to facilitate policy creation and change.
- Determine what all of the policy narratives have in common. What makes them different?

ADDITIONAL POLICY QUESTIONS

- Research social workers who have played a significant role in American history (for example, Frances Perkins, Harry Hopkins, Dorothy I. Height, Whitney M. Young Jr.). What policies would possibly be different without their advocacy?
- What are the organizations and agencies that affect policies for the social work profession (such as the Centers for Medicare and Medicaid Services, the U.S. Department of Health and Human Services, or state and local government agencies)?
- In what ways are the social work profession and workforce affected by policy and legislation? For instance, many social service agencies are publicly funded. Why is it important for social workers to understand advocacy for their organization and mission?
- What are the ethical obligations of social workers as they relate to policy making and advocacy?
- Select the legislative agenda of an organization you support. What kinds of legislation and policies are on that agenda and why?
- What social work skills naturally lend themselves to successful macro, policy-level work?
- Identify the professional social workers who are members of Congress or members of your state legislature. What social work skills do they exhibit that help them in their current position as leaders?
- What are some of the workforce challenges facing the profession of social work? How can they best be addressed through policy change?

- Identify special interest groups that address an issue you care about? What drives their work and how can you add to the discussion?
- Write your own practice to policy narrative. Do you consider your experience a success? What strengths can you build on and what would you do differently?

ADDITIONAL RESOURCES

- *Social Work Reinvestment Initiative:* http://www.socialworkreinvestment.org
  The goal of the Social Work Reinvestment Initiative is to secure federal and state investments in professional social work to enhance societal well-being.
- *Congressional Social Work Caucus:* http://socialworkcaucus-towns.house.gov/
  The Congressional Social Work Caucus (CSWC) was created in 2010 by Congressman and social worker Edolphus Towns (D-NY) to represent the interests of social workers, and the clients they serve, on Capitol Hill. The objectives of the CSWC are to initiate and support legislation to address the unique challenges and opportunities for professional social workers; monitor and evaluate programs and legislation designed to assist and support individuals, families, and communities who are coping with economic, social, and health problems, particularly those with limited resources; provide congressional staff members with educational tools and resources directed toward improving the social work profession and the people social workers serve; and assist in education and awareness efforts on the breadth and scope of the social work profession.
- *Social Work Policy Institute:* http://www.socialworkpolicy.org
  The Social Work Policy Institute examines issues that relate to the work of social workers, including how to serve people who have multiple or complex needs and how public agencies and other structures deliver health and human services.
- *NASW Advocacy:* http://http://socialworkers.org/advocacy/default.asp
  Learn about the key federal and state legislative and policy efforts of NASW. Find out more about NASW's political action committee, and learn about grassroots advocacy efforts.
- *NASW Practice Department:* http://socialworkers.org/practice/default.asp
  Social work practice consists of the professional application of social work values, principles, and techniques to one or more of the following ends: helping people obtain tangible services; counseling and psychotherapy with individuals, families, and groups; helping communities or groups provide or improve social and health services; and participating in legislative processes. The practice of social work requires knowledge of human development and behavior; of social and economic, and cultural institutions; and of the interaction of all these factors.
- *NASW Center for Workforce Studies:* http://workforce.socialworkers.org/
  The Center for Workforce Studies was created in 2004 to conduct studies of the current social work labor force as well as collect information from other sources

to serve as a unique clearinghouse for educators, policy makers, social workers, and public and private workforce planners; to enhance social work professional development through innovative training programs in emerging practice areas; and to disseminate timely information and resources on evidence-based practices.

- *NASW Legal Defense Fund:* http://socialworkers.org/ldf/default.asp
  The NASW Legal Defense Fund (LDF) was established in 1972 and provides financial legal assistance and support for legal cases and issues of concern to NASW members and the social work profession. LDF also supports educational projects and programs to improve the legal status and knowledge of the social work profession.
- *NASW Code of Ethics:* http://www.socialworkers.org/pubs/code/default.asp
- *NASW Social Media and Resources:*
  - Facebook: http://www.facebook.com/socialworkers
  - Twitter: http://www.twitter.com/nasw
  - LinkedIn: http://www.linkedin.com/groups?about=&gid=115089
  - YouTube: http://www.youtube.com/user/socialworkers
  - RSS Feed: http://www.youtube.com/user/socialworkers
  - Blog: http://www.socialworkblog.org
  - Chat: http://www.socialworkchat.org
  - Be A Social Worker: http://www.beasocialworker.org
  - Social Workers Speak: http://www.socialworkersspeak.org

INDEX

In this index, *n* denotes footnote.